SPIES, LIES, AND ALGORITHMS

SPIES, LIES, AND ALGORITHMS

THE HISTORY AND FUTURE OF AMERICAN INTELLIGENCE

AMY B. ZEGART

PRINCETON UNIVERSITY PRESS

PRINCETON & OXFORD

Published by Princeton University Press
41 William Street, Princeton, New Jersey 08540
99 Banbury Road, Oxford OX2 6JX

press.princeton.edu

First paperback printing, 2023
Paperback ISBN 9780691223070

The Library of Congress has cataloged the cloth edition as follows:

Names: Zegart, Amy B., 1967– author.
Title: Spies, lies, and algorithms : the history and future of American intelligence / Amy B. Zegart.
Description: Princeton ; Oxford : Princeton University Press, [2022] | Includes bibliographical references and index.
Identifiers: LCCN 2021011926 (print) | LCCN 2021011927 (ebook) | ISBN 9780691147130 (Hardback : acid-free paper) | ISBN 9780691223087 (ePub)
Subjects: LCSH: Intelligence service—United States. | Cyber intelligence (Computer security)—United States. | Terrorism—Government policy—United States. | Public-private sector cooperation—United States.
Classification: LCC JK468.I6 Z418 2022 (print) | LCC JK468.I6 (ebook) | DDC 327.1273—dc23
LC record available at https://lccn.loc.gov/2021011926
LC ebook record available at https://lccn.loc.gov/2021011927

British Library Cataloging-in-Publication Data is available

Editorial: Bridget Flannery-McCoy, Alena Chekanov
Jacket/Cover Design: Derek Thornton / Notch Design
Jacket/Cover Art: Shutterstock
Production: Erin Suydam
Publicity: James Schneider, Kathryn Stevens
Copyeditor: Elizabeth J. Asborno

This book has been composed in Arame and Arno Pro

Printed in the United States of America

For my children: Alexander, Jack, and Kate

and

For Craig, always

CONTENTS

TABLES

FIGURES

ABBREVIATIONS AND ACRONYMS

AI	artificial intelligence
BJP	Bharatiya Janata Party (Indian political party)
CIA	Central Intelligence Agency
COVID-19	Coronavirus disease of 2019
DCI	director of central intelligence
DIA	Defense Intelligence Agency
DNI	director of national intelligence
DOD	Department of Defense
FBI	Federal Bureau of Investigation
Five Eyes	Intelligence partnership between the United States, United Kingdom, Canada, Australia, and New Zealand
FOIA	Freedom of Information Act
GDP	gross domestic product
GEOINT	geospatial intelligence
GPS	global positioning system
HPSCI	House Permanent Select Committee on Intelligence
HUMINT	human intelligence
IAEA	International Atomic Energy Agency
IARPA	Intelligence Advanced Research Projects Activity
IC	Intelligence Community, a collection of eighteen U.S. federal agencies
INR	State Department Bureau of Intelligence and Research

INTs   intelligence missions and disciplines

IRA   Russia's Internet Research Agency

ISIS   The Islamic State of Iraq and Syria

JCS   Joint Chiefs of Staff

JSOC   Joint Special Operations Command

KGB   The Komitet Gosudarstvennoy Bezopasnosti, or the Committee for State Security (the Soviet Union's spy agency)

KSM   Khalid Sheikh Mohammed

MI5   Military Intelligence Section 5 (U.K. agency)

MI6   Military Intelligence Section 6 or the Secret Intelligence Service (SIS) (U.K. agency)

MICE   money, ideology, coercion/compromise, and ego

MID   Military Intelligence Division (later known as the Army's G-2)

NASA   National Aeronautics and Space Administration

NATO   North Atlantic Treaty Organization

NCAA   National Collegiate Athletic Association

NCRI   National Council for the Resistance of Iran

NCTC   National Counterterrorism Center

NGA   National Geospatial-Intelligence Agency

NIE   National Intelligence Estimate

NRO   National Reconnaissance Office

NSA   National Security Agency

ODNI   Office of the Director of National Intelligence

OPEC   Organization of the Petroleum Exporting Countries

OPM   Office of Personnel Management

OSINT   open-source intelligence

OSS   Office of Strategic Services

RT   Russia Today

SAPs   special access programs

SAR   Synthetic Aperture Radar (enables satellite imaging in cloudy conditions)

SATs   Structured Analytic Techniques

SCIFs   Sensitive Compartmented Information Facilities, or "Skiffs"

SEALs   Sea, Air, and Land (Naval Special Warfare combat forces)

SIGINT   signals intelligence

SSCI   Senate Select Committee on Intelligence

UN   United Nations

WMD   weapons of mass destruction

SPIES, LIES, AND ALGORITHMS

1

INTELLIGENCE CHALLENGES IN THE DIGITAL AGE

CLOAKS, DAGGERS, AND TWEETS

IN JUNE 2014, I was scrolling through my Twitter feed when I came across the following Tweet:

At first, I thought it was a joke. The Central Intelligence Agency (CIA) is notoriously secretive—so shadowy, even its public affairs officers don't always tell you their names. But the Tweet was real. America's cloak-and-dagger agency had finally joined the social media age. The Internet went wild. "Who knew?—they have a sense of humor," reported CNN.[1]

The CIA's Twitter debut was a light-hearted moment in a darkening landscape. New technologies such as artificial intelligence (AI), Internet connectivity, quantum computing, and synthetic biology are disrupting global economics and politics at unprecedented speed. Never before has the United States faced a more dynamic and dangerous world. For the CIA and the seventeen other agencies comprising the U.S. Intelligence Community (IC), this is a moment of reckoning.[2]

Artificial intelligence is transforming both commerce and defense in ways that could destabilize social orders and alter the global distribution of power. Computer scientist Kai-Fu Lee estimates that AI could eliminate up to 40 percent of jobs worldwide in the next fifteen to twenty-five years, in sectors ranging from trucking to the service industry.[3] AI is also poised to revolutionize how wars are fought—automating everything from logistics to cyber defenses to unmanned fighter jets that can sense and attack faster than humans.[4] As former Google CEO Eric Schmidt and former Deputy Secretary of Defense Robert Work wrote, "AI is accelerating innovation in every scientific and engineering endeavor."[5]

Not since electricity has a breakthrough technology ushered in so much potential promise and peril. Russian President Vladimir Putin has declared that whoever leads in AI development "will become the ruler of the world."[6] More than a dozen countries have launched national AI initiatives. And China has made no secret of its plans to become the global leader in AI by 2030, part of its strategy to challenge U.S. economic and military dominance.[7] American experts and policymakers are sounding the alarm. "We are in a strategic competition. AI will be at the center. The future of our national security and economy are at stake," noted the bipartisan National Security Commission on Artificial Intelligence in a 2019 report.[8]

AI isn't the only technology reshaping the world. Internet connectivity is supercharging politics, fueling protest movements like the Arab Spring and Hong Kong's Umbrella Movement, repressive crackdowns like China's persecution of the Uighurs, and Russian information warfare campaigns that reach deep into the societies of other nations. The so-called Internet of Things (everyday devices with Internet connections) is spreading to billions of toys, cars, appliances, and more—and bringing cyber vulnerabilities with it.[9] Facebook algorithms are deciding what news we read and influencing how we think, enabling the manipulation of populations at scale.

There is greater upheaval still to come. In 2019, Google announced it had achieved "quantum supremacy"—a computing breakthrough so powerful that a math problem a supercomputer would need ten thousand years to solve could be cracked by its machine in just three minutes and twenty seconds. Experts likened it to the Wright Brothers' first flight: the dawn of a technological era opening vast new possibilities. Not all of them are good. Quantum computing could eventually unlock the encryption protecting nearly all of the world's data today.[10]

Synthetic biology is enabling scientists to engineer living organisms and create new ones not found in nature, with the potential for revolutionary improvements in the production of food, medicines, and data storage, as well as new weapons of war.[11] Because living cells are programmable like computers, they could eventually be engineered to make just about anything. Potential uses include manufacturing plastics, creating plants that can detect chemical munitions by changing color, and even designing bioweapons that target individuals on the basis of their DNA.[12] Here, too, Chinese military leaders have made innovation a top priority, calling biotech the new "strategic commanding heights" of national defense.[13]

The COVID-19 pandemic accelerated many of these trends, sending entire economies and societies online and fueling the use of biosurveillance technologies like smart jewelry that tracks symptoms[14] and data analytics that can identify which rooms of a building an infected person used and whether they were wearing a face mask.[15]

We've seen technological advances before. But never have we seen the convergence of so many new technologies changing so much so fast. This moment is challenging American intelligence agencies in three profound ways.

First, technological breakthroughs are transforming the threat landscape by generating new uncertainties and empowering new adversaries. During the Cold War, America had one principal enemy: the Soviet Union. The Cold War was a dangerous time, but it was simpler. America's top intelligence priority was clear. Every foreign policy decision was viewed through the lens of "What would Moscow think?"

Now, a wide array of bad actors is leveraging technology to threaten across vast distances. China is launching massive cyberattacks to steal American intellectual property[16] and building space weapons to cut off U.S. military satellite communications before the fighting ever starts.[17] Russia is using Facebook, Twitter, and other social media platforms to wage information warfare.[18] Three dozen countries have autonomous combat drones and at least nine have already used them.[19] Terrorist groups are using online video games to recruit followers[20] and Google Earth to plan their attacks.[21] Despots in developing nations are employing high-tech repression tools.[22] Weak states and non-state actors can inflict massive disruption, destruction, and deception with the click of a mouse.

For most of history, power and geography provided security. The strong threatened the weak, not the other way around. Oceans protected countries from one another, and distance mattered. Not anymore. In this era, the United States is simultaneously powerful and vulnerable to a head-spinning number of dangers, all moving at the speed of networks. It's a far cry from the plodding pace of Soviet five-year plans from a few decades ago.

The second challenge of the digital age involves data. Intelligence is a sense-making enterprise. Agencies like the CIA gather and analyze information to help policymakers understand the present and anticipate the future. Intelligence isn't always right. But it beats the best alternatives: guesswork, opinion, and gut feel.

In the old days, spy agencies in a handful of powerful countries dominated the collection and analysis of information. They were the only organizations with the resources and know-how to build billion-dollar satellites, make and break sophisticated codes, and collect information at scale.[23] In 2001, the National Security Agency (NSA) intercepted about two hundred million foreign emails, phone calls, and other signals a day.[24] Few countries or companies could come close.

Now, data is democratizing, and American spy agencies are struggling to keep up. More than half the world is online,[25] conducting five billion Google searches each day.[26] Cell phone users are recording and posting events in real-time—turning everyone into intelligence collectors, whether they know it or not.[27] Anyone with an Internet connection can access Google Earth satellite imagery, identify people using facial recognition software, and track events on Twitter.

On January 6, 2021, when pro-Trump rioters violently attacked the U.S. Capitol to prevent congressional certification of the 2020 presidential election, causing the deaths of five people, online sleuths immediately started mining images and video posted on social media to help law enforcement agencies identify the perpetrators. One anonymous college student even created a website called Faces of the Riot. Using widely available facial detection software, the student scanned hundreds of videos and thousands of pictures shared by rioters and others on the social media site Parler and extracted images of those who may have been involved in the Capitol siege.[28]

The sheer volume of online data today is so staggering, it's hard to comprehend: in 2019, Internet users posted 500 million tweets, sent 294 billion emails, and posted 350 million photos on Facebook *every day*.[29] Some estimate that the amount of information on earth is doubling every two years.[30]

This kind of publicly available information is called *open-source intelligence* and it is becoming increasingly valuable. When U.S. Navy SEALs conducted their secret nighttime raid on Osama bin Laden's Pakistani compound, Pakistan's military didn't detect a thing. But a local information technology consultant named Sohaib Athar did. Hearing strange noises, he took to Twitter. "Helicopter hovering above Abbottabad at 1 A.M. (is a rare event)," he posted. Athar ended up live tweeting the operation, including reporting when an explosion shook his windows.[31]

Similarly, when Russia invaded Ukraine in 2014, the best evidence did not come from spies or secretly intercepted communications. It came from selfies: time-stamped photos taken by Russian soldiers and posted on social media with Ukrainian highway signs in the background. Social media has become so important, even the consoles at America's underground nuclear command center display Twitter feeds alongside classified information feeds.[32]

That's not all. Commercial firms worldwide are launching hundreds of small satellites every year,[33] offering low-cost eyes in the sky to anyone who wants them.[34] Some satellite sensors have resolutions so sharp, they can detect manhole covers from space.[35] Others can capture images at night, in cloudy weather, or through dense vegetation and camouflage.[36] And constellations of cheap, small satellites are offering something new: faster revisit rates over the same location to detect changes over time. Already, commercial imagery and machine learning tools are enabling some of my Stanford colleagues to analyze North Korea's trade relationship with China by counting the number of trucks crossing the border in hundreds of images over the past five years.[37] Commercial imagery is becoming so valuable that the National Reconnaissance Office, the American agency that builds and operates spy satellites, is spending $300 million a year to buy it rather than just building satellites of its own.[38]

In short, data volume and accessibility are revolutionizing sensemaking. The intelligence playing field is leveling—and not in a good way. Intelligence collectors are everywhere, and government spy agencies are drowning in data. This is a radical new world and intelligence agencies are struggling to adapt to it. While secrets once conferred a huge advantage, today open-source information increasingly does. Intelligence used to be a race for insight where great powers were the only ones with the capabilities to access secrets. Now everyone is racing for insight and the Internet gives them tools to do it. Secrets still matter, but whoever can harness all this data better and faster will win.

Secrecy and the Origins of Non-Denial Denials

The CIA's "We can neither confirm nor deny" response is part of the popular lexicon. While often used as a laugh-line in movies or on Twitter, that non-denial denial is real.[39] A CIA lawyer came up with it in 1975[40] when information about one of the agency's most highly classified covert operations leaked to the press.[41] The operation was code-named AZORIAN.[42] It involved billionaire Howard Hughes, a CIA ship posing as a commercial deep-sea mining vessel,[43] and a daring effort to hoist a sunken Soviet submarine—along with its nuclear missiles[44] and secrets[45]—from the bottom of the Pacific Ocean right as Soviet ships were passing by.[46] At the time, Cold War tensions were high, the risks of exposure were great, and reporters were barraging CIA officials with questions.[47] The agency did not want to be caught lying about what it was doing in the midst of Watergate, but it didn't want to reveal anything to the Soviets, either.[48] "We can neither confirm nor deny" has been used ever since.

The third challenge posed by emerging technologies strikes at the heart of espionage: secrecy. Until now, American spy agencies didn't have to interact much with outsiders, and they didn't want to. The intelligence mission meant gathering secrets so we knew more about adversaries than they knew about us, and keeping how we gathered secrets a secret, too.

Walk into CIA headquarters and you feel it. There's a gleaming white marble Memorial Wall covered with more than 100 stars, each denoting an intelligence officer who died in the line of duty.[49] A Book of Honor records their names, except for forty entries that have only blank lines.[50] For these CIA officers, service remains classified even in death.

Balancing secrecy and openness is an age-old struggle. Secrecy is vital for protecting intelligence sources and collection methods, as well as securing advantage. Openness is vital for ensuring democratic accountability. Too much secrecy invites abuse. Too much transparency makes intelligence ineffective.

In the digital age, however, secrecy is bringing greater risk because emerging technologies are blurring nearly all the old boundaries of geopolitics. Increasingly, national security requires intelligence agencies to engage the outside world, not stand apart from it.

It used to be that adversaries threatened from abroad and we could see them coming; military mobilization took time. Now they can attack privately owned critical infrastructure like power grids and financial systems in cyberspace—anytime, from anywhere, without crossing a border or firing a shot. In the twentieth century, economics and security politics were separate spheres because the Soviet-bloc command economies were never part of the global trading order. In the twenty-first century, economics and security politics have become tightly intertwined because of global supply chains and dramatic advances in dual-use technologies like AI that offer game-changing commercial and military applications. Until now, intelligence agencies focused on understanding foreign governments and terrorist groups. Today they also have to understand American tech giants and startups—and how malign actors can use our own inventions against us.

Securing advantage in this new world means that intelligence agencies must find new ways to work with private sector companies to combat online threats and harness commercial technological advances. They must engage the universe of open-source data to capture the power of its insights. And they must serve a broader array of intelligence customers outside of government to defend the nation.

These days, the National Security Agency isn't the only big data behemoth. Amazon, Apple, Facebook, Google, and Microsoft are, too. Although some companies have declared they will never use their technology for weapons, the reality is their technology already is a weapon: hackers are attacking computer networks through Gmail phishing schemes and Microsoft coding vulnerabilities, terrorists are livestreaming attacks, and malign actors have turned social media platforms like Twitter and Facebook into disinformation superhighways that undermine democracy from within.[51] American intelligence agencies have to find better ways to access relevant threat information held by these and other companies without jeopardizing civil liberties or firms' commercial success.

Intelligence agencies need the private sector more for innovation now, too. Analyzing massive troves of data, for example, will increasingly depend on AI tools. Technological advances (like the Internet) used to start in government and then migrate to the commercial sector.[52] Now that process is reversed, with breakthroughs coming from large companies like Google and Nvidia and from startups like Ginko Bioworks and Dataminr. Instead of developing technologies in-house, spy agencies now have to spot and adopt them rapidly from outside. That requires talent as well as technology, and the private sector is cornering the labor market, too, offering compensation packages and cutting-edge computing facilities that are hard for government agencies (or universities) to match. Companies have been hiring away so many top AI professors (forty-one AI faculty left academia in 2018 alone), experts are worried there won't be enough left to teach the next generation of students.[53]

Engagement and collaboration with the private sector don't come easily. Distrust of American spy agencies has a long history with some dark chapters. In the 1970s, revelations that intelligence agencies had been spying on Americans, infiltrating dissident groups, and assassinating foreign leaders prompted outcries and congressional oversight reforms. More recent controversies include CIA drone strikes and secret NSA surveillance programs revealed by a former agency contractor named Edward Snowden in 2013.

In the summer of 2014, a year after the Snowden revelations hit the press, I held a cyber boot camp for congressional staffers that included a visit to a major Silicon Valley tech company. As we filed into the conference room, the tension was palpable. One tech executive told the group he viewed the U.S. government just like China's People's Liberation Army—as an adversary that needed to be stopped from surreptitiously penetrating his systems. Jaws dropped. An intelligence committee staffer rushed outside to call the boss and relay the news: they had a lot more repair work to do. NSA's surveillance programs had been authorized, but in the eyes of tech executives, they had broken faith by secretly gathering customer data and making companies look weak, complicit, or both.

Intelligence agencies are still working hard to rebuild that trust. As the agency's first "neither confirm nor deny" Tweet went viral, Director John Brennan put out a press release explaining that he wanted a social media presence to "more directly engage with the public and provide information on CIA's mission, history, and other developments."[54] When secret agencies feel the need to engage and inform, you know times are changing. It's an important beginning.

As noted above, emerging technologies are also unleashing a whole new world of publicly available or open-source information—from Russian soldier selfies in Ukraine to satellite images of Chinese trucks in North Korea—that is challenging the primacy of secrets and the insight they provide. While open-source information has always been important, secrets have reigned supreme inside America's intelligence agencies. Not everything was secret, but secrets were everything. As former CIA analyst Aris Pappas noted, during the Cold War it was easy to slip into the attitude of "Gee, if they spent a trillion dollars to get this information, it must be a trillion dollars' worth of information."[55]

Technological breakthroughs are even challenging ideas about who counts as a decisionmaker. Until now, national security policy was the province of government. Important decisions were made by federal employees who wore badges, held security clearances, and knew how the Intelligence Community worked.

Not anymore. Increasingly, decisionmakers live worlds apart from Washington—making policy choices in living rooms and board rooms, not just the White House Situation Room. They are voters targeted by foreign influence campaigns to divide society and manipulate elections. And they are executives and employees working in technology companies where rewards come from inventing new products and finding new markets, not protecting society from nefarious uses and downside risks. Leaders in these companies may want no part of American national security policy or global politics, but their decisions unavoidably affect both.

In the digital age, business is not just business. Tech policy *is* public policy. Social media companies are deciding what presidential messages to the world can be blocked or shared. Software developers are affecting how vulnerable their global products will be to cyberattack. Cell phone and messaging app executives are making encryption decisions that determine how dissidents can operate and how law enforcement agencies can combat terrorists.

Leaders on both sides of the Silicon Valley–Washington divide must navigate this new world together. They cannot do it without intelligence about how the threat landscape is shaping the development and use of new technologies and how new technologies are shaping the threat landscape.

Serving a broader set of decisionmakers requires much more than declassifying old intelligence reports and conducting business as usual. This was one of the chief lessons of 2016. During that election cycle, intelligence officials detected many facets of Russian interference and became so alarmed, they decided to warn the public. On October 7, the director of national intelligence and the secretary of homeland security took the unprecedented step of issuing a joint press statement. But almost nobody noticed.

Why? In part because it was written in intelligence-speak. Here are the first few lines:

> The U.S. Intelligence Community (USIC) is confident that the Russian Government directed the recent compromises of e-mails from US persons and institutions, including from US political organizations. The recent disclosures of alleged hacked e-mails on sites like DCLeaks.com and WikiLeaks and by the Guccifer 2.0 online persona are consistent with the methods and motivations of Russian-directed efforts.[56]

To intelligence insiders, the message was serious and clear. To the public, not so much.

That same day, the infamous *Access Hollywood* audiotape—in which Republican nominee Donald Trump boasted about how easy it was for him to sexually assault women—hit the news. Guess which got more attention.

In the 2020 presidential election, intelligence officials became more active and creative, making video public service announcements, issuing more frequent press releases, and granting more media interviews.[57] One October video even included counterintelligence chief William Evanina and General Paul Nakasone, who led both the Pentagon's cyberwarriors and the super snoopers of the National Security Agency. Their message: election threats were real but their agencies were on the job.[58]

These steps have been important but insufficient. The 2020 video announcement, for example, received just 22,400 views on YouTube before election day.[59] Russia's state-run propaganda mill, RT America (formerly called Russia Today), had more than a million YouTube subscribers.[60] Meanwhile, intelligence itself became politicized, with Director of National Intelligence John Ratcliffe selectively using secrets and publicizing suspected Russian disinformation to support President Trump's campaign.

In the pages that follow, I hope to give readers a better understanding of intelligence as well as the challenges American spy agencies now confront. There are no easy answers, but one imperative is already evident: America's intelligence agencies must adapt or they will fail. The biggest surprise attacks in modern American history—Pearl Harbor,[61] 9/11,[62] and Russia's interference in the 2016 presidential election[63]—occurred because spy organizations did not change fast or fully enough to meet emerging threats. This juncture, too, requires dramatic change to harness new technologies better and faster than adversaries do.

This book draws on nearly thirty years of researching American intelligence agencies and advising the U.S. government; hundreds of interviews with current and former intelligence officials and policymakers; an undergraduate course I taught at UCLA; and focus groups I held more recently with high school and college students about what they wanted to learn about intelligence and why.

It's worth nothing that I am a visitor to the secret world of intelligence, not an inhabitant. Although I have served on the National Security Council staff and advised intelligence officials and policymakers, I have never worked inside an intelligence agency. I am a career academic who has examined spy agencies from the outside—looking at how they have evolved over time, why they have such a hard time adapting to new threats, and how they can improve. I often feel like an anthropologist who travels to the far reaches of Washington, D.C., to observe the foreign cultures of a rare and secret clan of people called intelligence officers.

Being an outsider has both drawbacks and benefits. On the one hand, I cannot examine what the classified record actually says about pivotal intelligence events. I can only study what happened after the fact. On the other hand, an outsider's perspective can bring healthy skepticism and independence. I am freer to ask uncomfortable questions—and come to unflattering conclusions—than an insider would be.

Chapter 2 starts by examining the crisis in intelligence education and its costs. Most Americans, including policymakers, have little idea how America's intelligence agencies actually work. Instead, fiction has played an outsized role. Years ago, a poll of my students led to a startling discovery: spy-themed entertainment seemed to be influencing attitudes on intelligence in significant ways. This chapter follows the trail, examining my national polling project, tracing the dramatic rise in "spytainment," and examining how Hollywood has fueled conspiracy theories and influenced policymakers from Supreme Court justices to soldiers on the front lines.

Chapter 3 covers American espionage from eighteenth-century invisible ink to twenty-first-century spy satellites. That may seem like a long time, but compared to the rest of the world, American intelligence history is quite short. George Washington's spies didn't come around until two thousand years after Chinese general Sun Tzu wrote his treatise on the use of intelligence in warfare, *The Art of War*. Today's vast intelligence enterprise emerged largely after World War II and reflects the country's evolving role in the world.

Chapter 4 covers intelligence basics. We examine what intelligence is, what it isn't, and how it operates—with a bird's-eye view of the decade-long hunt for Osama bin Laden and personal reflections by intelligence officials of their daily lives, ethical dilemmas, and best and worst moments.

Chapter 5 examines intelligence analysis and why it's so hard. From China's surprise attack in the Korean War to the mistaken reports around Iraq's weapons of mass destruction, analytic failures have common causes. Chief among them are what I call the seven deadly biases, or the cognitive traps that can lead even the smartest minds astray. We also explore the coming world of artificial intelligence, discussing which kinds of analysis machines can do better than humans and humans can do better than machines.

Chapter 6 turns to one of the most sensitive points for the Intelligence Community: traitors. What motivates trusted insiders to become turncoats? How can intelligence officers recruit spies in the digital age, and how can they identify possible double agents while still maintaining the trust necessary to do their work?

Chapter 7 explores covert action, what former CIA Director Leon Panetta once called "a hard business of agonizing choices."[64] We start in the deserts of Yemen, where an American citizen and infamous terrorist named Anwar al-Awlaki was killed in a covert drone strike without a trial, judge, or jury. We explore what exactly covert action is and why all presidents use it even though it so often fails. And we walk through one of these agonizing choices, examining a hypothetical covert action dilemma from different perspectives.

In chapter 8, we examine the contentious world of congressional oversight—how it's developed, why it matters, why it rarely works well, and what the future holds. We also delve into debates over the CIA's detention and interrogation program and the NSA's warrantless wiretapping program, two of the most heated oversight controversies in intelligence history.

Chapter 9 turns to nuclear sleuthing in the digital age. Thanks to the Internet, commercial satellites, and automated analytics, nuclear intelligence isn't just for superpower governments anymore. We trace the rise of the new nuclear sleuths—individuals and organizations outside of governments who are transforming how illicit nuclear activities are tracked. This new ecosystem highlights the dramatic changes in intelligence emerging today, including opportunities and risks.

Chapter 10 concludes with cyber threats—what they are, how they have evolved, what they mean for intelligence, and the key challenges they raise. In many ways, cyberspace is the ultimate cloak-and-dagger battleground, where nefarious actors employ deception, subterfuge, and advanced technology for theft, espionage, information warfare, and more. Cyber threats are hacking both machines and minds. This is only the beginning: artificial intelligence is creating deepfake video, audio, and photographs so real, their inauthenticity may be impossible to detect. No set of threats has changed so fast and demanded so much from intelligence.

For America's Intelligence Community, the digital age is filled with complexity and challenge. From catching traitors and undertaking covert action to understanding nuclear threats and operating in cyberspace, success requires a fundamental rethink about how to secure advantage in a radically new world. It starts by getting back to basics and depoliticizing intelligence again. But success also includes a mission shift that embraces open-source intelligence, develops new capabilities for both secret activities and open engagement, and rewards officials for doing things differently.

As we'll see, adapting to this technological era is an enormous paradigm shift. But it's essential.

2

THE EDUCATION CRISIS

HOW FICTIONAL SPIES ARE SHAPING PUBLIC OPINION AND INTELLIGENCE POLICY

The difference between fiction and reality? Fiction has to make sense.

—TOM CLANCY[1]

FOR FANS OF SPY MOVIES and television shows, a visit to CIA headquarters will be disappointing. The visitor center looks nothing like the cool, high-tech offices of Jason Bourne or Carrie Mathison. Instead, the entry to America's best-known intelligence agency has more of a shabby U.S. Post Office feel. There are teller windows with bullet-proof glass, soda machines, and an old-fashioned black landline phone mounted on the back wall. Once cleared by security, visitors head back outside, where they can walk down a winding road or take the rambling shuttle bus to the old headquarters building. There, lobby security has no retina scans or fancy fingerprint devices, just a few turnstiles and a friendly security guard who takes cell phones and hands out paper claim checks.[2]

Even the suite of executive offices where the CIA director sits seems strangely ordinary.[3] The only clue that this is not a typical government building is the burn bags.[4] Because classified documents cannot just be thrown away,[5] instead of trash cans, striped burn bags that look weirdly like Trader Joe's holiday shopping bags are scattered around the building to make incineration easier.[6]

The National Counterterrorism Center (NCTC) is another story. Created after 9/11 to fuse terrorism threat reporting across the U.S.

government,[7] NCTC has an ultra-modern operations center with giant wall monitors, an open floor plan, and computer stations tracking bad guys around the globe.[8] It looks like it came straight out of Hollywood. Because it did. Government officials actually hired an engineer from Walt Disney Imagineering to design the agency's offices, right down to the sleek consoles and lunchroom chairs.[9]

In intelligence, art is imitating life and life is imitating art. The implications of this shift are far more serious than they appear. In the past two decades, spy-themed entertainment, or "spytainment," has skyrocketed while spy facts remain scarce and university professors are teaching courses on just about everything other than intelligence. The result: spy-themed entertainment is standing in for adult education on the subject,[10] and although the idea might seem far-fetched, fictional spies are actually shaping public opinion and real intelligence policy.

This chapter begins by exploring how little Americans know about the real-life intelligence world. Next, we trace the rise of spytainment and the complicated relationship intelligence agencies have with Hollywood. Then we take a closer look at how classification policies, the Intelligence Community's culture of secrecy, and the incentives shaping what university professors study make spy facts hard to find.

Finally, we turn to consequences. As we'll see, since 9/11, "Deep State" conspiracy theories have spread like wildfire, many of them accusing intelligence agencies of waging a secret war against our own country—just like they do in the movies. Spytainment is also influencing policymaking elites, not just everyday Americans. From cadets at West Point to senators on the Intelligence Committee to Supreme Court justices, policymakers are contemplating Hollywood spies and plot lines to make real policy decisions.[11]

Intelligence about Intelligence

Most Americans don't know much about the secret world of intelligence because they have never interacted with it. Although many decry the growing gulf between civilians and the all-volunteer force, far more Americans interact with soldiers than with intelligence officers.[12] On a typical American street, military veterans live in two out of every ten houses.[13] But outside the Washington, D.C., area, almost no one lives next door to an intelligence official—or if they do, they don't know it.[14] Intelligence isn't a big part of Congress, either. In 2020, just 18 of the 535 Representatives and Senators serving in Congress had ever worked in an intelligence agency. In fact, the House and Senate had more doctors in their ranks than former intelligence officers.[15]

In 2009, I started hunting for polling data about Americans' knowledge of intelligence, as well as attitudes toward hot-button intelligence issues. There wasn't much, so I decided to gather my own small sample of rough data, surveying UCLA undergraduates enrolled in my class, U.S. Intelligence Agencies in Theory and Practice.

This wasn't exactly a ho-hum period for American intelligence agencies. The Iraq War, which began with faulty intelligence, was dragging on into its sixth year.[16] Controversy was still raging about the National Security Agency's "warrantless wiretapping" program, which collected telephone metadata on millions of Americans and intercepted international communications into and out of the United States of people with suspected links to terrorist organizations—all without court warrants.[17] Meanwhile the Senate Intelligence Committee was revving up a major investigation of the CIA's detention and interrogation of suspected terrorists at black sites around the world.[18]

With all these controversies, I expected protesters outside my class and empty seats inside. But when I walked into the lecture hall the first day, I was surprised to find that it was standing room only. Students, it turned out, were hungry to learn. The class was a wide mix of freshmen and seniors, doves and hawks, privacy activists and veterans. I asked them why they were taking the course. "I want to know why my buddy died in Iraq," said one. "I want to know why I was there." The room went silent. This student sat in the front row, right side, every class for the next ten weeks.

The class survey results were illuminating. I learned that my students, even those who followed the news closely, knew almost nothing about intelligence agencies and how they worked. What's more, there seemed to be a disconcerting connection between students' attitudes toward intelligence and spy-themed television. Those who said they always watched the hit show 24, which depicted torture often and favorably, were statistically more likely than their peers to approve of harsh interrogation methods like waterboarding, which simulates drowning and which many regard as torture.[19]

Of course, the survey couldn't *prove* that watching 24 caused these attitudes; my sample size was only about 100 and it was hardly representative. Maybe the show attracted viewers who were more pro-waterboarding all along and enjoyed seeing Jack Bauer do "whatever it takes" each episode. So in 2012 and 2013, I ran two national surveys through YouGov, a leading polling firm, gathering data from about a thousand respondents per survey from a nationally representative pool.

The YouGov findings ended up echoing my less scientific UCLA student poll and yielded two interesting results.[20] The first is that Americans' knowledge of intelligence is generally poor. To gauge understanding, I asked respondents some basic questions, such as how much intelligence in a typical report was secret and who was the most senior intelligence official in the United States. I also included some questions about the mission of the National Security Agency (NSA) in the midst of the Edward Snowden revelations, the agency's biggest crisis since its founding in 1952. To make it easier, I gave respondents options, so they didn't have to come up with answers out of thin air. They just needed to select the right multiple-choice answer, for instance:

About what percent of the information in a typical intelligence report comes from secrets?

☐ More than 75%
☐ 75%
☐ 50%
☐ 25%
☐ Less than 25%
☐ Not sure

The correct answer is less than 25 percent. Only about 20 percent of intelligence in a typical intelligence report comes from classified information, or secrets.[21] The rest is gleaned and synthesized from open sources, or publicly available information like foreign government reports and newspaper articles. (In the next chapter, we'll talk more about the different kinds of intelligence, and what intelligence agencies do with all of that open-source information that makes it valuable.)

The point is, if you got the question wrong, you are not alone. Nine out of ten Americans—or 93 percent to be exact—either didn't know how much intelligence in a typical report is secret or they marked the wrong choice. A quarter of Americans thought secrets comprised 75 percent or more of intelligence reports. Nearly half of respondents thought 50 percent of reports were secrets.[22]

Perhaps most interestingly, I found that Americans did not understand what the NSA did, even when media at the time was saturated with news stories about it. In May 2013, Edward Snowden, a former NSA contractor, illegally took and released a massive cache of highly classified documents detailing some of the agency's most important, and sensitive, collection programs.[23] Among other things, the documents revealed that the NSA was spying on foreign leaders of U.S. allies,[24] collecting millions of Americans' phone records or "metadata,"[25] and secretly accessing data from tech companies like Google and Yahoo.[26] Snowden became an international sensation when he fled to Hong Kong, then Moscow, and stories based on his materials began appearing in the *Washington Post*, the *Guardian*, the *New York Times*, and *Der Spiegel*.[27] Despite being in hiding and on the run, his face was everywhere. In the six months following the first disclosure, Snowden appeared in 395 articles in the *New York Times* and 716 articles in the *Guardian*, the newspaper that initially broke the story.[28] He later gave television interviews to Brian Williams at NBC News, John Oliver on HBO's *Last Week Tonight*, and Trevor Noah on Comedy Central's *The Daily Show*.

The Justice Department charged Snowden with violating the Espionage Act of 1917[29] and the State Department revoked his passport.[30] Snowden's revelations generated tremendous controversy. Although a presidentially appointed bipartisan review panel found "no evidence of illegality or other abuse of authority" within the NSA programs he disclosed,[31] Congress came under heavy pressure to more narrowly circumscribe the telephone metadata program, which it ultimately did.[32]

Many privacy advocates viewed Edward Snowden as a whistleblowing hero,[33] while many national security officials viewed him as a traitor.[34] When I asked former NSA Director Michael Hayden what he would ask or say to Snowden if he saw him, Hayden immediately answered: "You have the right to remain silent."[35]

Yet, according to my October 2013 survey, which was fielded in the middle of the Snowden media frenzy, most Americans didn't even know what the NSA did for a living. The crisis was unfolding against a backdrop of widespread public misperception and ignorance.

The NSA, which employs about forty thousand people, is one of America's most important organizations.[36] The agency intercepts and analyzes foreign signals intelligence, including email, telephone calls, and encrypted data transmissions.[37] The NSA is also, as its website declared, "home to America's codemakers and codebreakers."[38] This codemaking and breaking mission is essential for protecting information like U.S. nuclear codes and for penetrating foreign communications.

My survey asked respondents whether they thought the NSA conducted any of the following six activities: codebreaking, intercepting foreign communications, analyzing information, building spy satellites, interrogating terrorist detainees, and conducting operations to capture or kill foreign terrorists. The first three were true. The second three were false. The survey found that most Americans didn't know the difference. As table 2.1 illustrates, only half of respondents knew that the NSA is responsible for making and breaking codes. Large majorities harbored either ignorance or misperceptions about other aspects of the NSA's mission.

Americans' ignorance about the NSA wasn't an outlier. I found that even major events in the Intelligence Community don't always register with the public. During the week of September 3, 2009, the CIA released a landmark report about the use of waterboarding and other controversial interrogation techniques, but only 3 percent of Americans said that was the news story they followed most closely that week.[39] When

TABLE 2.1 YouGov National Poll 2013: What Activities Does the NSA Do?

Possible NSA Activities	Yes	No	Not Sure	True/False	Total Wrong
Break other countries' secret codes	51%	9%	40%	True	49%
Intercept foreign telephone and email communications	71%	4%	24%	True	28%
Analyze information	73%	4%	23%	True	27%
Build spy satellites	32%	22%	46%	False	78%
Interrogate detainees	35%	23%	42%	False	77%
Conduct operations to capture or kill foreign terrorists	32%	29%	39%	False	71%

Facebook listed the top forty most shared news stories of 2011, the killing of Osama bin Laden, one of the greatest intelligence successes in history, did not even make the list.[40]

Findings from my 2012 and 2013 YouGov polls also resonated with my less scientific student survey about the real influence of fictional spies. I found that the more frequently American viewers watched spy-themed TV shows and movies, the more likely they were to support aggressive counterterrorism tactics, including assassination, harsh interrogation techniques against suspected terrorists, and NSA surveillance of American citizens. Here are just a few examples of the statistically significant results from my 2012 YouGov poll:

- **Assassination:** 84 percent of frequent spy TV watchers were willing to assassinate known terrorists versus 70 percent of infrequent watchers.
- **Rendition:** 60 percent of frequent spy TV watchers thought that transferring suspected terrorists to a third-party country known for using torture (a practice called *rendition*) was right versus 45 percent of infrequent watchers; 53 percent of spy-moviegoers supported transferring suspected terrorists to a country known for using torture versus 41 percent of non-moviegoers.
- **Waterboarding:** 38 percent of frequent spy TV watchers believed that waterboarding suspected terrorists (which involves strapping someone on a board and forcing water into their cloth-covered

nose and mouth until they think they are drowning) was the right thing to do versus 28 percent of infrequent watchers.

My 2013 poll revealed that spytainment viewing habits were also highly correlated with opinions about the NSA. The more people watched spy-themed television shows and movies, the more they liked the NSA, the more they approved of NSA's telephone and Internet collection programs, and the more they believed the NSA was telling them the truth about its surveillance activities.[41] In many instances, the differences in opinion between spytainment viewers and the rest of the country were large. The statistically significant findings include these:

- **NSA favorability:** 58 percent of people who frequently watched spy movies in the previous year had favorable views of the NSA, but only 34 percent of infrequent spy moviegoers reported favorable views of the agency.
- **Approval of NSA surveillance programs:** 44 percent of people who watched spy TV shows frequently or occasionally said they approved of the NSA's Internet data and telephone records collection programs, but only 29 percent of those who rarely or never watched spy TV shows approved of these programs.
- **NSA telling the truth:** 23 percent of frequent/occasional spy TV watchers believed the NSA was telling them the truth about not listening in on telephone call content in the agency's metadata collection program, compared to just 15 percent of infrequent spy TV show watchers who thought the NSA was telling the truth.

Whatever one thinks about these activities—whether they are effective or ineffective, morally right or morally wrong—the fact that fiction may be significantly influencing public attitudes about them is unsettling.

Of course, in academia, we often warn that "correlation is not the same thing as causation." It could be that entertainment merely reinforces or reflects beliefs that people already hold.[42] Just because two things trend together doesn't mean one causes the other. Superstitious sports fans wear lucky T-shirts, but nobody really thinks the fashion choices of viewers determine which team wins the game.

In this case, however, there is good reason to believe the relationship between spytainment and beliefs could be causal. We know that entertainment has influenced popular culture and attitudes on plenty of other subjects. In the 1980s, law school applications skyrocketed when *L.A. Law* became a hit television show.[43] Prosecutors have bemoaned the "*CSI* effect"—how the popular television show has led jurors to expect fancy forensic evidence in court and to assume the government's case is weak without it.[44] And the 1986 blockbuster *Top Gun* became a Navy recruiting bonanza, boosting enlistments and applications to the Naval Academy; *Top Gun* made the Navy so popular, recruiters even began setting up tables outside movie theaters. As one columnist wrote, "America fell in love with Maverick, Iceman, and other high-fivin' silver-screen super-pilots as they traveled Mach 2 while screaming about 'the need for speed.'"[45] If art can affect life in the legal profession, criminal investigations, and the military, it's not much of a stretch to imagine the same thing could be happening in intelligence.

Evidence suggests that it does. Spytainment has ballooned in the past twenty years, becoming the predominant, and often only, way for Americans to understand the intelligence agencies that serve them.

The Rise of Spytainment

Spy-themed entertainment is everywhere these days—in Robert Ludlum novels, Tom Clancy video games, movie franchises like Bond and Bourne, and hit television shows like *Homeland* and *24*.

To be sure, spies have been big business for a long time. James Bond first appeared in Ian Fleming's 1953 novel, *Casino Royale*, and has been around so long that seven different actors have played him on the big screen. Tom Clancy's CIA hero, Jack Ryan, first appeared in his 1984 bestselling novel, *The Hunt for Red October*, and Jason Bourne first forgot his shady CIA past back in 1980, when Robert Ludlum published *The Bourne Identity*. In fact, America's first ever bestselling novel was a fictional account of a double agent during the Revolutionary War that was published in 1821 and aptly titled *The Spy*.[46]

The difference today is the quantity and variety of spy-themed entertainment surrounding us in a sea of fiction. A hundred years ago, American readers first discovered the allure of Spytainment. Now they can't get away from it.

Together, Clancy and Ludlum have sold roughly four hundred million books worldwide.[47] Clancy's novels have become such a common part of American culture that during the September 11, 2001, terrorist attacks, CNN anchor Judy Woodruff described the event as something "right out of a Tom Clancy novel," and the network interviewed Clancy about the similarities between his book and the 9/11 plot.[48] Ten years later, CNN host Eliot Spitzer used the same Clancy reference to describe the operation that killed Osama bin Laden.[49]

Everywhere you turn, fictional spies are there. For kids, there's Alex Rider, Anthony Horowitz's fourteen-year-old British agent who has appeared in twelve bestselling books, five graphic novels, and his own action figure line.[50] Tom Clancy spy-themed video games helped catapult the U.S. video game industry from a $2 billion business in 1996 to a $43.4 billion industry in 2018.[51]

Spies are cornering a larger share of television and movie audiences today, too. In the 1995–1996 television season, only two shows remotely related to intelligence—*The X Files* and *JAG*—made Nielsen's Top 100 list for the most watched programs. In the 2005–2006 season, there were twelve, a striking sixfold increase.[52] As households have switched from traditional TV to Internet streaming services, spy-themed shows have followed them, with Jack Ryan making his Amazon Prime debut in 2019. Today, Hollywood studios are releasing twice as many spy blockbusters as they did in the 1980s.[53]

Real spies have always had a complicated relationship with fictional ones. On the one hand, intelligence agencies have been courting Hollywood for decades in the hopes of getting favorable portrayals. On the other hand, they often decry the negative and unrealistic depictions that often result.

No one promoted an agency's reputation in the entertainment industry more assiduously than FBI Director J. Edgar Hoover. Presiding over
the Bureau from 1924 to his death in 1972, Hoover was a one-man public
relations machine who cooperated only with producers and reporters
that portrayed the Bureau in a positive light.[54] By the 1930s, there were
FBI-themed movies, radio shows, comic strips, even bubble gum
cards.[55] With the onset of the Great Depression, Americans were eager
for heroes, escapism, and the triumph of good over evil. In 1935, movies
regularly featured the FBI, including Warner Brothers' *G-Men*, starring
the biggest tough guy in Hollywood, James Cagney.[56] These films glori-
fied FBI agents as intrepid heroes, guns in hand, who worked the streets
to solve crimes and always got their man.[57] Although Hoover was quick
to say that he did not officially endorse *G-Men*, the Bureau was flooded
with fan mail after the movie's release.[58]

Today, the FBI, CIA, and Defense Department all have public affairs
officers or entertainment industry liaisons who work with Hollywood
writers, directors, and producers to try to favorably portray their organizations by "showing them the inside."[59] In 2008, the FBI sponsored a
special public relations seminar called "FBI 101" for the Writer's Guild
of America.[60] The CIA has developed and pitched its own list of story-
lines for screenwriters to consider.[61] The Army, Navy, Air Force, and
Marines have deployed to Los Angeles, setting up entertainment liaison
offices there.[62]

At Langley, movie posters decorate the public affairs conference
room.[63] In 2004, the CIA had *Alias* actress Jennifer Garner appear in a
recruitment video.[64] For years, the CIA's kid website featured a cartoon
spy named "Junior Officer Ava Shoephone," who wore bright red lip-
stick and a trench coat and spoke through a secret telephone embedded
in her high-heeled shoe.[65] The agency even named its venture capital
firm In-Q-Tel after Q, the gadgets master from James Bond; former CIA
general counsel Jeffrey Smith told National Public Radio, "We really
needed something that also had appeal to a wider audience and, frankly,
had some sex to it."[66]

At the same time, the CIA dislikes the sinister depictions of agency
life that ride shotgun with all the Hollywood glamour. In 2006, Robert

DeNiro starred in a film about the CIA's early days called *The Good Shepherd*. CIA officials were hoping it would be for the agency what *Flags of Our Fathers* was for the Marines: a glamorous glimpse of the country's unsung heroes. Instead, the movie tells a dark and disturbing fictionalized account of how a spycatcher named Edward Wilson (a character based very loosely on the CIA's dark and disturbing counterintelligence chief, James Jesus Angleton) loses his soul while serving his country. The film's only heroic figure was a Soviet KGB officer. CIA officers eventually published a history roundtable about the film. Needless to say, they weren't fans.[67]

Perhaps no movie captures the risks that arise when Hollywood writes history like *Zero Dark Thirty*, the Academy Award–nominated film about the CIA's ten-year hunt for Osama bin Laden.[68]

The film received significant assistance from the CIA and portrays the agency in a very flattering light.[69] According to declassified documents, CIA officials met with moviemakers on repeated occasions, reviewed draft movie scripts, and provided access to a number of key people involved in the hunt for bin Laden.[70]

Yet when the movie was released, it generated so much controversy about what was real and what wasn't that CIA Acting Director Michael Morell had to issue a memo to the CIA workforce clarifying the facts. "The film takes significant artistic license, while portraying itself as being historically accurate," Morell wrote. "What I want you to know is that *Zero Dark Thirty* is a dramatization, not a realistic portrayal of the facts."[71]

Morell didn't stop there. His memo directly disputed the movie's central claim: that harsh interrogation methods were pivotal to tracking bin Laden to his compound in Abbottabad, Pakistan. "The film creates the strong impression that the enhanced interrogation techniques that were part of our former detention and interrogation program were the key to finding Bin Laden. *That impression is false*," Morell wrote [emphasis mine]. "The truth is that multiple streams of intelligence led CIA analysts to conclude that Bin Laden was hiding in Abbottabad. Some came from detainees subjected to enhanced techniques, but there were many other sources as well."[72]

This was a big deal. Both the efficacy and morality of harsh interrogation techniques have been the subjects of intense debate, with defenders arguing that these methods produced some useful information that contributed to finding bin Laden, and critics emphasizing how harsh interrogations produced false and misleading information that hindered progress and raised deep ethical concerns.[73] Reality is nuanced. The movie was not. The result was deeply misleading.

Yet writer Mark Boal and director Kathryn Bigelow marketed *Zero Dark Thirty* as a faithful reporting of the facts, calling it a "reported film" and a "docu-drama."[74] The film's opening frame declares that it is "based on first hand accounts of actual events." These are strong words. Bigelow kept using them, repeating the "based on first-hand accounts" mantra as she defended her film in the press.[75] She even used them when she went on the comedy show *The Colbert Report*.[76] It was a surreal moment: a filmmaker masquerading as a journalist telling a comedian masquerading as a news anchor that her fictional film masquerading as a documentary was a "first draft of history."

Under fire, Bigelow eventually claimed that *Zero Dark Thirty* was just putting it out there for others to debate the issues. As she wrote in the *Los Angeles Times*, "Those of us who work in the arts know that depiction is not endorsement."[77] Those of us who work in the academy know something else: too often, depiction is shoddy education.

In Search of Spy Facts

While spy fiction has become ubiquitous, spy facts remain scarce. The Intelligence Community acknowledges the problem and has taken important steps to make more information public in recent years.[78] Still, new technologies, outdated classification policies, and the Intelligence Community's enduring culture of secrecy have made official information about American intelligence agencies hard to come by, while creating a bizarre information universe that is technically classified but widely known. The effect is a confusing labyrinth where it's hard to untangle what is real and what isn't.

Over-Classification, Declassification, and Reclassification

The current classification system arose during the Cold War, when government officials kept paper records and managed information by hand instead of computers. Even today, information is divided into three classification levels based on the degree of potential harm to U.S. national security if it is disclosed in an unauthorized manner:

- **Confidential** information could reasonably be expected to "cause damage" to U.S. national security.
- **Secret** information could reasonably be expected to cause "serious damage" to U.S. national security.
- **Top secret** information could reasonably be expected to cause "exceptionally grave damage" to U.S. national security.[79]

Protecting information, sources, and methods is critical to American national security; no democracy can be fully transparent. There's a reason Vice President Harry Truman didn't know anything about the Manhattan Project to build an atomic weapon until President Franklin Roosevelt died and he became president.

At the same time, officials have frequently complained that far too much information is classified unnecessarily, impeding information sharing between agencies, hindering collaboration between the government and outside experts, and undermining democratic accountability. In some sense, the problem is so severe precisely because it is no one's fault: bureaucracies naturally hoard information because revealing secrets can get bureaucrats into trouble but keeping them rarely does. When in doubt, it's better to classify.

Complaints about over-classification are nearly as old as the classification system itself. In 1956, the Coolidge Committee, led by Assistant Secretary of Defense Charles Coolidge, warned that "over-classification has reached serious proportions."[80] In 1997, a blue-ribbon commission on government secrecy chaired by Senator Daniel Patrick Moynihan found that there were no consistent guidelines or statutory standards for determining what should be classified. "Apart from aspects of nuclear energy subject to the Atomic Energy Act," Moynihan's commission concluded, "secrets in the Federal Government are whatever anyone with a stamp decides to stamp secret."[81] As Moynihan put it, "For the grunts, the rule is stamp, stamp, stamp."[82]

In 2005, Secretary of Defense Donald Rumsfeld wrote in the *Wall Street Journal*, "I have long believed that too much material is classified across the federal government as a general rule."[83] His own deputy secretary of defense for counterintelligence and security, Carol Haave, conceded during tough congressional questioning that half of all classification decisions are unnecessary over-classifications.[84] And in 2020, John Hyten, the four-star Air Force general serving as vice chairman of the Joint Chiefs of Staff, declared, "In many cases in the department, we're just so overclassified it's ridiculous, just unbelievably ridiculous."[85]

Much of the problem is that today's officials are operating with analog classification policies and tools in a world of digital records. The numbers are staggering:

- The classified universe has become so large, today nearly *four million* people have security clearances.[86] That's about the equivalent of the population of Los Angeles.[87]
- In 1996, there were six million total classification decisions.[88] In 2016, there were fifty-five million, thanks to new formats like graphical images, email, instant messages, and chat.[89]
- On average, the U.S. government declassifies a third as many pages today as it did in the 1990s.[90]

In its 2017 annual report, the Information Security Oversight Office of the National Archives starkly warned that America's archaic classification system was overwhelmed and in desperate need of modernization. "Still resource-intensive and paper-based, the declassification processes in place cannot meet the demands imposed by large volumes of paper records needing timely review, let alone the deluge of electronic records already well underway," it noted. The report didn't mince words: the current system was unsustainable; it was hampering good policymaking; and it was eroding trust in government.[91]

Classification absurdities abound. Until the early 2000s, the phrase "offensive cyber operations" was classified. Not what it might mean, or what targets might be considered, or what technologies might be used. Just the phrase itself.[92]

In September 2011, when President Obama announced the killing of an American terrorist in Yemen named Anwar al-Awlaki, the president could not say the words *drone* or *CIA* in his speech.[93] That information was classified[94] even though the CIA's drone program had already been widely covered in the press.[95]

In early 2010, Army PFC Chelsea Manning illegally downloaded hundreds of thousands of classified documents about the wars in Iraq and Afghanistan onto a fake Lady Gaga CD while lip syncing to the song "Telephone" and handed them over to WikiLeaks.[96] The trove included sensitive diplomatic cables with foreign partners; the names of Iraqi and Afghan civilians who had been working with U.S. troops, putting their lives at risk;[97] and video of a U.S. helicopter attack in Baghdad that mistakenly killed civilians, including two journalists.[98]

U.S. government personnel with security clearances were told not to click on the WikiLeaks files, even though they were plastered all over the news.[99] Diplomats, soldiers, and others weren't supposed to read the documents on their home computers or on their personal time, either; at one point, the Air Force even tried to ban the children of Air Force personnel from accessing the Manning WikiLeaks files at home and blocked the *New York Times* and twenty-five other sites that were running news stories about the documents from unclassified office computers.[100]

Why all the fuss? Because the WikiLeaks documents were technically still classified, so accessing them without a legitimate reason would be a security violation for anyone with a security clearance.[101] The documents were public but secret. These classification rules meant that any undergraduate without a security clearance had greater access to leaked information about actual American policies and communications than many U.S. government officials.

Then there is reclassification. In 2006, the National Archives found that government agencies had reclassified more than twenty-five thousand documents since 1995. That's right. Classified, then declassified, then classified again—years, and sometimes decades, later. The Archives found that agencies were releasing information that should have stayed secret and reclassifying information that should have stayed public.[102]

De-Re-Classification: A Tale of Two Documents

In 1971, the Pentagon released a document titled "Nixon Strategy for Peace." It lists specific numbers of nuclear weapons, including Minuteman missiles (1000), Titan II missiles (54), and submarine-launched ballistic missiles (656). Four secretaries of defense mentioned these numbers publicly in the 1960s and 1970s.[103]

In 2006, more than a decade after the Cold War ended, Defense Department and Energy Department officials decided that these numbers should be classified. They re-issued the same document with redacted sections blacking out the well-known numbers of missiles that had been in the public domain for nearly fifty years.

"We've always known about overclassification," said Thomas Blanton, director of the nonprofit National Security Archive. "But reclassification of previously public data crossed the line into absurdity, and now our protests have established a whole new feature of the secrecy system: de-re-classification!"[104] After the National Security Archive appealed, the redactions were removed.

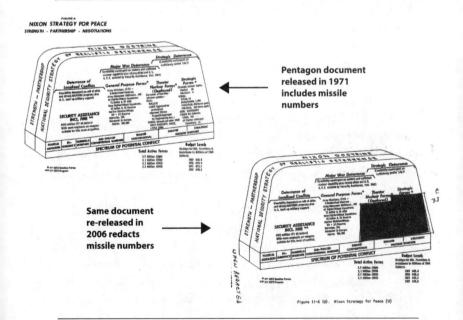

NIXON STRATEGY FOR PEACE
STRENGTH - PARTNERSHIP - NEGOTIATIONS

Pentagon document released in 1971 includes missile numbers

Same document re-released in 2006 redacts missile numbers

Figure II-6 (U).   Nixon Strategy for Peace (U)

These classification problems are funny, but they are also deadly serious. Under-classification is dangerous because it leaves the nation vulnerable to enemies. But over-classification can be dangerous, too. Hyten, the four-star Air Force general, has publicly worried that over-classification undermines deterrence—if adversaries don't know U.S. capabilities, they can't foresee what punishment they'll receive if they cross a redline. "You can't deter people if everything you have is in the black," said Hyten.[105]

Overclassification also raises the risks of marooning pieces of information in different places so that analysts cannot connect the dots in time, hiding bureaucracies from scrutiny for all the wrong reasons, and eroding trust in government about what's really going on. In a world of excessive classification, it doesn't take much to see how doubts could emerge and citizens start wondering: If the federal government is going to such great lengths to hide things everyone already knows, perhaps it's hiding more. If spy agencies are so cagey about information that shouldn't be classified in the first place, how can they ever be trusted? When it takes so long for documents to get declassified, after memories fade and key players are gone, how can we ever be sure we know the full story? The bottom line is that when spy facts are sparse, cynicism and suspicion are more likely to grow.

The Culture of Secrecy

A second barrier to understanding intelligence lies in the culture of secrecy embedded in the Intelligence Community. American intelligence agencies are world class when it comes to separating themselves from the outside world. They've had to be. Intelligence officials work in secure locations apart from the rest of us. Their writings are classified. They cannot speak freely about what they do with family, friends, or neighbors. Talk to anyone who works in an intelligence agency, and you will quickly realize that this is no ordinary workforce. It is filled with members who know their successes will probably stay secret but their failures will probably make headlines. Intelligence officials speak often of "the mission." Always in serious tones. No elaboration. They know what it means.

In such a cloistered world, culture has a powerful grip. And nothing is more central to intelligence culture than secret service to country.

While a great deal of secrecy is necessary for intelligence officials to do their jobs, a great deal is not. Insiders have often said that the National Security Agency's acronym stood for "No Such Agency," because the federal government flatly denied its existence for years.[106] When I and a group of academics were invited to visit NSA after the Snowden revelations, an NSA public affairs officer joked that her primary job used to be watching the phone ring—and not answering it.[107] Once, a CIA public affairs officer even refused to tell me his last name or hand me a business card. This wasn't some undercover operation to a dangerous place. It was an out-in-the-open outreach visit to an American university campus. Several agency analysts were with him, running a simulation for my students that they designed. Still, the person in charge of public affairs was uncomfortable being public. It was telling.

Why does this penchant for secrecy matter? Because intelligence officials often have discretion over what information the public knows even when it's not classified. I got a front-row seat to this gatekeeping power when I wrote a book examining why the CIA and FBI failed to adapt to the rising threat of terrorism before the 9/11 attack. In 2004, I contacted the FBI director's office to request an unclassified version of the Bureau's 1998 strategic plan.[108] Through interviews, I had heard that the strategic plan warned about terrorism and called for radical FBI reforms three years before 9/11, but those reforms were never implemented.[109] If true, the document was a compelling piece of evidence showing that senior officials saw the emerging terrorist threat and tried to adapt but did not succeed. I needed to see the strategic plan for myself. So I called.

The director's office sent me to public affairs, which told me I would probably need to file a Freedom of Information Act Request, the legal process used for requesting declassification (more on that below).[110] "But the document I want is not classified," I told them. "You've got a more recent strategic plan posted on your website right now. I just need the old one." I was told somebody would send it to me, along with some other unclassified materials I'd requested. Sure enough, a few weeks later, a large envelope arrived in the mail. I tore it open, excited. But instead of the documents I had requested, the FBI had filled the package with random photocopies of web pages from its public website.

It took months and a lot more digging, but I eventually got a copy of the unclassified 1998 strategic plan without the Bureau's help.[111] It was, indeed, compelling—revealing a massive effort to transform the FBI's counterterrorism capabilities that failed.[112] Ironically, the FBI later used the book I wrote, *Spying Blind*, to train new agents about its own history.

Missing in Action: Intelligence Education

Few professors study or teach intelligence. One of the biggest reasons why is data. As the FBI strategic plan saga suggests, evidence is the lifeblood of academic research, and data-driven evidence is usually much easier to find on other topics. Congress scholars, for example, have a treasure trove of historical data about committee assignments, roll call votes, hearings, legislation, and elections. Legal scholars have the full corpus of U.S. court cases and judicial opinions at their fingertips.[113] But intelligence scholars have to rely on whatever gets declassified whenever the government decides to declassify it or whatever unclassified information they can get their hands on. Even basic information like phone directories and annual budgets remains hidden from outsiders. For years, there was a cottage industry of people who scoured news stories just to try to estimate the total intelligence budget because the official number was secret.[114]

The Freedom of Information Act (FOIA) enables anyone to request the release of classified documents, and by law federal agencies must respond to all requests within twenty business days.[115] But "respond" doesn't mean "hand over the document." It only means providing a status report of the request.[116] Sometimes, information comes fast. Often it doesn't. In 2019, simple requests to the CIA took an average processing time of 225 days, complex requests took an average of 530 days, and the ten oldest requests had been pending for nine years or more.[117] The NSA took even longer.[118] This uncertainty provides strong incentives for professors to steer clear of intelligence research. With ticking tenure clocks, few career-minded academics are willing to risk their futures betting that research materials are on the way.[119]

The publishing record shows that most don't take this risk. Between 2001 and 2016, the three most highly regarded academic journals in political science—*American Political Science Review, American Journal of Political Science,* and *Journal of Politics*—published a total of 2,780 articles.[120] Only five articles—a miniscule 0.02 percent—discussed topics even tangentially related to intelligence.[121] In the post-9/11 world, while intelligence issues have been dominating headlines and policymaker attention, political scientists continue to ignore them.

Since professors teach what they know, intelligence courses to educate the next generation are also in short supply. In 2006, just four of the top twenty-five universities[122] offered any undergraduate courses on U.S. intelligence topics.[123] Ten years later, eight of the top twenty-five did.[124] While that's progress, it's still not much. I found that during that same ten-year period, a majority of the top twenty-five universities offered courses on the history of rock and roll, giving undergraduates at America's top universities a better chance of learning about U2 the rock band than the spy plane with the same name.[125]

In short, most Americans cannot learn about intelligence even if they want to. Spytainment is all they have.

Why a Little Knowledge Is a Dangerous Thing

The proliferation of spytainment has generated two policy problems. The first is a public mindset that sees intelligence agencies as far more powerful, capable, and unaccountable than they actually are. In its most extreme form, the tendency to believe intelligence agencies are omnipotent has fueled conspiracy theories that a Deep State is out there, running rogue. The second problem is a policymaking elite that invokes fictional spies and unrealistic scenarios to formulate real intelligence policy. From the heartland to the beltway, a little knowledge of intelligence turns out to be a dangerous thing.

Deep State versus Weak State: The Rise of Conspiracy Theories

Spytainment is chock-full of conspiracy theory plot lines, from Carrie Mathison's one-woman battle against corrupt CIA and White House officials on the television show *Homeland* to Jason Bourne's action-packed escape from CIA hit men in the streets of New York in the movies. Conspiracy theories make for great entertainment.

The problem is that conspiracy theories are also increasingly believed by Americans in real life. Years ago, two of the leading 9/11 conspiracy theorists admitted their popular online 9/11 "documentary," *Loose Change*, started off as a fiction screenplay based on the idea that 9/11 was an inside job.[126] For David Ray Griffin and other 9/11 conspiracy theorists who call themselves the 9/11 Truth Movement, intelligence agencies are depraved and unstoppable.[127] According to them, intelligence officials knew that al Qaeda was planning to strike New York and Washington on 9/11 and that Saddam Hussein really had no weapons of mass destruction, but a cabal of evildoers inside the secret corridors of power let tragedy strike anyway. Scratch the surface of these conspiracy theories and you find intelligence agencies are too high-tech, too powerful, too secret, and reach too far to make mistakes. Bad events don't just happen. They are intended and carefully planned. The government's penchant for secrecy is used as further proof; conspiracy theorists argue that if government officials were telling the truth, they'd let us see the classified documents.

Conspiracy theories about 9/11 aren't fringe. A 2006 Scripps poll found that 36 percent of Americans considered it "likely" or "somewhat likely" that U.S. government officials either carried out the 9/11 attacks or knowingly allowed them to occur. As *Time* magazine reported, "Thirty-six percent adds up to a lot of people. . . . It is a mainstream political reality."[128] Ten years later, a YouGov-*Economist* public opinion poll found that 25 percent of Americans still believed it was "probably" or "definitely" true that the "U.S. government helped plan the attacks of 9/11" despite no evidence that it's true and overwhelming evidence that it's not.[129]

More recently, connective technologies have created an online ecosystem tailor-made for spreading false narratives at lightning speeds and unprecedented scale.[130] The Internet has become a misinformation superhighway where conspiracy theories can be conjured up by anyone, posted on social media, spread by hashtag, amplified by bots, and picked up by mainstream media—all at the touch of a button. In this new arena, conspiracy theories are being peddled by everyone from radical bloggers to Kremlin cyber proxies.

The Trump administration pushed high-tech conspiracy theories into overdrive, accusing U.S. intelligence agencies of being part of a Deep State that was secretly working to undermine the Trump presidency at every turn.[131] President Trump used the phrase "Deep State" repeatedly,[132] accused the FBI without evidence of "spying" on his campaign,[133] and said that he trusted Russian President Vladimir Putin's denials of interfering in the 2016 presidential election more than the judgments of his own intelligence agencies.[134] President Trump also accused intelligence agencies of "running amok" and appointed loyalists without intelligence experience to, in his words, "rein them in."[135]

Conspiracy theory catchphrases and arguments about the Deep State peppered President Trump's tweets and press conferences during his term. In a single day (May 10, 2020), Trump posted nearly a hundred conspiracy-oriented tweets,[136] including several about "OBAMAGATE," which he said "makes Watergate look small time!"[137] and was "the biggest political crime in American history, by far!"[138] In a nationally televised press conference the next day, Trump repeated the claims, describing a vague and sinister plot against him. Asked by *Washington Post* reporter Philip Rucker exactly what crime had been committed, Trump replied, "Obamagate. It's been going on for a long time. . . . And from what I understand, that's only the beginning. Some terrible things happened and it should never be allowed to happen in our country again."[139] As former CIA historian Nicholas Dujmovic wrote, "The president's own rhetoric, more than any other factor, fans the flames of Deep State thinking."[140]

Those flames spread. A 2017 *Washington Post*–ABC News poll found that nearly half of all Americans (48 percent) believed that a Deep State of "military, intelligence and government officials who try to secretly manipulate government policy" exists; only 35 percent thought the Deep State was an unfounded conspiracy theory.[141] A 2019 *Economist*-YouGov poll found that 51 percent of Americans had heard of the Deep State. Among Republicans who had heard of the Deep State, 83 percent believed it was working to overthrow President Trump. Even 10 percent of Democrats who said they had heard of the Deep State thought it was trying to remove Trump.[142]

In the 2020 presidential election, Trump's conspiracy theories threatened the democratic transfer of power for the first time in American history. Refusing to concede, Trump insisted without any evidence that the election had been "rigged" and that he'd rightfully won.[143] Most Republicans believed him. In reality, democratic candidate Joseph Biden won both the electoral college and the popular vote by large margins, and judges across the country threw out more than sixty baseless lawsuits filed by Trump's legal team alleging voter fraud for lack of evidence.[144] On January 6, 2021, the day Congress met to certify the electoral college results, Trump delivered a speech to thousands of followers insisting the election had been stolen from him. Shortly after, a pro-Trump mob attacked the Capitol, forcing Representatives and Senators to evacuate to a secure location. Days later, the House of Representatives impeached Trump for "inciting an insurrection" in a bipartisan vote—making him the only president to be impeached twice.

The 2020 election revealed the powerful grip of conspiracy thinking and the very real dangers that it poses. For intelligence agencies, the themes of conspiracy theories are always the same: intelligence agencies are too powerful, secret, and rogue—just like they are in the movies. No amount of evidence will ever be enough to prove that suspicions are unfounded and bureaucrats are just trying to do their jobs.

In 2021, Senate Intelligence Committee Vice Chairman Marco Rubio (R-FL) was so concerned about myths and misperceptions, he gave a short tutorial about what intelligence actually is during the committee's public intelligence threat hearing. "There's a lot of TV shows about intelligence, there's a lot of movies," warned Rubio. "The work of our intelligence agencies is depicted in all kinds of ways in the popular culture, in the media, in the darkest recesses of the internet."[145]

I do not mean to suggest that intelligence agencies and officials never overstep their legal authorities, keep information from Congress, or engage in objectionable activities. They have. I discuss some of the more disturbing chapters in intelligence history in chapters 7 and 8. And it's worth noting that even programs deemed to be legal—such as CIA

drone strikes targeting American citizens without judicial review[146]—
raise unsettling issues about ethics and policy. But the allure of conspiracy theories and Deep State thinking raises serious questions about
how well intelligence agencies can fulfill their mission in the future if
large swaths of the public, and even the president, view them with such
suspicion. So long as citizens believe that intelligence agencies can track
anyone, go anywhere, and do anything—whether for good or for ill—
real intelligence weaknesses are less likely to get fixed and real excesses
are more likely to go unchecked.

Invoking Fake Spies to Make Real Policy

Fictional spies are influencing policymakers, too, from soldiers fighting
on the front lines to justices sitting on the nation's highest court.

In the fall of 2002, Lt. Col. Diane Beaver, the Staff Judge Advocate
General at Guantanamo Bay, ran a series of brainstorming sessions
about interrogation techniques that might be used on terrorist detainees held there. She later admitted that Jack Bauer, the lead character on
the hit Fox television drama 24 "gave people lots of ideas."[147] Bauer, a
federal counterterrorism agent played by Kiefer Sutherland, repeatedly
used torture to elicit information that would save the United States from
imminent terrorist attack, using the mantra, "Whatever it takes." Beaver
ultimately approved the use of dogs, sexual humiliation, waterboarding,
and other controversial interrogation techniques.[148] The dean of the
U.S. Military Academy at West Point, Army Brig. Gen. Patrick Finnegan,
became so concerned that 24 was hurting cadet training by glamorizing
the efficacy and morality of torture, he visited the show's creative team
in Los Angeles to request that they produce episodes where torture
backfires. In a truth-is-stranger-than-fiction moment, the show's crew
thought that General Finnegan, who came wearing his military uniform,
was an actor.[149]

Other military educators reported similar concerns that soldiers in
the field could not differentiate what they were seeing on television—in
shows that included 24, Lost, The Wire, and Alias, where interrogators
faced imminent threats and torture always worked—from how they

were supposed to behave in the field. This led to an unusual partnership between military educators, Hollywood producers and writers, and the nonprofit organization Human Rights First to create a military training film aimed at educating junior soldiers about the differences between fictionalized interrogations and their real-life jobs.[150]

The military is not suffering this problem alone. Members of Congress, presidential candidates, and even former CIA Director Leon Panetta have all debated serious issues of policy by contemplating Jack Bauer plot lines, particularly ones involving ticking time bomb scenarios where a suspected terrorist in custody is thought to hold vital information about an imminent threat to large numbers of people. In reality, these ticking time bomb situations have never occurred, and national security experts have long argued that they are unrealistic.[151] According to Jack Cloonan, who spent twenty-five years as an FBI special agent and interrogated several al Qaeda members in the 1990s, even the Israelis, who have been dealing with terrorism for decades, have never faced a ticking time bomb situation. "A show like *24*," Cloonan notes, popularized the ticking time bomb and "makes all of us believe that this is real. It's not," said Cloonan. "Throw that stuff out. It doesn't happen."[152]

And yet, both Jack Bauer and ticking time bombs have been real considerations in national security policy. In 2005, the Senate Judiciary Committee delved into ticking time bombs during its confirmation hearing of Alberto Gonzales to become the attorney general.[153] In a 2006 Heritage Foundation panel discussion of *24*, former Secretary of Homeland Security Michael Chertoff praised Jack Bauer and the show as "reflecting real life."[154] John Yoo, the George W. Bush administration lawyer who authored the memos justifying the use of waterboarding and other harsh interrogation techniques, wrote a book about his time in government that referenced Jack Bauer and considered the ticking time bomb scenario to be plausible.[155]

During the 2008 presidential campaign, Jack Bauer was a major topic of conversation on Washington's most venerated Sunday news show, *Meet the Press*. The week's guest was not a Hollywood producer or actor, but former President Bill Clinton, who was asked to comment on public statements made by his wife, presidential candidate Hillary Clinton, on interrogation policy.[156] In 2009, several members of the Senate Select Committee on Intelligence pressed CIA director nominee Leon Panetta about what interrogation techniques he might use if confronted with a "ticking time bomb situation."[157] Panetta took the hypothetical seriously, telling the intelligence committee that he would seek "whatever additional authority" he needed to get information that would protect Americans from imminent harm. The press quickly dubbed the policy the "Jack Bauer exception" to President Obama's ban on the use of harsh interrogation techniques.[158]

The late Supreme Court Justice Antonin Scalia even suggested—twice, in public—that he would turn to TV operative Jack Bauer to resolve legal questions about interrogation methods. At a 2007 international conference on torture and terrorism law, a Canadian judge offhandedly remarked, "Thankfully, security agencies in all our countries do not subscribe to the mantra, 'What would Jack Bauer do?'" Scalia rushed to the fake intelligence officer's defense, referring to details of the show's season two plotline, where Bauer tortures a suspected terrorist to prevent a nuclear attack on Los Angeles. "Jack Bauer saved Los Angeles," Scalia remarked. "He saved hundreds of thousands of lives." Arguing that law enforcement officials deserve latitude in times of crisis, Justice Scalia challenged the panel, "Are you going to convict Jack Bauer? . . . I don't think so."[159]

The following year in a BBC News interview, Scalia again invoked 24, arguing that the Los Angeles ticking time bomb scenario creates an exception to the Constitution's Eighth Amendment prohibition of cruel and unusual punishment. "Is it really so easy to determine that smacking someone in the face to find out where he has hidden the bomb that is about to blow up Los Angeles is prohibited under the Constitution?" Scalia asked. "Because smacking someone in the face would violate the 8th amendment in a prison context. . . . Is it obvious that what can't be done for punishment can't be done to exact information that is crucial to this society?" When the BBC reporter pointed out that a ticking time bomb situation was completely unrealistic, Scalia defended it anyway.[160]

Spy fiction has also affected congressional policymaking. Tom Clancy's *Red Storm Rising* inspired Vice President Dan Quayle's support for the development of anti-satellite weapons during his time in the Senate.[161] Of Clancy's stories, Quayle said, "They're not just novels. . . . They're read as the real thing."[162] Quayle later recommended Clancy as a consultant for the White House Space Council.[163]

At a Senate Intelligence Committee hearing in June 2017, Senator Tom Cotton (R-AR) compared the "fantastical situations" of spy fiction to the allegations that Attorney General Jeff Sessions colluded with the Russians during the 2016 presidential elections. Cotton began his inquiry by asking whether Sessions enjoyed espionage entertainment. Sessions quickly responded that he had "just finished" David Ignatius's bestselling espionage thriller, *The Director*.[164]

The Trust Challenge

Spytainment isn't all fun and games. Mounting evidence suggests that fiction too often substitutes for fact, creating fertile ground for conspiracy theories to grow and influencing the formulation of real intelligence policy. Most Americans, including members of Congress, cabinet officials, and judges making policies affecting national security, don't know much about the secret world of intelligence. The costs are hidden but significant.

In the twenty-first century, the tip of the spear isn't a spear. It's intelligence—the ability to find, acquire, and analyze information to give us decision advantage against adversaries in physical space, outer space, and cyberspace. But secret agencies in democratic societies cannot succeed without trust. And trust requires knowledge. As former CIA and NSA Director Michael Hayden once put it, "The American people have to trust us and in order to trust us they have to know about us."[165]

3

AMERICAN INTELLIGENCE HISTORY AT A GLANCE

FROM FAKE BAKERIES TO ARMED DRONES

> There is nothing more necessary than good intelligence to frustrate a designing enemy, and nothing that requires greater pains to obtain.
>
> —GEORGE WASHINGTON, JANUARY 5, 1756[1]

IN THE SUMMER OF 1781, Gen. George Washington tricked the British with a bakery. The deception was part of a huge gamble that would change the outcome of the Revolutionary War.

The war had been raging for six years. Benedict Arnold, one of Washington's ablest generals, had recently betrayed the cause, switched sides, and tried to hand over the rebels' strategic garrison at West Point.[2] As the Continental Army and allied French forces camped outside of New York, money grew tight, and morale was low. "Our affairs were then in the most ruinous train imaginable," Washington later wrote.[3]

On August 14, Washington finally received some good news: French naval allies were sailing from the Caribbean toward the Virginia peninsula.[4] It was the chance he'd been waiting for. At that moment, British forces were split into two large contingents. One occupied New York City under the command of Gen. Henry Clinton. The other, about seven thousand men led by Lord Cornwallis, had marched south, capturing Charleston and Savannah before landing in Yorktown, Virginia. If Washington could reach Yorktown before British reinforcements from New York arrived, he could defeat Cornwallis and score a decisive victory.

It was a big if. Somehow, Washington had to convince Gen. Clinton in New York that the Continental Army was remaining in the area while it was actually marching two hundred miles south. In addition to designing fake communications to fall into British hands, Washington decided to go one step further, devising an elaborate deception that included the construction of French bake ovens.[5] Because French bread was a major source of food, bake ovens were a telling indicator of troop movements.

Washington ordered that large brick bake ovens be built in Chatham, New Jersey—an ideal stopping point en route to Yorktown but still close enough to New York to look like it was part of a permanent encampment.[6] Men were dispatched to buy as many bricks for the bake ovens as they could, in the hopes they would be seen by Loyalists and reported to Clinton. Washington even sent a guard unit to protect the construction of the ovens. The bakery started churning out three thousand loaves a day.[7] Days after the Continental Army left, the ovens were still baking and the guards were still guarding them to keep up the ruse.[8]

It worked. Clinton was convinced that Washington's troops were staying put even as they headed to Yorktown. Without reinforcements, Cornwallis was forced to surrender in Virginia. It was the last major battle of the war.

———

Espionage has always been part of American history. This chapter briefly traces 250 years of American intelligence, highlighting the major patterns, key events, and intelligence organizations that have influenced the way intelligence operates today.

Two and a half centuries may seem like a long time, but the United States is a relative newcomer to intelligence. George Washington's skillful use of espionage during the Revolutionary War came more than two thousand years after Chinese general Sun Tzu wrote *The Art of War*, the first book to describe how to use intelligence in warfare.[9] Ivan the Terrible used intelligence to quell dissent in Russia two centuries before the American Revolution (1533–1584).[10] French intelligence flourished under the hand of Cardinal Richelieu (1624–1642), who created the first Black Chamber (cabinet noir), a government office responsible for intercepting, opening, decrypting, and copying correspondence. Many hallmarks of Britain's modern intelligence system—including its recruitment of promising university students, the close integration of intelligence and statecraft, the use of codebreaking alliances with other nations, and the existence of intelligence leaders who "spoke truth to power"—date to the reign of Elizabeth I (1558–1603).[11] When British codebreakers at Bletchley Park cracked Hitler's ciphers in World War II, it was the third time in 350 years that British codebreaking prevented a foreign invasion.[12]

In comparison, America's intelligence history is remarkably short and has been marked by three distinct overarching patterns: halting development, organizational fragmentation, and democratic tensions.

Halting Development

The development of U.S. intelligence capabilities has evolved in fits and starts, driven largely by wartime necessity and America's evolving role in the world.

Until the mid-twentieth century, intelligence was considered a strictly wartime endeavor, not a peacetime capability to help policymakers gain advantage in international affairs. George Washington's sophisticated intelligence apparatus helped win the revolution but did not outlast his presidency. The United States had no permanent intelligence organizations until the 1880s, when the Army and Navy established small units. Even these organizations faced boom-and-bust cycles, expanding when warfighting necessitated and demobilizing when hostilities ended.

It was only after World War II that permanent, robust peacetime intelligence capabilities took hold.[13] In 1947, Congress passed legislation creating a Central Intelligence Agency to coordinate the activities of different intelligence offices in the military services, the Justice Department, and the State Department.[14] Collectively known as the United States Intelligence Community (IC), these disparate intelligence organizations have grown in number over time. By 2000, the IC included a dozen federal agencies and an estimated $30 billion budget.[15] Since 9/11, the number of agencies has ballooned to eighteen, with a new Office of the Director of National Intelligence to oversee and coordinate them all.

The growth of U.S. intelligence largely reflects America's changing role in geopolitics. In the eighteenth and nineteenth centuries, America was a fledgling nation separated from Europe by a vast ocean. Geography mattered. Europe was a rough neighborhood with close borders and hostile powers nursing age-old grievances and vying for advantage.[16] America stayed away from great power politics both because it had to and because it could.

Instead, American presidents were focused on national survival, securing their new union from European encroachment and expanding westward by seizing more Native American lands. Thomas Jefferson declared in his first inaugural address that he sought "peace, commerce, and honest friendship with all nations, entangling alliances with none."[17] America did not venture abroad "in search of monsters to destroy," as John Quincy Adams famously put it in 1821—because it was too busy nation-building at home.[18] As historian David Kennedy notes, "isolation represented the most obvious strategic choice for a relatively small, weak state, and one that leveraged the peculiarities of its uniquely insular geography."[19]

Aversion to standing armies or permanent intelligence capabilities ran deep. "While Americans were willing to fight when necessary in the nineteenth century, and were more than comfortable expanding national power through military force," writes political historian Julian Zelizer, "most politicians and citizens were unwilling to commit to a permanent national security state. They would fight a war, and then when it was done, they put away their arms and set their minds to other things."[20]

That changed after World War II. Two world wars had left eighty million dead[21] and ravaged the economies and societies of Europe. The Japanese attack on Pearl Harbor in 1941 brought the United States into the war, which helped transform the nation from a reluctant global power into an undisputed one. The early post-war years saw the rise of a new international order led by the United States, with new organizations designed to secure the peace, promote prosperity, and spread democratic values. These included the United Nations, alliances such as the North Atlantic Treaty Organization (NATO), the World Bank and International Monetary Fund, the General Agreement on Tariffs and Trade (the precursor to the World Trade Organization), and a number of treaties and conventions.[22]

At the same time, even before the war ended, U.S. leaders grew concerned that the Soviet Union would spread Communism by force, by proxy, and by propaganda throughout Eastern Europe, war-torn Western Europe, and Asia, threatening U.S. allies and interests. As allied forces met at Yalta in 1945 to frame the new European order, the contours of the post-war world—the devastation of Europe, the economic and military primacy of the United States, and the rising Communist threat—were already apparent. In 1946, just months after the peace treaty was signed, Winston Churchill delivered his Iron Curtain speech, warning that Europe was fast becoming divided into two spheres: a totalitarian bloc under Moscow's control and free Western democracies.[23] To lead the world in the fight against Communism, the United States would need stronger national security organizations and capabilities, including intelligence. As Senator Henry M. "Scoop" Jackson (D-WA) put it in 1959, "Organization by itself cannot assure a strategy for victory in the cold war. But good organization can help, and poor organization can hurt."[24]

Fragmented Organizations

The second recurring pattern of American intelligence history is organizational fragmentation. Presidents, their advisors, and military commanders have always struggled to coordinate intelligence collection and analysis. In part, coordination challenges are inevitable: getting the right information in the hands of the right people at the right time is hard, especially when different pieces of intelligence reside in so many different large bureaucracies, each with its own headquarters, workforce, cultures, classification procedures, and competitive inclinations.

In part, these coordination challenges reflect the proliferation of intelligence methods—described in chapter 4—as well as the wide array of intelligence needs of individual decisionmakers. Specialization has benefits. In the 1880s the Army and Navy each created their own intelligence units because they had different needs. Today, the National

Reconnaissance Office builds and maintains spy satellites, the CIA recruits spies, and the National Security Agency intercepts electronic communications and breaks codes. Those are very different mission sets requiring tailored skills and capabilities.

Specialization also ensures that intelligence customers get the information they most need and want. Good intelligence for the Navy is different from good intelligence for the Army, or the secretary of defense, or the president. Even within an organization, intelligence needs vary widely. An infantry officer needs to know whether the road up ahead is still passable. The commanding officer needs to know where the enemy is moving across the battlefield, how fast, and why. The chairman of the Joint Chiefs of Staff has to understand adversary capabilities and movements across the world and whether today's battlefield decisions affect America's preparedness elsewhere.

Each intelligence agency tailors intelligence for specific customers. Doing so, and doing it well, has its advantages, but the tradeoff is that tailored intelligence makes the whole system much harder to coordinate. The danger of fragmentation is that dots don't get connected because they are often collected and then marooned in different parts of the sprawling Intelligence Community. In 2017, the Office of the Director of National Intelligence reported that four million people held security clearances, 1.3 million of which were top secret.[25] There were hundreds of special access programs (SAPs) requiring clearances above top secret.[26] Information was so compartmented, even senior leaders didn't know about all the programs. "There's only one entity in the entire universe that has visibility on all SAPs—that's God," said former Director of National Intelligence James Clapper.[27]

Democratic Tensions

The third recurring pattern in American intelligence history has been the consistent, uneasy tension between secrecy and democracy, between the need for a government strong enough to provide security but restrained enough to protect individual rights.

Modern-day concerns over NSA surveillance, data privacy, and counterterrorism policies have deep roots. When President Truman signed the law creating the CIA in 1947, he feared creating an American Gestapo and insisted the new intelligence agency have no domestic intelligence-gathering or law enforcement capabilities.

More than a century and a half earlier, the Framers had also struggled to reconcile the tension between democracy and security. The chief architect of the Constitution, James Madison, was deeply conflicted about how to strike the right balance, going "back and forth over the course of his long career . . . about how security should inflect the powers we invest in government," write Benjamin Wittes and Ritika Singh. "In Madison's vacillations . . . we see fascinating harbingers of our own."[28]

History, in short, casts a long shadow. The organizational capabilities, challenges, and controversies of today's intelligence agencies are rooted in America's founding debates, the nation's evolving role in the world, and age-old coordination challenges.

Revolutionary Beginnings

America's founding owes much to intelligence.[29] George Washington, Benjamin Franklin, and other Founding Fathers are remembered today as virtuous creators of a bold new democracy. But they were also cunning spymasters and manipulators of their information environment—a side of the founding story that has often been overlooked.

George Washington's inability to tell a lie is a lie. The cherry-tree fable—in which young George admits to his father that he did, indeed, chop down the tree with his hatchet—was invented by a Washington biographer named Mason Locke Weems in 1806 to boost his book sales. In truth, Washington was an avid spymaster with a talent for deception that would remain unequaled by American presidents for the next 150 years.

During the Revolutionary War, Washington had his own secret code number (711) and made frequent use of ciphers and invisible ink.[30] His extensive network of spies included Paul Revere, the not-so-able Nathan Hale (see box), and the most successful espionage cell of the day, the Culper spy ring of operatives in Long Island who made

Nathan Hale: America's First Fallen Spy

In August 1776, British forces drove George Washington's Continental Army out of Long Island. Desperate for information about British troop strength and plans, Washington instructed Colonel Thomas Knowlton to send a spy behind enemy lines. A twenty-one-year old captain from Connecticut named Nathan Hale courageously volunteered.

Hard facts are scant, but evidence suggests the operation was botched from the start. The mission was announced and volunteers solicited in a meeting of several officers—poor operational security.[31] Hale used his real name[32] and brought his Yale diploma with him, presumably to bolster his cover story that he was an unemployed school teacher looking for work—except that unemployed school teachers didn't usually hang around British fortifications. In addition to Hale's flimsy cover, Hale was known to be exceptionally trusting, a poor quality for a spy. Even before he left, Hale discussed the assignment with an old Yale classmate, Captain William Hull, who believed Hale was too honest to lie about anything and tried to talk him out of the mission.[33]

Hull was right. A few days after landing in Long Island, Hale made the crucial and amateurish blunder of trusting a stranger who turned out to be British Major Robert Rogers. Pretending to be a fellow colonial spy, Rogers got Hale to confide over dinner in a tavern, then promptly captured him the next morning.[34] Hale was hanged in present-day midtown Manhattan on September 22, 1776, becoming the first American spy executed in the line of duty. He is famous for allegedly declaring just before his death, "I only regret that I have but one life to lose for my country," though there is substantial doubt about whether he actually said those words.[35] Nevertheless, for two hundred years, Hale has been lionized as a symbol of American patriotism, an inept spy but a noble and brave man. As the CIA's historical review program noted, "Hale is what he is in the American pantheon not because of what he did, but because of why he did it."[36] A statue of Nathan Hale stands outside the CIA's headquarters building today.

secret signals by hanging laundry on clotheslines. Their successes included helping to unmask Benedict Arnold's treachery and preventing the British from ambushing French troops in Rhode Island in 1780, which could have had disastrous consequences.[37]

Washington employed all sorts of schemes to protect his forces, confuse his adversaries, and gain advantage. These included filling gunpowder casks with sand to make the British think his munitions were well supplied when they were nearly empty and writing fictitious reports inflating his troops' strength that were designed to fall into the hands of traitors within his own ranks. During the brutal winter of 1777–1778 at Valley Forge, with his troops starving, freezing, and dwindling in number, Washington successfully employed this subterfuge, writing documents referring to phantom infantry and cavalry regiments to convince British general Sir William Howe that the American rebels were too strong to attack. It worked. Had Howe known the truth and pressed his advantage, the Continental Army might not have survived the winter.[38]

A ragtag band of patriots defeated the most powerful country in the world because Washington used intelligence to figure out when and where *not* to fight.[39]

It wasn't just Washington who was enamored with deception. Benjamin Franklin waged a covert propaganda campaign from his Paris basement, where he set up a printing press and wrote articles designed to sway opinion across Europe. A printer by trade, Franklin even imported European paper and type to make his documents look more authentic.[40]

Some of Franklin's writings were outright lies. In 1777, for example, he wrote a fake letter from a German prince to the commander of mercenary troops fighting with the British in America. The prince complains that he is being cheated out of money owed to him and tells the commander to let wounded soldiers die so the British will pay more. The letter created an uproar in Europe over Britain's use of mercenaries.

In 1782, Franklin created a convincing forgery of a Boston newspaper that included fake local news and even fake advertisements. The main story quoted a letter from Captain Samuel Gerrish of the New England militia claiming that the British royal governor of Canada was paying Indian allies for American scalps and that many of the scalps sold were from women and children. The story was picked up and used by Whig opponents of the war in Britain. Franklin's use of deception was so skillful, the CIA named him a founding father of American intelligence.

Future Supreme Court Justice John Jay led America's first fledging counterintelligence effort, rooting out Tory sympathizers and spies. His investigative efforts included exposing a British plot to recruit traitors to sabotage American defenses in the New York area and a plot to recruit George Washington's personal bodyguard to betray the cause and kill the American leader.[41] Future Vice President Aaron Burr volunteered to disguise himself as a priest and travel behind enemy lines in Canada to deliver an urgent request to General Montgomery for reinforcements during the winter of 1775–1776.[42]

Early Failures

Although America's founders are generally credited with having greater intelligence and deception operations than the British during the war, their intelligence system also suffered from many weaknesses and failures. During this early period, America's intelligence system, from collection to analysis to counterintelligence, was largely a do-it-yourself operation. General Washington frequently served as his own spymaster and chief analyst, setting up production for invisible ink,[43] advising assets on how to maintain operational security, planting false information for suspected double agents, and assessing the value of the information that came in.

Because Washington was enmeshed in running so many intelligence and military operations, he sometimes found it difficult to keep track of everything. In 1777, he wrote to one of his agents, "It runs in my head that I was to corrispond [sic] with you by a fictitious name, if so I have forgotten the name and must be reminded of it again."[44] In 1775, Washington ordered a secret paramilitary mission to seize gunpowder stores in Bermuda. The men arrived to find no gunpowder but several enemy ships. It turns out another American group had already raided the depot but never told Washington.[45] These kinds of coordination challenges would bedevil American intelligence for the next two and a half centuries.

Washington also experienced his share of outright intelligence failures. Nathan Hale ended his mission empty-handed and at the gallows.

The Continental Army's devastating 1777 defeat at Brandywine Creek, which resulted in the deaths of 10 percent of Washington's force, stemmed in large part from the failure of local militia to detect the English advance.[46]

When Gen. Benedict Arnold became a turncoat and joined the British, Washington was stunned by his comrade's treachery—but he should not have been. It was well known that the British were trying to recruit American military commanders. Rumors were swirling that a patriot general had switched sides. Washington's intelligence chief, Benjamin Tallmadge, had received word that there was a highly placed British spy in American ranks. And Arnold, one of Washington's most talented generals, was known to be greatly disgruntled, politically besieged, severely injured, and in financial trouble. He had also recently married Peggy Shippen, the daughter of a well-known Tory sympathizer in Philadelphia.[47]

Benjamin Franklin's delegation in Paris was also penetrated by a British secret agent, none other than Franklin's delegation secretary, Edward Bancroft, who transmitted details of Franco-American diplomacy to his handlers in London faster than they reached the U.S. Congress. Bancroft's espionage would not be uncovered until a century later, when secret documents were revealed in British archives.[48]

Nevertheless, on balance, the patriots' intelligence successes were impressive, particularly for a new nation with so little experience in espionage.

After the war ended, as president, George Washington continued to devote significant attention to intelligence, setting a number of important precedents. In 1790, just three years after the Constitutional Convention, Congress acknowledged an executive prerogative to conduct intelligence operations and gave President Washington a secret unvouchered fund for it. (In fact, Washington dispatched Gouverneur Morris overseas even before Congress provided the funding, making Morris the first intelligence officer sent abroad under the Constitution.[49])

The secret intelligence fund received $40,000 in the first year, but within two years, the amount had risen to $1 million, or a whopping 12 percent of the federal budget. (To put that into perspective, 12 percent of the 2019 federal budget would be about $528 billion; intelligence spending in 2019 was approximately $82 billion.[50]) Notably, Congress required the president to certify the sums he spent from that first secret fund but allowed him to keep secret both the purposes and the recipients of payments. This set a strong precedent of secrecy for protecting "sources and methods," or the specific means by which intelligence is acquired.[51]

On-Again, Off-Again Intelligence

Washington's administration would prove to be an anomaly in the country's early intelligence history. His successors devoted relatively little attention or resources to intelligence.[52] Although sporadic espionage missions continued, the U.S. government did not establish any peacetime intelligence collection or analysis organizations for nearly a hundred years following Washington's presidency. Instead, from the late eighteenth century to the mid-twentieth century, U.S. intelligence was generally poor, with bursts of action to improve capabilities during wartime followed by long periods of neglect.

Even during wartime, intelligence efforts often fell short. During the War of 1812, military intelligence was so poor that the British threat to Washington, D.C., was not realized until enemy forces were just sixteen miles away. On the night of August 24, 1814, as British troops closed in, First Lady Dolley Madison barely had time to rescue the original draft of the Declaration of Independence and Gilbert Stuart's portrait of George Washington hanging in the state dining room. British officers arrived to find the Madisons' dinner and wine left on the table. They ate the meal, then proceeded to torch the house, along with much of the city.[53]

When the Civil War began in April 1861, neither the Union nor the Confederacy had any substantial intelligence capabilities. Instead, generals on both sides scrambled to gather information on enemy strength, plans, and troop movements by recruiting spies; monitoring newspapers; interrogating prisoners of war, deserters, and refugees; retrieving documents from corpses on the battlefield; and sending scouts or messengers behind enemy lines.

Both sides also invented new intelligence methods. These included using hot air balloons to conduct overhead reconnaissance (presaging

the modern-day use of satellites, spy planes, and drones) and pioneering
the use of a flag signaling system to communicate from hilltop observation stations over great distances during battle. At the first Battle of Bull
Run, a Confederate soldier standing on top of a hill saw something
gleaming in the distance. Believing Union troops were attempting a
flanking maneuver, he signaled his commanding officer using the "wig-
wag" flag system for the first time.[54] It worked. The Confederates ended
up making a surprising show at Bull Run, suggesting the war would not
be as short-lived as many expected and that signals intelligence would
remain vital for any and all future warfare.[55]

By the war's end, Union intelligence outperformed Confederate intelligence for mundane bureaucratic reasons rather than heroic ones. In
the South, various intelligence activities were not coordinated into "all-
source" intelligence. General Robert E. Lee and his predecessor never
had a single staff officer devoted to intelligence. Lee and his staff maintained such poor records that enemy organization charts were apparently kept in their heads instead of on paper.[56]

The North maintained a similarly fragmented intelligence system
for the first two years of the war, splintering responsibilities for collection and analysis among various groups. There were balloonists sending
reports of troop movements;[57] messenger, telegraph, and intelligence
activities conducted by various battlefield commanders at their own
discretion;[58] rival "secret service" detective units established by Allan
Pinkerton and Lafayette Baker;[59] and even activities directed and
paid for by President Lincoln himself.[60] Perhaps most significantly,
there was no clearinghouse unit to put pieces together and provide
the big picture—an issue that would haunt American intelligence
nearly a century later. Each organization sent reports to different people,
and coordination was so disjointed that in at least two instances,
Pinkerton and Baker operatives arrested or conducted surveillance on
each other.[61]

In 1863, however, when Maj. Gen. Joseph Hooker was given command of the Army of the Potomac, he ordered the creation of the Bureau
of Military Information, which became the first all-source intelligence
since George Washington ran spies during the Revolutionary War.

Although coordination was fiercely resisted in some quarters and challenges remained, the bureau succeeded in producing reports that culled information from a variety of sources.[62] Gen. Ulysses S. Grant found it so useful, he moved the bureau into his own headquarters at City Point, Virginia, and said that its work enabled him to "keep track of every change the enemy makes."[63]

Despite its success, the Bureau of Military Information was disbanded after the war. Not until the 1880s did the Navy and Army move to establish permanent intelligence organizations—the Office of Naval Intelligence and the Military Intelligence Division (MID, later known as the Army's G-2).

Both of these military intelligence organizations had modest beginnings. The Office of Naval Intelligence began with four officers, the Army's MID had one.[64] Both also experienced boom-and-bust cycles over the next several decades. They were utilized in the Spanish-American War and World War I, only to be largely demobilized when hostilities ended. In 1908, MID was essentially relegated to providing a map library at the Army War College.[65] By 1916, it had only three people. Then, when World War I erupted in 1917, MID staff ballooned to more than 1,400 and its contingency fund budget hit $2.5 million. By 1919, however, MID's contingency fund fell again, to just $225,000.[66]

World War I and Domestic Subversion

In July 1914, the First World War erupted in Europe, with Germany and Austria-Hungary fighting the British, French, and Russians. America tried to remain neutral. Neutrality, however, meant that the United States became an intelligence target for both sides. German intelligence agents orchestrated an elaborate subversion campaign to keep American munitions and materiel from reaching the Allies, while British agents tried to draw the United States into the war. As a result, American intelligence efforts focused on countering foreign espionage activities at home.

German plots included using local dockworkers to plant time bombs on ships ferrying supplies to the Allies,[67] establishing front companies to purchase explosive ingredients so they could not be used by their enemies to make munitions, and smuggling deadly germs to infect American horses bound for the war.[68] On July 29, 1916, German agents set fire to the Black Tom Island munitions depot in New York harbor. At the time, it was filled with two million tons of war materials bound for Europe—including explosives, weapons, and fuel.[69] The explosion was so large, it severely damaged the main building at Ellis Island, shattered windows across lower Manhattan and New Jersey, sent shrapnel tearing into the Statue of Liberty, and had the force of a 5.5 earthquake on the Richter scale. People as far away as Maryland felt the ground shake.[70]

The British, too, established extensive intelligence operations in the United States that included intercepting and decoding top secret cables from President Woodrow Wilson and leaking Germany's infamous Zimmerman telegram—which promised a German alliance to Mexico if war broke out between Germany and the United States—to draw the U.S. into the war.

Congress passed the Espionage and Sedition Acts to counter espionage and sabotage—laws that since have drawn intense criticism for their infringement on freedom of speech. President Wilson also turned to two law enforcement organizations for help: the Treasury Department's Secret Service and a relatively new organization in the Department of Justice called the Federal Bureau of Investigation (FBI).[71]

The Secret Service had been around for some time. It was founded in 1865 to combat pervasive counterfeiting, though over time, its mission evolved. After President William McKinley was assassinated in 1901, the agency assumed responsibilities for protecting the president. When World War I erupted, Wilson directed the Secret Service to investigate foreign espionage inside the United States.[72]

The FBI, by contrast, was just a few years old, created by U.S. Attorney General Charles Bonaparte to investigate possible violations of federal laws on U.S. soil.

From the beginning, the Secret Service and FBI were rivals. In fact, it was Attorney General Bonaparte's growing frustration over the necessity of borrowing Secret Service agents to investigate the rising wave of crime sweeping the country—agents that answered to the treasury secretary instead of him—that led him to begin hiring his own.[73]

During the war, the Secret Service and FBI launched uncoordinated, aggressive, and rival campaigns to root out German spies, sabo-
teurs, and immigrants suspected of disloyalty. Justice Department
efforts included forming a 250,000-member volunteer vigilante group
called the American Protective League, which committed a number
of civil liberties abuses while never actually catching a spy.[74] With the
Bolshevik Revolution of 1917, worries about radicalism grew, and
counterintelligence efforts spread to Communists, anarchists, and
other radicals.

It was during this period that the United States launched the first
nationwide domestic intelligence program in history. Government officials tapped telephones and opened mail, and in 1919 the FBI began
rounding up thousands of people, arresting hundreds, and deporting
dozens in what would be dubbed the "Palmer raids," named after Attorney General A. Mitchell Palmer.[75] Many of these domestic intelligence activities and arrests later proved to be unfounded, others outright illegal.

Although members of Wilson's administration warned that bitter bureaucratic rivalries between the Secret Service and FBI were harming
both the effectiveness of counterintelligence and the protection of civil
liberties,[76] the president took no action, commenting later that he felt
"derelict in not having sought a remedy."[77] The president who championed openness, democracy, and human rights abroad oversaw widespread surveillance operations and infringement of civil liberties at home.

This period, known as the First Red Scare, would be the first of several instances over the coming decades when the FBI would be mired
in controversy for overstepping its legal authorities.[78]

As counterintelligence efforts proliferated during the 1920s, peacetime foreign intelligence again languished. The Army's codebreaking
unit closed after the war, and although the State Department soon created a jointly funded peacetime civilian replacement called, aptly, the
Black Chamber, this effort lasted just ten years and achieved few successes. The Black Chamber's signature achievement was breaking several Japanese codes before the 1921 Washington Navy conference to
negotiate naval disarmament among the great powers. But the Black

Chamber was never as adept as its European counterparts, never broke Soviet diplomatic codes, and did not decrypt British, German, or French ciphers after 1921.[79]

Instead, the office deteriorated thanks to presidential inattention; budget reductions; reluctance by telegraph companies to share their cable traffic with the government; the Radio Communications Acts, which made radio traffic interception difficult; and opposition from Secretary of State Henry L. Stimson, who believed that spying on diplomatic communications was simply not something that civilized nations did, especially in peacetime. As he famously put it years later, "Gentlemen do not read each other's mail."[80]

Pearl Harbor: The Attack That Changed Everything

As the sun rose on December 7, 1941, hundreds of Japanese warplanes attacked the U.S. Pacific Fleet anchored at Pearl Harbor, Hawaii. By day's end, more than three thousand Americans lay dead or wounded, nearly two hundred American warplanes were destroyed, and the Pacific Fleet was in ruins. President Franklin D. Roosevelt thundered that the day would "live in infamy" and declared war against Japan.[81]

Pearl Harbor had several important consequences for U.S. intelligence. First, the attack helped spark the creation of a new wartime intelligence unit called the Office of Strategic Services (OSS).[82] The agency was the brainchild of William "Wild Bill" Donovan, whose statue stands inside the CIA headquarters lobby today. A Congressional Medal of Honor recipient, Donovan became convinced during a 1940 European tour with Roosevelt that the existing U.S. intelligence system—which left intelligence units in the War, Navy, State, Justice, and Treasury Departments to their own devices—was incapable of providing integrated analysis or operations. He had been pressing the president for an agency that would not only coordinate these disparate intelligence components but combine intelligence, collection, analysis, and clandestine foreign operations under one roof.

After Pearl Harbor, Donovan got his agency and the opportunity to lead it. By the war's end, OSS employees numbered in the thousands and were engaged in everything from guerilla warfare to clandestine activities to strategic analysis.[83] The agency proved daring and creative, sending agents directly into Germany (where all but two were killed), recruiting future celebrities to its spy ranks (see box), and even testing whether bats could be dropped over Tokyo with bombs strapped to their backs.[84] Many of these feats proved unsuccessful, others outlandish. Yet OSS and its cowboy culture heavily influenced four men in its ranks—Allen Dulles, Richard Helms, William Colby, and William Casey—all of whom would become future CIA directors. The spirit of OSS still influences the CIA's clandestine arm.[85]

Another important consequence of Pearl Harbor was that the surprise attack laid bare the dangers of uncoordinated intelligence and the need for greater centralization to ensure the right information got to the right places at the right time.

In the aftermath of Pearl Harbor, investigations found that the United States had been blindsided not because intelligence was missing but because it was poorly integrated.[86] Japan's true intentions were signaled repeatedly, but these signals were lost amidst the noise. They were scattered across different agencies and buried in a crushing flow of information and misinformation that pointed to other locations, timetables, and plans.

Much attention has been paid to this "signals-to-noise" problem in intelligence,[87] which has grown exponentially worse with time. But the signals-to-noise problem is not just about information flow; it is about organizational fragmentation. As the congressional investigation into the Japanese attack concluded, "the system of handling intelligence was seriously at fault and . . . the security of the Nation can be insured only through continuity of service and centralization of responsibility in those charged with handling intelligence."[88] There was no clearinghouse to put all the information together, the investigation concluded. America needed a central intelligence agency.

Finally, Pearl Harbor made clear that preventing surprise attack was the most important mission, the raison d'être, of intelligence. As the congressional Pearl Harbor inquiry put it, the one "enigmatical and paramount question" after December 7, 1941, was "Why, with some of the finest intelligence available in our history, with the almost certain

Famous Americans Who Were Secret OSS Officers

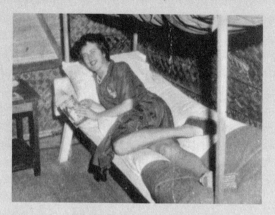

Julia Child in Kandy, Ceylon
Credit: Central Intelligence Agency

What do a famous chef, a professional baseball player, and a Supreme Court justice have in common? They all secretly served in the Office of Strategic Services, the CIA's forerunner, during World War II. Thanks to 750,000 pages of documents declassified by the National Archives in 2008, we now know the names and some of the activities of nearly twenty-four thousand people who worked in the wartime intelligence agency. Famous French cuisine chef Julia Child, Chicago White Sox catcher Moe Berg, and Supreme Court Justice Arthur Goldberg were among them. OSS officers also included the sons of both President Theodore Roosevelt and author Ernest Hemingway.[89]

Child joined OSS in 1942 under her maiden name, Julia McWilliams, becoming one of 4,500 women serving in the spy agency during the war. She held a top secret clearance and was posted overseas to China and Ceylon (present-day Sri Lanka), where she is pictured in the photograph above. Child helped track operatives around the world. She also was tasked with cooking up a recipe for shark repellent, which was used to help protect Navy personnel in shark-infested waters and to coat explosives that targeted German U-boats. Without the repellent, sharks would sometimes accidentally run into the explosives, detonating them before they reached their target. Julia met her husband, Paul Child, in the OSS, where he was also an officer.[90]

knowledge that war was at hand, with plans that contemplated the precise type of attack that was executed by Japan on the morning on December 7—why was it possible for a Pearl Harbor to occur?"[91] After the
war ended, preventing another Pearl Harbor would become the over-
riding priority of the newly minted Central Intelligence Agency.

The Central Intelligence Agency

When most people think of the CIA, they think of clandestine activities,
spy gadgets, secret raids, and Hollywood movies.[92] "Those spooky
boys," as Secretary of State Dean Rusk called them[93] did, in fact, design
exploding cigars to assassinate Cuban leader Fidel Castro, mine Nicaraguan harbors in contravention of U.S. law in the 1980s, plant Soviet
moles, and sponsor coups from Guatemala to Iran to Vietnam.[94] After
9/11, the agency continued its secret operations in the war on terror.
Activities included landing in Afghanistan just days after the terrorist
attacks to turn the tide against the Taliban, finding and killing Osama
bin Laden in Pakistan, and detaining, interrogating, and targeting suspected terrorists for drone strikes.

Yet today's CIA looks nothing like the agency originally envisioned
and created by the National Security Act of 1947. In fact, President Truman wasn't much interested in a CIA when he signed that law. His focus
was on other provisions of the National Security Act, which sought to
combine the Navy and War Departments (which housed the Army and
its air forces) into a single Department of Defense. Military unification
was one of the president's top priorities, and it sparked heated debate
and tremendous conflict. On October 20, 1945, the *New York Times* described the battle as a "brass knuckle fight" between the two military
departments and their congressional supporters.

The proposal for a peacetime intelligence agency to centralize intelligence got caught in the middle of this battle. In the end, Truman hoped
to get a small intelligence unit that would serve essentially as a global
news clipping service—coordinating, evaluating, and disseminating
intelligence that other agencies gathered from around the world.

The CIA was never supposed to collect its own intelligence. Nor
was it supposed to engage in sponsoring coups, influencing foreign

elections, or conducting other covert operations.[95] The National Security Act of 1947 charged the CIA only with "coordinating the intelligence agencies of the several Government Departments and agencies" and provided no language explicitly authorizing it to collect intelligence or conduct covert operations. As President Truman later wrote, "It was not intended as a 'Cloak & Dagger Outfit'!"[96]

The CIA may not have started out as a cloak and dagger outfit, but it quickly became one thanks to pressing security demands and loopholes in the National Security Act, which included vague language authorizing the agency to conduct "additional services of common concern" and perform "such other functions and duties related to intelligence affecting the national security."[97] By the end of 1947, Communists had come to power in Poland, Hungary, and Romania. Germany was divided. Millions across war-ravaged Europe were starving. As former Secretary of State Condoleezza Rice later reflected, "The question wasn't will Eastern Europe go communist. It's will Western Europe go Communist?"[98] Truman and his advisors viewed these developments as a grave threat to American security and demanded new options between diplomacy and war.

On December 17, 1947, Truman's National Security Council granted the CIA authority to conduct "covert psychological operations designed to counteract Soviet and Soviet-inspired activities."[99] Within a year, the CIA would be engaged in covert activities to influence Italy's election and would operate a permanent unit with official guidance by the National Security Council to conduct espionage and counterespionage operations abroad. By 1952, the CIA's clandestine ranks numbered nearly six thousand, with activities spanning forty-seven countries and a budget of $82 million.[100]

Between 1961 and 1974, the CIA conducted more than nine hundred major covert actions and thousands of smaller ones.[101] Among them: the botched Bay of Pigs invasion of Cuba in 1961; coups and assassination plots to oust left-leaning leaders in Cuba, the Congo, Brazil, and elsewhere; and a daring covert operation to exfiltrate six American diplomats hiding in the Canadian Embassy in Iran after the 1979 revolution by posing as filmmakers scouting locations for a fake movie.[102] The operation was depicted—with significant creative license—in the Academy Award–winning Ben Affleck movie, Argo.[103]

Meanwhile, the CIA still struggled to coordinate intelligence across the rest of the Intelligence Community. This was no accident. When the agency was created in 1947, the Departments of War, Navy, State, and Justice all lobbied to keep it weak so they could retain control and autonomy over their own intelligence activities. As Thomas Troy writes in his classic history of the CIA, the idea of a permanent and powerful central intelligence organization generated "intense hostility" from these "old-line" intelligence agencies.[104]

The National Security Act of 1947 gave the director of central intelligence two jobs—running the CIA and coordinating the intelligence activities of everyone else. But the statute made one of those jobs impossible. By law, the director of central intelligence was not granted exclusive access to the president, had no control over the budgets or personnel of any intelligence agency outside the CIA, and operated "under the direction of the National Security Council," which meant he reported to the very cabinet secretaries who wanted the CIA to stay out of their business. A winning organizational design this wasn't.[105] And that was the point. In 1948, just a year after the CIA's creation, the *New York Times* called the CIA "one of the weakest links in our national security."[106]

Over the next several decades, three things happened that would drastically change American intelligence.

First, the CIA developed its own collection and analysis capabilities, so it didn't have to rely so much on others. The agency's Directorate of Intelligence began conducting all-source analysis of intelligence, producing intelligence products rather than serving as a clearinghouse. And the Directorate of Operations quickly began collecting clandestine human intelligence and running covert operations.[107]

Second, presidents started to compensate for CIA weaknesses by creating even more agencies. Harry Truman became so frustrated by the CIA's poor attention to signals intelligence, he created the National Security Agency in 1952. His secret executive order gave NSA undisputed responsibility for all communications intelligence such as eavesdropping and codebreaking.[108] Within five years, NSA had nearly nine thousand employees and ran the most sophisticated computer complex in the world.[109]

In 1961, President John F. Kennedy's secretary of defense, Robert McNamara, ordered the creation of the Defense Intelligence Agency (DIA) to reduce overlap and parochialism among the Army, Navy, Air Force, and Marine Corps intelligence services.[110]

As the word *community* suggests, the Intelligence Community has never been a tight organizational structure with one boss in the corner office and clear authorities about who does what, how, and why. It's more akin to a loose federation of semi-autonomous, sometimes warring regions—each with its own leader, culture, and specialty products. Intelligence agencies serve different bureaucratic bosses, specialize in different intelligence missions and disciplines (called INTs), operate with vastly different cultures, and compete against each other for resources. Yet they have to work together to be effective. The setup is supposed to balance centralization and decentralization—providing both unity of effort and freedom of action for each component. Except that unity of effort has always been an uphill battle.

The third major development affecting the trajectory of American intelligence was the discovery of abuses in the 1970s, which led to the creation of new congressional oversight mechanisms. As we discuss more in chapter 8, intelligence agencies faced a dark moment of reckoning beginning in 1974, when the *New York Times* reported that they had been spying illegally on Americans for years.[111] A sweeping congressional investigation of intelligence abuses ensued, led by Senator Frank Church (D-ID). The Church Committee's work ultimately ushered in new laws, organizations, and practices to set limits and improve accountability, including the creation of permanent House and Senate intelligence oversight committees.

The Cold War Ends, a New Threat Emerges

After the collapse of the Soviet Union in 1991, the Intelligence Community was faced with dwindling resources, strategic confusion, and ongoing turbulence. In search of a "peace dividend," intelligence budgets in the 1990s were cut more than 20 percent. The Intelligence Community lost a third of its all-source analysts and a quarter of its human intelligence collectors, and it relied on satellites that were beyond the end of their design lives for imagery and signals intelligence.[112] "It was the leanest of times," wrote former CIA Deputy Director Michael Morell.[113]

Many policymakers questioned the need for intelligence at all; the Cold War was over, the United States had won, and peace was here to stay. "The United States has never been less threatened by foreign forces than it is today," noted William Hyland, one of the deans of U.S. foreign policy circles, in May 1991.[114] Former NSA chief Lt. Gen. William Odom and Senator Daniel Patrick Moynihan (D-NY), one of the most powerful members of the Senate, recommended abolishing the CIA.[115]

Meanwhile, fragmentation flourished, just as it had from the earliest days of the republic. Intelligence agencies developed their own budgets, set their own priorities, hired and trained their own staffs, communicated by separate email systems, and kept intelligence in incompatible databases.

Each agency even had its own security badge, making it impossible for officials to physically enter buildings outside their home organization. When Director of Central Intelligence George Tenet issued a directive mandating that all intelligence agencies use a standard blue security badge to improve collaboration, officials ignored, slow-rolled, and circumvented the order. Some agencies kept their own security badges and required both badges for entry.[116] Some employees simply refused to carry the new blue badges out of loyalty to their home agencies. One NSA official told me he superglued the laminate on his green NSA badge and refused to give it up until he was barred by security officers in the NSA lobby. "I worked for NSA, not the Community," he said.[117]

The Intelligence Community's lack of integration was a tragedy waiting to happen, and many experts, intelligence officials, and policymakers knew it. Between the Soviet Union's collapse in 1991 and the September 11, 2001, terrorist attacks, a dozen major unclassified reports were issued by bipartisan commissions, government studies, and think tanks examining the Intelligence Community and U.S. counterterrorism efforts (see table 3.1).

Each of these studies focused on different issues, tapped different experts, and issued recommendations. But their overall consensus was

TABLE 3.1 Unclassified U.S. Intelligence and Counterterrorism Studies, 1991–2001

Study Name	# Intelligence Reform Recommendations	Date Issued
National Performance Review (Vice President's Reinventing Government Initiative, Phases I, II)	35	1993, 1995
Commission on the Roles and Capabilities of the United States Intelligence Community (Aspin-Brown Commission)	38	1996
Council on Foreign Relations Task Force	29	1996
House Permanent Select Committee on Intelligence Staff Study (IC21)	74	1996
20th Century Fund Task Force on the Future of U.S. Intelligence	17	1996
National Institute on Public Policy Report on Modernizing Intelligence (Odom Report)	34	1997
FBI Strategic Plan, 1998–2003	54	1998
Commission to Assess the Organization of the Federal Government to Combat the Proliferation of Weapons of Mass Destruction (Deutch Commission)	17	1999
Advisory Panel to Assess Domestic Response Capabilities for Terrorism Involving Weapons of Mass Destruction (Gilmore Commission), Reports 1, 2	14	1999, 2000
Commission on the Advancement of Federal Law Enforcement (Webster Commission)	10	2000
National Commission on Terrorism (Bremer Commission)	12	2000
U.S. Commission on National Security in the 21st Century (Hart-Rudman Commission), Phase III Report	6	2001
Total	340	

Source: Zegart, Spying Blind, 29–33.

stunning in its simplicity: they all believed that intelligence reform was urgently needed. Together, they issued 340 intelligence reform recommendations. Seventy-five percent of these proposals focused on tackling the same three overarching problems: (1) coordination weaknesses across the IC, (2) personnel and information sharing problems, and (3) a lack of strategic direction setting intelligence priorities.[118]

Yet almost none of these reforms were implemented before the 9/11 terrorist attack. To be exact, 79 percent of the total, or 268 recommendations, produced no action of *any* kind—no phone call, no meeting, no memo. Only 35 recommendations, or 10 percent of the total, were fully implemented, and nearly all of those were throwaway "study the problem more" suggestions.[119]

These studies also made clear that in the decade between the collapse of the Soviet Union and 9/11, the terrorist threat was grave, rising, and imminent. And yet counterterrorism efforts remained split across forty-six organizations without a central strategy, budget, or coordinating mechanism. Director of Central Intelligence George Tenet wrote a memo declaring war on Osama bin Laden nearly three years before 9/11, urging that "no resources or people [be] spared," but only a few agency heads received the memo and all of them ignored it. Nobody knew how many intelligence analysts worked in the IC or what expertise they had. The FBI said that terrorism was its top priority, but on 9/11 only 6 percent of FBI personnel were working counterterrorism issues, and new agents got more time for vacation than counterterrorism training. Resistance to interagency collaboration was so engrained that when the CIA and FBI began swapping deputy directors to each other's counterterrorism centers in the late 1990s to improve collaboration, people called it the "hostage exchange program."[120]

As 9/11 approached, the CIA and FBI had twenty-three opportunities to penetrate and possibly unravel the plot.[121] They missed them all, including three chances—starting as early as twenty months before the attacks—to track down one of the hijackers before he flew Flight 77 into the Pentagon. Khalid al-Mihdhar tripped the wire when the CIA surveilled him attending a January 2000 al Qaeda planning meeting in Malaysia and discovered he held a multiple-entry U.S. visa in his passport. But nobody at the CIA told the FBI about al-Mihdhar until nineteen days before the attack. We now know that al-Mihdhar went directly from that meeting to the United States, where he lived for the next year and a half under his real name and made contact with an FBI informant. All of this was unknown to the FBI before 9/11.[122] With an intelligence structure that did not give anyone the power to deploy resources against priorities and knock bureaucratic heads together, the IC didn't have much of a chance. As former National Security Advisor Brent Scowcroft told congressional investigators after the attacks, "I was not surprised. I was horrified."[123]

The Iraq WMD intelligence failure soon followed.

As the United States edged toward war in 2002, the Intelligence Community issued a National Intelligence Estimate of Iraq's WMD programs.[124] It was the critical assessment at the critical moment. And nearly every judgment was wrong.[125]

The postmortem conducted by the bipartisan WMD Commission found that intelligence agencies collected too little information and shoddy information; relied on sources known to be unreliable, including an Iraqi defector code-named, incredibly, Curveball; clung to old hypotheses even in the face of new evidence; and vastly overstated the certainty of their judgments.[126]

Intelligence errors "were not the result of simple bad luck, or a once-in-a-lifetime 'perfect storm,'" the WMD Commission concluded in a damning report. "Rather, they were the product of poor intelligence collection, an analytical process that was driven by assumptions and inferences rather than data, inadequate validation and vetting of dubious intelligence sources, and numerous other breakdowns. . . . In many ways, the Intelligence Community simply did not do the job that it exists to do."[127]

As CIA Director Tenet later reflected, "Everything that could go wrong did go wrong. We have to live with the fact that on a high-consequence issue our analysis was used to enable war."[128]

Intelligence Reform and Creation of the DNI

By the fall of 2004, pressures for reform were intense. The 9/11 Commission's final report became a national bestseller, and it issued a blistering review of intelligence failures. At the same time, the Senate Select Committee on Intelligence issued a scathing report criticizing pre-war intelligence assessments of Iraq's weapons of mass destruction. And CIA Director George Tenet resigned, leaving the Intelligence Community without a strong public advocate to defend itself.

On December 10, 2004, Congress passed the Intelligence Reform and Terrorism Prevention Act,[129] the most consequential restructuring of the nation's intelligence services in half a century. Its most significant change was the creation of a new director of national intelligence (DNI) to integrate the agencies of the Intelligence Community and serve as the president's principal intelligence advisor. The DNI was supposed to lead with a strong hand—improving information sharing, standardizing procedures, and deploying budgets across agencies more effectively. A new DNI would also free up the CIA director to concentrate on running the CIA.

Government reform, however, is nearly always a zero-sum game. Empowering one bureaucratic actor requires weakening another, as well as its champions in Congress. In intelligence, a powerful, independent DNI threatened the discretion, budgets, and autonomy of all the other intelligence agencies. One former senior intelligence officer joked at the time that the CIA should be renamed "The Agency formerly known as Central." The Defense Department had the most to lose, with four of the six largest intelligence agencies and the lion's share of the intelligence budget under its aegis.[130]

In a replay of the CIA's creation, existing intelligence agencies and their congressional champions fought back, stripping the reform bill of its most important measures to strengthen the DNI: control over intelligence agency budgets and personnel. As Representative Chris Shays (R-CT) put it, Secretary of Defense Donald Rumsfeld "just trashed everything about the national intelligence director" in private meetings on Capitol Hill.[131] Other lawmakers from both parties issued similar assessments. As Jane Harman (D-CA), the ranking member of the House Intelligence Committee and one of the chief architects of the bill, later remarked, "No one missed the big fights when we were doing the intel reform law with the Pentagon. If any of you missed it, I'm not sure what planet you were on."[132]

A compromise bill passed, but the resulting director of national intelligence position was considered such a loser, it was hard to get anyone to take it. Robert Gates turned down the job to stay on as president of Texas A&M University before later becoming secretary of defense—apparently believing it would be easier to reverse the flailing Iraq War than unify the intelligence enterprise.[133] Keeping a DNI in the job proved to be difficult, too. Four different people served as DNI in the organization's first five years.

When James Clapper was asked to serve as DNI in 2010, his first response was, in his words, "a flat no." As Clapper later reflected, "I'd watched three successive DNIs in less than five years struggle with the responsibility of occupying a Cabinet-level position without congruent legislative authorities." With fifteen of the agencies the DNI was supposed to oversee reporting to six different cabinet secretaries, Clapper "wasn't sure it was possible to actually *do* the job of DNI."[134]

Indeed, turnover in the job was so bad, at Clapper's confirmation hearing, Senator Kit Bond (R-MO) joked off-mic to Senator Dianne Feinstein (D-CA), "Welcome to our *annual* DNI confirmation."[135]

The director of national intelligence has gradually grown more effective since then. With about two thousand employees, it now includes a DNI staff; several cross-community mission centers in counterterrorism, counter-proliferation, cyber threat intelligence, and counterintelligence;[136] a program to conduct technology research for community intelligence missions called the Intelligence Advanced Research Projects Activity (IARPA); and the National Intelligence Council, which used to be housed in CIA and is responsible for producing longer-range community-wide intelligence assessments on topics like Iran's nuclear weapons program.[137]

Yet the yawning gap between the DNI's responsibilities and its actual authorities still exists, and its overall effectiveness remains a work in progress. Even now, three quarters of the annual intelligence budget still goes to agencies inside the Department of Defense.[138]

As former CIA Director Leon Panetta observed, "The problem with the position is that the director of national intelligence doesn't really have a staff to produce his own information, so he is regularly caught between wanting information and having to rely on others to get it."[139] It was the same dynamic the CIA faced in 1947.

Today, the Central Intelligence Agency is still central, serving as the premier agency that collects human intelligence (HUMINT), analyzes intelligence from all sources, and conducts covert operations.[140] As one DNI official put it, "If the CIA is the New York Yankees, we're the

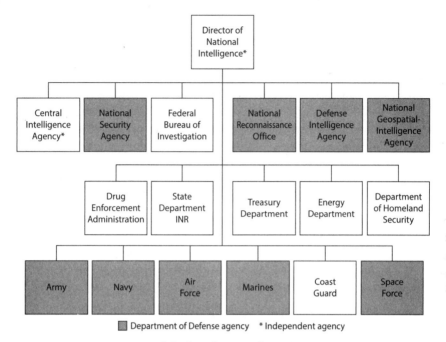

FIGURE 3.1 Who's Who in the U.S. Intelligence Community
Source: Office of the Director of National Intelligence, "Members of the IC."

Commissioner's Office. We don't have any fans, and no one buys our jerseys."[141] In the 2019 annual intelligence threat hearing held by Congress, the DNI sat next to five other intelligence agency leaders at the witness table: the directors of the CIA, FBI, Defense Intelligence Agency, National Security Agency, and National Geospatial-Intelligence Agency.[142] In the Bush, Obama, and Trump administrations, both the DNI and the CIA director attended National Security Council meetings.[143] Even now, the CIA and DNI's office vie for influence and power. The question "Who's in charge of intelligence?" is still not easy to answer.

Figure 3.1 shows why: the Intelligence Community is vast, varied, and complex, with eighteen agencies in all. Nine reside within the Defense Department, consuming the majority of the intelligence budget.

Two—the CIA and the Office of the Director of National Intelligence—are independent, answering to no cabinet secretary. The rest are housed within five other departments: the Departments of Energy, Homeland Security, Justice, State, and Treasury.

Six agencies are considered "top tier" intelligence organizations that serve national policymakers.[144] The CIA is the nation's premier agency for human intelligence and all-source analysis, and it has unique covert action capabilities and authorities. The National Security Agency intercepts foreign signals intelligence (SIGINT) such as emails and telephone calls. It is also responsible for the making and breaking of codes and is believed to be the largest employer of mathematicians in the United States.[145]

The National Reconnaissance Office designs, builds, and operates spy satellites. The FBI, which is part of the Justice Department, is responsible for domestic intelligence (by law, the CIA cannot collect intelligence inside the United States). The Defense Intelligence Agency collects military intelligence on foreign capabilities and intentions.

The National Geospatial-Intelligence Agency (NGA) is one of the newest agencies and hardest to understand. Originally descended from photo imagery intelligence, NGA says it processes and exploits "imagery and geospatial information that describes, assesses, and visually depicts physical features and geographically referenced activities on the Earth."[146] In English, this means the agency handles everything from satellite photographic imagery to drone footage to imagery built not by photographs but by reflections from spectral analysis that cannot be seen in the visible light spectrum. Together, all of these are part of an intelligence discipline called geospatial intelligence, or GEOINT.[147]

Other cabinet departments have specialized intelligence units with deep expertise, such as the Department of Energy (which focuses on securing departmental laboratories at home and assessing nuclear proliferation abroad) and the State Department's Bureau of Intelligence and Research (INR), which supports the secretary of state. Finally, each military service has its own intelligence agency that tailors collection and analysis to particular service missions.

Intelligence in the Twenty-First Century

Today's threat landscape is more complicated than ever, with global threats like pandemics and climate change; great power competition between the United States, Russia, and China; and threats like terrorism and cyberattacks that are waged by the few on the many. In a world of dangerous uncertainties, the side that prospers is the one that sees what's coming first— and bends the arc of history in its favor. That requires intelligence.

As former Principal Deputy Director of National Intelligence Susan Gordon noted, "The one thing that intelligence best drives . . . is advantage. Ruthless advantage. Disproportionate advantage. Relentless advantage. That's all there is. You have to know a little bit more a little bit faster, or we won't get where we need to go."[148]

Intelligence helped create America in the eighteenth century, secure it in the nineteenth, and lead a new international order in the twentieth. In the twenty-first century, the intelligence mission demands all that, and more. New missions include securing cyberspace and satellites in outer space, protecting our own democracy from foreign interference, gaining competitive economic advantage, and tracking disease and climate disruption.

We're a long way from French bake ovens.

Today's policymakers aren't just government employees, either. Some of the most important decisions affecting American national security are being made by executives at Google, Microsoft, Twitter, Facebook, and Apple, all of whom have global shareholders and no voters holding them accountable in elections. They are instead driven, as all companies are, by financial interests. Tech companies are giving rise to threat vectors, making privacy decisions, and empowering everyone— good citizens and bad actors alike. Intelligence agencies must find ways of working productively with them, too.

New threats and technologies also raise new dilemmas about how intelligence agencies can safeguard American security while upholding American values. It's always been a difficult balance to strike. A century ago, there was the Red Scare. In the 1940s, Truman feared creating an American Gestapo. The 1970s reckoned with the repercussions of illegal domestic spying and secret assassination plots of foreign leaders. More recently, controversies have erupted over drone strikes killing American citizens without judicial review and NSA's warrantless wiretapping program. But for all the concern about intelligence agencies growing too strong, Pearl Harbor, 9/11, and the Iraq WMD failure remind us that bad things also happen when intelligence agencies grow too weak.

Finding the right balance between risks to security and restrictions on liberties will always involve hard choices and heated debates. It should. In authoritarian regimes, intelligence agencies wield the power of the state at their will. In democracies, intelligence agencies wield the power of the state at the *people's* will.

4

INTELLIGENCE BASICS

KNOWNS AND UNKNOWNS

Seek the truth and speak the truth. That's our mission.

—DANIEL COATS, DIRECTOR OF NATIONAL
INTELLIGENCE, 2017–2019[1]

THIS WAS IT. Decision time. On April 28, 2011, President Obama gathered his top foreign policy advisors in the White House Situation Room.[2] After months of meetings so secret that not even the secretary of homeland security or FBI director knew about them,[3] Obama was about to make one of the most consequential decisions of his presidency: whether to green-light a Navy SEAL team raid to capture or kill a man the CIA believed might be Osama bin Laden.[4]

For months, a small circle of intelligence officials had been watching a man they called the Pacer inside his walled compound in Abbottabad, Pakistan, a city thirty-five miles north of Islamabad. While the CIA thought he might be the infamous al Qaeda leader, they were far from sure. There had been no direct sighting, no DNA evidence, no eavesdropped phone call to or from him, no intercepted email, no human source who had come forward and said, "I saw him. He's there."[5]

All they had was circumstantial evidence. The Pakistani compound was very unusual, more like an expensive fortress than a house, with high perimeter walls topped by barbed wire.[6] Even the second-floor balcony had a seven-foot-tall privacy wall.[7] There was no Internet connection or telephone landline, and the residents who lived there burned all their trash.[8] Three families lived inside but none of the children went to school. The owner who was listed in property records lived in a guest house, not the nicest part of the main residence.[9] And the Pacer never ventured outside the compound. Ever. He just walked around the vegetable garden, back and forth, underneath a tarp.[10] Satellite imagery never captured a picture of his face,[11] but analysis of his height based on his gait and the shadows he cast during his garden walks[12] suggested the Pacer could be tall, anywhere from five feet eight to six feet eight.[13] Bin Laden was thought to be six four.[14]

What happened next is now well known: President Obama authorized the CIA covert operation[15] to raid the compound with a Navy SEAL team.[16] Osama bin Laden was killed, his identity confirmed, and his body buried at sea. Commandos retrieved an enormous stash of the terrorist leader's papers and computer files.[17]

The covert operation did not stay covert for long. Within hours, President Obama went on television and announced, "Tonight, I can report to the American people and to the world that the United States has conducted an operation that killed Osama bin Laden, the leader of al-Qaida and a terrorist who's responsible for the murder of thousands of innocent men, women, and children."[18]

The bin Laden raid is a thrilling story and an intelligence success, but it's also a rare chance to see how intelligence actually works. What exactly led to that fateful meeting in the White House Situation Room? What constituted intelligence and how was it collected? Why was it so hard for analysts to find bin Laden and how did they finally succeed after ten years of searching? And why did the president choose a CIA covert operation to kill bin Laden rather than a larger, overt military strike?[19]

This chapter seeks to lift the veil on this secret world by examining intelligence basics through three lenses—an analytic lens, a human lens, and an operational lens. Without the Intelligence Community's unique sense-making mission, its people, and its capabilities, operations like the bin Laden raid couldn't exist.

We start by laying out what intelligence is and is not. Next we look at the human dimension of intelligence through personal reflections of current and former intelligence officials whose careers included briefing the president, catching traitors, handling defectors, and writing the first report warning about the threat posed by an obscure Saudi millionaire named Osama bin Laden.[20] Finally, we revisit the bin Laden operation to see the three core missions of the U.S. Intelligence Community in action: *intelligence collection, intelligence analysis,* and *covert action.*

An Analytic Lens: What Intelligence Is, and Is Not

Put most simply, intelligence is information that gives policymakers an advantage over their adversaries.[21] We've come a long way from ancient days when gathering intelligence meant divining the will of the gods rather than understanding the intentions and capabilities of humans. In the fifth century B.C.E., Chinese general Sun Tzu was one of the first to realize what now seems obvious: better information makes for better decisions. Rather than consulting oracles, interpreting dreams, and reading portents from animal entrails, Sun Tzu suggested gathering real data to outwit adversaries. "If you know the enemy and know yourself, you need not fear the result of a hundred battles," he wrote.[22] Knowledge never guarantees perfect decisions, but it does reduce uncertainty, which makes better decisions more likely.

In the case of the bin Laden raid, intelligence was successfully used to kill the mastermind of 9/11. But it would be a mistake to think of intelligence only as a tool that supports violence. Intelligence plays a crucial role in every aspect of statecraft and every kind of decision, from diplomacy to trade, coercion to cooperation. A tank commander under fire has to know whether the bridge up ahead will collapse if crossed. A diplomat needs to know whether the Iranians are adhering to or cheating on the Nuclear Non-Proliferation Treaty. The national security advisor has to get a handle on what the cyber threat landscape looks like and how it's changing as she develops a new government-wide cyber strategy. The president, seeing an opportunity to negotiate a multinational free trade agreement in the Asia-Pacific, needs to anticipate how China might react. At its essence, intelligence is information that helps policymakers.

Intelligence Is Understanding Knowns and Unknowns

In his February 12, 2002, press briefing, Secretary of Defense Donald Rumsfeld described the limits of intelligence in the Iraq War when he famously started talking about "known knowns" and "unknown unknowns." Critics had a field day. Some thought it was a gaffe. Others called it convoluted thinking. Some even set his comments to music.[23] Here's what he said:

> Reports that say that something hasn't happened are always interesting to me, because as we know, there are known knowns; there are things we know we know. We also know there are known unknowns; that is to say we know there are things we do not know. But there are also unknown unknowns—the ones we don't know we don't know. And if one looks throughout the history of our country and other free countries, it is that latter category that tends to be the difficult ones.[24]

But Rumsfeld wasn't rambling. He was popularizing ideas that intelligence officials have been writing about for years.[25] Sherman Kent, a Yale history professor and the founding father of the CIA's analytic branch, distinguished between three types of information in a 1964 essay (see Table 4.1). First, there are "indisputable facts," what Rumsfeld referred to as "known knowns." These are questions with definitive answers that U.S. intelligence officials have found. For example, whether China has an aircraft carrier is a knowable fact, and it is known by U.S. intelligence agencies: China's first aircraft carrier, the *Liaoning*, was purchased from Ukraine in 1998.[26]

Kent described a second type of information as "things which are knowable but happen to be unknown to us," or what Rumsfeld called the "known unknowns." How exactly does the *Liaoning* maneuver at sea under various conditions? That information exists, but it requires firsthand knowledge on board the ship over long stretches of time. Chinese sailors know it, but U.S. intelligence agencies may not.

Kent called the third type of information "things which are not known to anyone," or Rumsfeld's "unknown unknowns." These are things that are simply not knowable. How long, for example, will the

TABLE 4.1 Three Types of Intelligence

	Known Knowns	Known Unknowns	Unknown Unknowns
Description	Indisputable facts: things that are knowable and known by U.S. intelligence agencies	Things that are knowable but unknown to U.S. intelligence agencies	Things that are not knowable to anyone
Example	Existence of Chinese aircraft carrier	Performance of Chinese aircraft carrier at sea	Longevity of the Chinese Communist Party's rule
Difficulty	Hard	Harder	Hardest

Chinese Communist Party remain in power? Not even Chinese leader Xi Jinping has the answer. Leaders' intentions often fall into the unknown unknown category, too—because they are not clear even to the leaders themselves.[27]

Getting inside someone's head is actually difficult, even for them. To see why, consider the following vacation prediction exercise I give my Stanford students.

On a piece of paper, write down what you plan to do for your next vacation. Now imagine that we reconvene in a year and compare what you wrote down to what you actually did. How many of you might do something different? Why?

At this point in class, hands shoot up. Many admit they probably won't end up doing what they planned because they haven't made the decision yet. Over time, events happen and preferences change. Students might get a job or lose a job, meet a boyfriend or break up with one, discover a new passion or suffer a family emergency. They come up with dozens of reasons why their plans probably won't pan out as they expect.

"That's you predicting you," I remind them. It's the best-case intelligence scenario. Nobody can predict your intentions better than you can. Next I ask them to imagine predicting the vacation plans of the student sitting next to them. "That's so much harder!" someone usually says. Finally, I ask them to imagine what it would be like to predict their neighbor's plans when the neighbor is doing everything possible to conceal or lie about them. That's the world of intelligence unknown unknowns.

The vacation prediction exercise suggests why getting good intelligence is so much harder than it looks.

Intelligence Is Vast and Varied

The U.S. Intelligence Community (IC) is vast, comprising eighteen federal agencies and roughly one hundred thousand people[28] that do everything from identifying strange gases in suspect buildings to eavesdropping on terrorists to compiling information for the President's Daily Brief each morning. A *Washington Post* investigation found that in 2010, thirty-three building complexes for top secret intelligence work had been built in the Washington, D.C., area since 9/11 with total square footage equivalent to nearly three Pentagons. At these and other secure locations, intelligence analysts churned out fifty thousand intelligence reports a year.[29] For 2021, the total intelligence budget was an estimated $85 billion.[30] To put that number into perspective, it's more than the GDP of half the countries in the world. U.S. intelligence, in a word, is big.

Intelligence is also varied. Major intelligence agencies specialize in disciplines called INTs. The National Security Agency collects foreign signals intelligence, or SIGINT—which includes telephone calls, texts, and email. The National Geospatial-Intelligence Agency collects and processes satellite imagery and other intelligence from space known as GEOINT.[31] The Defense Intelligence Agency collects human intelligence, or HUMINT—sometimes overtly, through defense attachés posted abroad, and sometimes clandestinely.[32] The CIA is the nation's premier clandestine HUMINT collector, with case officers recruiting and running foreign assets—a.k.a. spies. Many believe that publicly available information, or open-source intelligence (OSINT), has become so important in the Internet age that it needs its own agency.[33]

The point is that intelligence is highly specialized. Just like doctors, intelligence officials develop expertise in different areas. Nobody wants their dermatologist performing heart surgery or their heart surgeon detecting skin cancer. Intelligence is no different. If you've ever tried to judge whether a satellite image is showing a railroad line or a highway or whether the coding quirks behind a cyberattack indicate a particular culprit, you'll appreciate how much specialized intelligence expertise matters.

American Intelligence Is Outward-Looking

Many countries' intelligence services spy on their own citizens. In 2018, China spent more on internal security than external defense.[34] Russian domestic surveillance and political repression have such a long history, the country celebrated the 100th anniversary of the Soviet secret police in 2017. During the Cold War, domestic spying operations became so large, the Soviet Union's spy agency, the KGB, established a special directorate to handle them.[35]

American intelligence, by contrast, sharply distinguishes between foreign and domestic targets. Almost all American intelligence is aimed abroad, at foreign allies and adversaries. Only one of the eighteen intelligence agencies has domestic intelligence collection as a core mission: the Federal Bureau of Investigation, which is housed within the Department of Justice and operates with extensive legal and policy constraints, judicial review, and congressional oversight to protect American rights.[36] The National Security Act of 1947 explicitly prohibits the CIA from exercising any "police, subpoena, law-enforcement powers, or internal-security functions."[37]

That's not to say there aren't violations. The NSA, CIA, and FBI were all found to have spied illegally on American citizens in the twentieth century. NSA's SHAMROCK program intercepted American communications from the end of World War II until 1975.[38] The FBI spied on, infiltrated, and disrupted political dissident groups from the 1950s to the 1970s—a program Congress found to be "far beyond" the bounds of what was "intolerable in a democratic society." The CIA's HTLINGUAL program illegally opened hundreds of thousands of letters to and from U.S. citizens during the same time period.[39] All of these activities violated American law. But that's the point: domestic laws forbid this kind of surveillance on Americans. U.S. intelligence agencies were set up to protect the nation from external threats, not to maintain internal political control.

That's what intelligence is. It's equally important to know what intelligence isn't. Misperceptions abound. Below, we tackle three big ones—involving secrets, the news, and the relationship between intelligence and policy.

Most Intelligence Is Not Secrets

Contrary to popular belief, secrets in intelligence are rare. Intercepted phone calls, stolen documents, and first-hand reports by spies are always important. But since the Cold War's end, it is estimated that more than 80 percent of information in a typical intelligence report is *not* secrets.[40] It's publicly available information—what intelligence officials call open-source intelligence, or OSINT for short. OSINT includes a wide range of information and sources—everything from routine bureaucratic documents published by obscure foreign government agencies to televised speeches by foreign leaders to maps available on Google Earth and ISIS decapitation videos posted online.

As we'll discuss more in chapter 9, OSINT is growing dramatically. Online connectivity, artificial intelligence tools, the proliferation of small commercial satellites, and other technologies are giving ordinary citizens, non-state actors, and foreign governments more information and more analytic capacity than ever before. There is both promise and peril in this OSINT revolution. New technologies offer intelligence agencies more potential information and analytic tools. But they are also leveling the intelligence playing field and making open democratic societies more vulnerable.

To give just one example, President Trump's Twitter feed became an open-source intelligence gold mine for foreign actors, providing a steady stream of information about the president's opinions on matters from the frivolous (whether he liked the latest *Saturday Night Live* episode) to the consequential (whether the secretary of state should negotiate with North Korea).[41] The tweets conveyed what Trump thought, felt, and prioritized; what actions or words elicited different responses from him; and whose opinion he valued. It's believed about half of Trump's tweets came directly from him.[42] The U.S. Intelligence Community can only dream of having that kind of insight into the thinking of leaders in authoritarian regimes that censor the Internet and tightly restrict the flow of information, like China's Xi Jinping or North Korea's Kim Jong-Un.

Intelligence Is Not Google or CNN

All intelligence is information, but not all information is intelligence. If the United States Intelligence Community only stated the obvious or passed along the same news stories as CNN or the *Wall Street Journal*, it wouldn't add much value, especially for the estimated $85 billion per year it costs.[43] Today, with so much more information online and more real-time information at decisionmakers' fingertips, it's worth asking what makes intelligence valuable.

First, intelligence *tailors information to a policymaker's needs*. Intelligence agencies don't just spit out the same responses to everyone, like Google searches. They answer the specific and often highly classified informational demands of "customers" like the tank commander, the diplomat, the national security advisor, and the president. And they have to be timely, delivering information when policymakers need it—before a missile launches, or a summit convenes, or the National Security Council makes a decision. "When you're doing negotiations, knowing as much as you can about what the other side is thinking is very useful," said Michael McFaul, who served as ambassador to Russia in the Obama administration. "We have some tremendous capabilities. . . . There's just no replacing that."[44] Continuous interaction between policymakers and the IC is essential. "When you are in continuous conversation," noted former National Security Advisor H. R. McMaster, policymakers can "clarify what you need to know and work hard on collection and analysis" that fills gaps, reveals weaknesses, and advances policy.[45]

Sometimes, serving policymakers' needs means telling them what they don't want to hear or never thought to ask. This is known as *speaking truth to power* and it's a core part of the intelligence mission. As former Director of National Intelligence Dan Coats put it, "We strive to know the truth and we have an obligation to speak the truth. Anything short of that is a disservice to policymakers and to our country."[46] Coats did just that in 2019, when he delivered the IC's annual threat briefing to Congress, which offered a different assessment of threats than President Trump, including a far more pessimistic assessment of prospects for North Korean denuclearization.[47] In authoritarian regimes, intelligence services often tell leaders what they want to hear. In the United States, intelligence agencies strive to tell leaders what they need to know—a role that can lead to friction, as I discuss more below.

The second way intelligence adds unique value to policymakers is by *turning information into insight.* Raw data isn't worth much without analysis. These days, we are swimming in data; some estimate the total amount of information in the world is doubling every twenty-four months.[48] Much of it is wrong, incomplete, misleading, contradictory, poorly sourced, poorly argued, even deliberately deceptive. To this seeming chaos, intelligence analysis brings logical reasoning skills— assessing the credibility of information and what it means. The goal isn't to predict the future with 100 percent certainty. Nobody can do that. It's to reduce uncertainty about present conditions and what possible futures could unfold. Analysts wield hypotheses, not crystal balls, asking what explanations could possibly account for the information they have. Analytic tradecraft seeks to uncover broader patterns and reveal cause-and-effect relationships that help anticipate where events are likely to head, and why.

Analysts do this by synthesizing open-source information and secrets. Even though secrets constitute a small percentage of most intelligence reports, those classified nuggets can be priceless. In the hunt for bin Laden, one key breakthrough came in 2010 when the National Security Agency intercepted a telephone call from bin Laden's former courier to a friend suggesting the courier might be back in the game, working with bin Laden.[49] By putting this together with other secrets and open-source information, analysts eventually found the courier, tracked him to Abbottabad, and planned the operation that killed the al Qaeda leader.

It's worth noting that intelligence analysis also drives intelligence collection, surfacing what crucial information is missing that needs to be gathered. Intelligence analysis is often described as connecting the dots. That's only half-right. Good analysis suggests what dots should be collected, too.

Intelligence Is Not Policymaking

One of the most common misperceptions is that intelligence agencies make policy. They don't. And they shouldn't.

Former CIA Director George Tenet experienced this misperception during a 2007 *Daily Show* interview with comedian Jon Stewart. Tenet was promoting his memoir, but at the time anger over the Iraq War was running high, and Stewart was pulling no punches as he questioned Tenet about the Iraqi WMD intelligence failure and the decisions that led to war.

But Stewart did not understand the role of intelligence. He kept pushing Tenet about Bush administration policy choices. Would Tenet fire Vice President Dick Cheney if he could? Did Tenet give intelligence to the White House to help sell the war to the American people? Did the United States go to war with Iraq because some in the administration wanted war more than Tenet and Secretary of State Colin Powell opposed it? As Stewart fired away, Tenet grew visibly frustrated. Intelligence and policymaking is a contact sport, he explained, but the boundaries matter. "Jon, it's important for you to understand that when you're the director of central intelligence, you don't make policy. Your job is to give people data. When you start crossing those lines, then your analysis becomes suspect."[50] The intelligence-policy divide was news for Stewart and his viewers.

Intelligence agencies were never designed to be just another set of policy advisors. Their job is to present the available intelligence, not make the case for policy A or B. In fact, intelligence officials are trained to *not* make policy recommendations even when asked. As former Director of National Intelligence James Clapper wrote, the number one unwritten rule of intelligence is "leave the policy making to the policymakers." If intelligence officials weigh in on policy debates, Clapper noted, they risk compromising their credibility as "impartial, unbiased bearer[s] of intelligence truth." He made a strict practice of staying out of policy discussions during National Security Council meetings, so much so that he once waited until after a meeting was over to tell President Obama a personal anecdote about his time serving in Vietnam out of worry his story might have swayed the discussion had he mentioned it during the meeting.[51] Intelligence leaders have not always hewed to this rigid boundary, but they cross it at their peril.[52]

Even in the best of circumstances, tension between policymakers and intelligence officials is inevitable. Because intelligence success is hard and mistakes are so costly, policymakers are right to be skeptical about the intelligence assessments they receive.

Friction also arises because policymakers and intelligence officials come from different worlds and serve different roles. Policymakers are natural optimists. Presidents, after all, campaign on promises to build a better future. Intelligence officials, by contrast, are natural skeptics. There's an old joke that when an intelligence officer smells flowers, she looks for a coffin.[53] Policymakers are political appointees with short time horizons. Intelligence officials are career appointees with long time horizons. For policymakers, the imperative is getting things done. For intelligence officials, the imperative is getting things right.

In every administration, intelligence officers must walk a fine line between responsiveness and independence. They have to gain the president's trust without sacrificing credibility and support the nation's elected leader while relaying information he may not like or want to hear. Susan Gordon, the nation's number two intelligence official from 2017 to 2019, noted that "every president wishes intelligence could say things that it can't, and every president is vexed by intelligence because we steal their decision space."[54]

Little wonder all presidents have issues with the intelligence agencies that bring them news of unwelcome surprises, tell them how their favorite policies may backfire, and caution that they are unable to predict the future with telepathic accuracy. President Kennedy so distrusted CIA Director John McCone, he ignored McCone's warnings about the Soviet military buildup in Cuba in 1962 until it was nearly too late.[55]

President Richard Nixon nursed deep suspicions of the Central Intelligence Agency, questioning the agency's loyalty as well as its competence: "What the hell do those clowns do out there in Langley?" he once asked.[56] He ended up firing CIA Director Richard Helms in 1972. President Bill Clinton's relationship with his CIA director, James Woolsey, was so bad that when a small plane crash-landed on the White House lawn in 1994, aides joked it was Woolsey trying to get a meeting with the president. "At first that kind of stung," Woolsey later reflected, "but the more I thought about it, the more I thought, 'What the hell, that's really exactly what the situation is.'"[57] As former CIA Director and Secretary of Defense Robert Gates put it, "Few Presidents have anything good to say about the CIA or the intelligence they received."[58]

President Trump's relationship with his intelligence agencies was especially turbulent and public, raising concerns about the potential for lasting damage to intelligence capabilities, credibility, and morale. Trump called intelligence officers "Nazis"[59] and tweeted that his intelligence chiefs should "go back to school" after they publicly contradicted his claims about Iran, North Korea, and ISIS in congressional testimony.[60] When Director of National Intelligence Daniel Coats stepped down in August 2019, Trump nominated a congressional loyalist with no significant intelligence experience to replace him and ominously tweeted that America's intelligence agencies needed to be "reined in,"[61] by which it appears he meant that they should start agreeing with him more regardless of what the facts said.[62] The nominee, John Ratcliffe, withdrew under fire when news surfaced he had lied on his résumé but was renominated a few months later and confirmed by a party-line vote.[63]

Trump's hostility toward the Intelligence Community prompted unprecedented reactions from former intelligence officials.[64] Former CIA and NSA Director Michael Hayden wrote in the *New York Times* in April 2018, "We in the intelligence world have dealt with obstinate and argumentative presidents through the years. But we have never served a president for whom ground truth really doesn't matter."[65] Former CIA Director John Brennan was especially acerbic, criticizing Trump in deeply personal terms.[66] He called Trump "a national disgrace,"[67] characterized Trump's acceptance of Putin's denials of election interference as "nothing short of treasonous,"[68] and suggested that Trump's "venality, moral turpitude and political corruption" would relegate him to a "disgraced demagogue in the dustbin of history."[69] Nobody knows what the long-term effects of this hyper-political moment will be for U.S. intelligence agencies.

A Human Lens: Life in the Intelligence Community

Intelligence also has a human dimension that's rarely seen. Who works in this secret world, and why? How do they deal with secrecy in their daily lives? How do they think about ethics? What are their toughest and proudest moments? I put these questions to nearly two dozen current and former intelligence officers and examined the memoirs of others. Here are glimpses into their world.

Who Works in Intelligence and Why?

Bill Phillips was an African American progressive student and activist in law school in the 1970s when he noticed two men who seemed out of place at a career fair. They weren't students and didn't look like lawyers. Phillips was president of the student bar association at the time. He decided he should ask who they were.

The answer was CIA recruiters. "You're at the wrong law school," Phillips told them. "Our school is known for being involved in activist law like women's rights and civil rights. You need to go down the road to that other more traditional law school." The recruiters said they'd stay anyway. And by the way, what was his name? It was a spot interview. Phillips assured them he had no interest in joining the CIA.[70]

A few years later, Phillips received a letter in an unmarked envelope with vague instructions about a job interview in suburban Northern Virginia. Thinking the agency wanted to hire him in the general counsel's office, he went. But the interview was for the clandestine service. "Look at me. I've got this big Afro. I've been a student activist in the

1960s. I said you really don't want me. They said yes we do." It turns out Phillips had spent part of his childhood in Pakistan and had some familiarity with languages, studying German and Amharic and picking up a little Urdu before college.[71]

He ended up jettisoning his legal career and spent the next twenty-five years as a CIA case officer—recruiting foreign spies, conducting counter-narcotics operations, preparing the groundwork for an invasion, and leading the agency's offices in several countries. But he never told his mother he worked at the CIA until his retirement ceremony. "I didn't think my parents would actually understand why I left my career as a budding lawyer to become a spy," Phillips told me.[72]

Michael Morell had never traveled overseas. He'd hardly left Ohio. When it came time for college, he stayed close to home, attending the University of Akron. An economics whiz, he planned on getting his doctorate and going into academia. He still seems like a professor—with wire-rimmed glasses and a careful way of thinking through any question. He applied to the CIA "on a lark" when one of his professors suggested it. Morell would eventually serve as President George W. Bush's daily briefer, run the CIA's analytic branch, and help lead the hunt for bin Laden.[73]

Former Director of National Intelligence James Clapper grew up in military intelligence—his father was an Army signals intelligence officer. Clapper enlisted as a Marine Corps reservist and eventually became a three-star Air Force general. But he started his signals intelligence career at the age of twelve, using toothpicks and his grandparents' television set to intercept communications of the Philadelphia Police Department and tracking their activities, codes, and call signs on a homemade "database" of index cards.[74]

Gina Bennett is one of the world's leading terrorism analysts. In 1993, she wrote the first intelligence assessment warning that Osama bin Laden was a rising terrorist threat. She's also a mother of five kids who once went into labor while briefing National Security Advisor Condoleezza Rice. Bennett started her career as a State Department clerk typist because it was the first paying job she could get. "I'm still a really fast typist today," she told me. Her boss quickly realized that Gina's talents extended far beyond fast typing, promoted her, and told her to get a job in intelligence.[75]

Robert Baer spent his childhood getting into trouble, skipping school, dreaming of becoming a professional skier, and roaming across Europe with his adventure-seeking mother. "I managed to make it through Georgetown, but not by much," Baer wrote. His pranks included rappelling off the Kennedy Center during a performance and infamously riding his motorcycle through the Georgetown library during exam week, where he was spotted by a classmate named George Tenet. Baer became a decorated CIA case officer who spent two decades running agents in the Middle East. Tenet worked on the Senate Intelligence Committee staff, the National Security Council staff, and eventually became CIA director. When the two ran into each other years later at a White House meeting, Tenet told Baer, "This is the last place I ever thought I'd run into you."[76]

As these vignettes suggest, intelligence officers are an eclectic bunch. If you were asked to pick one out in a room full of people, you'd probably get it wrong. The workforce has come a long way since the 1950s, when it was mostly White, male, and plucked from Ivy League campuses.[77]

Intelligence officers are so varied in part because intelligence agencies are. Each of the IC's eighteen agencies has a unique role and a culture that comes with it. NSA, for example, employs legions of mathematicians because its mission involves intercepting foreign communications, codemaking, and codebreaking. As former NSA senior official Bill Nolte put it, "NSA is not an intelligence organization. It's a cryptologic agency."[78]

Each agency has sub-cultures, too. The CIA combines two vastly different worlds. The agency's human intelligence collectors, or case officers, tend to be risk takers with exceptional interpersonal skills who enjoy running toward the sound of gunfire, working in dangerous places, manipulating foreigners, evading surveillance, and gathering information in secret. As Phillips put it, they're "the fighter jocks of the agency . . . the pointy end of the spear."[79]

The agency's analysts couldn't be more different. They tend to have exceptional intellectual skills and enjoy solving vexing puzzles, working in cubicles, developing hypotheses, challenging assumptions and sources, and finding insight from disparate pieces of information. John McLaughlin headed the CIA's analytic branch and is widely admired as one of the agency's best analysts. His hobby isn't motorcycles. It's magic. A world-class amateur magician, McLaughlin's nickname around the Intelligence Community is "Merlin."[80]

Why do intelligence officers serve? When I asked Bill Phillips why a Black activist from the 1960s would give up a legal career to join the CIA, he didn't hesitate: "Because every male in my family on both sides has been a U.S. service member. Every male. My father was a World War II Navy vet. Both of his brothers were Korea vets. Both of my mother's brothers were in the Army in Korea. My brother was a naval officer. All of us had this thing in us about service to America."[81] One former official was drawn to the NSA because "you stand on the front lines of protecting the country."[82] Michael Morell says he often thinks about something a defense official once told him: "When you go home, would you rather tell your family you sold more trucks than anybody else in the world or you stopped a terrorist attack?"[83] The mission is a powerful draw for linguists, mathematicians, terrorism analysts, daredevils, and civil rights activists alike.

Daily Life in a Secret World

Gina Bennett tracks terrorists around the globe, but the CIA makes it hard to keep tabs on her own children. Not because of the long hours or the sudden crises. It's the phones. For security reasons, cell phones aren't allowed inside the building and office phone numbers change frequently. What's more, whenever CIA employees take on a new role, they change desks, and whenever they change desks, they have to get a different telephone number. In one assignment, Bennett moved desks four times in the span of a few months, and her children couldn't remember her work telephone number. "I teach my kids not to answer a call they don't know. So my kids wouldn't answer when I called them," she said.[84]

Working in the IC is not a normal job. Secrecy and security touch every part of daily life in ways most people cannot imagine. It's hard to get medical test results without a regular office telephone number.

Intelligence officers spend a lot of time in parking lots, because that's the best place to check the news on social media. Résumés have to be officially approved each time they are updated. Kids are often taught to be wary—looking for anything that might be out of place.[85]

Years ago, Bennett's son got worried. He'd been working at a coffee shop and a pretty girl kept coming in. Eventually, she asked him out and he learned she was from Afghanistan. "She's completely out of my league," he told his mother. "I think she's trying to get to you through me." Security investigated and found nothing amiss. "Your son probably just has a confidence problem," they told Bennett.

Intelligence officers can't reveal much to their families about what they do. There's no spousal privilege for sharing classified information. The day of the bin Laden raid, Michael Morell missed his daughter's final high school choral performance. His wife was furious. "Whatever you're doing can't be that important," she told him. All he could do was apologize. When President Obama announced the raid on national television later that night, she knew what had kept him at the office.[86]

Intelligence officers operating undercover may not even be able to tell their families where they really work. Most others have much more discretion; the CIA lets officers decide whether and when to tell their kids the truth.[87] The agency also hosts an annual family day, when kids can try on disguises, see polygraph machines, and play with disappearing ink.

Bennett told her oldest son when he was five, after she took him to the office one weekend and he started asking questions about all the posters of terrorist events on the walls. She explained her job was sending tips to police about where to find bad guys. "Wow, you are like Batman," he said.[88]

Bill Phillips revealed that both he and his wife worked at the CIA when his oldest son was eleven and they were living in a South Asian country. "Terrorism was in full bloom," explained Phillips. "We wanted the kids to know, not the details, but who their parents worked for. They might hear things in school that might be ugly. They should ignore them and tell daddy and mommy if they heard something." In another foreign country, after he received a vague death threat to his family, Phillips taught his children how to be safe on the streets. "I wanted them to be able to detect when things were not normal. We'd play a game. 'See the guy with the balloon cart down the street? Was he there yesterday? What's he have on?'" His older son remembered thinking it was cool that his parents worked in intelligence.[89]

Not everyone reacts so well. Former CIA counterterrorism chief James Olson recounted how one CIA friend revealed the truth to a daughter. She slammed the door to her room and cried for hours. "Unfortunately, this sense of betrayal is not uncommon among CIA children when they find out the truth," noted Olson.[90]

Spouses and children sometimes know without ever being told. Aris Pappas was a lead CIA military analyst on Poland during the Cold War, when Poland was ground zero for any military conflict involving the Soviet Union. One of his most valuable sources was a Polish colonel named Ryszard Kuklinski, who narrowly escaped capture and execution when his cover was blown. The CIA exfiltrated him and resettled him in the United States.

Kuklinski and Pappas worked closely together and became friends. Pappas never told his family who he was, but they all knew. "Here I was a thirty-something-year-old analyst and suddenly I'd developed a friendship with a fifty-year old Polish guy. And my wife was reading about this Polish colonel in the U.S. My wife never had a briefing. She didn't need one," said Pappas. "My kids knew it was serious and that he was not to be spoken of—ever." They called Kuklinski "George." As Pappas put it, "George was a friend. George came to dinner. George went on boats. And nobody talked about George."[91]

Ethical Dilemmas

If you ask intelligence officers what misperceptions bother them most, odds are they'll mention ethics. "People think we're lawbreakers, we're human rights violators," said former CIA counterintelligence chief James Olson, who wrote a book about intelligence ethics.[92] When Gina Bennett first offered to teach a Georgetown University course on intelligence ethics, one of her future academic colleagues asked, "Are there ethics in intelligence?"

Actually, intelligence officers think about ethics a lot because they operate in a profession filled with ethical dilemmas—where the trade-offs are complicated, often agonizing. The NSA did not cavalierly decide to collect telephone call records of millions of Americans after the September 11 terrorist attacks. As I discuss more in chapter 8, intelligence officials and policymakers carefully considered the program. They sought, and received, presidential approval. They got legal guidance. And they vigorously debated the ethical dimensions of a massive new intelligence collection program targeting the data of Americans. One official resigned in protest, later noting, "It was the wrong thing to do for the right reasons."[93]

Ethical dilemmas don't just involve high-profile, high-stakes programs. They're part of everyday life. How do intelligence officers weigh action versus inaction? Keep a collection stream going or capitalize on the information it provides and lose the source forever? How far should they go to speak truth to power—when speaking out may lead policymakers to shut out intelligence altogether? Where does loyalty to the president end? Where do they draw their own moral lines, regardless of how many legal memos say an action is Constitutional? "We take upholding the Constitution very seriously," said Bennett, "especially those of us who have been overseas and have seen governments who would just as soon kill somebody as let them speak. Those discussions really can get very deep and we have them a lot."[94]

One former NSA official recounted being asked to recruit a foreign émigré he knew. Recruiting human assets was far outside his normal job, which was analyzing signals intelligence like emails and intercepted telephone calls. The manipulation made him deeply uncomfortable. "I'm making friends with this guy so I can exploit him," he said. When the émigré asked to have dinner with their wives, it was too much. "He was a nice guy," said the official. "I had to go to my handlers and say we're done."[95]

Bill Phillips faced the opposite ethical problem: what to do when a junior CIA case officer suddenly has qualms about recruiting a spy in a foreign country—which is exactly what case officers are hired to do. "If you don't manipulate people you won't be successful at recruitment," said Phillips. "You have to have the mental acumen to do it without hesitation." Second-guessing in the field wasn't just ineffective. It was dangerous. Phillips sent the junior case officer home. "These are good questions, heavy and thoughtful questions," he advised. "You should have a way of resolving these questions in your mind. But it's not going to be here."[96]

Ethical dilemmas abound. In his book *Fair Play*, Olson lists fifty scenarios "taken from the real world of espionage and covert action" that U.S. intelligence practitioners "currently face or could conceivably face in the future." Among them: a foreign asset violates human rights or requests "payment" in the form of prostitutes or drugs; an asset working to penetrate a foreign terrorist organization seeks approval for a terrorist attack to prove his bona fides; a former CIA officer defects to an enemy, leading to the deaths of other CIA officers and assets and you have to decide whether to try to kidnap him; an opportunity arises to create an anti-American terrorist chat room but it may identify American citizens who are radicalizing.[97]

Intelligence officers grapple with these and other ethical dilemmas in different ways. Many told me their ethical guide is imagining what the American public would think if the secret became public—as one put it, "Would I be proud to tell the American people that we did that?"[98] That's exactly how CIA Director Leon Panetta presented the bin Laden raid to President Obama. "If I asked the average citizen, 'If you knew what I knew, what would you do?'" Panetta asked. "In this case, I think the answer is clear. . . . If we don't do it, we'll regret it."[99]

Regardless of the outcome, the decisions linger. As one official put it, "Ethical questions will put scars on your soul that you can never get rid of."[100]

Best and Worst Moments

For CIA analyst Aris Pappas, a highlight of his career came one day when he walked into a Virginia safe house and met the Polish agent whose intelligence he'd been using for years—a man who had risked everything to help the United States. "It dawned on me. Oh my God! This is the agent! This is the source!" he said.[101]

Dan Coats's best day as director of national intelligence came on his one-year anniversary in the job. Morale was low. Coats was under attack. The Intelligence Community was being pilloried by the president. Coats invited anyone who wished to take the constitutional oath of office with him online. Hundreds did, from agencies across the Intelligence Community. "No matter what happens," he reflected, "we have to be faithful to that oath."[102]

For Susan Gordon, who spent more than thirty years in the IC and served as the number two intelligence official, the best and worst days were the same: meeting the coffins of intelligence officers killed in the line of duty abroad. "I thought I should finish these patriots' trip home," she told me. Gordon would go to Dover Air Force Base, often alone, in the middle of the night, to be with the families of the fallen. "God, the families were always young," she recalled. "It was awful. They were wracked with pain. They'd have their babies, their little girls, six, four, and two, in tow." In some cases, Gordon was the one who had sent the intelligence officers on the assignments that got them killed. "And always in the middle of me comforting these families, they comforted me," she said, choking up. "They said, 'He wanted to be there. Don't worry. This is what he chose.' The grace shown to me on their worst day was my best day," said Gordon. "I carry those men and their families with me."[103]

This is the human side of intelligence.

An Operational Lens of Intelligence in Action: The Hunt for bin Laden

For intelligence officials, 9/11 was personal. A sign hanging above the entrance to the CIA's Counterterrorism Center sent a daily reminder of the price of failure and the importance of the mission: "Today's date is September 12, 2001."[104] They would end up hunting the al Qaeda leader for a decade. Although much remains shrouded in secrecy, information released to date offers a valuable glimpse into the workings of intelligence collection, analysis, and covert operations that led to one of the greatest intelligence successes in American history.

Finding Signals in the Noise: Intelligence Collection

The hunt for bin Laden started with a botched raid in the mountains of Tora Bora.[105] Soon after the September 11, 2001, terrorist attacks, CIA officers, U.S. special forces, and Afghan militia fighters had al Qaeda on the run, chasing bin Laden and about one thousand of his men to a maze of tunnels and caves high in the icy peaks of the Hindu Kush. By December 2001, allied forces were closing in. With bombs pummeling Tora Bora from above, bin Laden wrote his last will and testament, telling his wives not to remarry.[106] Gary Bernsten, the CIA officer leading the team, thought he had him.[107] But for reasons that are still unclear, the raid went sideways. In the dark hours of night, bin Laden handed his satellite phone (which he suspected was being tracked by the CIA) to an aide and slipped away.[108]

Days stretched into weeks, then years. The working theory was that bin Laden was holed up somewhere in the lawless mountain passes along the Afghanistan-Pakistan border.[109] But the terrain was punishing and the trail grew cold.

It was certainly not for lack of trying. Intelligence agencies went into collection overdrive, using all of the INTs. Experts mined open-source information, including two dozen audio- and videotapes issued by bin Laden—assessing whether the voice was really his and examining details (like the background images or whether he was holding a weapon by his left or right side) that might suggest his location or his health.[110] The CIA even enlisted the help of geologists and botanists to examine foliage and rock formations in the videos that might give clues to bin Laden's whereabouts.[111]

The National Security Agency kept its ears trained on terrorist communications hoping to intercept signals intelligence that could lead to bin Laden. But with 1.7 billion phone calls, emails, radio signals, Tweets, and text messages intercepted every day, it was akin to finding a needle in an enormous and ever-growing haystack.[112] And in any case, al Qaeda's leader and his trusted lieutenants had ditched their cell phones and satellite phones so their conversations wouldn't be intercepted.[113] After Tora Bora, they abandoned cell phones, satellite phones, and the

Internet, resorting to a small circle of trusted couriers who hand-carried communications to his network and released the occasional video and audio messages.[114]

President Bush directed the CIA to "flood the zone" with human intelligence collectors.[115] CIA officers poured into Afghanistan and Pakistan in the hopes of recruiting a foreign asset who might know where bin Laden was hiding.[116] U.S. airplanes dropped flyers with bin Laden's face behind bars and offered a $25 million reward for anyone who helped turn him in.[117]

Other terrorists were captured, detained in CIA black sites, and subjected to harsh and controversial interrogations to learn more about al Qaeda's operations and bin Laden's whereabouts. CIA Director Leon Panetta later noted that some of the information detainees provided was valuable, while some of it was intentionally false or misleading.[118] Unmanned aerial vehicles flew the skies over Afghanistan and Pakistan, surveilling, hunting, and striking.[119]

In the end, there wasn't one "aha" moment or lucky break. For years, there were only fragments and whispers—potential clues surrounded by false leads and dead ends, painstakingly collected, dissected, and resurrected. In 2002, a detainee not in CIA custody provided the nom de guerre of a bin Laden courier: Abu Ahmed al-Kuwaiti.[120] While analysts knew that targeting bin Laden's courier network was important, it would take years before anyone learned the courier's true name or location. But evidence increasingly suggested he was a promising lead.

CIA records show that by 2007 more than twenty detainees had discussed al-Kuwaiti's ties to senior al Qaeda leaders, including his role as bin Laden's courier and his close relationship with al Qaeda's third-in-command, Abu Faraj al-Libbi. Other information came from what detainees did *not* say. When interrogators ran al-Kuwaiti's name by Abu Faraj al-Libbi, he denied ever knowing him.[121] Another senior al Qaeda leader in custody, Khalid Sheikh Mohammed (KSM), downplayed the courier's importance—leading intelligence officials to suspect that both terrorists were trying to conceal just how important al-Kuwaiti was. "The coup de grace," wrote former CIA Deputy Director Michael Morell, was "when KSM returned to his cell after the questioning and communicated to other prisoners that they should not mention anything about 'the courier.' . . . Our interest in the courier was now sky-high."[122]

Somehow—intelligence officials have never revealed the details—in 2007, they learned the courier's real name and later discovered the general area where he operated.[123] In 2010, the National Security Agency intercepted a phone call he made to a friend. "I'm back with the people I was with before," said the courier, indicating he could be working with bin Laden or another high-level al Qaeda figure again.[124] Eventually, intelligence officers identified the courier's white Suzuki and tracked it to the Abbottabad compound.[125]

For the next several months, agencies inside the IC collected every piece of information they could about the compound and who lived there—without tipping them off. The National Reconnaissance Office sent satellites to capture images of the Pacer taking his walks. The National Geospatial-Intelligence Agency (NGA) used reference points from the images to estimate his height as well as the genders and heights of others living there.[126] NGA used other sensing devices to create 3D models of the compound.

The CIA's open-source center scooped up public information about the city of Abbottabad, but to keep operational security tight, officials requested research on several Pakistani cities.[127] The CIA also set up a safe house in Abbottabad with a small team to establish "patterns of life" at the compound.[128] Their activities included spying on the laundry hanging outside to determine the number of residents, their genders, and whether they were adults or children.[129]

All of this does indeed sound like something out of a Jason Bourne film. And because we know how the story ends, success seems inevitable. But it's important to bear in mind that the IC never got conclusive evidence that bin Laden was hiding there: his tradecraft was too good; the task was too hard; the timing was too tight; and the risks of discovery—which could blow the best chance to get bin Laden since Tora Bora—were too high. Many collection efforts were considered but never tried. Others failed or were thwarted by countermeasures.

CIA Director Leon Panetta kept pressing for more creative ideas, asking whether sewers could be tapped to collect DNA from the waste or whether surveillance cameras could be placed on the trees just outside the compound. (As Panetta himself recounts, it was a good thing CIA veterans shot down that idea—since the trees were trimmed not long after and any cameras would likely have been discovered).[130] The CIA's most ambitious plan to confirm bin Laden's identity involved a phony local vaccination program. The aim was to get DNA samples from people inside the compound that could be compared with bin Laden family member DNA on file at the CIA. But the scheme failed and the Pakistani doctor leading it was arrested and sentenced to thirty-three years in prison.[131]

To thwart NSA surveillance, the terrorists never called from the compound itself, instead traveling an hour and a half away before even putting a battery in a cellphone.[132] "You've got to give him credit for his tradecraft," said one former CIA official involved in the manhunt. Ten years earlier, bin Laden "had bodyguards, multiple SUVs and things like that. He abandoned all of that."[133] Which made him harder to find.

When President Obama made his go/no-go decision on the SEAL team raid, estimates that the Pacer was actually bin Laden ranged from 40 to 95 percent. Even with the full might of the $85 billion intelligence enterprise, nobody could be certain that he was there.

Challenging Intelligence Analysis

Analyzing intelligence in the hunt for bin Laden was just as challenging as collecting it. Analysts had to deal with two major questions. The first was "What should we be looking for?" The second was "What does our intelligence mean and how credible do we think it is?"

While the courier network ultimately led to success, it wasn't the only path. Analysts looked at multiple possibilities and took a systematic approach to locating him.[134] One focused on bin Laden's sprawling family (he was known to have four wives and about twenty children)[135] and the chance that a relative might contact the al Qaeda leader, eventually leading officials to his location. The CIA succeeded in identifying one of bin Laden's sons and learning that he had been under house arrest in Iran. But by then, the son, Saad bin Laden, had been released and left

Iran, so the agency had to track him all over again. By the time they located his whereabouts in Pakistan, he was dead.[136]

CIA analysts also sought to identify signatures of bin Laden's lifestyle that could help track him down—like the medicines he might need for chronic health problems, his hobbies, and how he liked to move or live.[137] According to Panetta and his CIA chief of staff, Jeremy Bash, the questions for the bin Laden manhunt focused on how and where he would be hiding—including what security he would be using. "The working hypothesis," they later wrote, "was that he was located in the tribal areas in Western Pakistan, probably in a cave or a rural area, separated from his family. The hypothesis was that well-armed guards surrounded him. There was also a suggestion that his health was failing and that he may have been hooked up to a makeshift kidney dialysis machine."[138]

Almost everything about that working hypothesis turned out to be wrong. Bin Laden's compound wasn't in some remote mountain cave; it was in a suburban neighborhood in a city of about a million residents. Abbottabad wasn't even known as a stronghold for Islamic extremists. When analysts considered likely locations for bin Laden, "Abbottabad wouldn't be on that list," said one former intelligence official involved in the manhunt.[139] Bin Laden also wasn't separated from his family as analysts expected. He was living with them—three wives and a dozen of his children and grandchildren. Nor was he surrounded by well-armed sentries and layers of security. Instead, he lived with chickens, goats, rabbits, and the families of two trusted couriers who had a handful of weapons.[140] His hideout didn't have any booby traps or escape tunnels. His security depended on staying off the grid while living in the middle of the grid—hiding in plain sight. The SEALs didn't find a dialysis machine inside the Abbottabad compound, either, but they did find hair dye for men.[141]

For the Abbottabad lead to be right, the analytic team hunting bin Laden had to be willing to challenge their prevailing hypotheses. That's a very hard thing to do. As I'll discuss more in chapter 5, psychology research has long shown that humans are highly susceptible to confirmation bias, trusting more in information that confirms their prior beliefs and discounting information that doesn't. There were many good reasons to believe that bin Laden was camped out in a fortified rural stronghold like Tora Bora, hidden by the rugged terrain, protected by his followers, and disconnected from the rest of the world. After all, he had done it before. And it was well known that bin Laden enjoyed rural life[142] and that he was intimately familiar with the ravines, paths, and caves of the area, having fought the Soviets there in the 1980s.[143]

Admitting that the hypotheses guiding the ten-year hunt for the world's most wanted terrorist could be wrong was a heavy analytic lift and a major breakthrough. Panetta and Bash write that agency analysts "were willing to admit that the Agency had been wrong. And they were willing to dedicate finite resources to an entirely new theory, one that upended all previous assumptions, and to imagine that bin Laden's plan to 'hide in plain sight' was more brilliant than we had ever guessed he'd be."[144] Bin Laden's hiding strategy deviated completely from what he had done before, and it was likely an unexpected change, even for him. It was an unknown unknown.

Then there was the problem of assessing the significance of the intelligence that came in. Detainees were known to lie and distract, sending interrogators on wild goose chases. Sometimes they provided truthful information but often they didn't. Pulling intelligence threads led to both dead ends and renewed hopes. At one point, for example, the CIA heard the courier they were tracking had been killed in Afghanistan, but it turned out to be his brother.[145] Among the most vexing challenges was that the same facts could support different theories. The Pacer could be bin Laden. That's what everyone hoped. But he might also be another al Qaeda figure, or a warlord, or a drug runner, or nobody of interest at all. To make sure wishful thinking wasn't clouding the analysis, the National Counterterrorism Center assigned a "red team" of fresh analysts to review the intelligence, scrub all of the assumptions, and play devil's advocate, challenging everything. They did not reach a consensus.[146]

The president's advisors didn't agree, either. When Obama asked how likely it was that the Pacer was bin Laden, the lead analyst put the odds at 95 percent.[147] Several others answered between 60 and

80 percent.[148] Michael Morrell, the deputy CIA director, told the president he was more certain that Saddam Hussein had weapons of mass destruction than he was that bin Laden was in that compound.[149] Michael Leiter, the head of the National Counterterrorism Center, was even more pessimistic. He put the probability at 40 percent, though he noted, "that's 38 percent better than we have ever had before."[150] It was a stunning range of answers based on the exact same information.

"People don't have differences because they have different intel," the CIA's Morell later explained. "We are all looking at the same things." Instead, Morell concluded the variation stemmed from different experiences. Counterterrorism specialists were optimistic because they were coming off a string of recent successes in locating and killing top terrorist targets. But Morell and others who had lived through the intelligence failures of 9/11 and Iraq WMD were far more cautious.[151] "Even if we had a human source inside the compound and that source told us that bin Laden was there, I would not be at 95 percent," Morell recalls telling the president, "because sources lie and get things wrong all the time."[152] Former CIA Deputy Director John McLaughlin also believed the Iraqi WMD failure played a large role. "In a curious and ironic way," he told me, "the Bin Laden estimate may have been right because of the Iraq failure—the caution it planted and the sensitivity to rigorous [analytic] tradecraft."[153]

Still, all that watching, collecting, analyzing, scrubbing, and red-teaming could only reduce uncertainty, not eliminate it. By April 2011, the intelligence was as good as it was ever going to get. The president had to decide.

Covert Action

Covert action, as we'll see in chapter 7, is reserved for the toughest situations. It involves activities intended to "influence political, economic, or military conditions abroad, where it is intended that the role of the United States Government will not be apparent or acknowledged publicly."[154] Covert operations are led by the CIA. All presidents use them because they offer a third option between doing nothing and going to war. But precisely because they are tools of last resort in difficult circumstances, covert operations have a high rate of failure.

Confronted with intelligence about the Pacer, President Obama considered four options.[155] Each had serious drawbacks. A large air strike would obliterate the compound but would be an overt military action against a sovereign partner that could ignite a political, and potentially kinetic, firestorm. It was also estimated to cause 50 to 100 deaths[156] and would provide no proof that bin Laden had been killed.

A drone strike with a small missile could hit the Pacer during his walk and avoid other casualties, but the munition was experimental and could not be guided after launch. If it missed, bin Laden would vanish again. If it hit, U.S. officials would not be able to confirm bin Laden had been killed or retrieve any intelligence from the compound.[157]

Waiting for more intelligence might confirm the Pacer's identity but increased the risks of a leak tipping off the Pakistanis or bin Laden.[158]

A covert special forces operation deep inside Pakistani territory risked the lives of two dozen men, could ignite a shooting war with a putative ally, might not get bin Laden, could kill innocents, and could fail, triggering a domestic political crisis akin to President Carter's after the failed Iranian hostage rescue mission of 1980. But a raid offered the best chance of confirming bin Laden's identity, retrieving intelligence, and providing potential deniability, however thin, if bin Laden wasn't there.[159]

Two days later, under a moonless sky, choppers carrying American commandos secretly flew over the Pakistani border. Fifteen thousand feet overhead, an RQ 170 stealthy drone beamed real-time footage to command centers at the CIA, White House, and Pentagon.[160] President Obama and his senior advisors huddled in a cramped room as CIA Director Leon Panetta narrated the unfolding operation. The tension of the moment was captured in an iconic White House photograph (figure 4.1)

"They've reached the target," said Panetta.[161]

Then things went south, fast. The first chopper was forced to crash land. A second was supposed to hover over the compound's roof but

FIGURE 4.1 President Barack Obama and his national security team receive
an update on the bin Laden operation as it unfolds, May 1, 2011.
Credit: Pete Souza, Official White House Photographer

had to jettison that plan when the other one crashed, so it landed across
the street instead.[162] This meant that instead of assaulting the compound from above and below simultaneously to maintain surprise and
speed, SEALs had to work their way slowly through the house, clearing
rooms as they moved up to the third floor, where they believed bin
Laden was living.[163] All the noise woke neighbors, who started ap-
proaching the compound to see what was going on.[164] Minutes passed.
Shots were fired. Officials said it felt like years. "Eternity is defined as
the time between when you see something go awry and that first voice
report," said one special operations officer.[165] Then the news: "We have
a visual on Geronimo," said Panetta.[166] And finally, "Geronimo EKIA"—
enemy killed in action. In the Situation Room, it was silent. Then
Obama said, "We got him."[167]

5

WHY ANALYSIS IS
SO HARD

THE SEVEN DEADLY BIASES

There is no perfection in our business.
—GEORGE TENET, CIA DIRECTOR 1997–2004[1]

THE AMBUSH CAME on an icy November night. In 1950, United Nations forces led by American and South Korean troops were marching north toward the Yalu River border separating North Korea from China. Their mission: rout the North Koreans, reunify the Korean peninsula, and score a decisive win against Communism. In the mountains, temperatures dropped below zero, freezing American tank treads to the ground and cracking the windshields of reconnaissance aircraft flying overhead.[2] From the distant comforts of his Tokyo headquarters, Gen. Douglas MacArthur directed troop movements that spread his men and supply lines dangerously thin. Although some worried that his northern gambit might provoke China to intervene in the war, MacArthur didn't. Intelligence reports from the CIA and Joint Chiefs of Staff estimated that China's new Communist regime would likely limit its interference to covert assistance of North Korea, since large-scale intervention risked igniting World War III between the Soviet Union and the United States.[3] MacArthur's own intelligence division in Far East Command believed that at most, China could send fifty thousand to sixty thousand troops across the border. And even if that happened, Chinese forces would eventually be defeated, since they were ill equipped, poorly trained, and operating without air support. "There would be the greatest slaughter," MacArthur assured President Harry Truman a few weeks earlier. MacArthur was so convinced victory was around the corner, he told Truman the troops would be home by Christmas.[4] Some of his men were already planning a victory parade in Tokyo.[5] They would never get one. Instead, nearly forty thousand would return home in coffins.[6]

On the night of November 26, approximately three hundred thousand Chinese troops began swarming out of the snow-covered peaks, blaring bugles, hurling mortars, firing machine guns, and hammering UN forces. It turns out that Chinese soldiers had been hiding undetected for a month, attacking in small skirmishes that concealed their numbers and lured MacArthur's men into the trap.[7] The effect was devastating. Within weeks, UN forces lost thousands of men, two hundred miles of territory, and the advantage in the Korean War. MacArthur was sacked—an inglorious end to a storied military career. When the fighting ended in 1953, it left a Cold War geopolitical deadlock, a divided Korean peninsula, and a brutally repressive Communist North Korean regime in place.

China's surprise entry into the Korean War was a "hinge of history" moment. Over the next half century, North Korea would grow more destitute and dangerous, dedicating its resources to building a clandestine nuclear weapons program and incarcerating more than one hundred thousand political prisoners in a vast gulag[8] while leaving three million people (12 percent of its population) to starve to death. Today, South Korea is a wealthy democratic ally of the United States with per capita GDP of $39,000. North Korea is one of the most impoverished and repressive states in the world, with a per capita GDP of just $1,700[9] and a growing nuclear arsenal.[10] While history is always filled with uncertainties, the trajectories of the two Koreas reveal the enormity of one critical juncture—and the monumental price of intelligence failure.

China's surprise attack highlights the pitfalls of intelligence analysis. In the fall of 1950, there were plenty of clues about China's actual intentions and capabilities picked up from prisoner-of-war interrogations;

human intelligence from North Korean locals; reports from Chinese Nationalists; intercepted communications; photo reconnaissance; captured enemy documents; diplomatic messages transmitted through the Indian ambassador to China, K. M. Panikkar; and even public statements by Chinese Premier Zhou Enlai himself.[11] The failure came in interpreting what all those signals meant. MacArthur and his G-2 intelligence chief at Far East Command, Maj. Gen. Charles Willoughby, misread nearly all of the intelligence they received. Others did, too.[12] The question is why.

Many have laid the Korean War intelligence failure at the vainglorious feet of General MacArthur. It is certainly true that MacArthur lived in a "dreamworld of self-worship," as historian William Stueck put it.[13] But there's more to the story. There usually is. Whenever disaster strikes, it's tempting to blame individuals, but the sources of intelligence failure almost always lie deeper.

This chapter takes a closer look at intelligence analysis, examining why it's often so hard to see what there is to be seen. The answer lies in two sets of factors: natural variations in the predictability of human events and the limitations of human cognition. The world out there is inherently hard to understand and human brains are not wired to understand it well.

As we'll see, MacArthur suffered an extreme case of very common afflictions. He allowed optimism to cloud his assessment of facts, discounted evidence that contradicted his prior beliefs, and built a team around him that discouraged dissent. The most important lesson from Korea isn't that MacArthur failed in unique ways. It's that he failed in ordinary ones. The cognitive filters that all humans use to process information can lead even the most determined leaders in the most important moments to fail. In recent years, researchers and intelligence officials have been seeking ways to better spot and avoid these kinds of cognitive traps. Advances in artificial intelligence also offer promising ways to help analysts find new insights and contend with a crushing volume of data in the digital age. But vexing challenges remain.

Estimating the Future Is a Hazardous
Occupation—in Many Occupations

Everyone knows that predicting the future is hard. Even experts with access to the best data are often wrong. Doctors offer incorrect diagnoses. Bankers get initial stock prices wrong—as we saw when Uber, Peloton, and Lyft went public. Hollywood executives are surprised by sleeper hits (*Little Miss Sunshine*) and blockbuster bombs (*Green Lantern*). Political pollsters get surprised on election day. In the 1948 presidential election, analysts were so sure New York Governor Thomas Dewey would defeat incumbent President Harry Truman that the *Chicago Tribune* emblazoned its oversized headline "Dewey Defeats Truman" when it went to press.[14] Truman had a field day when the election results came in. In 2016, pollsters with advanced data analytics didn't do any better. Four models tracked by the *New York Times* gave Republican candidate Donald Trump a 15 percent, 8 percent, 2 percent, and less than 1 percent chance of winning against Democratic candidate Hillary Clinton. Even statistics guru Nate Silver put the odds of a Trump victory at just 29 percent.[15]

But we often forget that some things are much easier to predict than others. The foreseeability of the world out there varies in systematic ways for systematic reasons.

The Predictability Spectrum: Four Key Factors

As figure 5.1 shows, predictability lies along a spectrum. Sports contests sit on the easier end of the spectrum. Assessing how national security threats will unfold over time sits on the opposite, much harder end. Four factors explain the difference and why intelligence analysts have a much tougher job than other professions that peer into the future.

DATA! DATA! DATA!

Data is a key ingredient to predicting the future of anything. Analysis is an exercise in *causal inference*—understanding what causes are likely to produce what outcomes. But not just any data will do. To be useful, data has

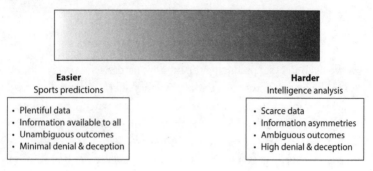

Easier	Harder
Sports predictions	Intelligence analysis
• Plentiful data • Information available to all • Unambiguous outcomes • Minimal denial & deception	• Scarce data • Information asymmetries • Ambiguous outcomes • High denial & deception

FIGURE 5.1 The Predictability Spectrum

to cover comparable events or circumstances. The more similar situations you can see, the more insight you can gain about likely causes and effects.

Sports competitions are data-rich. They involve repeated play, consistent rules, long-running programs or competitors, and statistics covering just about everything—from the post positions of Kentucky Derby winners to the batting averages of every professional baseball player since 1871.[16] Sportscasters don't always get it right. But comparable data reduces uncertainty and increases prediction accuracy. In sports, winning against the odds is exciting precisely because the odds are usually right. Exactly how often in the past eighty-plus years has the worst-ranked team in an NCAA men's basketball bracket won it all? Never. History is not destiny, but in sports it's a pretty good guide.

Intelligence analysts, by contrast, usually don't have anywhere near that kind of rich comparable data to help them assess future geopolitical trends. When the Korean War began in June 1950, data to help discern the intentions of China's new Communist regime stretched back just eight months: Mao Zedong had won China's civil war and established the People's Republic of China on October 1, 1949. No American intelligence analyst could look at the history books to get a good read on how Mao had dealt with past foreign invasions of neighboring states who were ideological allies at the dawn of a Cold War, because none existed.

Or consider the current nuclear crisis with Iran. Only ten countries have ever acquired nuclear weapons.[17] Five got the bomb so long ago, hand-held calculators hadn't been invented yet. North Korea is the most recent nuclear rogue, but the Hermit Kingdom's ruling family hardly seems a generalizable model for anything. And even if it were, how much do we really know about how North Korean leader Kim Jong-Un thinks? North Korea has been such a hard intelligence target, as late as 2009, the CIA was building its dossier on Kim through the second-hand reports of a sushi chef.[18] South Africa is the only country that has ever developed a nuclear arsenal and then voluntarily dismantled it.[19] But that's not a generalizable case, either; at the time, apartheid was crumbling and the outgoing White regime feared putting the bomb in the hands of a Black government.

While sports analysts can estimate this year's outcomes by leveraging literally thousands of data points, nuclear analysts trying to mine history for insights about Iran have a grand total of ten unique cases over seventy-five years.

ASYMMETRIC INFORMATION

The second factor making some things easier to estimate than others is asymmetric information. In sports, the same information is generally available to everyone. Coaches may have inside knowledge about the mood of their team or how good they looked in practice, but critical information is in the open; nobody is hiding this year's rankings or a season-ending injury. The only real limiting factor to obtaining data is time—how much of it you want to spend watching ESPN or digging through statistics.

In geopolitics, the same information is *not* available to everyone, regardless of how much time they have. Intelligence is in the business of unlocking other people's secrets and protecting our own. Asymmetric information is the name of the game. And in a world of asymmetric information, prediction is much more difficult and miscalculation much more likely.

Douglas MacArthur had some intelligence about China's troop movements and willingness to intervene in the war. But he found out too late that it wasn't the full picture. On October 15, 1950, just as MacArthur was reassuring President Truman that China "would have the greatest difficulty of getting more than 50 thousand across the river," tens of thousands of Chinese forces were secretly doing just that.[20] By October 19, 260,000 Chinese fighters were hiding in the Korean mountains. The Chinese were working hard to conceal their movements, including wearing their jackets inside out so the white blended in with the snow.[21] China's surprise attack relied on asymmetric information.

Asymmetric information problems don't just come from adversaries. Even within the Intelligence Community, the same information isn't available to everyone. In part, this stems from classification rules that tightly restrict who has access to what.

There are good security reasons for this kind of need-to-know compartmentalization, including limiting the risks that an intelligence target (like Osama bin Laden) could be tipped off and slip away and mitigating the damage of a potential cyber breach or mole. The downside of need-to-know, however, is that analysts frequently have different pieces of information and face enormous barriers to sharing it.

Imagine scattering twenty years of NCAA basketball tournament data across a thousand people. Now imagine that most of them do not know each other, and many don't know the value of the particular piece of information they possess. Some have no idea how the game of basketball is played because their expertise lies in other sports. They're all told that if they share anything with the wrong person, they could be disciplined, fired, even prosecuted. But to succeed, they somehow have to collectively pick this year's winning team.

Many factors explain why the right information often does not get to the right people at the right time in the intelligence world—including bureaucratic turf protection, agency cultures, career incentives, ingrained habits, and a desire for autonomy. In the Korean War, MacArthur and Willoughby, his intelligence chief, deliberately kept the CIA out of the loop because they didn't trust the fledgling intelligence agency and because they wanted total control over their wartime intelligence. As one scholar wrote, MacArthur didn't want "second-guessing by his subordinates or outside interference by Washington," even though second-guessing is exactly what good intelligence analysts are supposed to do.[22]

Fifty years later, the FBI and CIA failed to share information about vital clues that could have unraveled the 9/11 plot because working across agency lines was an unnatural act for both agencies, and it had always been that way.[23] "At the FBI . . . agents are not trained to share information with other agencies," Attorney General Janet Reno told the bipartisan 9/11 Commission that investigated the tragedy. "Nor are they evaluated and rewarded based on their ability to generate and share information that other agencies might find useful."[24] While counterterrorism intelligence sharing has improved significantly since 9/11, information asymmetries still abound. As one senior intelligence official put it, "No one's career is ever ruined by being too restrictive about classified information."[25]

WHEN IS A WIN A WIN?

The third factor influencing predictability is whether outcomes are fast and clear. This is a big deal. Rapid, unambiguous outcomes make it possible to develop feedback loops for analysts to improve their predictions over time. It's easier to learn from your mistakes when you know you've made them.[26]

Wharton psychologist Phil Tetlock, the leading scholar on expert judgment, is a fan of feedback loops. As he and Dan Gardner wrote in their book, *Superforecasting*, "To learn from failure, we must *know* when we fail. The baby who flops backward does. So does the boy who skins his knee when he falls off the bike. And the accountant who puts an easy putt into a sand trap. And because they know, they can think about what went wrong, adjust, and try again."[27]

Failing is easier to see in some areas than in others. One reason meteorologists have gotten so much better at weather forecasting is that they have great feedback loops. Gauging accuracy is fast and obvious. In weather forecasting, *long-term* means next week. It snows or it doesn't. Nobody's ever unsure whether there are hurricane winds gusting outside.[28] Meteorologists make many predictions, can tell easily and quickly whether each one was right or wrong, adjust their models, and try again the next day.

In sports, too, outcomes are unambiguous and instantaneous. Everyone knows when a win's a win. Analysts can look at their prediction track record and examine whether they put too much weight on the wrong variables or let their biases skew their judgment (more on that below).

In foreign policy, though, winning and losing are almost never clear. Is ISIS on the ropes or on the rise? Is maximum pressure against North Korea working? Will the U.S. war in Afghanistan ever succeed? Who got it right or wrong? It's hard to say. And the answer today may be different in a month, a year, a decade, or a century.

Success is especially hard to see in intelligence because so many factors influence policy outcomes and because intelligence success sometimes means preventing bad events from occurring in the first place. As former CIA Deputy Director John McLaughlin told me, success is "sometimes woven invisibly into the fabric of a successful policy—the Balkans, the uniting of Germany within NATO—and sometimes success is nothing happening—an embassy is not attacked because intelligence warns and no one ever hears anything."[29]

It's difficult for analysts to get better at predicting when they don't know if their past predictions were ever any good.[30]

DENIAL AND DECEPTION

The fourth factor affecting the prediction spectrum is denial and deception—or efforts to conceal what you're doing and deceive the other side.[31] Sports coaches engage in some denial and deception, using codes to hide their play calls or using a trick play in a big game, for example. But this is small-time compared to what countries and transnational actors do to conceal their intentions and capabilities and lead other intelligence services astray.

In 2016, North Korean leader Kim Jong-Un staged a fake missile test by doctoring old video. During the 1962 Cuban missile crisis, Russian leader Nikita Khrushchev outright lied to John F. Kennedy, assuring the American president that Soviet arms shipments to Cuba were purely defensive in nature.[32] In the Korean War, Mao's troops went to extraordinary lengths to cloak their movements across the Yalu River, including disguising themselves as refugees, avoiding all radio, telegraph, and telephone communications, and constructing wooden bridges that were painted the color of water and submerged just below the surface.[33] During the Revolutionary War, Gen. George Washington created phantom camps, wrote phony battle plans and letters designed to fall into enemy hands, and even shipped fake gunpowder casks filled with sand to trick the British into thinking the Continental Army was bigger and better armed than it was.

Denial and deception efforts are not rare occurrences in international politics. They're everyday life. Wars are won and lost and countries are helped or hurt by how well they can hide critical information and manipulate the other side into believing things that are not true.

Nobody doubts sports data. A homerun is a homerun. But in geopolitics, data is always suspect.

In short, there are predictable reasons why everything in the world is not equally predictable. For intelligence analysts, the degree of difficulty is high. Data shortages, asymmetric information, weak win-loss feedback loops, and the prevalence of denial and deception activities make geopolitical trends and events much harder to predict than other things.

The Seven Deadly Biases

The problem isn't just the world out there. Sometimes, the problem is us.

Psychology research finds that humans rely on mental shortcuts to process all the information bombarding them each day. These shortcuts are extremely useful, enabling faster thinking and efficient decisionmaking. We use them without even thinking about it—skimming Yelp reviews to pick a restaurant, watching shows recommended by Netflix's search algorithm, and voting party-line tickets rather than carefully assessing each candidate for every local position. But mental shortcuts are also prone to error.[34]

To see this in action, consider one of the early and controversial experiments conducted by Amos Tversky and Daniel Kahneman, pioneers in the psychology field. Participants were given the following description about an imaginary woman named Linda:

> Linda is 31 years old, single, outspoken and very bright. She majored in philosophy. As a student, she was deeply concerned with the issue of discrimination and social justice, and also participated in antinuclear demonstrations.

They were then asked which was more probable:

> Linda is a bank teller; or
> Linda is a bank teller and is active in the feminist movement.

Between 85 and 90 percent of participants in the study chose (2). Kahneman described this outcome as totally "contrary to logic." All feminist bank tellers are also bank tellers, so (1) always has a higher probability of being true.[35] The math doesn't lie but the brain often does.

Economists and psychologists have discovered so many cognitive biases, Wikipedia currently lists nearly two hundred.[36] Seven are especially pervasive and consequential for intelligence analysis. I call them the Seven Deadly Biases.

Confirmation Bias

Humans are not objective, no matter how hard they try to be. Researchers have found that people are wedded to their initial beliefs and will rationalize like nobody's business to cling to them even in the face of contrary evidence. People tend to seek and latch on to information that confirms their pre-existing beliefs while avoiding, disregarding, or minimizing evidence that challenges them.

In a now-famous psychology experiment, my Stanford colleagues Lee Ross and Mark Lepper, along with psychologist Charles Lord, recruited twenty-four undergraduates who supported capital punishment and twenty-four who opposed it. All forty-eight students were then shown two studies with equivalent evidentiary standards. One contained evidence that capital punishment deterred future crime; the other contained evidence that it did not. Ross, Lepper, and Lord found that students discounted whichever study conflicted with their already-held beliefs about capital punishment and accepted the study that confirmed their policy preferences.[37] Students' objective analysis of facts was colored by their prior beliefs, and they didn't even know it.

Confirmation bias has dogged good analysis for centuries. In Roman times, the imperial physician Galen was so confident in his remedies, no evidence could prove him wrong. He famously wrote, "All who drink of this treatment recover in a short time, except those whom it does not help, who all die. It is obvious, therefore, that it fails only in incurable cases."[38] Francis Bacon warned of the dangers of confirmation bias in 1620, writing, "The human understanding when it has once adopted an opinion . . . draws all things else to support and agree with it."[39]

Three centuries later, in the Korean War, Maj. Gen. Charles Willoughby suffered from such severe confirmation bias that even when UN forces started encountering Chinese troops on the battlefield weeks before the massive November ambush, Willoughby invented ways to downplay and dismiss the information.[40] On October 25, the first Chinese prisoner was captured. He told interrogators that he was a regular soldier in the Chinese Communist Army and that there were tens of thousands of Chinese soldiers in the mountains nearby. The report immediately went up the chain to Willoughby, who sent word back that the prisoner must be a Korean resident of China who had volunteered to fight. Over the next several weeks, American and South Korean forces took more Chinese prisoners who reported that they had crossed the Yalu River in large numbers. Each time, Willoughby minimized the significance of their reports.[41]

In 2002, as war was brewing in Iraq, confirmation bias again led to intelligence failure. In October, Congress received a National Intelligence Estimate (NIE) about Iraq's weapons of mass destruction (WMD) programs. NIEs are the most authoritative assessments produced by the Intelligence Community. They are considered the gold standard, harnessing the best insights from the best information across the entire Intelligence Community. This particular NIE contained several alarming assessments. Among them: Iraq was at that moment reconstituting its nuclear weapons program and seeking a nuclear device; had restarted its production of chemical weapons, including mustard, sarin, and VX, and had probably amassed substantial chemical weapons stockpiles; and had expanded and advanced its bioweapons capability since the first Gulf War, including developing mobile biological weapons production facilities that could evade detection.[42]

Every single one of these judgments turned out to be wrong.[43] After the United States invaded, the CIA and Defense Department organized an international fact-finding team to hunt for evidence of weapons of mass destruction and any associated research or infrastructure. Called the Iraq Survey Group, the team never found evidence of a reconstituted nuclear program.[44] They found a trace amount of chemical weapons believed to be left over from the Iran-Iraq war and not enough to be militarily significant.[45] They concluded that Saddam Hussein had destroyed his bioweapons program back in the 1990s.[46] The mobile bioweapons capability that could evade detection was actually a phantom peddled by an unreliable human source code-named, of all things, Curveball.[47] Former CIA Director John Brennan called Curveball a "fabricator" and the estimate "seriously flawed."[48]

How could so many smart and dedicated intelligence analysts have been so wrong? The bipartisan Silberman-Robb Commission conducted a postmortem that reviewed thousands of documents and interviewed hundreds of experts inside and outside the Intelligence Community. Its unanimous report identified many causes of failure. Confirmation bias was a big one. "It appears that in some instances analysts' presumptions were so firm that they simply disregarded evidence that did not support their hypotheses," the report concluded. "As we saw in several instances, when confronted with evidence that indicated Iraq did not have WMD, analysts tended to discount such information. Rather than weighing the evidence independently, analysts accepted information that fit the prevailing theory and rejected information that contradicted it." On the basis of what coalition forces discovered after the First Gulf War, intelligence analysts knew that Iraqi leader Saddam

Hussein had developed clandestine WMD programs in the past. A decade later, they assumed he was probably developing weapons of mass destruction again. It wasn't an unreasonable assumption, but it was an untested one. And that made all the difference. "Analysts began to fit the facts to the theory rather than the other way around," the commission concluded.[49] It was a classic case of confirmation bias.

Optimism Bias

Optimism bias is a close cousin of confirmation bias. Put simply, optimism bias is wishful thinking. It's everywhere. Researchers have found that people believe good events will happen to themselves more than others,[50] that their own investments will outperform the average,[51] that their favorite sports team has a higher chance of winning than it actually does,[52] and that their preferred presidential candidate will win even when the polls say otherwise.[53] People are also wildly optimistic about themselves. Large majorities believe they are smarter, more talented, better looking, and even better drivers than the average—even though it's statistically impossible for that many people to beat the average at anything.[54]

Optimism bias has its benefits. Without it, college dropouts like Bill Gates and Steve Jobs would never dream of risking it all to start Microsoft and Apple. Optimism bias helps drive humans to overcome failure and try again, but in the realm of foreign policy, it can be deadly. Politicians can be highly susceptible to policy proposals claiming favorable estimates of success, whether it's humanitarian intervention in Somalia, war in Libya, or renewed sanctions against Iran.

The leaders of nearly every country involved in World War I predicted that victory would be swift and easy. "Give me 700,000 men and I will conquer Europe," said Gen. Noël de Castelnau, chief of staff for the French Army at the outbreak of the war.[55] Castelnau got 8.4 million men—more than ten times that number he said he needed—but Europe wasn't conquered. It was decimated. The war took the lives of nearly forty million people and ravaged economies and societies.[56]

In the Korean War, Douglas MacArthur and Charles Willoughby were so hopeful for victory, no amount of intelligence suggesting otherwise was sufficient to change their minds. According to an expert review of the Korean War intelligence, both men, along with other intelligence officers, received numerous reports that Chinese forces were massing in Manchuria—as many as 450,000 men. MacArthur and Willoughby agreed that China was deploying large numbers of troops, yet still concluded that China was unlikely to intervene in a major way.[57] Optimism bias kept them from considering bad outcomes that might have been avoided if only they had been recognized.

Optimism bias more often affects policy decisions than intelligence analysis because intelligence officials are naturally prone to pessimism. Their mission is considering downside risks and seeing dangers before it's too late. CIA Director John Brennan brought bad news to the White House so often, President Obama took to calling him Dr. Doom.[58] Nevertheless, intelligence analysts are not immune to this cognitive trap.

Availability Bias

Humans are atrocious at understanding probabilities. Ever wonder why people are more afraid of dying in a shark attack than a car crash, even though fatal car accidents are about sixty thousand times more likely?[59] Or why tornadoes are seen as more frequent killers than asthma, even though asthma causes twenty times more deaths?[60] It's not because people are stupid; even smart people with advanced degrees miscalculate probabilities. Instead, the problem is availability bias: people naturally assume something they can easily recall is more likely to occur. The human brain confuses the availability of a past memory with the likelihood of its future occurrence. Even though they're statistically less likely, vivid, horrifying events (like shark attacks) are generally easier to remember than everyday occurrences (like car accidents).

Intelligence analysts, like everyone else, have to contend with the risk that availability bias can skew their judgment in hidden ways. We can see the powerful grip of recent experience in how different intelligence analysts viewed information about whether the Pacer walking around a suspicious Pakistani compound in 2011 was Osama bin Laden. As recounted in chapter 4, estimates about whether they had found the al Qaeda leader ranged from 40 to 95 percent.[61] Those who had lived through the intelligence failure of overestimating Saddam's WMD programs were more skeptical of the intelligence and issued lower probability estimates that the Pacer was bin Laden, while those coming off recent counterterrorism successes put more stock in the intelligence and issued more optimistic assessments.[62] What you predict depends on what you've experienced.

The Fundamental Attribution Error

The fundamental attribution error is the tendency to believe that others behave badly because of their personality while we ourselves behave badly because of factors beyond our control. People often jump to blaming others while letting themselves off the hook. Drivers think that someone cutting them off must be a jerk rather than wondering if there's an emergency or some other reason requiring them to drive that way. College students often say "I got an A!" when they do well in a course but "The professor gave me a C!" when they do poorly.

In foreign policy, the fundamental attribution error fuels misperception. As Kahneman and Renshon wrote:

A policymaker or diplomat involved in a tense exchange with a foreign government is likely to observe a great deal of hostile behavior by that country's representatives. Some of that behavior may indeed be the result of deep hostility. But some of it is simply a response to the current situation as it is perceived by the other side. What is ironic is that individuals who attribute others' behavior to deep hostility are quite likely to explain away their own behavior as a result of being "pushed into a corner" by an adversary.[63]

History is filled with crises in which one country either overestimated the hostile motives of another or underestimated how threatening its own actions could appear to the other side, or both.[64] Take, for example, the First Gulf War and the Iraq War, in which both the United States and Iraq largely misunderstood the other's view. Iraq underestimated the United States' risk tolerance following the Cold War and 9/11, and the United States failed to see that Saddam was much more concerned about the Iranian threat than the American one. In both 1990 and 2003, an incomplete picture of the other side's intentions and motives led to costly conflict between the two countries.[65]

During the Korean War, many U.S. officials believed that marching through North Korea toward the Chinese border would not be seen as threatening to China. "Washington authorities, most notably the JCS [Joint Chiefs of Staff], seemed to believe that as long as direct clashes along the Yalu could be avoided, so too could war with China—hence proposals by Army Chief of Staff General J. Lawton Collins that MacArthur stop five miles from the border," noted Eliot A. Cohen in his 1988 analysis of the intelligence failure.[66] Secretary of State Dean Acheson went so far as to claim that "no possible shred of evidence could have existed in the minds of the Chinese Communists about the non-threatening intentions of the forces of the United Nations."[67] American leaders knew that their own intentions toward China were not hostile and assumed that Chinese leaders knew it, too. And even when China entered the war, American officials attributed it to China's inherent hostility toward the United States rather than to it being a reaction to MacArthur's advance beyond the 38th parallel.

Mirror Imaging

Mirror imaging is estimating how someone else will behave by projecting what you would do in the same situation.[68] Framing your assessment with "If I were Xi Jinping" or "If I were a Russian intelligence officer" is one the greatest pitfalls in intelligence analysis and foreign policy decisionmaking. As former CIA analyst Frank Watanabe warned in his Fifteen Axioms for Intelligence Analysis, "Just because something seems like the logical conclusion or course of action to you does not mean that the person or group you are analyzing will see it that way."[69]

In May 1998, India tested a nuclear device for the first time in twenty-four years. U.S. intelligence agencies were so taken by surprise, they learned about the test in an Indian press release.[70] It was a major intelligence failure.

A high-level review found that mirror imaging played a significant role.[71] Although the Indian government engaged in extensive denial and deception to hide test preparations, intelligence analysts were also deceived by their own thinking.[72] They had assumed that the campaign promise of India's hardline Bharatiya Janata Party (BJP) to test a nuclear weapon if it came to power was just talk.[73] On the basis of the American experience, campaign pledges shouldn't be taken too seriously. Analysts reasoned the BJP would be unlikely to conduct an atomic test—risking economic sanctions and international opprobrium—since no American government in the same situation would. As review chairman Adm. David E. Jeremiah put it, "We should have been much more aggressive in thinking through how the other guy thought."[74]

Mirror imaging also led MacArthur, other policymakers, and CIA analysts astray in the Korean War. They believed the Chinese saw the costs and benefits of intervening just like they did—namely, that air power gave American forces a decisive advantage over Chinese troops and that Moscow would be reluctant to approve China's entry for fear of risking a global war between the two nuclear superpowers.[75]

And in the Cuban missile crisis of 1962, mirror imaging led both the Soviets and Americans to miscalculate, leaving the world at the nuclear brink. American estimators failed to see the world or weigh the costs and benefits of the missile deployment through Soviet eyes. And the Soviets appeared to make the same mistake when estimating how the United States would react.

Between January and October 1962—when American U-2 spy planes discovered smoking gun evidence of nuclear missile sites in Cuba—the U.S. Intelligence Community produced four National Intelligence Estimates about Cuba.[76] All of them assumed the Soviets' principal aim was defending Cuba from an American attack. Surely, analysts reasoned, the Soviets knew that deploying nuclear weapons to Cuba involved unacceptably high risks of discovery and nuclear war with the United

States. The Soviet Union "would almost certainly never intend to hazard its own safety for the sake of Cuba," noted the March 21, 1962, estimate.[77] None of the assessments considered whether Soviet leader Nikita Khrushchev saw *benefits* to a nuclear deployment, such as gaining leverage over the status of a divided Berlin, embarrassing President Kennedy, exerting psychological pressure by basing nuclear weapons in the neighborhood just as the United States had done to the Soviets in Europe, or compensating for Moscow's small and unreliable long-range nuclear arsenal by parking some of its more plentiful and reliable shorter-range missiles just ninety miles from the American homeland.[78]

Less is known about Soviet intelligence assessments,[79] but it is clear that Soviet leader Nikita Khrushchev reasoned he could get away with a nuclear fait accompli in Cuba without triggering a dangerous American response, exactly the opposite of what American intelligence analysts and policymakers actually thought.[80] As Raymond Garthoff concluded, "If Khrushchev and his colleagues had realized that Kennedy would do what he did do, they would never have made their decision to deploy the missiles."[81]

President Kennedy said he believed the odds of superpower nuclear war were "somewhere between one out of three and even."[82] Historian Arthur Schlesinger Jr. called the Cuban missile crisis "the most dangerous moment in human history."[83] Why? Because each side believed the other thought like they did.

Framing Biases: The Trouble with Numbers and Words

Different people perceive the same numbers or words in very different ways. How a question is asked or how statistics are presented can lead to varying interpretations of likelihood and risk.

When we moved from Los Angeles to Palo Alto, my eight-year-old daughter thought Northern California might finally give her the chance to see snow. Each morning, Kate would scour the weather forecast before breakfast and then inspect the car windshield, looking for frost, before we headed off to school. One day, she ran into the kitchen and declared excitedly, "It's going to snow! It's finally going to snow!" The weather forecast had indeed predicted a 10 percent chance of snow flurries. Ten percent didn't seem particularly likely to me, but for an eight-year-old hoping to make her first snow angel, 10 percent looked promising.

Kate's snow hopes always remind me that information is never just information. For years, former Secretary of State Condoleezza Rice and I taught a course on global risk management to Stanford MBAs. We sent this point home with an in-class experiment called the Beauty Pill exercise. We asked students to imagine that we had invented a pill that could make them look their all-time best, forever—whatever weight, hair style, or age that might be. Our beauty pill was rigorously tested and found to be 99.9 percent safe, with no side effects. How many would take it? Hands shoot up. Typically, all but one or two skeptical students jump at the chance to take the pill. Next we tell them, "What if we said there's a 1 in 1,000 chance that if you take this beauty pill, you will drop dead, right here, right now? How many of you would still take it?" This time, not many hands go up—even though statistically speaking, *99.9 percent safe is exactly the same as a 1-in-1,000 risk of death.* But 99.9 percent safe sounds a lot better than a 1-in-1,000 risk of instant death. With numbers and words, communication is rarely straightforward. Framing biases get in the way.[84]

(The one exception I encountered was when I ran the Beauty Pill exercise with a couple hundred business executives in Texas and found a woman who kept her hand raised proudly in the air the whole time. She understood the statistics. "Oh hell, I might die," she blurted, "but at least I'd die beautiful.")

Intelligence analysts have to deal with framing challenges all the time. Whether they are writing a National Intelligence Estimate or briefing the White House, analysts are asked to estimate the likelihood that something will or won't occur, even though the same words and numbers of estimative probability have different meanings for different people.

Sherman Kent noticed this phenomenon early in his CIA career. In March 1951, Kent and his team produced a National Intelligence Estimate on whether the Soviets would invade Yugoslavia after the Communist government there broke from the Soviet Union. Kent and his

TABLE 5.1 Sherman Kent's "Words of Estimative Probability"

100%		Certainty
93%	Give or take almost 6%	Almost certain
75%	Give or take about 12%	Probable
50%	Give or take about 10%	Chances about even
30%	Give or take about 10%	Probably not
7%	Give or take about 5%	Almost certainly not
0%		Impossibility

Source: Sherman Kent, "Words of estimative probability," *Studies in Intelligence* (1964).

team concluded that there was a "serious possibility" that the Kremlin would launch an attack on Yugoslavia. A few days later, a State Department official who had read Kent's estimate casually asked him what his team meant by a "serious possibility." Kent had thought it was pretty clear and told him he felt the odds were about 65 to 35 in favor of a Soviet attack. His colleague was startled, and said he took it to mean much lower odds. Confused, Kent went back to his team to ask what odds they each thought "serious possibility" indicated. The responses ranged anywhere from 80–20 in favor of an attack to the exact opposite.[85] Kent wondered how it was possible they had all agreed on the same terminology and yet had come to such different conclusions. Horrified, Kent set out to make a chart, giving terms like *certain* and *almost certain* numerical values of estimated probability.[86] Table 5.1 is what he produced.

The chart was never used. Some felt that reducing judgments to numbers seemed awkward and made intelligence estimates seem too much like gambling. Others raised concerns that numbers give a false sense that a judgment is an objective fact rather than a subjective probability estimate. Perhaps the most serious objection is what Tetlock calls the "wrong-side-of-maybe fallacy," the risk of being charged with "failure" when an event doesn't happen even when the intelligence estimate claimed there was only a 70 percent chance that it would. When it comes to likelihood, we tend to conflate *maybe* with *sure thing*.[87]

After the Iraq WMD failure, the Intelligence Community overhauled its analytic tradecraft and the way in which National Intelligence Estimates were put together. In 2007, Intelligence Community Directive 203 established a number of new standards. Reforms required that analysts provide alternative analysis in the body of NIEs when appropriate, clearly express uncertainties and confidence levels in judgments, clearly denote existing assumptions in judgments, and include analysis about the quality and reliability of sources.[88] But the IC still presents judgments with words, not numbers. There's no easy way around framing biases. Words leave room for confusion, but numbers do, too.

Groupthink

All six of the seven deadly biases discussed so far afflict individuals. The seventh, groupthink, distorts *collective* judgment. Group dysfunction takes many forms for many reasons—clashing bureaucratic interests, poor leadership, and personality conflicts, to name a few. All of us have experienced unpleasant and unproductive groups in which leaders are too passive or too domineering, the group is too stressed out or too laid back, or some members argue too much or contribute too little. Although *groupthink* has become a popular catchphrase for bad group decisions of all kinds, it refers to a particular psychological pathology. When groupthink strikes, even smart, motivated, well-intentioned, rational individuals working in highly cohesive groups make poor collective decisions. How can this be? Because cohesion turns out to be a double-edged sword. The problem isn't that there's too much friction in the group. It's that there's too little.

Irving Janis, the psychologist who coined the term *groupthink* in his classic study of the Vietnam War and other U.S. foreign policy fiascoes, found that in high-pressure, high-stakes situations, the need for group affiliation and cohesion can assume overwhelming importance, fostering over-optimism, sloppy thinking, and an inflated sense of the group's morality. Maintaining group cohesion in the face of external pressures drives members to shy away from questioning, dissenting, and exploring alternative viewpoints—even though these are precisely the types of behaviors found to improve analysis.[89] When groupthink arises, the whole becomes *worse* than the sum of the parts. The group runs smoothly into failure.[90]

One of the best-documented cases of groupthink within the Intelligence Community was, once again, the assessment about Saddam Hussein's weapons of mass destruction program in Iraq.[91] The 2002 National Intelligence Estimate put it plainly, stating, "We judge that Iraq has continued its weapons of mass destruction programs in defiance of UN resolutions and restrictions."[92] As discussed earlier, that sentence, and many of its crucial underlying judgments about Saddam's nuclear, chemical, and biological programs, turned out to be dead wrong.[93]

Michael Morell, who led the CIA's analytic branch from 2010 to 2013, wrote in his memoir that groupthink played a large role in the Iraq WMD intelligence failure. "There were no outliers, no group with a different view, no one to force a broader debate that might have led to a more rigorous assessment on the part of the analysts," he wrote. "Groupthink turned out to be a part of the problem."[94] Other postmortems found that nobody ever created red teams or devil's advocates to challenge the prevailing views or surface alternative possibilities.[95] In twelve years, not a single intelligence product examined whether anything might cause Saddam to destroy his weapons of mass destruction. As the Silberman-Robb Commission reported, "failing to conclude that Saddam had ended his banned weapons program is one thing—not even considering it as a possibility is another. . . . An intellectual culture or atmosphere in which certain ideas were simply too 'unrespectable' and out of synch with prevailing policy and analytic perspectives pervaded the Intelligence Community."[96]

To be sure, groupthink wasn't the only problem. The Iraq intelligence estimate suffered from a number of other weaknesses, including insufficient intelligence collection and poor vetting of information from unreliable human sources like Curveball. But groupthink played an important role, sending analysts down a path without sufficient skepticism about their evidence, assumptions, and arguments.

When the calls are tough, the stress is high, and the evidence is murky, conformity feels reassuring. But it's a dangerous delusion. When everyone's agreeing, you shouldn't be comforted. You should be worried.

"What do we got on the spacecraft that's good?"

Between the predictability spectrum and the seven deadly biases, intelligence analysis may seem a hopeless endeavor. It isn't. In the movie *Apollo 13*, when all hope seems lost after the spacecraft suffers a crippling explosion, NASA Tiger Team leader Gene Kranz turns to his engineering group at mission control and asks, "What do we got on the spacecraft that's good?" Realizing that it's not all bad is a useful place to start. Much about the human brain, and collective decisionmaking, works pretty well. The key is figuring out how to capitalize on those strengths and develop interventions that keep people from avoiding the pitfalls.

Academics have been trying to figure out how to "debias" people and avert cognitive malfunctions for years, with mixed results. They've found that simply informing people of their own cognitive biases isn't enough; mental ruts are stubborn things.[97] One of the most famous examples of how our brains play tricks on us is the Müller-Lyer illusion, which was discovered by a German psychologist named Franz Carl Müller-Lyer back in 1889. To see how it works, look at figure 5.2. Which of the two lines is longer?

For most people, the top line appears to be longer than the bottom one—even though they are exactly the same length. Now that you know the truth, it's still hard to believe, right? That's the point—knowing is not enough! Even when our brains know better, the optical illusion persists.

So if knowing isn't enough, what debiasing efforts work better? The short answer appears to be three sets of things: processes that nudge people to check their own biases and re-perceive what they see;

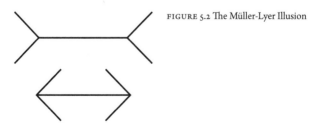

FIGURE 5.2 The Müller-Lyer Illusion

formatting information in ways to increase understanding; and super-forecasting training that includes practice and robust feedback.

Scenarios, Devils, and Other Re-Perceiving Tools

Business leaders, military officers, and intelligence officials use many process tools to check cognitive bias and better anticipate the future. Scenario planning is one of the most popular and best known.[98] A 2014 Bain & Company global survey found that 18 percent of businesses said they used scenario planning already and 60 percent said they expected to use it in the future.[99]

Developed by Ted Newland and Pierre Wack at Royal Dutch Shell in the 1970s, scenario planning is a systematic process that envisions three or four stories of alternative future worlds, each carefully researched to draw on diverse perspectives from a wide range of sources. The goal isn't to pinpoint the future. It's to view the future differently, getting analysts out of their mental ruts, identifying key drivers of change, and better understanding uncertainties. Newland and Wack's first scenario planning exercise in 1971 imagined a world where oil prices spiked, something most considered unthinkable at the time. But their exercise revealed a price hike was more likely than most people imagined because optimistic projections were based on questionable assumptions about both demand and supply. A year after they finished, the Organization of the Petroleum Exporting Countries (OPEC) did raise oil prices dramatically, triggering an energy crisis. Thanks to scenario planning, Shell was the only company that was prepared for it—operationally, strategically, and emotionally.

It's important to emphasize that scenarios are learning tools, not prediction tools. They are designed to help analysts re-perceive the world around them to see causes, connections, and uncertainties in new ways.[100] Scenario planning did not give Newland and Wack a crystal ball. It never even suggested when or why a price hike might occur. But the process did provide insight into macro forces that made a price hike more likely than most people assumed: American energy needs were rising, domestic supply was not, and OPEC consisted mostly of Arab countries in the unstable Middle East who had opposed Western support of Israel in the 1967 Six-Day War.

Thinking like an outsider is another popular tool, especially for intelligence and defense officials. Red teams are groups that play the part of skeptics, competitors, or enemies. Some red teams are tasked with penetrating cyber security systems. Some pretend to be terrorists testing airport security procedures.[101] Others scrub intelligence assessments, challenging every assumption, piece of information, hypothesis, and judgment. After 9/11, CIA Director George Tenet created a CIA Red Cell whose job was to generate out-of-the-box thinking that challenged conventional wisdom. Members were hand-picked and given wide latitude. As former Red Cell co-director Paul Frandano put it, "Tenet charged us to piss off senior analysts. If we weren't doing that, we weren't doing our jobs."[102]

Devil's advocates, like red teams, are designed to challenge conventional views, though usually in a less formalized, less structured way. The term originated in 1587 to improve the saint-making process of the Catholic Church. The advocatus diaboli served as the designated opponent to a sainthood candidate in an extensive process that often stretched over years, even decades.[103] Today, devil's advocates are designated in-house dissenters. Although real devils are better than designated ones (genuine dissent is more powerful than ritualized dissent), devil's advocates can still play a useful role.[104]

For years, the Intelligence Community has used these and other process tools to confront cognitive bias. Together, these methods are called Structured Analytic Techniques (SATs).[105] They include everything from simple checklists, designed to surface and validate implicit assumptions, to "alternative competing hypotheses," a process that arrays each piece of evidence and every reasonable hypothesis in a matrix so that analysts can see whether pieces of information could be consistent (or inconsistent) with multiple hypotheses. "Using the analytic techniques contained in this primer will assist analysts in dealing with the perennial problems of intelligence: the complexity of international developments, incomplete and ambiguous information, and the inherent limitations of the human mind," notes the CIA's 2009 analytic tradecraft primer.[106] However, it's hard to gauge the effectiveness of any of these tools. Combatting one bias (like overconfidence) may leave analysts vulnerable to another (like underconfidence).[107]

Information Format Matters

Psychologists have found that the way in which problems are presented can activate or overcome cognitive biases. As we saw in the Beauty Pill exercise, information format matters. This is especially true when it comes to probabilities that tend to stump even highly educated experts. Consider this classic example:

> *The probability of breast cancer is 1 percent for a woman at age forty who participates in routine screening. If a woman has breast cancer, the probability is 80 percent that she will get a positive mammography. If a woman does not have breast cancer, the probability is 9.6 percent that she will also get a positive mammography. A woman in this age group had a positive mammography in a routine screening. What is the probability that she actually has breast cancer?*[108]

Students, doctors, and even the staff at Harvard Medical School had trouble answering the question correctly. One study found that 95 out of 100 doctors estimated the probability to be between 70 and 80 percent.[109] The correct answer is 7.8 percent. That's not a typo. In this hypothetical, the probability that a woman who has tested positive for breast cancer in a routine mammography actually has breast cancer is less than 8 percent.

In their seminal paper, Gigerenzer and Hoffrage find that the way in which probability problems like the breast cancer diagnosis are usually presented makes it harder to understand base rates and get the right answer. Standard probability looks like this:

$$p(C) = .01 \text{ (1 percent probability of cancer)}$$

$$p(M/C) = .80 \text{ (80 percent probability of cancer AND positive}$$
$$\text{mammogram)}$$

$p(M/-C) = .096$ (9.6 percent probability of positive mammogram BUT no cancer)

p (cancer if you have a positive mammogram) =

$$\frac{.01 \times .80}{(.01 \times .80) + (.99 \times .096)} = .078$$

It's pretty basic math but still not intuitive to most people. Gigerenzer and Hoffrage found that when probabilities were presented as natural sampling schematics like the one in figure 5.3, the math became much easier to see, and estimating errors declined significantly.[110] A quick glance shows why.

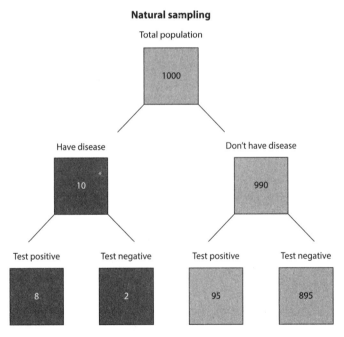

FIGURE 5.3 Visualizing Probabilities in Cancer Testing
Source: Gerd Gigerenzer and Ulrich Hoffrage, "How to improve Bayesian Reasoning without instruction: Frequency formats," *Psychological Review* 2, no. 4 (1995):684–704.

Here, a 1 percent probability rate of cancer is visualized graphically as a total population of 1,000: 10 with cancer, 990 without. Like all testing, mammography isn't perfect, sometimes missing people with cancer (false negatives) and sometimes returning results showing that perfectly healthy people have cancer (false positives). Here, the assumption is that mammography is 80 percent accurate. That means eight of the ten people who actually have cancer will receive mammogram results showing cancer—but two cancerous patients will go undetected. Now consider the 990 people who don't have cancer. If the false positive rate is 9.6 percent, 95 people who don't have the disease will test positive for it, while 895 will test negative.

So if you test positive, what are the odds that you actually have cancer? Take the number of people with cancer who tested positive (8) and divide it by the total number of positive tests (8 + 95). That's how you get 7.8 percent.

The Secrets of Superforecasting

After the Iraq WMD intelligence failure, the U.S. Intelligence Community launched several initiatives to improve intelligence analysis.[111] One of them was commissioning a National Research Council study by academic experts from different fields to examine the most promising ideas in the social sciences and recommend ways for the IC to adopt them.[112] I was one of the experts on the study, and I jumped at the chance to spend two and a half years examining how the IC could improve its thinking about thinking. It's not every day that secret intelligence agencies ask outsiders for help. And it's not every day that a political scientist like me gets the chance to collaborate with and learn so much from psychologists, historians, engineers, lawyers, and intelligence leaders.

One of our recommendations was that the Intelligence Community needed to test its analytic methods in a rigorous way to see whether, how, and why some approaches worked better than others. It's hard to improve intelligence analysis if you don't know what works and what doesn't. We even recommended the creation of a recurring IC Analytic

Olympics to send home the message that fostering a culture of continuous evaluation and learning should be championed.[113]

There are about twenty thousand analysts across the Intelligence Community making thousands of estimates about geopolitical developments every year.[114] And yet the IC had never assessed which of these forecasts were right, which weren't, and why. There were understandable reasons why this didn't happen. As noted above, judging success or failure in the intelligence business is tricky to say the least. It's also politically charged. It doesn't take much to imagine how a well-meaning evaluation effort could be misconstrued and misused—conjuring headlines like "CIA analysis of Country X found to be deficient" or "New study finds Y percent of intelligence analysts don't understand probabilities." Evaluating debiasing tools in university experiments with undergraduate volunteers is one thing. Evaluating real-life analytic methods used by career intelligence professionals confronting high-stakes national security threats is quite another. No undergraduate has ever been charged with failing the country, been hauled before Congress, or suffered a major career setback for answering a few questions one day in exchange for a $10 Amazon gift card.

Still, the lack of testing meant that intelligence analysts lacked robust feedback loops to learn from the past and improve their accuracy in the future. Instead, performance was measured by whether analysts used the right processes—like considering alternative explanations and making their assumptions explicit.

To their credit, several intelligence officials ran with the idea of testing after our report came out. They approached one of our panel members, Phil Tetlock, the expert judgment expert. Tetlock at the time had recently finished a twenty-year study examining how well experts forecasted the future. It was the first large-scale scientific experiment of judgment ever conducted. In it, Tetlock asked a group of nearly three hundred experts to make thousands of predictions about economic and political issues of the day, nearly eighty-two thousand predictions in all. His main finding was depressing: the average expert was about as accurate as a dart-throwing chimpanzee, and their predictions were about the same as random guessing. The chimpanzee discovery made headlines and became something of a sensation. Less noticed was Tetlock's other find-ing: predicting the future wasn't just lucky guessing. Some people did much, much better than average.[115] He called them superforecasters.

In 2011, the IC launched a forecasting tournament to better under-stand what makes some people better forecasters than others. Over the next four years, five teams competed, answering questions every morn-ing ranging from the price of oil at a given time to the prospects of conflict between China and Japan in the East China Sea. There were nearly five hundred questions in all. The winner was the team with the best accuracy at predicting things that did not happen as well as things that did happen.

Tetlock and his colleague Barbara Mellers put together a team of thousands of volunteers called the Good Judgment Project. The Uni-versity of Michigan and MIT each fielded a team. The IC did, too. The fifth team was a control group. "By varying the experimental conditions, we could gauge which factors improved foresight, by how much, over which time frames, and how good forecasts could become if the best practices were layered on top of each other," Tetlock later reflected.[116]

By the end of the second year, the results were staggering: Tetlock's volunteer team was winning by a lot. They outperformed other university-affiliated teams at Michigan and MIT by such large margins (30–70 percent), the other schools were dropped from the competition. Tetlock's team also beat professional intelligence analysts with access to classified data.[117]

The best of the best on Tetlock's team, the superforecasters, weren't geniuses with multiple PhDs. They were artists and scientists, students and retirees, "Wall Streeters and Main Streeters," as Tetlock put it.[118] They included a retired IBM computer programmer who liked to drive his red Mazda Miata around and an Agriculture Department bureaucrat who lived in Nebraska and loved birdwatching.

Tetlock found that the secret to success wasn't sky-high brilliance or a *Jeopardy!*-like mastery of news and facts. It wasn't what superforecast-ers knew. *It was how they thought.* Superforecasters are far more open-minded, curious, careful, and self-critical than the average bear. They believe that reality is complex, that nothing is certain or inevitable, and that ideas should always be subjected to evidence, testing, and updating. They have what Tetlock calls "Dragonfly eyes"—the ability to see a problem with the thirty thousand lenses of a dragonfly's eye. While high-functioning groups harness the wisdom of different perspectives that each member brings, superforecasters can harness the wisdom of different perspectives from within, all by themselves.

Perhaps most encouraging, Tetlock and his colleagues have since found in their experiments that superforecasting skills can be learned through training, practice, measurement, and feedback. One basic sixty-minute tutorial improved accuracy by 10 percent through a tournament year.[119] That may not seem like a lot, but imagine if your financial advisor told you she could guarantee a 10 percent better return on your investments than anyone else. Or imagine if you had a 10 percent better chance of getting a promotion at work than all the other candidates. Or imagine you're an eight-year-old hoping for snow in California. When it comes to forecasting important things, 10 percent can be larger than you think—and cause for optimism.

Artificial Intelligence and the Future of Analysis

Humans are also getting help from machines. Advances in artificial intelligence offer potential game-changing capabilities to process volumes of data at radically new speeds and scales, identify patterns across data sooner and more easily, and empower human analysts in new ways.

As noted in chapter 1, intelligence has gone from a world of information scarcity to information overload. Today, data is everywhere—captured by cameras on city streets, selfies on social media, sensors in space, and billions of communications transiting the Internet each day. According to the World Economic Forum, 44 zettabytes of data have already accumulated in the digital universe.[120] That's a number so big, it has twenty-one zeros. It's forty times more bytes of data than stars in the observable universe.[121] We're a long way from Douglas MacArthur's days of paper reports and typewriters.

Sense-making increasingly requires sifting the wheat from the chaff of this vast digital world, and AI tools are well equipped to assist. Already,

algorithms can recognize patterns in vast amounts of data at superhu-
man speeds. In a 2017 U.S. intelligence pilot program, for example, an
algorithm identified Chinese surface-to-air missile sites over a thirty-
five-thousand-square-mile area eighty times faster than the human
team, with the same level of accuracy.[122]

During 2020–2021, I served on an expert task force that examined future
intelligence challenges and opportunities arising from emerging technologies. The task force's research included dozens of interviews and deep-dive
sessions with technology leaders and intelligence experts across the U.S.
government, private sector, and academia. We found that AI and its associated technologies (such as cloud computing, advanced sensors, and big
data analytics) could transform every core intelligence mission. For analysis, machine learning algorithms could summarize streams of news articles,
highlighting issues that intelligence analysts might not otherwise notice or
have time to read. Algorithms could more rapidly mine foreign social
media data for crisis monitoring and analyze data more continuously to
detect smaller changes in patterns suggesting something might be afoot.
They could offer algorithmic red teams to test human analysis against
machine-derived patterns and insights. And more.[123]

We also found that the greatest promise of AI comes from augment-
ing human analysts, not replacing them. By automating mundane tasks
that absorb tremendous amounts of time, AI has the potential to free
human analysts to concentrate on higher-level thinking that only
humans can do well—like assessing an adversary's intentions, considering broader context, examining competing hypotheses, and identifying
what evidence may be missing.[124]

Harnessing the power of artificial intelligence and other new technologies to improve analysis will not be easy, both because there are
always weaknesses in technologies and because there are always deep-
seated impediments to adopting them, however beneficial they might
be. Even the most advanced AI algorithms have severe limitations, including the inability to explain how they reach results and the tendency
to fail unexpectedly in the face of seemingly small changes—like mis-
taking a picture of a sloth for a race car when imperceptible changes are
made to the image.[125] AI also raises important ethical concerns that

warrant careful consideration about uses, policies, and limits. And adoption requires overcoming large technical, bureaucratic, and cultural hurdles inside the IC, from bespoke computer systems that cannot operate across agencies, to archaic technology-acquisition policies that take too long and make buying new products too hard, to cultural aversion to change.

No organization adapts easily. Companies fail to adjust to market conditions, competitors, and new technologies so often that on average 550,000 businesses fail in the United States each year.[126] That's more than a company every minute. Even leading organizations are not immune. Bethlehem Steel, Blockbuster Video, Enron, and Lehman Brothers were all one-time giants that didn't survive. Government agencies have an even harder time adapting than companies because they lack the three most powerful tools for success: control over their own mission and budgets, leeway to make rapid changes in the workforce, and a market imperative to adapt or die.

Yet these barriers must be overcome for American intelligence agencies to succeed. A new sense-making race has already begun, with adversaries rapidly adopting AI and other new technologies, leaving U.S. intelligence agencies behind the curve.[127] "If you want to know my great fear about China," said Susan Gordon, who served as the second highest official in the Office of the Director of National Intelligence from 2017 to 2019, "it's that because they both steal and collect so much data and they now have essentially equivalent computing capability, they're getting practice with data that we're not." In a world of ubiquitous data, AI will transform how analysis is done and who will gain the edge. As Gordon put it, "How does an intelligence community not be the best in the world of data? How are we not better at using it, finding it, assessing it, protecting it, insuring it, than everyone else?"[128]

Trying Not to Fool Ourselves

Physicist Richard Feynman once said that analysis is how we try not to fool ourselves.[129] He's right. Estimating the future will always be a hazardous occupation, especially in intelligence. No analyst, however skilled, can ever fully know the internal pressures, thinking, aims, and maneuvers of an adversary. The world outside is hard to predict, and the world inside our own minds is prone to error. But failure is not inevitable. Trying not to fool ourselves is a worthy endeavor, and evidence suggests it is likely to get better as we learn more about the processes and practices that make some individuals and groups more accurate than others and as new technologies enhance the quest for insight.

6

COUNTERINTELLIGENCE

TO CATCH A SPY

Never go home at night without wondering where the mole is.
—ROBERT GATES, CIA DIRECTOR, 1991–1993[1]

ROBERT HANSSEN SEEMED an unlikely traitor. The son of a Chicago police officer, he majored in chemistry and went to graduate school in dentistry before getting his MBA from Northwestern University. In 1976, after stints as an accountant and a police officer, Hanssen joined the FBI, where he worked for the next twenty-five years.[2] Colleagues found him socially awkward but smart, with a strong interest in computers. Hanssen was a devoted husband, a father of six children, and a devout Catholic who went to Mass almost every day. He walked the family dog and lived in a modest split-level home in suburban Virginia. "He was a great dad," said his daughter.[3]

Hanssen was also a great liar. He started spying for the Soviet Union back in 1979, not long after joining the FBI,[4] and lived a double life for nearly half his life. Then, one cold night in 2001, that double life came to an end.

On February 18, just five weeks before his retirement, Hanssen walked into Foxstone Park, a quiet leafy area near his house, and hid a small garbage bag under a bridge. The bridge was a dead drop—a prearranged location for him to pass secret documents to his Russian spymasters without risking a face-to-face meeting.[5] Ten FBI agents were secretly watching in the woods. As soon as Hanssen placed his package, the arrest team surrounded him, cuffed him, and read him his Miranda rights. After a fifteen-year mole hunt, they had finally caught their traitor. Hanssen pleaded guilty to spying for Moscow on and off for twenty-two years—throughout his FBI career—and was sentenced to life in prison without the possibility of parole.

The damage was substantial. Hanssen was found to have betrayed at least four Russian agents working for U.S. intelligence, three of whom were executed as a result of his treachery. Using dead drops around New York and Washington, Hanssen had handed over more than six thousand pages of classified documents and twenty-six computer diskettes detailing U.S. nuclear war preparations, U.S. operations and techniques to recruit Soviet intelligence officers and evaluate double-agent operations, dozens of other technical and human intelligence operations, and the existence of a billion dollar eavesdropping tunnel beneath the Soviet Embassy in Washington.[6] Hanssen is still considered the most damaging mole in FBI history.[7] In return for spilling America's secrets, he received gems and up to $1.4 million in cash, some of which he used on lavish trips, jewelry, and a silver Mercedes-Benz for a stripper named Priscilla.[8]

Traitors have always held a special fascination in the public conscience while creating a special challenge for intelligence professionals. When trusted insiders become turncoats, the damage can be devastating. The betrayal is personal, and the job of catching them is painful. As former CIA counterintelligence chief James Olson noted, "Counterintelligence can be an excruciatingly frustrating profession. You lose when you win. You feel good about uncovering spies in our midst, but you are then inevitably hit with the cutting follow-up questions: How could you let that happen? Wasn't it your job to prevent things like that?" As Hanssen was being arrested, the notoriously arrogant FBI agent took the time to deliver a final insult to his counterintelligence colleagues, asking them, "What took you so long?"[9]

This chapter examines counterintelligence from the old days to the cyber age. As we'll see, catching traitors is just one part of the counterintelligence mission. We begin by taking a step back and examining what counterintelligence is and how it's done, from mundane procedures to exotic devices and operations. Then we will tackle a burning question: What motivates people to betray their country or cause? Finally, we examine three key counterintelligence challenges: trust, paranoia, and technology.

What Is Counterintelligence?

As its name suggests, counterintelligence is the art of countering the intelligence activities of others—by protecting your own secrets through security and guile, disrupting others' intelligence operations, penetrating their organizations, and manipulating their perceptions and activities. Intelligence and counterintelligence are two sides of the same coin. Intelligence seeks to collect and analyze information to give one side insight and advantage. Counterintelligence seeks to protect those capabilities and deny them to others. One side's intelligence success is the other side's counterintelligence failure.

Hollywood often gets the real world of espionage wrong, and the use of the word *spy* is a prime example. Spies are not CIA officers who meet their Chinese or Russian sources in dark alleyways. Spies *are* the Chinese or Russian sources. Spies are also often called *assets* or *agents*. They are people who betray their home country's cause for a foreign one. Intelligence officers who manage spies for a living are called *handlers* or *spymasters*. At the CIA, these officers are members of the national clandestine service, and they are officially called *operations officers* or *case officers*.[10]

The primary job of a case officer isn't to steal secrets herself. It's to convince foreign nationals to steal secrets and hand them over. Why? Because foreign nationals live on the inside of an intelligence target. They can get into positions of power or proximity granting them access to streams of sensitive foreign information that would be difficult or impossible to obtain any other way. Spies can be a foreign engineer working on next-generation missile systems, a foreign jihadist operating inside a terrorist cell, a foreign military officer, or a foreign leader's cook, half-brother, or mistress, to name a few. The job of a case officer is to identify, recruit, and run spies—figuring out how to keep them working and keep them safe from detection. It's an intimate, complicated, and high-stakes relationship. Spies who get caught are imprisoned or executed.

From a counterintelligence perspective, one nation's spy is another nation's mole or traitor. Robert Hanssen was a spy for the Soviets and Russians. He was a mole and a traitor to the United States.

It's also important to remember that everyone spies, and counterintelligence must be aimed not just at adversaries but at allies as well. As the CIA's former counterintelligence chief James Olson notes, in counterintelligence "there are friendly countries, but there are no friendly intelligence services. With only a handful of exceptions, everyone spies on everyone else, friends and foes alike."[11] The handful of exceptions are the Five Eyes partners who share a very close intelligence relationship: United States, United Kingdom, Canada, Australia, and New Zealand. Otherwise, it's an intelligence jungle out there.

At least eighty countries are known to have conducted intelligence operations against the United States, including allies like France, South Korea, and Israel.[12] In the 1980s, Israel strained relations with the United States for the next thirty years by running an American spy named Jonathan Pollard.[13] A civilian Navy intelligence analyst, Pollard passed hundreds of classified documents to the Israelis, including American assessments of the military capabilities of Israel and other Middle Eastern states. Then one day an alert coworker saw Pollard carrying what looked like a classified envelope into the parking lot and reported him.[14] Pollard was arrested in 1985 and became the only American ever sentenced to life in prison for spying on behalf of an ally.[15] For years Israeli leaders lobbied for his release and for years American leaders refused. In the 1990s, Israel even tried to make Pollard's freedom part of Middle East peace talks, prompting then CIA Director George Tenet to threaten to resign if President Clinton agreed. In 2015, after serving thirty years of his life sentence, Pollard was released from prison, and in 2020 his parole ended, clearing the way for him to move to Israel.[16]

Today, according to former U.S. intelligence officials, two to three million people are engaged in espionage around the world, most of them aiming at the United States.[17] China, Russia, Cuba, and Iran are the most aggressive foreign intelligence services seeking to steal American secrets.[18] Of them, China stands apart as the most serious counterintelligence threat. American military experts have said that there isn't a single major Chinese weapons system that isn't based on stolen U.S. technology.[19] In 2015, China was behind the most damaging counterintelligence cyberattack yet known: a hack that stole over twenty-one million security clearance records from the Office of Personnel Management, the agency that oversees federal human resources management, including background investigations for security clearances.[20] It was a counterintelligence nightmare for the United States, giving China highly sensitive information about Americans serving in government, including their debts, medical records, foreign friends, relatives, and other information that could be used to coerce them.

Government agencies are not the only targets. Chinese cyber and human espionage activities have penetrated corporations and universities, too—seeking to steal everything from COVID-19 research to missile chips. By the summer of 2020, Chinese spying had become so rampant, the FBI was opening a new China-linked counterintelligence investigation about every ten hours.[21]

China is active but not alone. The 2019 threat assessment issued by the Office of the Director of National Intelligence warned that the United States "faces a complex global foreign threat environment" and that technological advances are enabling more states and non-state actors to steal information "to the detriment of U.S. interests."[22] The 2016 National Counterintelligence Strategy noted that global supply chains and communications have made information and assets essential to American national security more distributed and vulnerable. At the same time, hostile intelligence services have more tools at their disposal for stealing and exploiting sensitive data.[23]

Defensive and Offensive Counterintelligence

Counterintelligence can be divided roughly into two sets of activities: defensive or passive counterintelligence, which consists chiefly of security measures, and offensive counterintelligence, which involves infiltrating a hostile intelligence service to understand how it operates and thwart its activities through disruption and deception. It's important to note that counterintelligence is not just about blocking and tackling to protect our own side. Done well, counterintelligence opens new opportunities to gather information, deceive the opponent, and gain advantage.

DEFENSIVE COUNTERINTELLIGENCE

Defensive counterintelligence measures range from the mundane to the exotic. Safes, locked rooms, checkpoints, armed guards, electric fences, motion detectors, hydraulic anti-truck devices, and attack dogs are common features at intelligence facilities.[24] Classified documents never get tossed into regular garbage cans; they are placed in burn bags to be incinerated at the end of every workday.[25] Visit a classified facility like CIA headquarters or the nuclear command bunker at United States Strategic Command in Nebraska, and you'll find the desks are weirdly clean; nobody leaves their classified work open on a computer screen or on a table when someone without a clearance is around. Visitors can feel a bit like criminals. They are never left alone. And in some classified facilities, red lights flash in the hallways when someone "un-cleared" is inside, just to make sure everyone knows.

Of course, work has to get done in all sorts of places outside these secure facilities. Because foreign policy never sleeps, senior government officials often have to work from home, late at night. Presidents and their foreign policy teams travel overseas. Members of the congressional intelligence committees need to view classified documents near their offices. Defense contractors have to make and discuss classified weapons systems in their factories. Sensitive Compartmented Information Facilities (SCIFs, called "Skiffs") are special rooms designed and built to keep secrets secret in these and other far-flung locations. Built according to strict construction guidelines that include acoustic protections, SCIFs are often located inside otherwise open or ordinary buildings like offices, homes, or hotels. SCIFs can be permanent or temporary. They have been built in boats,[26] trailers,[27] even tents.[28] Cell phones are not allowed inside a SCIF to ensure classified information cannot be duplicated and conversations cannot be recorded. There are often cubbies (watched by a guard) outside SCIFs for depositing phones and other connective devices.

Other defensive counterintelligence measures aren't so visible. In his 2008 book, *The Shadow Factory*, James Bamford recounts some of the counterintelligence measures built into National Security Agency headquarters. It sounds fictional but it's all real:

> Modern and boxy, it has a shiny black-glass exterior that makes it look like a giant Rubik's Cube. But hidden beneath the dark reflective finish is the real building, a skinlike cocoon of thick, orange-colored copper shielding to keep all signals—or any other type of electromagnetic radiation—from ever getting out. Known by the code name Tempest, this protective technique . . . was designed to prevent electronic spies from capturing any escaping emissions. . . . [The windows of the director's office] contained hair-thin copper wires to seal in even the faintest electronic whisper. And to prevent sophisticated laser devices from capturing the telltale vibration of [the director's] voice on the glass, music played between the panes.[29]

Defensive counterintelligence also involves people, not just buildings. Vetting your own employees—through background investigations and security clearances—is essential and difficult. One challenge is scale. In 2017, four million people in the United States held security clearances giving them access to classified information.[30] That's more than the entire population of Los Angeles. While clearance backlogs have been shrinking, in 2019 the number of people awaiting security clearances was about half a million, and the *fastest* top secret clearances still took more than a year to process—468 days, to be exact.[31]

A second challenge is identifying the best methods to assess trustworthiness. Polygraphs, or lie detector tests, are widely used but controversial, drawing support from many intelligence and law enforcement officials but deep skepticism from the scientific community.[32] The tests record physiological responses to yes/no questions—typically by measuring the respondent's respiration, heart rate, blood pressure, and skin sweatiness. But polygraphs do not test deception directly, and contrary to conventional wisdom, there is no unique physiological response known to indicate lying. In fact, the test itself can produce anxiety that leads respondents to fail even when they are being truthful. At the same time, others who do not exhibit expected physiological responses can pass polygraph tests even when they are being deceptive. Aldrich Ames, a CIA officer who secretly worked for the Russians, passed two polygraphs while he was betraying some of America's most important secrets—treachery that led to the deaths of at least ten people.[33] Ana Belen Montes, a Defense Intelligence Agency analyst who spied for Cuba, also passed polygraph tests, as did two dozen Cubans who American officials thought were spying for the United States but were in fact double agents spying for Havana.[34]

In 2003, an expert panel from the National Academy of Sciences conducted a comprehensive study examining the scientific validity and reliability of polygraphs for employment screening. The study concluded that there is "little basis for the expectation that a polygraph test could have extremely high accuracy" and that "polygraph testing [is] intrinsically susceptible to producing erroneous results" in both directions, failing people who are telling the truth (false positives) and passing people who are lying (false negatives).[35]

When it comes to these kinds of tests, you can't have it all. The better the test becomes at reducing one kind of error, the more likely it will fail to catch the other type. Table 6.1 illustrates the dilemma. In a hypothetical employee population of 10,000 people that includes 10 traitors, a polygraph test with 80 percent accuracy at catching deceivers would fail more than 1,600 truthful employees and catch only 8 of the 10 actual traitors. If the test were set to reduce the number of false alarms (loyal employees who fail the test) to just 40 people, then 8 of the 10 moles would pass and remain uncaught.[36]

"Given its level of accuracy, achieving a high probability of identifying individuals who pose major security risks in a population with a very low proportion of such individuals would require setting the test to be so sensitive that hundreds, or even thousands, of innocent individuals would be implicated for every major security violator correctly identified," the expert study noted. "The only way to be certain to limit the frequency of 'false positives' is to administer the test in a manner that would almost certainly severely limit the proportion of serious transgressors identified."[37]

TABLE 6.1 The Problem with Polygraph Tests: False Positives and False Negatives

If polygraph threshold detects 80% of spies, there are many false positives: 1,598 truth tellers are seen as liars

Examinee's True Condition

Test Result	Spy	Nonspy	Total
"Fail" test	8	1,598	1,606
"Pass" test	2	8,392	8,394
Total	10	9,990	10,000

If polygraph threshold detects 95% of truth tellers, there are false negatives: 8 spies go undetected

Examinee's True Condition

Test Result	Spy	Nonspy	Total
"Fail" test	2	39	41
"Pass" test	8	9,951	9,959
Total	10	9,990	10,000

Source: National Research Council 2003, The Polygraph and Lie Detection, 5.

Yet many intelligence agencies still use polygraphs.[38] In fact, the FBI expanded the use of polygraphs after the Hanssen case.[39] Defenders say the test provides a helpful deterrent and one input into a broader system designed to identify past or ongoing behavior (such as debts, alcoholism, marital troubles) that could indicate that an employee might be susceptible to working for a hostile intelligence service, terrorist group, or other organization operating against the United States government. As former CIA Director William Colby put it, "I don't believe in the polygraph . . . but it sure as hell helped us. My security people told me that, faced with the polygraph, people told us things that caused us not to hire them. As far as I'm concerned, it paid for itself right there."[40]

OFFENSIVE COUNTERINTELLIGENCE

Offensive counterintelligence is more aggressive and dynamic. It involves uncovering how foreign intelligence services operate against American officers, detecting American traitors, and penetrating hostile intelligence services and organizations with our own spies—foreign nationals willing to betray their country or cause for ours. Good counterintelligence also looks ahead, imagining and planning for all the devious scenarios adversaries might use in the future to recruit American traitors. And it requires asking whether any source, however valuable the information may seem, can really be trusted. Former CIA Director Michael Hayden referred to his regular counterintelligence briefings—which reviewed cases, leads, and suspicions—as "the most depressing ninety minutes on my calendar."[41]

In counterintelligence, the most vulnerable moments usually come when spies are trying to communicate with their handlers.[42] Tradecraft to hide these communications is designed to reduce the risks of discovery. Techniques include surveillance, dead drops,[43] coded communications, and signal sites, where a case officer places a predetermined mark (often with chalk or tape) in a public location to let a spy know that a package is ready to be picked up or that the spy needs to make contact.[44] These techniques take considerable training and time to develop. Observing an opposition intelligence service without "being made" is "excruciatingly difficult," wrote Olson, the former CIA counterintelligence chief. Olson insisted his teams have at least a year in the city of operation before he would allow them to start surveillance operations there. A single twenty-four-hour FBI surveillance operation of one terrorist suspect or foreign intelligence officer takes more than two dozen people.[45]

The best way to uncover traitors at home is by penetrating hostile intelligence services abroad. As counterintelligence officials have noted, it takes a mole to catch a mole.[46]

That's how the FBI ultimately caught Robert Hanssen. For years before Hanssen's 2001 arrest, the FBI and CIA knew that someone in the U.S. government was handing over vital secrets to the Russians. They worked furiously to find the mole, without success, spending three years chasing the wrong man, a CIA officer named Brian Kelley. It wasn't until the FBI paid a former Russian intelligence officer $7 million for a KGB intelligence file about an American mole that counterintelligence officials got the leads that broke the case. Even that required an elaborate counterintelligence effort: To get the file, the FBI narrowed down the list of KGB intelligence officers who might have known the mole's identity, focused on any who had retired (since active officers would have been even more difficult to recruit), found one who fit the criteria and had started a business in Moscow, and then convinced an American business executive to send a sham invitation inviting the Russian to meet him in the United States to discuss expanding the business. It worked. When the Russian landed in New York, he was met by FBI agent Mike Rochford, who recruited him to give up the goods.[47]

The Russian file did not have Hanssen's name because Hanssen, well versed in counterintelligence tradecraft, had never given his name to his handlers, referring to himself only as "B" or a pseudonym, Ramon Garcia, in his communications. He also refused to meet with Russian intelligence officers in person for two decades, sending messages and materials only by dead drops. And Hanssen used his position in counterintelligence at the FBI to check computer files about whether he was under suspicion. But the $7 million file did contain three gold nuggets. The first was an audio recording of the unidentified mole's voice talking with a KGB officer. The second was the mole's fingerprint, which was lifted from one of the garbage bags used to wrap his dead drop materials. The third was a set of notes showing the mole had twice referred to an off-color quote by Gen. George S. Patton. The voice matched Hanssen's. The fingerprint was run through the FBI database and came back a match for Hanssen. And an FBI analyst remembered Hanssen using the same Patton quote in conversations at work.[48]

What Makes Traitors Tick?

Why did they do it? That's the question family, friends, colleagues, and counterintelligence officials invariably ask when a trusted insider goes bad. Human motives are complex, and spies often try to justify their actions after the fact. Yet most counterintelligence experts find four major types of motives that conveniently fit into the acronym MICE: money, ideology, compromise, and ego.[49]

Greed has long been a powerful driver for all sorts of human behavior. America's first known traitor, Benjamin Church, sold secrets to the

British to support his mistress and his otherwise costly lifestyle.[50] More recently, a Defense Department study found that more than two hundred Americans have been convicted of espionage-related charges from 1947 to 2015. Money was at the top of that list, too, serving as the sole or primary motive for nearly half of them[51]—including Robert Hanssen; Aldrich Ames, who received $4.6 million from the Russians; and Kevin Mallory, a former employee of the CIA, Defense Intelligence Agency, State Department, and U.S. Army with a top secret clearance, who was indicted in 2018 for turning over classified information to the Chinese. "[Y]our object is to gain information," he texted his Chinese handlers, "and my object is to be paid for [it]."[52]

Ideology has also been a common motive. In the 1930s and 1940s, a number of Americans and British betrayed their countries because they sympathized with the Communist cause. These included the infamous Cambridge Spies—Donald Maclean, Guy Burgess, Harold "Kim" Philby, Anthony Blunt, and John Cairncross, all students at Cambridge University who went on to serve in the British government and used their positions to pass secret information to the Soviets for years. Their espionage included betraying some of the most sensitive American secrets and operations, such as plans for the atomic bomb, military strategies for the Korean War, and American counterintelligence operations. Eventually all five Soviet spies were caught, but it took three decades to uncover Philby, after he had served in some of the most senior and sensitive positions in British intelligence. He had even been interrogated by MI5 and MI6 in 1951 after Burgess and Maclean were uncovered, but he was exonerated. It wasn't until 1962 that British agents finally confronted him and offered him immunity from prosecution if he told what he knew. Philby agreed but then fled to Russia on a ship sent by the KGB. He became a Russian citizen and was buried with the honors of a KGB general after his death in 1988.[53]

Belief in a foreign cause also drove Julius Rosenberg (who joined the Young Communist League when he was growing up) to reveal atomic secrets of the Manhattan Project to develop the atomic bomb. More recently, Jerry Chun Shing Lee, a Hong Kong native and naturalized

U.S. citizen who served in the CIA for more than a decade, was moti-vated by ideology to spy for China.[54] The Defense Department study of American traitors found that ideology (which included divided loyal-ties to another country or cause) ranked second, constituting the sole or primary motive for 25 percent of convicted spies.[55]

Others end up spying for foreign powers for a host of reasons, includ-ing coercion by a foreign intelligence service that has compromising information on them; because they feel disgruntled, unappreciated, and unrecognized at work; because they seek the sheer thrill of it; or because they are trying to ingratiate themselves with someone, perhaps a roman-tic interest or an admired friend.

Motives, of course, are often tangled. Benedict Arnold was known to have an extraordinary ego, deep grievances over politically motivated investigations against him, financial pressures, and a young new loyalist wife he wanted to impress. Aldrich Ames, the former CIA officer who spied for Russia, did it to pay off debts accumulated by his luxurious lifestyle. But ego also played a role. As he later explained in interviews, "I did it for the money . . . not because of what it could buy but because of what it said about me. . . . It said Rick Ames was not a failure."[56]

Evidence suggests that motives have been shifting since the Cold War's end, with ideology or divided loyalties playing a larger role than it once did and money declining in importance. As figure 6.1 shows, during the Cold War, money was the sole or primary motive for 54 percent of those convicted of committing espionage-related crimes, but since 1990, it has been the primary motivation for just 37 percent of traitors. By contrast, ideological commitment to another cause was re-sponsible for just 20 percent of espionage-related convictions of Ameri-cans during the Cold War but 35 percent of spy cases since 1990.[57]

A few other demographic factors are worth noting. American traitors are almost always men. Since 1947, only 18 of 209 American spies con-victed of espionage-related crimes have been women. Traitors also tend to be middle-aged and married. And 57 percent of the time, they volun-teered to become spies rather than being recruited by foreign intelli-gence services.[58]

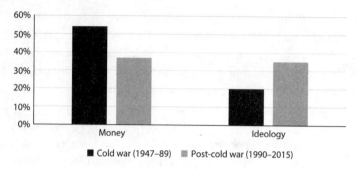

FIGURE 6.1 The Changing Motives of Traitors
Source: Katherine Herbig, "The Expanding Spectrum of Espionage by Americans, 1947–2015," Defense Personnel and Security Research Center (PERSEREC), Office of People Analytics, 2017.

Three Key Counterintelligence Challenges: Trust, Paranoia, and Technology

Counterintelligence faces three major challenges. The first is trusting too much, which makes warning signs hard to see and traitors hard to stop. The second is trusting too little, which can breed debilitating paranoia that ruins careers and casts wrongful doubt on good intelligence. The third challenge comes from advances in technology, which can create new vulnerabilities and enable insider threats to operate at vastly greater speeds and scale.

Trusting Too Much

Every organization trusts its own people, and intelligence agencies in some ways trust their employees more than most. Security procedures, the mission, and secrecy tend to breed a close sense of camaraderie and a false sense of comfort that make it hard to see or report red flags when a colleague is breaking bad.

Guards, guns, and gates serve as a physical dividing line between insiders and outsiders. Nobody just walks into the CIA or NSA headquarters. There's a zone of trust inside, and then there is everywhere else. What's more, every employee, whether it's the director or the janitor, must be investigated, vetted, and cleared before the first day on the job—a process that can take months, even years. Cleared employees also must undergo periodic reinvestigations. These security procedures are necessary, but they can have the unintended effect of providing reassurance that lowers the guard.

In addition, as discussed in chapter 4, working in an intelligence agency is not a job. It's a mission. The sense of shared purpose breeds strong bonds and a natural insularity that secrecy reinforces. Intelligence work is more dangerous and more insulated than the average day job, giving rise to a "clubby" culture that leans toward trusting insiders even in the face of evidence that something big seems amiss.

The perils of trusting too much were brought home to the CIA in 1994, when Aldrich Ames, a veteran case officer, was arrested as he drove his Jaguar to work. Ames soon confessed to having spied for the Soviet Union for nearly a decade, compromising more than 100 American and allied intelligence operations, passing thousands of secret documents—which he carried in shopping bags to dinners with his Russian handlers[59]—and blowing the covers of every important Soviet intelligence officer working for the United States.[60] Ames's treachery led to the execution of at least ten Soviet sources of the CIA and FBI.[61]

The most important of them was Gen. Dmitri Polyakov, code name TOP HAT, who served as a senior officer in Soviet military intelligence while sending secrets about Soviet moles, weapons systems, and more to his American handlers for two decades.[62] TOP HAT supplied hard evidence of the Sino-Soviet split that President Nixon leveraged to make his opening to China in 1972.[63] TOP HAT's intelligence about Soviet anti-tank missiles enabled American forces to defeat them when they were used by Iraq in the 1991 Gulf War. And his intelligence was voluminous, filling twenty-five file drawers at CIA headquarters. It was "like Christmas" whenever his packages arrived, said one CIA officer. Former CIA Director James Woolsey called TOP HAT "the jewel in the crown" of Cold War spies.[64]

After Ames revealed Polyakov's identity as an American spy, the Russian was arrested and, on March 15, 1988, executed. Nobody knows where he is buried. As CIA veterans Sandra Grimes and Jeanne

Vertefeuille wrote, "the loss of this man was inexpressible" to those who supported the operation and to many CIA officers who never met him. Polyakov never asked for money. He spied out of conviction. His years of service and his contributions "had become a legend" inside Langley.[65]

Perhaps most upsetting about the entire ordeal was the fact that Ames's betrayal was not difficult to pull off. This was no superspy who worked tirelessly to hide his activities and outwit his CIA colleagues at every turn. Ames was a flagrantly incompetent case officer who routinely violated security policies and received poor performance reviews while serving in some of the CIA's most important Soviet and counterintelligence offices abroad and at headquarters. Frequently rated toward the bottom of his cohort, Ames was described as lazy, careless, weak, a bad leader, and unsuited for operations overseas. He forgot to lock his office safe and failed to submit reports about his contacts with Soviet officials. He once lost a briefcase filled with classified papers in a New York subway. He was personally and professionally sloppy. One annual performance review noted that his clothes were disheveled and his teeth were rotting.[66]

Ames was also an alcoholic who often came back from lunch too drunk to work.[67] He once passed out in a gutter in Rome until local police found him and took him to a hospital.[68] In Mexico City he got into a traffic accident while so inebriated that he couldn't answer police questions or recognize the American embassy officer sent to help him.[69] Even the KGB warned Ames about his drinking.[70] Yet while his struggle with alcohol dogged him for years across multiple assignments, Ames's CIA superiors never seriously counseled him, disciplined him, reprimanded him, or moved him into less sensitive positions. As a bipartisan Senate Intelligence Committee review concluded, "Obviously, something went terribly wrong." Ames clearly had "serious suitability problems" from the beginning of his CIA career. "Supervisors were aware of his personal and professional deficiencies but did not make his problems part of his official record, nor act effectively to correct them," the study concluded.[71]

Counterintelligence red flags about Ames were obvious but went unreported and unaddressed. After Ames began spying for the Soviets in 1985, his lifestyle changed considerably. In 1986, while stationed in Rome, the normally shabby Ames started wearing expensive Italian suits and Gucci watches and began jetting off to European cities with his new wife, Rosario. Everyone in the office noticed that he seemed to have a lot of money;[72] one officer described his spending as "blatantly excessive."[73] When Ames moved back to Langley, he started driving Jaguars, moved into a fancy $540,000 house, and hired a maid. Ames later admitted, "I didn't conceal my funds in any real way. . . . I sloshed my money around pretty good." His spending clearly exceeded his government salary but nothing was ever put in his file. One CIA officer, after a visit to his house, reported him to the counterintelligence center, but a cursory investigation was opened and quickly closed.[74]

Why did Ames go undetected for so long by so many? And why was a boozy incompetent ever put in positions inside the CIA's Soviet division and counterintelligence branch that gave him access to some of the nation's most important secrets?

Trust was a major factor. On June 13, 1985, when Ames assembled his first cache of secrets for the KGB, he stuffed six pounds of classified documents into his briefcase and just walked out the door. Nobody searched him as he left CIA headquarters. According to *New York Times* reporters Tim Weiner, David Johnston, and Neil A. Lewis, the agency had stopped searching employees a few years earlier.

"Trust was the watchword of the day," they wrote.[75] Words like *fraternity, brotherhood,* and *club* were often used to describe the CIA's tight-knit, largely male national clandestine service where Ames worked. Trust in the brotherhood made it unthinkable that one of their own could be spying for the enemy. Trust in the brotherhood also fostered a deep reluctance to confront or report a colleague, no matter how incompetent or suspicious his conduct. The Senate Intelligence Committee's review concluded, "All too often an officer who has been through training, gone through the polygraph examination, and had an overseas assignment, is accepted as a 'member of the club,' whose fitness for assignments, promotions, and continued service becomes immune from challenge." The review found the CIA suffered from "a system and culture unwilling and unable particularly in the early years of Ames' betrayal to face, assess, and investigate the catastrophic blow Ames had dealt to the core of its operations."[76]

Former CIA counterintelligence chief James Olson felt this cultural pull deeply and personally. Decades after Ames's arrest and sentencing to life in prison, Olson is still haunted that he never said anything to the CIA's office of security about Ames's obvious performance issues and drinking problems when the two worked together. "The fact that I didn't step forward . . . torments me," Olson told me in 2020. "But it's so counter-cultural to rat out a colleague, even a friend."[77]

Trusting Too Little: Paranoia

The second counterintelligence challenge is trusting too little. Skepticism—always questioning whether a source is credible, whether an asset has been turned, whether reality is what it seems, whether someone is trying to deceive you—is a job requirement for good counterintelligence.

But there's a fine line between healthy skepticism and destructive paranoia. Taken too far, skepticism can create a debilitating, distrustful culture where suspicions run wild, careers get destroyed, and the truth gets lost. "It's a very dark side of the intelligence profession," noted Bill Phillips, a CIA case officer whose twenty-five-year career included stints in counterintelligence. "I suspect that is why you do not find a lot of intelligence professionals spending their entire careers in the CI sub-specialty. You can lose sleep, you can lose your sense of balance if you're not careful and if you do it for too long. You begin to see spy ghosts and double and triple agent ghosts in every case."[78]

That's exactly what happened during the Cold War, when for twenty years the CIA was caught in growing paranoia of the agency's infamous first counterintelligence chief, James Jesus Angleton.

Tall and lanky, with a gaunt face, thick glasses, and spidery fingers that clutched the Virginia Slims he chain-smoked in a darkened office,

Angleton was a larger-than-life figure to supporters and detractors alike. From 1954 until he was fired in 1974, Angleton ran agency counterintelligence. His curtains were always drawn, his desk covered with personal super-secret files that never made it into the CIA's official records system.[79] An insomniac, Angleton often worked late into the night, his mind racing to find deceptions, double-crosses, and secrets within secrets waged by America's enemies. Angleton once described his counterintelligence world as a "wilderness of mirrors," a phrase he took from a T. S. Eliot poem. He cultivated an aura of brilliance, secrecy, and mystery—a man with an encyclopedic knowledge of Soviet operations and an unnerving habit of saying nothing at all in meetings. He grew exotic orchids at home, tied elaborate flies for his fishing trips, was fond of poetry, and was one of the CIA's heaviest drinkers.[80]

Angleton was convinced the Soviets had orchestrated a massive campaign to tie allied intelligence services in knots by sending false defectors and planting moles inside allied governments. In his view, almost every Soviet defector was a fake sent to peddle misleading information, lead U.S. intelligence officials on wild goose chases, and obscure the truth. While effective early in his career at building important counterintelligence capabilities, Angleton's suspicions grew more untethered to reality over time.

To be sure, Angleton had some good reasons to be suspicious. He cut his teeth in World War II working for America's wartime intelligence service, the Office of Strategic Services. His posting to London gave Angleton a front-row seat to Britain's Operation Double Cross, a brilliant operation that identified nearly all of Germany's secret agents in England and used them to send phony information about allied landing plans and locations so that the actual D-Day landing at Normandy would be a surprise.[81]

After the war, thanks to a secret American program named VENONA, codebreakers were able to intercept and decrypt Soviet communications. Angleton saw the transmissions that revealed the Soviet Union had placed more than two hundred agents and sources inside the U.S. government, defense industries, and the media, as well as the Manhattan Project to build the atomic bomb in World War II.[82]

In 1963, Angleton was betrayed by one of his closest friends in the intelligence inner circle, none other than British intelligence officer and double agent for the Soviet Union, Kim Philby of the Cambridge Spies. Philby and Angleton had worked together since the war. It was Philby who taught Angleton the intelligence business, served as his mentor, confidant, and drinking companion for two decades. "It was a bitter blow he never forgot," said Angleton's wife, Cicely. Philby's treachery affected him "terribly, deeply."[83] Angleton's CIA colleagues shared his wife's assessment. "It seems almost certain that the revelation of Kim Philby's duplicity in 1963 and the experience in 1951 of uncovering four other Soviet agents in the service of the British had a profound effect on Angleton and his views of the KGB's capability and his propensity to believe it likely that CIA had also been penetrated at high levels," concluded a 2011 CIA study.[84]

Angleton's obsessions grew progressively worse and his actions more destructive. When a mid-level KGB officer named Anatoliy Golitsyn defected to the United States in 1961 and echoed some of Angleton's conspiracy theories, Angleton was hooked. He became convinced Golitsyn had to be believed and that the vast plot was real. Angleton's obsession with Golitsyn and what critics dubbed the Monster Plot led Angleton and his counterintelligence staff to spend years doubting some of the most valuable intelligence of the Cold War and ruining the lives of several CIA officials in a fruitless quest for a fictitious mole nicknamed Sasha.

One of Angleton's casualties was a Soviet spy named Yuri Nosenko, who defected to the United States in 1964. From the start, Angleton believed that Nosenko was a fake defector, a Soviet plant sent to trick the United States. As a result, the CIA reneged on its deal with him and imprisoned him for nearly four years, holding him in solitary confinement in the attic of a CIA safe house in the United States. There, Nosenko was subjected to hostile interrogations by CIA officers seeking to get him to confess to being a Soviet ruse. He wasn't. In fact, Nosenko provided important information about Soviet agents in American and European embassies, Russian bugs planted in the American embassy in

Moscow, and the Soviet file on Kennedy assassin Lee Harvey Oswald, who had lived in the Soviet Union in the 1950s and 1960s.[85]

After three and a half years of interrogation sessions and polygraph tests, the CIA finally determined that Nosenko was telling the truth and released him with a new name and $80,000.[86] Nosenko spent the rest of his life somewhere in the southern United States until his death in 2008. KGB records later conclusively showed that Nosenko was a genuine defector, who was considered so damaging to Soviet operations, the KGB planned on executing him.[87]

By the time James Schlesinger became CIA director in 1973, Angleton was trapped in his own wilderness of mirrors, trusting almost no one and suspecting almost everyone. He was cagey, uncontrollable, isolated, and drunk. Schlesinger was so concerned that he sent a special assistant named Sam Hoskinson to talk with him. Hoskinson found Angleton in his office, chain-smoking in the dark, a single desk lamp on. Angleton spent the next forty-five minutes spinning a bizarre Soviet conspiracy theory that ended by accusing the new CIA director of being a Russian spy. Stunned, Hoskinson said he would have to tell the director what Angleton had just alleged. Angleton glared back at him and replied, "Well then, you must be one of them, too."[88]

Angleton's paranoia took a heavy toll on the agency. In his elusive quest for Sasha, the counterintelligence chief launched a massive mole hunt under the code name HONETOL that investigated more than fifty employees. At least sixteen were treated as serious suspects. The careers of three CIA officers—Richard Kovich, S. Peter Karlow, and Paul Garbler—were so damaged, Congress eventually passed a law known as the Mole Relief Act to clear their names and compensate them financially.[89]

Angleton never found a Soviet mole in America. Meanwhile his suspicions chilled efforts to recruit spies inside the Soviet bloc. Many CIA officials, including former CIA Director William Colby, say Angleton's excessive distrust all but paralyzed the CIA's Soviet operations during the Cold War.[90] Former CIA Director Robert Gates, who joined the agency as a Soviet specialist, wrote that "Angleton by the end of his career had become a caricature of a counterintelligence officer." His "personality and behavior became an obstacle to serious consideration of the very real problem of determining whether CIA or the U.S. government had been penetrated by a foreign intelligence service or whether a recruited spy was real and his information valid."[91]

It is generally acknowledged that after Angleton's firing, the counterintelligence pendulum swung too far in the other direction, breeding a laxness and reluctance to raise counterintelligence alarms, one of the reasons Hanssen and Ames were able to go undetected for so long.[92]

Technology Challenges

The third major counterintelligence challenge is technological. New technologies are usually a double-edged sword for all aspects of the intelligence business. Counterintelligence is no exception. Massive increases in storage and computing power enable analysts to comb through data at speeds and scales unimaginable even a decade ago. But these advances also enable turncoats to do more damage because they have more information at their fingertips. New developments in encryption and Internet communications make it easier to recruit and run spies from afar, but these technologies also inject new ways for foreign counterintelligence services to discover American assets.

BREACHES ARE GETTING BIGGER, FASTER, BETTER

In the old days, stealing secrets took effort. Before the Internet, traitors had to sneak into files, snap pictures with hidden mini-cameras, and smuggle documents out of secure buildings in their pant legs or a tissue box. The digital era has supersized the damage that one person can inflict. Today, insiders can steal classified information in terabytes, not trash bags, and do the job in days, not decades. As former CIA counterintelligence chief Olson put it, "The risk to us now as counterintelligence professionals has been greatly increased" by technology. "I was worried about disloyal people only walking out the door with documents. Now they walk out the door with disks."[93]

It took Robert Hanssen more than twenty years to ferret out six thousand documents and hand them to the Russians, one small garbage bag at a time. By contrast, in 2010, Army Private First Class Chelsea Manning downloaded the contents of 250,000 classified State Department cables on a fake Lady Gaga CD while lip syncing to the song "Telephone." Former National Security Agency contractor Edward Snowden stole an estimated 1.5 million documents containing some of the most highly classified programs in the U.S. government in just ten months before hightailing it to Hong Kong and then Moscow in 2013.[94] The trove was so huge, if the documents were printed and physically stacked, the pile would be three miles high.[95]

Snowden claims he was a whistleblower who acted out of conscience, not a traitor who acted in cahoots with a foreign power. But Snowden did not just copy what he happened to see on his desktop. A bipartisan review by the House Intelligence Committee found that Snowden sought access to classified programs by tricking coworkers into giving him their security credentials and by searching their network drives without their permission, downloading away. The "vast majority of the documents he stole," the report concludes, "have nothing to do with programs impacting individual privacy interests—they instead pertain to military, defense, and intelligence programs of great interest to America's adversaries."[96] Snowden managed to download a mother lode with some clicks and clever social engineering, all from the comfort of his own desktop.[97]

The breaches keep coming. In the past few years, former CIA officer Kevin Mallory was sentenced to twenty years in prison for spying for China,[98] and an NSA contractor named Hal Martin pleaded guilty to hoarding 50 terabytes of classified materials—that's five hundred million pages of information—in his house, garden shed, and car.[99] A mysterious group calling itself the Shadow Brokers somehow stole (either through a cyberattack or a human penetration) many of the National Security Agency's most valuable hacking tools and dumped them on the Internet, where they have been used in global cyberattacks by North Korea and others.[100] These stolen tools could be used for years to come, by an array of nefarious actors; once bad code is "in the wild," it never really goes away. One of these weapons is called Eternal Blue, which is perhaps exactly how NSA employees are feeling in the wake of this breach.[101]

Technological breakthroughs are also introducing new computer vulnerabilities that put American assets and their handlers at risk and make mole-hunting even more complicated. America's recent counterintelligence crisis in China makes this challenge all too clear.

HOW DID AMERICA'S SPY NETWORK
IN CHINA GET BLOWN?

It was late 2011 and the informant was worried. Everyone he knew in China who was secretly helping the U.S. government was getting caught by Chinese authorities and turned into double agents. Or killed. "He was nervous," recalled a former U.S. official.[102] That meeting kicked off a special joint CIA-FBI counterintelligence investigation that would last years and leave lingering questions unanswered even after the arrest of a suspected Chinese mole named Jerry Chun Shing Lee. What is known is that over a two-year period, nearly all of America's spies in China were blown. The lucky ones were imprisoned. At least twenty were eventually executed. One was shot in the courtyard of a government building in China, right in front of his colleagues, just to make sure coworkers got the message. According to one account, the CIA launched secret rescue operations to ferry spies out of China. Some made it. Others didn't. The last CIA case officer to meet with sources in China reportedly handed them large sums of cash; it was all that could be done.[103] America's spy network had taken years to build—and it had suddenly turned to ash. "They wiped us out in China. All the networks we had were gone," said one former American official.[104] The CIA had to temporarily suspend human intelligence collection in China and permanently overhaul its electronic communications system with assets worldwide. China may have shared information with Russia that blew and possibly even killed American sources there, too.[105]

What caused this monumental collapse? Some believed one or more moles inside the United States government were responsible. Two

American intelligence officials came under suspicion. One, a senior CIA case officer who had served in China when the network was recruited, was cleared in 2013. The other was Jerry Chun Shing Lee, a naturalized American citizen who was born in Hong Kong, grew up in Hawaii, served four years in the U.S. Army, and spent thirteen years as a CIA case officer, from 1994 to 2007. His job was recruiting foreign spies to spill secrets to the United States. But instead of creating moles, evidence suggests that Lee became one.

After leaving the CIA, Lee moved to Hong Kong, where he worked for a tobacco company and tried to start his own cigarette import business but failed. In 2010, two Chinese nationals approached Lee at a dinner in Shenzhen and said they were aware of his background, were in the same profession, and would give him a gift of $100,000 and take care of him for life in exchange for his help.[106] The next month, Lee began receiving written taskings from Chinese intelligence officers asking about sensitive CIA information.

Meanwhile, Lee started depositing hundreds of thousands of dollars in his bank account. In 2012, the FBI lured him back to the United States with a fake CIA job offer and conducted a court-authorized search of his belongings while he was staying in hotels in Hawaii and Virginia. FBI agents found two little books filled with secrets that included the true names of Chinese assets, operational notes from clandestine meetings, and covert facility locations.[107] In 2019, Lee pleaded guilty to one charge of conspiring to commit espionage and was sentenced to nineteen years in prison.[108]

Yet mounting evidence suggests humans were not the only weakness: the CIA's main Internet-based clandestine communications system had also been penetrated. A 2018 *Foreign Policy* investigation citing "five current and former intelligence officials" first reported that the CIA had found serious technical flaws that linked a temporary communications system—meant to contact un-vetted new sources—with the main one. The two systems were supposed to be completely separate. But they weren't. As one former official colorfully put it, the CIA "fucked up the firewall."[109]

Penetration testing conducted by the NSA and FBI found that cyber experts with access to the interim system could find their way into the main one used to communicate with vetted sources. Because the two systems were first used in war zones in the Middle East, they were not designed to withstand the sophisticated cyber capabilities and heavily surveilled online environments of countries like China.[110] Some former intelligence officials believe that only a technical breach could explain the speed and scope of the blown network in China. (Iran, it should be noted, also breached the same shoddy communications system.[111])

In short, the China case suggests that counterintelligence challenges in the digital age are likely to grow more difficult, not less. The age-old human vulnerabilities of trust and paranoia are not going away. Meanwhile, human frailties are being joined by technical ones. Hidden vulnerabilities in information systems are likely to require new skills and faster action. While technical tools like signals intelligence have long played a role in counterintelligence, the twenty-first-century counterintelligence battleground is growing ever more vast—encompassing everything from garbage bags under bridges to computer code in the far corners of cyberspace.

7

COVERT ACTION

"A HARD BUSINESS
OF AGONIZING CHOICES"

Are some covert actions effective? Yes. But most are not.

—MICHAEL MORELL, CIA ACTING DIRECTOR (2011, 2012, 2013) AND DEPUTY DIRECTOR (2010–2013)[1]

THE SUN WAS RISING OVER the Yemeni desert on September 30, 2011, when Anwar al-Awlaki sat down outside his Bedouin-style tent for breakfast.[2] Tall, skinny, and wearing wire-rimmed glasses, Awlaki looked more like a professor than a killer.

Someone must have heard the buzzing. Awlaki and his men started racing for their trucks. They knew what that sound meant; they knew what was coming.

From another desert 8,500 miles away, at Creech Air Force Base just outside of Las Vegas, drone operators sitting inside a darkened trailer launched Hellfire missiles. They watched in eerie quiet, lights dim and monitors glowing, as the trucks were incinerated.[3] Awlaki was killed, as were the three men with him, later identified as another American Jihadi propagandist named Samir Khan and two tribesmen.[4] The nondescript trailers at Creech gave nothing away. To a passerby, they weren't noteworthy in the least. But the sign at the base entrance made it clear what kind of business took place here: Home of the Hunters.[5]

Anwar al-Awlaki was full of contradictions. He was an American who liked playing soccer and going fishing. Born in New Mexico to a moderate Yemeni family, Awlaki studied engineering at Colorado State

University and spent half his life in the United States. Eventually he became an imam at a prestigious mosque outside of Washington, D.C., where he was considered a leading voice of modern Islam. With three kids and a Dodge minivan, he seemed the picture of an Americanized cleric. He was invited to preach at the U.S. Capitol and the Pentagon. Shortly after 9/11, the *New York Times* featured Awlaki as part of "a new generation of Muslim leader capable of merging East and West."[6]

But Anwar al-Awlaki also had a dark side that grew darker with time. He was a spiritual advisor to several of the 9/11 hijackers,[7] a preacher who liked prostitutes, and an inspirational leader who increasingly targeted his own countrymen for death.[8]

A few years after 9/11, Awlaki moved to Yemen, where he assumed a leading role in al Qaeda's offshoot there[9] and became the most influential Jihadi propagandist in the world.[10] His radical sermons preaching hate and violence could be found all over the Internet—on YouTube videos, Facebook posts, and even a glossy, English-language online Jihadist magazine called *Inspire*, which included an article titled "Make a Bomb in the Kitchen of Your Mom."[11] By 2009, Awlaki had moved from inspiration to operation, recruiting suicide terrorists and planning attacks. These included the "underwear bomber" plot to blow up Northwest Flight 253 over Detroit on Christmas Day, which was foiled when an alert passenger noticed the bomber trying to detonate his underwear.[12]

The 2011 targeted killing of Anwar al-Awlaki marked the first time since the Civil War that the U.S. government trained its firepower to hunt and kill one of its own citizens without any charges or trial.[13] Awlaki was also the first American citizen ever marked for death by a drone strike.[14] The operation had been conducted as a CIA covert action, which meant it didn't need congressional or judicial approval.[15] In the strange post-9/11 legal landscape, wiretapping an American terrorist required a court order, but killing one didn't.[16]

Although the drone pilots were hunkered down in a trailer near Las Vegas, the drones themselves were launched from a secret CIA base in Saudi Arabia.[17] Sometime in 2010, Awlaki had been put on a secret CIA kill list and his death was approved by President Obama. But the kill list didn't stay secret for long.[18] After word leaked to the press, Awlaki's father, a prominent Yemeni who had served as minister of agriculture,[19] sued in U.S. court to get his son taken off the list. It was an extraordinary moment: a foreign national suing in American court to save the life of his American son who was plotting to kill other American citizens. In December 2010, Awlaki's father lost his court case.[20] Nine months later, the CIA tracked down his son and carried out the drone strike that killed him.[21]

No intelligence topic is more charged than covert action. Drone strikes are only the most recent controversy, drawing both widespread public support and fierce opposition.[22] As former CIA Director Leon Panetta wrote, covert action "is a hard business of agonizing choices."[23]

This chapter begins by examining what covert action is and how it works. Next we explore why all modern presidents have used it. Then we turn to a central question—How do you judge whether covert action is worth it?—and the debates it raises about efficacy and morality. Finally, we look at new challenges for intelligence posed by drone technologies and the global war on terror.

Shedding Light on Dark Corners

Covert action conjures up images of "dark corner of the room" activities that make people uneasy. For years, the Central Intelligence Agency has worked covertly to overthrow regimes in far-flung places.[24] And until 1976, the CIA's covert action portfolio included targeting foreign leaders for assassination. Fidel Castro was the subject of at least eight plots, including bizarre schemes involving Mafia hit men and exploding seashells.[25]

Some CIA officers use imagery that adds to the mystique or discomfort of covert action, depending on your view. Cofer Black, who directed the CIA's Counterterrorism Center, once told a colleague that he wanted Osama bin Laden's head shipped back in a box of dry ice.[26] Black also assured President George W. Bush after 9/11, "When we're through with them, they will have flies walking across their eyeballs."[27] Among Bush's closest advisors, Black came to be known as the "flies on the eyeballs guy."[28]

Yet this picture misses a lot. Yes, covert action includes lethal and controversial programs, but it also includes a wide spectrum of activities, from old-fashioned propaganda to high-tech cyber sabotage.[29] Perhaps even more striking, every modern president has resorted to covert action, even those who made human rights and democratic values pillars of their foreign policies. When different leaders with different political philosophies facing different enemies in different eras turn to the same toolkit, it's time to put preconceived notions aside and dig deeper. As we'll see, covert action is complicated and frequently misunderstood.

Defining Covert Action: Three Words, Four Types

The National Security Act of 1947 established the CIA but never originally mentioned covert action. Instead, for years covert action was conducted on the basis of a vague catch-all clause in that law authorizing the CIA "to perform such other functions and duties related to intelligence affecting the national security as the National Security Council may from time to time direct."[30] It wasn't until the 1991 Intelligence Authorization Act that covert action was defined: "an activity or activities of the United States Government to influence political, economic, or military conditions abroad, where it is intended that the role of the United States Government will not be apparent or acknowledged publicly."[31]

There are three key words in this definition. The first is *influence*. Covert action encompasses activities that are intended to affect outcomes in foreign countries—like swaying public opinion,[32] assisting rebels,[33] and sabotaging illicit nuclear weapons programs.[34] Covert action and espionage are both done in secret, but they are not the same. Covert action is active; its aim is to produce or affect outcomes. Espionage is more passive; its purpose is acquiring information.

The second important word is *acknowledged*. What makes something a covert action isn't the activity being carried out. *It's the secret U.S. sponsorship of the activity.* Covert action is designed so that the role of the U.S. government is not apparent or acknowledged. There needs to be "plausible deniability": if something happens or some aspect of a covert operation becomes known, U.S. officials can make a believable case that they had nothing to do with it.

Preserving deniability helps to minimize negative effects for the United States. It also enables nations to assist who otherwise might not—because helping the United States would be unpopular domestically or provoke retaliation by other foreign powers.

Of course, many covert operations become open secrets, making plausible deniability not so plausible. And the United States often conducts the exact same activities overtly that it does covertly—including killing terrorists with drones. The point is that hiding official U.S. involvement is one of the most important features setting covert action apart from other intelligence and military activities. (The other important feature is who actually conducts these activities—the CIA or the Defense Department. More on that later).[35]

The third crucial word is *abroad*. By law, the CIA is not allowed to conduct covert action inside the United States.[36] That's not the case in many other nations, where intelligence services work to influence political activities not just outside their borders but also within them.

Covert activities can be classified into four broad types. The first is *propaganda,* or *information operations,* which seeks to influence the beliefs and actions of a target group by disseminating information that can be true, incomplete, or deliberately false.[37] In the Cold War, the CIA dropped propaganda from balloons and secretly funded radio broadcasts to stir dissidents behind the Iron Curtain.[38] According to Leon Panetta, who ran the agency from 2009 to 2011, more recent CIA covert operations have sometimes tried to influence foreign media messages to "change attitudes within the country" before important elections.[39]

The second type of covert action is *political action,* which seeks to shift the balance of political forces in another country by helping friends and undermining foes, often by providing secret funding or training to political leaders, parties, or opposition groups.[40] One of the CIA's first covert operations sought to combat Communism at the polls. When the agency was created in 1947, Communists had assumed power in Poland, Hungary, and Romania and were making fast electoral inroads in Italy and France.[41] Truman and his advisors were convinced that something had to be done.

The CIA got to work, laundering over $10 million in captured Axis funds and funneling it to Italy's Christian Democratic Party to win the national election.[42] The agency covertly funded Italian politicians for the next twenty years, spending more than $65 million, or $582 million in today's terms.[43]

Italy was seen as an instant success and became a model for expanding covert election influence operations in countries around the world.[44] Operations included supporting anti-Allende groups in Chile in the 1960s and 1970s and Milosevic's opposition in Serbia in 2000.[45]

Political action also includes riskier and more controversial activities, like overthrowing governments directly or through surrogates, as the CIA did in Iran and Guatemala in the 1950s and in Chile in the 1970s[46] and as it attempted in Iraq in the 1990s.[47]

The third kind of covert activity is *economic covert action*, which seeks to disrupt and destabilize the economies of unfriendly regimes.[48] These activities have included counterfeiting currency, destroying crops, and, in the case of Nicaragua in the 1980s, secretly mining harbors to impede commercial shipping.[49]

Fourth and finally, *paramilitary operations* are the riskiest and most controversial kinds of covert action because they tend to be larger-scale and violent. This is the "flies on eyeballs" part of the portfolio—activities like arming, training, and advising insurgencies in secret wars and targeted killing with drones.[50]

According to public records, during the Cold War, the CIA backed guerillas, sponsored insurgents, and engaged in secret wars in more than twenty nations.[51] The best known of these are the failed Bay of Pigs operation in Cuba in 1961,[52] the secret arming of Afghan rebels after the Soviet Union invaded in 1979,[53] and the Contra war against the Sandinista regime in Nicaragua in the 1980s.[54]

The CIA also engaged in covert assassination plots of foreign leaders until they were discovered by Congress and banned by a presidential executive order in 1976.[55] In addition to Fidel Castro, the Senate Select Committee to Study Governmental Operations with Respect to Intelligence

Activities, better known as the Church Committee, unearthed evidence that the CIA's assassination portfolio included plans to kill Congolese leader Patrice Lumumba with a special poison that simulated a local disease.[56] The agency's chief scientist, Sidney Gottlieb, flew with the poison in his carry-on luggage and delivered it to Larry Devlin, the senior CIA officer in Leopoldville. Devlin was supposed to inject it into Lumumba's food or drink or toothpaste, but he couldn't go through with it. He ended up burying the poison vials in the banks of the Congo River.[57]

After 9/11, paramilitary operations turned toward renditions (secretly seizing suspected terrorists abroad who are wanted by the United States and transporting them to third party countries for detention and interrogation outside the judicial process)[58] and drone strikes.[59]

As we'll discuss later, it is getting harder to know just where the CIA's role ends and the military's role begins. Both conduct drone strikes against suspected terrorists—sometimes in the same country, sometimes against the same target, sometimes on the same team.[60] This much, however, is clear: drone strikes have been a major tool of the past three presidential administrations. According to one expert study, President George W. Bush authorized approximately fifty drone strikes in Yemen, Pakistan, and Somalia during his presidency, which killed nearly three hundred terrorists and nearly two hundred civilians.[61] The Obama administration carried out more than five hundred drone strikes in those countries, killing more than three thousand terrorists and nearly four hundred civilians over eight years.[62] And in the first two years of the Trump administration, approximately two hundred strikes were carried out against targets there, killing an estimated one thousand people.[63] None of these figures count drone strikes on the "hot battlefields" of Iraq, Afghanistan, or Syria.

Covert Action and Its Overt Counterparts

One of the biggest misperceptions of covert action is that it involves a unique set of bad activities that are so troubling, they must be hidden from view. In reality, nearly all covert activities have overt counterparts;[64] we just don't think about them.

During the Cold War, propaganda behind the Iron Curtain was produced both by Radio Free Europe and Radio Liberty,[65] which were covertly backed by the CIA and by the Voice of America, which was openly sponsored by the U.S. government to "tell America's story."[66]

The CIA has covertly funneled support to pro-democracy political candidates and groups abroad. Meanwhile, the congressionally financed National Endowment for Democracy has been doing the same thing openly since the 1980s.

Covert economic action seeks to undermine foreign economies; economic sanctions are imposed openly and deliberately for the same goal: hitting them where it hurts.

Covert regime change operations are called coups. Overt ones are called wars. When American troops fight in places like Korea, Vietnam, Iraq, Afghanistan, and Libya, the reason usually isn't to keep existing leaders in power.

In 1998 Congress even passed a law called the Iraq Liberation Act, which telegraphed bipartisan intent to oust Iraqi leader Saddam Hussein. "It should be the policy of the United States to support efforts to remove the regime headed by Saddam Hussein from power in Iraq and to promote the emergence of a democratic government to replace that regime," the law declared. To help get the job done, Congress authorized $97 million to support Iraqi opposition groups.[67] Regime change does not get much more overt than that.

Even paramilitary operations come in both covert and overt varieties. The CIA launched covert operations to assassinate Castro and Lumumba. In 1986 President Ronald Reagan ordered air strikes that narrowly missed killing Libyan strongman Moammar Gaddafi.[68] Reagan went on national television just to make sure everyone knew the strikes were retaliation for a Libyan-sponsored terrorist attack in West Berlin that had targeted American service members.[69]

In recent years, the United States has tried to roll back suspected nuclear weapons programs by using covert cyber operations against Iran[70] and by openly declaring war against Iraq.

While many drone strikes off the hot battlefield—in places like Yemen, Pakistan, and Somalia—have been carried out by the CIA as covert action,[71] in 2020, a drone strike killing Qassim Suelimani, Iran's top military and intelligence official, was carried out openly by the U.S. military.[72] The Trump administration took full and immediate responsibility.[73]

Why Go Covert?

If covert action looks so much like overt action, then why do presidents ever use it? And why has every modern president found it so indispensable?

It's not because American presidents are so much alike. Thirteen presidents have served from the end of World War II to 2020. Seven were Republicans, six were Democrats. They hailed from every region of the country and had a wide range of prior careers—in acting, farming, law, real estate, academia, the military, even men's clothing. One (Eisenhower) was a four-star general and war hero, while several (Clinton, Obama, Trump) never served in the military. George H. W. Bush was steeped in intelligence, having previously served as CIA director and vice president. Donald J. Trump had no exposure to intelligence and had never served in any governmental office before becoming president. Eight presidents held office during the Cold War. Five served after the Soviet Union collapsed, when terrorists, rogue states, failed states, cyber dangers, global climate change, and rising competitors like China filled the threat landscape. Yet despite these differences, every president from Truman to Trump has authorized covert action, even the "dark corner of the room" variety.

If you had to bet which presidents would embrace covert action, you'd probably put your money on hawkish Republicans. And you would be wrong. Well, not entirely wrong. Ronald Reagan increased the use of covert action in the 1980s.[74] But Jimmy Carter and Barack Obama, both Democrats who made averting wars and promoting human rights mainstays of their foreign policy agendas, turned to covert action as much as or more than their Republican predecessors.

In 1976, Carter ran for president against the national disgraces of "Watergate, Vietnam, and the CIA" and vowed never to "do anything as

President that would be a contravention of the moral and ethical standards that I would exemplify in my own life as an individual."[75] He initially slashed covert action budgets.[76] But the Iranian hostage crisis and Soviet invasion of Afghanistan changed his mind.

On November 4, 1979, Iranian revolutionaries sacked the U.S. embassy in Tehran and held fifty-two American diplomats and other government employees hostage for 444 agonizing days. The hostage crisis consumed the nation. Across America, yellow ribbons were everywhere—an homage to the 1973 hit song about a prisoner coming home, "Tie a Yellow Ribbon Round the Ole Oak Tree."[77] CBS News anchor Walter Cronkite signed off each nightly broadcast by counting the number of days the hostages had been in captivity. Carter vowed not to travel abroad or campaign for re-election until they were freed. To many, it seemed that Carter had become a hostage, too.

Negotiations went nowhere and the administration looked feckless. CIA Director Stansfield Turner wrote that "it was little consolation to the American public that we had frozen Iran's assets."[78] The president had to do more. He turned to secret operations, authorizing the CIA's daring rescue of six Americans hiding in the Canadian embassy and a second military rescue to free the other hostages inside the U.S. embassy. But the big rescue operation, code-named EAGLE CLAW, ended in fiery disaster when a helicopter collided with a C-130, killing eight service members before they ever reached Tehran.[79]

The hostage crisis coincided with a superpower crisis: the Soviet invasion of Afghanistan, which Carter described as "the most serious threat to the peace since the Second World War."[80] Two days after Soviet troops rolled into Kabul and killed Afghan leader Hafizullah Amin, Carter authorized his first covert action to arm Afghan Mujahidin rebels.[81]

"Our ultimate goal," wrote National Security Advisor Zbigniew Brzezinski in a January 2, 1980, memo, "is the withdrawal of Soviet troops from Afghanistan. Even if this is not attainable, we should make Soviet involvement as costly as possible."[82] It would become the largest covert operation of the Cold War,[83] costing billions[84] and leading to a Soviet withdrawal.[85]

By the time Carter left office, he had approved nearly as many covert operations as Nixon and Ford had.[86] Carter's CIA director, Stansfield Turner, later wrote that "the Carter Administration, despite its dedication to human rights and its considerable reservations about the morality of covert actions, turned easily and quickly to covert devices to respond to some of these despotic acts."[87]

Barack Obama was another president who spoke passionately about promoting human rights. Obama, a former constitutional law professor, ranked among the more liberal Democratic members of the Senate when he ran for president.[88] He also vowed to make American democratic values a cornerstone of American foreign policy. "We can hold true to our values, and in so doing advance those values abroad," he declared in a major foreign policy campaign speech.[89] Obama was determined to end America's wars in Iraq and Afghanistan, wind down the CIA's controversial detention and interrogation program, and combat terrorism.

Meeting all three goals left few options. Obama turned to drone strikes because, as he put it, "doing nothing is not an option" and "by narrowly targeting our action against those who want to kill us . . . we are choosing the course of action least likely to result in the loss of innocent life."[90] Three days after taking office, he authorized his first CIA drone strikes in northwest Pakistan. Obama ended up dramatically expanding the targeted killing program, authorizing ten times more drone strikes against suspected terrorists than his Republican predecessor, George W. Bush.[91]

The Enduring Allure of Covert Action

Three reasons explain the enduring allure of covert action.[92] First, covert action offers presidents a third option in between doing nothing and sending in the Marines. It's a toolkit to get things done when combat looks too risky and other policy levers look too weak.

Presidents may be unique in many respects, but they are alike in one important way: they have a preference for action. They know that legacies are made by big changes and new directions, not maintaining the status quo. "President Jones carefully kept everything exactly the same" is never the description a president wants in history books. Imagine, for example, how history would have remembered Carter if the Iran hostage rescue mission had succeeded.

Nor are presidents comfortable sitting idly by while adversaries invade neighbors, harm Americans, and destabilize the world. It's one thing to consider covert action on the campaign trail, quite another in the Oval Office. Shouldering the responsibilities of office has a way of changing perspective. Senator Frank Church (D-ID), who led the congressional committee investigating CIA abuses in the 1970s, wrote that "once the capability for covert activity is established, the pressures brought to bear on the President to use it are immense."[93]

The second factor is feasibility. Concealing the U.S. government's role through covert action is sometimes the only possible path to success. If the United States had openly financed Italy's Christian Democratic Party in 1948, voters would have seen the party as an American puppet and the Communists would likely have won the election.[94] In 1979, if word ever got out that the "Canadian movie team"[95] traveling to Tehran to make a movie named *Argo* was actually a covert operation to rescue six Americans who had taken refuge in the Canadian embassy during the Iranian revolution, the diplomats could have been captured or killed.[96] Covert action is never a president's first choice of action. Sometimes, however, it's the only viable choice.

The third reason for the enduring allure of covert action is that the plausible deniability of U.S. involvement in a covert action can limit retaliation and escalation. Particularly during the Cold War, when the two superpowers were locked in a global geopolitical and ideological battle and were pointing nuclear warheads at each other's cities, the pressure was on to find ways of competing without unleashing nuclear war. Plausible deniability proved valuable even when it wasn't terribly plausible. Both the United States and the Soviet Union engaged in proxy wars in which both sides knew the other was secretly backing local groups but officially pretended they did not know in order to manage escalation risks.

During the Korean War, for example, Soviet pilots covertly engaged in air-to-air combat against Americans—and U.S. intelligence agencies knew it.[97] Yet to prevent crisis escalation, neither side let on that direct combat was occurring. Similarly, the massive American covert operation to support the Afghan Mujahidin against the Soviets became an open secret by 1984, and yet the Reagan administration refused to officially acknowledge U.S. support for two more years. Officials even insisted on supplying the Mujahidin with Soviet-made weapons to maintain the cover story.[98] Why? Because even the pretense of covertness kept the conflict from escalating into a superpower war and provided cover for partners like Pakistan and Egypt to assist U.S. efforts without facing retaliation by the Soviets.[99] As Berkowitz and Goodman wrote, "The fact that . . . covertness is sometimes no more than a fig leaf does not necessarily alter the fact that it is a useful fig leaf."[100]

The useful fig leaf played a role in the 2011 bin Laden operation, too. Robert Gates, who was serving as secretary of defense at the time, wrote that regardless of whether the raid succeeded or failed, sending an American military team into sovereign Pakistani territory without Pakistani knowledge or permission could "jeopardize an already fragile relationship . . . and thus the fate of the war in Afghanistan." If the operation was carried out under Department of Defense authorities, the U.S. government could not deny involvement. But if the CIA was in charge, it could. Conducting the raid as a CIA covert operation offered "at least a fig leaf—granted, a very small leaf—of deniability," Gates wrote.[101] One CIA official involved in the hunt for bin Laden put it more directly: "If the military did it, we could have been at war with Pakistan."[102]

Is Covert Action Worth it?

Judging whether covert action is worth it involves three related issues: *efficacy, morality,* and *accountability*. Efficacy requires examining the probability of success and the magnitude of desired outcomes that might result compared to the costs. Morality requires judgments about what values matter most to our society and why. Even if a covert action is likely to succeed, there may be good moral reasons why the United States should not undertake it. Accountability requires balancing the need for secrecy against the potential for abuse and the idea that political leaders should bear responsibility for their actions.

The Efficacy of Last Resorts

In public policy classes, I teach students that good decisionmaking is rational: policymakers should systematically assess the costs and benefits of their options and pick the one that yields the best overall result. Sounds straightforward.

It isn't. For starters, covert action often fails because it's used only for the toughest foreign policy challenges—the ones that keep presidents awake at night, those in which the stakes are high and the odds of success are inherently low. Academics call this a *selection bias* problem. It's one thing to judge a failure rate when your sample is representative, but quite another when the sample is skewed.

Imagine judging Michael Jordan's basketball record only by how many half-court shots he made. Retrieving a sunken Soviet nuclear sub and its hidden secrets,[103] arming foreign fighters against Soviet soldiers, and rescuing American hostages are the half-court shots of foreign policy. There's no such thing as an easy or low-risk covert action. If presidents are authorizing covert action, they're in last resort territory: policymakers believe something has to be done and all the other options are worse. The risk of failure is high, but this choice is the best they've got. Presidents often green-light covert action knowing it probably won't work. But if it does, the payoff could be large—like bringing bin Laden to justice.

What's more, presidents often underestimate the domestic political costs at home when covert action goes south. Kennedy's disastrous Bay of Pigs invasion didn't just fail to overthrow Fidel Castro. It dealt Kennedy a serious political blow early in his presidency. "How could I have been so stupid to let them go ahead?" he famously remarked.[104]

Similarly, the Reagan administration's covert action in the 1980s to overthrow the leftist Sandinista regime in Nicaragua ended up severely damaging Reagan's presidency. When word leaked in the *Wall Street Journal* that CIA activities included mining Nicaraguan harbors, Congress was incensed; the CIA had not notified the congressional intelligence committees of the operation as required by law, and the mines ended up striking ships from six different countries, including a Soviet oil tanker. Senator Barry Goldwater (R-AZ), a CIA stalwart and Republican chairman of the Senate Intelligence Committee, was furious. "I am pissed off!" he wrote in a letter to CIA Director William Casey. "The President has asked us to back his foreign policy. Bill, how can we back his foreign policy when we don't know what the hell he is doing? . . . Mine the harbors in Nicaragua? This is an act violating international law. It is an act of war. For the life of me, I don't see how we are going to explain it."[105]

Congress passed new laws cutting off funding for the Contra rebels. These prohibitions, in turn, prompted Reagan administration officials to carry out an ill-conceived, illegal plan—secretly funneling money to the Contras by selling arms to Iran in exchange for the release of American hostages. Dubbed the Iran-Contra affair, the scheme deceived Congress, sparked congressional and independent investigations, and mired the Reagan presidency in scandal.[106] The president's public approval rating plummeted.[107] "Reagan wasn't just a lame duck, he was a dead duck," an aide later reflected.[108] National Security Advisor John Poindexter was forced to resign and several other officials were convicted of crimes.[109]

Covert action also poses the risk of unintended consequences down the line. In 1953, the CIA helped the Shah overthrow Prime Minister Mohammad Mossadegh in Iran.[110] Installing a pro-American regime in an oil-rich nation located in a strategic stretch of the Middle East during the throes of the Cold War appeared to be a success. But the picture looked a lot different two decades later. Ultimately the Shah's rule gave rise to religious extremism, a revolutionary overthrow, the American hostage crisis, severed ties, regional instability, and today's rising nuclear dangers.

Likewise, U.S. Cold War support for the Afghan Mujahidin succeeded in expelling the Soviets, but the rebels' foreign benefactors eventually morphed into al Qaeda, made Afghanistan a terrorism stronghold, launched the deadliest terrorist attack on American soil in history, and drew the United States and allies into war.

Of course, history is filled with contingency, and policymakers can only fight the enemies they have here and now. "People have criticized the CIA effort in Afghanistan because we gave weapons to Islamic fundamentalists," said Milt Bearden, a CIA field manager involved in the program. "Well, I don't know how many Presbyterians there are over there. The implication is that if only some history professor could have told us who to give the weapons to, we would have found the Methodists and the Presbyterians. You can try, but you can't do that very well. It's their rebellion."[111]

Bearden makes an important point. Better options may not have existed, even with the benefit of 20/20 hindsight. Still, Iran and Afghanistan are cautionary reminders about the long arc of history. In both cases, covert action seemed successful in the moment but unleashed a chain of events that proved even more dangerous later. Judging the success or failure of a covert action is murky business.

Moral Dilemmas

In 1984, *Harper's* magazine hosted a roundtable conversation about covert action called "Should the U.S. Fight Secret Wars?" Participants included legislators, CIA officials, diplomats, and journalists. The discussion got hot, fast. Moral questions were at the center of the debate. Even the CIA officials disagreed with each other.[112]

Covert action is highly charged and morally complex. Thoughtful people come at the issues from different vantage points. Many Americans are deeply uncomfortable with the idea of secretly meddling in the domestic affairs of other countries. To them, covert action runs counter to American values of transparency, accountability, respect for the rule of law, and human rights. George Kennan, veteran diplomat and author of the famous "X" article on containment, wrote:

> Excessive secrecy, duplicity, and clandestine skulduggery are simply not our dish. . . .
> One may say that to deny ourselves this species of capability is to accept a serious limitation on our ability to contend with forces now

directed against us. Perhaps; but if so, it is a limitation with which we will have to live.[113]

Kennan came to believe that even though the Soviets took the gloves off and engaged in covert action during the Cold War, the United States shouldn't, except in extreme and rare circumstances.[114]

For others, covert action is morally problematic because it lacks democratic accountability. These concerns are especially acute when covert action involves violence. As former Defense Department official Morton Halperin noted in the 1984 *Harper's* roundtable:

> Covert operations commit the United States to major foreign policy initiatives—to wage war—without public debate, without congressional debate, and without giving citizens the opportunity to express their views either by petitioning the government or by voting against a president because they don't approve of his policies. In a democratic society, it is unacceptable for the president to engage in operations that cannot be tested in the marketplace—in Congress or at the ballot box.[115]

Oversight has certainly improved since the Wild West days of the 1950s, when plausible deniability meant not telling the president things he might not want to know and when congressional committees preferred not to ask too many questions. But classification still makes oversight difficult for Congress. Legislators can object, but they have to do it in secret. Covert action requires secrecy for success—the more, the better. Yet democratic accountability requires openness—the more, the better. And there's the rub.

Finally, some find the secret use of force inherently unfair or dishonorable. Using force openly on a battlefield is one thing. Secretly killing people in ways designed to obscure America's involvement is another.

Defenders of covert action note that *all* foreign policy involves influencing the domestic politics of other nations.[116] Broadcasting pro-American messages over the airwaves, providing aid to fledgling democracies, training foreign militaries, signing free trade agreements, waging counterinsurgency operations, declaring war—these and other overt foreign policy tools are also designed to interfere in the domestic politics of other nations to advance American interests. Covert action isn't some special bag of dirty tricks in an otherwise pristine world. Foreign policy is a meddling business. All nations do it, and all leaders know it.

Others believe that governments have a moral imperative to protect the lives and well-being of their citizens, and covert action serves that purpose. Achieving the greater good in a dangerous world sometimes requires tough choices and tactics. To do less is foolish, dangerous, and unjust.

Former CIA Deputy Director Ray Cline captured this reasoning in the 1984 *Harper's* roundtable when he talked about the Cold War. "The United States is faced with a situation in which the major world power opposing our system of government is trying to expand its power by using covert methods of warfare," he noted. "Must the United States respond like a man in a barroom brawl who will fight only according to the Marquis of Queensberry rules?"[117] Presidents George W. Bush and Barack Obama felt the same way about al Qaeda after 9/11. Both presidents devoted considerable attention and resources to hunting bin Laden. The terrorist leader wasn't playing by any gentleman's rules; the only way to stop him was to capture or kill him.

Defenders also note that in some cases, covert action can *lower* the risk of casualties for American soldiers and foreign non-combatants. Which option is more moral: The military strike that is overt and democratically accountable but kills more people? Or the covert action that is secret and less accountable but saves more lives of combatants and innocent civilians? Fairness, moreover, looks different on the battlefield than it does in a classroom. When I asked one senior Navy officer what he thought of arguments that covert drone strikes were not fighting fair, he replied, "When I'm asking my sailors to risk their lives against terrorists, I don't want a fair fight."

To get a feel for these moral dilemmas, consider the following scenario:

A notorious international drug trafficker has just ousted the democratically elected leader in a foreign nation and declared a state of war against the United States. The country is strategically located along a vital waterway. Its political turmoil comes during a critical negotiation with the United States.

Years ago, the drug trafficker was a paid CIA asset whose assistance included funneling support for pro-American rebels in neighboring nations. But he was also known to assist American adversaries and is suspected of orchestrating a number of political murders in his own country.

The U.S. Justice Department has indicted him on money laundering and drug charges, which provides legal justification for bringing him to the United States to stand trial.

What do you do?

One option is to take no action. This is a domestic political problem in a foreign country, and the United States should not interfere as a matter of principle. But doing nothing lets one of the world's most notorious drug kingpins operate freely. It will likely result in the deaths of thousands of innocent people seeking democracy under his brutal rule. And it throws your relationship with this strategic country into crisis at a pivotal moment. If the foreign country seizes control of the waterway, U.S. economic and security interests could be severely impacted.

A second option is to authorize the CIA to help wage a coup. But using covert action to oust this man and restore democracy would be advancing a secret foreign policy without accountability to Congress or American voters. The operation might end up killing him, which could be interpreted as violating the U.S. executive order banning political assassinations. There are also sensitivities around America's history of controversial action in the region. Launching a covert action to foster regime change now, even if it's for a good cause, could backfire, stoking anti-Americanism in the country and the broader region.

The third option is to overtly deploy American troops to restore democracy and bring the man to trial in the United States. But military action would risk many more American lives than a covert action, and it could trigger wider civil strife. Even a fast and small invasion would require several thousand troops and probably result in the deaths of hundreds of civilians. There's always the risk that the Pentagon could get bogged down in a protracted conflict. And U.S. forces cannot be everywhere at once: any sizable deployment would reduce the Defense

Department's capacity to deal with other crises and contingencies around the world.

What choice do you make?

If limiting casualties is most important to you, then covert action is the best option. If transparency and accountability matter more in your moral calculus, launching an invasion is best. If you deeply value non-interference in the domestic affairs of other nations, you'll opt for doing nothing.

This scenario isn't some hypothetical I dreamed up. It actually happened. In 1989, a shady former CIA asset named Manuel Noriega annulled the results of a democratic election and seized power in Panama.[118] This wasn't just any country, and Noriega wasn't just any strongman. Panama was strategically important to the United States because of its U.S.-built canal connecting the Pacific and Atlantic Oceans. The fifty-two-mile canal played such a vital role in commercial and military transit, it had been controlled by the United States ever since its construction in 1914, though there were plans to return it to Panamanian control by the year 2000.[119]

Noriega had helped U.S. intelligence in the past, but he was no Boy Scout. CIA assets usually aren't. Noriega was known to play both sides, funneling information to American enemies. He was one of the world's biggest drug traffickers, providing logistical support and financial safe havens for Pablo Escobar's cocaine empire. And he was notorious for brutalizing his domestic political opponents in Panama with anti-riot squads wielding steel pipes and baseball bats.[120] Noriega was widely believed to have murdered political opponents, including Hugo Spadafora, whose headless body was found in a mail bag along the Costa Rican border.[121]

In 1988, he was organizing anti-U.S. demonstrations where he brandished a machete and shouted, "Not one step back!"[122]

To ramp up pressure, the U.S. Justice Department indicted Noriega on drug trafficking and money laundering charges and imposed economic sanctions. President Reagan also approved covert action to provide non-lethal aid to Panamanian opposition forces to get Noriega to leave Panama voluntarily.[123] None of it worked. Noriega ousted the democratically elected leader, declared himself "maximum leader," and got Panama's National Assembly to declare that the United States and Panama were in a "state of war."[124]

Reagan seriously considered ousting Noriega by force through covert action. He even issued an authorization and briefed Congress. But the Senate Intelligence Committee was deeply concerned that if Noriega somehow died during a CIA-backed overthrow, it could be considered a peacetime assassination, which was banned by executive order.[125]

Even if Justice Department lawyers had believed it was legal, was it a good idea? Did policymakers want to set the precedent of an "incidental" assassination in light of the CIA's past assassination scandals and its overthrow of other Latin American leaders?[126] "The CIA's history in Latin America is not entirely a proud one," noted former CIA Director Leon Panetta.[127]

The conflict stretched into the next administration. President George H. W. Bush—a former CIA director—opted to go overt, sending more than twenty-five thousand troops to Panama in a military operation called JUST CAUSE.[128] It was the largest American combat operation since the Vietnam War.[129]

As troops fanned out, Noriega, reportedly disguised as a woman, took refuge inside the Vatican's embassy. After a two-week siege in which U.S. forces blared rap and rock music (which Noriega reportedly hated) twenty-four hours a day, he finally surrendered.[130] But not before twenty-three American soldiers and several hundred Panamanian civilians were killed.[131]

Although a covert action likely would have produced fewer casualties, even former CIA Director William Colby believed that overt military action was probably the right call. Why? Because of the moral opprobrium that would have resulted from being seen to violate the political assassination ban. There is something different, and dishonorable, about killing a leader secretly in peacetime compared to killing him openly in wartime. "You'd still be hearing about the assassination of Noriega for the next hundred years—and you will not be hearing about the attack on Panama for the next hundred years," noted Colby.[132]

Accountability and "Edgy Things"

Former CIA Director Michael Hayden calls covert operations "edgy things."[133] He's right. These activities lie in tough legal, moral, and political terrain. Covert action offers presidents immediacy and secrecy. Democratic accountability requires deliberation and transparency. Oversight of covert action has to reconcile these competing needs. The picture hasn't always been pretty.

Until the 1970s, deliberations inside the White House and National Security Council assumed an air of "Who will rid me of this meddlesome priest?"[134] in which presidents preferred not to ask about specifics and intelligence officials and policy advisors preferred not to give them.[135] Discussions used oblique language. Presidents Eisenhower and Kennedy never said, "Go kill Fidel Castro with an exploding seashell." Instead, covert operations proceeded on the basis of general approvals—like "get rid of the Castro regime."[136]

Procedures and decisions were poorly documented.[137] An internal CIA memorandum described covert action authorization procedures in the 1950s and 1960s as "somewhat cloudy" and "based on the value judgments" of the CIA director. The system was geared to provide the president a secondary layer of plausible deniability: even if a U.S. covert action were exposed, presidents were less likely to be held accountable for it if they never explicitly ordered it. All that circumlocution and vagueness fostered confusion—masking presidential decisions and preventing successive presidents from being fully informed about operations.[138]

Congressional oversight was even looser.[139] The House and Senate did not have dedicated intelligence committees. Instead, intelligence issues were handled by sub-panels of existing committees, which took little interest and spent little time on them.[140] The general view was that CIA covert operations were better left alone. In the 1970s, Congressman Leslie Aspin Jr. (D-WI) asked CIA Director William Colby what happened in the past when oversight committees objected to a CIA operation. "He was stunned," recalled Aspin. "The question had never come up before. The committees preferred not to get involved."[141]

Reforms since the 1970s have tightened and improved many aspects of oversight. Today, foreign assassinations are still prohibited by executive order, though there's ongoing debate about what constitutes an assassination and the conditions under which the prohibition can be waived.[142] Specific processes (like how drone kill lists are determined) typically remain classified,[143] but presidents are now required by law to approve every covert action personally, in writing, and transmit a "finding" to the congressional intelligence committees stating how the approved activity "is necessary to support identifiable foreign policy objectives of the United States and is important to the national security of the United States."[144]

To be sure, there are still large loopholes. In exceptional circumstances,[145] findings may be transmitted orally and limited to a handful of members.[146] When this happens—as it sometimes does—legislators cannot discuss what they learn even with other members of the intelligence committees or their own professional staffs. Senator John D. Rockefeller IV (D-WV), who chaired the Senate Intelligence Committee from 2007 to 2009, complained that the limited briefings were a way to "muzzle" Congress.[147]

And just because a presidential finding has to be written down doesn't mean it has to be clear. In the late 1990s, President Clinton issued several findings authorizing CIA proxies to capture Osama bin Laden in operations where he might be killed. But what exactly did that mean? Could the CIA's proxies just go out and kill bin Laden? Or did they have to try capturing him? Clinton later told the 9/11 Commission he wanted bin Laden dead.[148] But that's not what the CIA thought. Every CIA official interviewed by the commission, including Director George Tenet, "believed that the only acceptable context for killing Bin Ladin was a credible capture operation."[149]

Notably, Congress does not have the power to approve or veto a covert action.[150] It never has. Nevertheless, Congress has to approve annual funding, which means it may know well in advance before a covert action begins.[151] While presidents retain unilateral authority to authorize covert action, Congress must be informed, and congressional views do matter. As former CIA official Mark Lowenthal writes, "Should committee members or the staffers raise serious questions, a prudent covert action briefing team reports that fact to the executive branch. This should be enough to cause the operation to be reviewed."[152] According to press reports, for example, congressional opposition led President George W. Bush's administration to rescind an authorized covert operation that would have supported certain candidates during the 2005 Iraqi elections.[153]

None of these reforms guarantee that covert action will be legal, moral, wise, or effective. But they do make it more likely that Congress stays informed, that CIA operations are more clearly limited and permitted by standard presidential authorization procedures, and that presidents are held more accountable.[154]

Drones, Terrorists, and Blurring Lines

When Gen. David Petraeus became CIA director in 2011, he made his Langley office look like the Pentagon. Iraqi weapons, military challenge coins, and wartime photographs were everywhere—visual reminders that Petraeus was a career warrior, not an intelligence officer.[155] The retired four-star Army general had revolutionized counterinsurgency doctrine in the battlefields of Iraq and Afghanistan, and it showed.

Petraeus's military mementos also signaled something deeper, a momentous shift years in the making: never before had the lines between military action and intelligence become so blurred. Even as Petraeus was moving to Langley, his CIA predecessor, Leon Panetta, was moving to the Pentagon to become secretary of defense.

Before 9/11, who did what was clear. Activities conducted with official U.S. involvement were carried out by the military. Those requiring that U.S. sponsorship be hidden were conducted by the CIA as a covert action. But two decades spent fighting terrorism with new technologies have blurred those lines.

Intelligence and on-the-ground combat have become much more tightly integrated. When the United States invaded Afghanistan in 2001, the first troops weren't troops. They were CIA officers carrying boxes full of cash to recruit Afghan warlords before special operations forces landed.[156] The first covert CIA teams landed just sixteen days after 9/11.[157] Weeks later, as Osama bin Laden fled to the mountains of Tora Bora, the "commandos" hunting him were CIA officers working alongside special operators and local Afghan militias operating out of an abandoned schoolhouse and calling in air support from behind enemy lines. That degree of battlefield integration was new. CIA Director George Tenet called Afghanistan "the CIA's finest hour."[158]

CIA-military collaboration took root. Today, the work of spies and warriors has become indistinguishable in many ways. Drone strikes are carried out by the CIA and the Pentagon's Joint Special Operations Command (JSOC), sometimes separately and sometimes together.[159] JSOC has increasingly carried out black operations against terrorists that look a lot like covert action.[160] At the same time, the CIA is engaging in covert operations that look a lot like military action conducted in the open—like killing Anwar al-Awlaki.[161]

The good news is that intelligence and warfighting are now much more connected. The bad news is that intelligence and warfighting are now much more connected.

Let me explain. To the outside world, intelligence and defense don't seem so different—they're both national security-ish. But looks are deceiving. The Pentagon and CIA were set up separately for a reason. The Defense Department's primary mission is fighting. The CIA's primary mission is understanding. Military officers are trained in the management of violence.[162] CIA officers are trained in the management of information—how to get it, analyze it, hide it from the wrong people, and share it with the right ones.

Remember, covert action is just part of what the CIA does. The agency is the U.S. government's premier human intelligence agency. Its officers recruit foreign spies to spill their secrets and betray their causes. The CIA is also the place where analysts assess all types of intelligence—from images and sensors to intercepted phone calls and human reports. They didn't name it the Central Intelligence Agency for nothing.

No organization can do it all. The more CIA people are hunting, the less they are gathering. Paramilitary activities, however successful they may be at taking terrorists off the battlefield, take time and resources away from the CIA's core job: giving the president decision advantage. As former CIA Acting Director Michael Morell recounted, "Covert action takes your focus. We used to have three meetings a week with the Counterterrorism Center because it was deeply involved in covert action. I often wondered what if we'd spent that much time with Russia collectors or China collectors?"[163] Too much attention to today's priorities leaves the nation vulnerable to nasty surprises tomorrow.

8

CONGRESSIONAL
OVERSIGHT

EYES ON SPIES

We are like mushrooms. They [the CIA] keep us in the dark and
feed us a lot of manure.

—NORMAN MINETA, MEMBER OF THE HOUSE PERMANENT
SELECT COMMITTEE ON INTELLIGENCE, 1983[1]

[T]he Senate of the United States and the House of the United States
is [sic] not doing its job. And because you're not doing the job, the
country is not as safe as it ought to be.

—LEE HAMILTON, FORMER CONGRESSMAN AND 9/11
COMMISSION VICE CHAIRMAN, 2007[2]

CIA DIRECTOR JOHN BRENNAN had a crisis on his hands. On January 15, 2014, he held an emergency meeting with Senate Intelligence Committee chair Dianne Feinstein (D-CA) and vice chair Saxby Chambliss (R-GA). The senators were told they could each bring just one senior staff member. Carefully reading through his talking points, Brennan delivered stunning news: CIA employees had secretly searched the computers of Feinstein's Senate Intelligence Committee staff.[3] These weren't just any computers. They belonged to Democratic staff investigators examining the CIA's controversial terrorist detention and interrogation program.[4]

Weeks later, Feinstein learned the CIA had filed a crimes report to the Justice Department accusing her staff of improperly accessing an internal CIA document about the detention and interrogation program called "the Panetta review."[5] Then came the press stories with anonymous sources whispering that her staff had "hacked" the CIA.[6] It wasn't true. An independent CIA investigation later found that CIA employees were the ones who had behaved inappropriately, surreptitiously accessing congressional staff computers, accusing congressional investigators of violating the law with "no factual basis," and in some cases lying after the fact about what they had done.[7]

Aides wrote Feinstein a public speech. For weeks, she could not bring herself to give it. The California Democrat had been a longtime supporter of the agency, even sometimes breaking with party ranks. "I can honestly say I don't know a bigger booster of the CIA than Senator Feinstein," said Senator Martin Heinrich, another Democrat on the intelligence committee.[8]

Feinstein did not like public fights and didn't believe in grandstanding. She had seen enough hate up close in her time. In 1978 when she was president of the San Francisco board of supervisors, a colleague murdered Mayor George Moscone and Supervisor Harvey Milk. Feinstein found Milk in his office down the hall from hers, lying in a pool of blood.[9]

By March 11, 2014, after her questions to Brennan went unanswered, she'd had enough. Feinstein went to the Senate floor and gave the speech. The CIA had spied on her committee's investigation and made bogus charges to intimidate her staff, Feinstein said. The CIA may have violated the Constitution; it had certainly violated her trust. The Agency's actions had threatened the very foundation of congressional oversight. "Mr. President, the recent actions that I have just laid out make this a defining moment for the oversight of our Intelligence Community," Feinstein fumed. "How Congress responds and how this is resolved will show whether the Intelligence Committee can be effective in monitoring and investigating our nation's intelligence activities, or whether our work can be thwarted by those we oversee."[10]

Brennan apologized.[11] But the oversight crisis wasn't anywhere close to being over.

At issue was how history would judge one of the CIA's most controversial programs. From 2002 to 2008, the agency held more than 100[12] suspected terrorists[13] at secret black sites around the world and interrogated many of them with harsh methods[14] that included water-boarding, prolonged confinement in coffin-sized boxes, and involuntary "rectal hydration."[15] Some CIA personnel were so disturbed by what they witnessed, they cried.[16]

Feinstein's Democratic staff claimed to be writing the definitive account of that painful chapter. Dubbed "The Torture Report," the study argued that the CIA program had been illegal, inhumane, out of control, and ultimately ineffective at producing valuable intelligence.[17]

But to many intelligence officials and Senate Intelligence Committee Republicans, Feinstein's report was a hit job that distorted the facts and cast the CIA in the worst possible light. Six of the seven Republicans on the Senate Intelligence Committee wrote a 167-page dissenting report.[18] The CIA released its own study of the Democratic staff study with a point-by-point rebuttal.[19] Former intelligence officials launched a media campaign with op-eds[20] and a website and Twitter hashtag #CIAsavedlives.[21]

They argued the Senate report was partisan, analytically flawed, and flat wrong on key points. Although Feinstein's investigation began with strong bipartisan support,[22] Republican committee members said they lost faith as investigators interviewed no CIA officials, held no hearings, and issued no recommendations.[23]

What's more, they noted, evidence showed the CIA detention and interrogation program was lawful.[24] It had been approved by the president, deemed legal by the attorney general, overseen by the executive branch at the highest levels, and briefed to Congress more than thirty times, including graphic details.[25] Not one legislator objected back then; some even worried the CIA wasn't going far enough.[26] Defenders believed that some in Congress were conveniently forgetting the past, now that political winds were shifting. The agency was being hung out to dry.[27]

Defenders also claimed the CIA program was effective, providing "unique intelligence that helped the US disrupt plots, capture terrorists, better understand the enemy, prevent another mass casualty attack, and save lives."[28]

In the end, nobody was satisfied. Instead of the definitive account, Feinstein's study produced dueling reports and even more unanswered questions.

Incidents like this battle between the CIA and Feinstein offer a rare glimpse into the private world of public accountability. As the episode suggests, congressional intelligence oversight is often contentious, with the executive and legislative branches sparring over everything—what information congressional overseers get, when they get it, how they access it, and what conclusions they draw. There's rarely consensus about what really happened or who's to blame. These fights usually play out behind closed doors, in classified briefings and documents that remain locked in safes.[29]

As we'll see, oversight rarely works well. Sometimes the battles get too fierce; often they aren't fierce enough—because Congress is focused on the wrong intelligence issues or not focused on any intelligence issues at all. In the media glare, partisan politics can get in the way.

This chapter asks four questions: (1) What does good congressional intelligence oversight look like? (2) How well has Congress overseen intelligence throughout history? (3) What makes congressional oversight of intelligence different from, and harder than, other policy areas? (4) What does the future hold?

It's worth emphasizing that I view these questions through a political science lens. Most histories and press accounts trace oversight ups and downs as a series of personality clashes; the usual story is all about who's in charge and how well they get along. Although these interpersonal dynamics certainly matter, political scientists find that other factors often matter more. General explanations are powerful things, shedding light on root causes that transcend individuals and moments in time.

In this case, three underlying factors have driven oversight dynamics no matter who's been in the White House or chairing congressional intelligence committees: *information*, *incentives*, and *institutions*. The oversight headline isn't variation over time; it's continuity. Intelligence oversight has always been challenging for reasons that have nothing to do with who liked whom or which party was in power.

From a policy perspective, this is bad news because it suggests the limits of individual leadership. Even with the best leaders, oversight challenges are hard to overcome and likely to stay that way. What's more, emerging technologies are likely to strain congressional oversight in new ways.

What Does Good Congressional Oversight Look Like?

James Madison famously wrote in *Federalist 51*, "If men were angels, no government would be necessary. If angels were to govern men, neither external nor internal controls on government would be necessary."[30] The Framers divided power so that each branch was checked by another. Although never explicitly mentioned in the Constitution, oversight of executive branch agencies has always been a core part of Congress's duties. As historian Arthur Schlesinger wrote, the Framers believed "the power to make laws implied the power to see whether they were faithfully executed."[31]

That makes congressional oversight sound more neutral and technocratic than it is. In reality, fights about oversight are really fights about policy outcomes. The best offshore drilling regulations look different to the Sierra Club than to British Petroleum. To NSA leaders, the agency's post-9/11 intelligence programs were well overseen by all three branches of government. To civil libertarians, they weren't.[32] What constitutes good oversight often lies in the eye of the beholder.

That's not to say that anything goes. I have asked dozens of current and former intelligence officials, legislators, and Capitol Hill staffers, "What does good oversight look like to you?" They agreed on more than you might think.

The general refrain goes like this:

Oversight is essential. As former CIA Deputy Director Michael Morell put it, "Oversight of intelligence I think is particularly important because the community is made up of a group of organizations that are secret organizations operating in a democracy, and there has to be a process to assure the American people that they are operating the way they should."[33]

Done well, congressional oversight is nonpartisan and big-picture. It ensures that intelligence agencies get the resources they need and deploys them to maximum effect. It sets agencies' strategic priorities and pushes them to improve by asking tough questions and demanding better answers. It maintains accountability, ensuring compliance with the law and generating public confidence in agencies that must, by necessity, hide much of what they do.

Done poorly, oversight micromanages, distracts, and blames. It mires everyone in the day-to-day, drawing time and attention away from bigger and more important questions—like what American intelligence agencies should be doing, how well they are doing it, and where they should be heading. Ineffective oversight consumes energy but produces little benefit, demanding reports that aren't read and briefings that aren't well attended.[34] It blames agencies when things turn ugly and cameras start rolling rather than working with them to prevent mishaps in the first place.

More specifically, everyone I interviewed believed that good oversight requires legislators to serve four distinct roles, though different people emphasized different ones to different degrees:

(1) **Police officer:** Ensuring that intelligence policies and activities fall within the bounds of the law.

(2) **Board of directors:** Setting strategic guidance and ensuring that resources are matched against priorities.

(3) **Coach:** Continuously examining and improving current programs and practices by asking good questions and demanding good answers.

(4) **Ambassador:** Generating public trust and support for the vital functions that secret intelligence agencies play in U.S. national security.[35]

Respondents also agreed that however oversight was defined, it usually didn't work well.

A Tale of Three Eras

A closer look at history finds that congressional intelligence oversight has always struggled, but in different ways at different times.

Intelligence oversight can be divided into three eras. From the nation's founding until the 1970s, oversight was so infrequent, it could be more aptly described as "undersight." The 1970s brought routinization—the rise of permanent oversight committees with greater statutory powers. Finally, the Cold War's end ushered in a changing threat landscape that laid bare Congress's strategic oversight weaknesses. These deficiencies contributed to 9/11, and many remain unaddressed even now.

The Undersight Era: 1770s–1970s

For nearly two hundred years, congressional intelligence oversight did not amount to much. In part, this reflected the sporadic development and use of intelligence. As noted in chapter 3, until the Cold War, intelligence agencies developed in boom-and-bust cycles, growing dramatically during wartime only to be demobilized again when hostilities ended.

Even so, intelligence activities encountered little congressional interest or oversight until the 1970s. Presidents had strong incentives to keep information about their intelligence operations from Congress, and Congress had weak incentives and institutional mechanisms to demand more.

When Congress gave President George Washington a secret intelligence fund in 1790, for example, it required him to certify the sums he spent but not what, or who, he spent them on.[36] In the 1840s, some legislators suspected President James Polk was secretly paying provocateurs to provoke a war with Mexico that would allow the United States to annex California and Texas. But when they asked Polk to turn over an accounting, he refused.[37] Keeping information from Congress gave him a freer foreign policy hand. "The experience of every nation on earth has demonstrated that emergencies may arise in which it becomes absolutely necessary for the public safety or the public good to make expenditures, the very object of which would be defeated by publicity," Polk argued.[38] And that's pretty much how it went.

After World War II and the establishment of the CIA, Congress became more involved, but not much. There were no dedicated House or Senate Intelligence Committees. Instead, oversight was divvied up between subcommittees of the powerful Appropriations and Armed Services Committees, which had little time for intelligence and less interest in it.[39]

Two or three times each year, a handful of leaders met informally to discuss intelligence issues, always in secret. In 1951, the CIA subcommittee of the Senate Armed Services Committee met just once.[40] In 1957, the Senate Appropriations Committee's panel didn't meet at all.[41] "It is not a question of reluctance on the part of the CIA officials to speak to us," said Senator Leverett Saltonstall (R-MA), who served on both the Senate Appropriations and Armed Services Committees during the

1950s. "Instead it is a question of our reluctance, if you will, to seek information and knowledge on subjects which I personally, as a Member of Congress and as a citizen, would rather not have."[42]

The House wasn't any better. One former House Armed Services Subcommittee member recalled, "We met annually—one time a year, for a period of two hours in which we accomplished virtually nothing."[43]

Congressional oversight scholar Loch Johnson called it "blue moon frequency" and noted, "the CIA, with its thousands of employees, large budget, and risky operations spanning the globe, was subjected to roughly twenty-four hours of legislative 'probing' in both chambers over an entire year."[44]

In fact, the CIA struggled to get more congressional attention. Walter Pforzheimer, the agency's first liaison officer to Congress, recalled, "There were very loose reins on us at the time because the Congress believed in what we were doing. It wasn't that we were attempting to hide anything. Our main problem was, we couldn't get them to sit still and listen."[45] William Colby, who ran the CIA from 1973 to 1976, admitted that lax oversight contributed to excesses. "It was a consensus that intelligence was apart from the rules. . . . That was the reason we did step over the line in a few cases, largely because no one was watching. No one was there to say don't do that."[46]

The Era of Routinization: 1970s–1990s

The 1970s brought a period of unprecedented congressional activism and dramatic changes to intelligence oversight.

The Vietnam War was roiling the nation and breeding a deep distrust in government. In June 1972, a five-man team with links to the CIA was caught trying to bug the Democratic National Committee headquarters in the Watergate building in a late-night break-in.[47] President Nixon lied to cover it up and was eventually forced to resign. Then came news reports that the CIA was running a covert operation to subvert Salvador Allende's democratically elected Marxist regime in Chile.[48] And on December 22, 1974, the *New York Times* ran a bombshell story by Seymour Hersh reporting that the CIA had engaged in "a massive, illegal domestic intelligence operation" against American anti-war protesters and other dissidents during the Nixon administration.[49] Congress's undersight era had created a permissive environment for egregious intelligence violations.

Suddenly, intelligence scandals seemed to be everywhere, and investigations weren't far behind. There was a special commission chaired by Vice President Nelson Rockefeller, an internal 693-page CIA review of dirty deeds called "The Family Jewels"[50] (see box) and a House investigation led by Representative Otis Pike (D-NY). But it was the Senate investigation chaired by Idaho Democrat Frank Church that captured national attention and produced lasting change.

The Family Jewels

In 1973, CIA Director James Schlesinger wanted to know just how bad it was. He ordered CIA employees to report any activity that might have ever violated the agency's statutory charter. Aptly called "The Family Jewels," the compilation was declassified in 2007. It's a trove of trivia and scandal—everything from mundane bureaucratic records to salacious details about CIA domestic wiretapping, break-ins, and mind-control experiments.[51]

One of the most tantalizing documents was a memo to the CIA's deputy director for management and services that included the words, "Hunt requests a lockpicker." Hunt was the infamous E. Howard Hunt, the CIA Cold-Warrior-turned-Nixon-hatchet-man who oversaw the botched Watergate break-in of the Democratic National Committee headquarters. The break-in and its cover-up eventually led to the resignation of President Nixon.

Whether Hunt's lockpicker request was related to the Watergate break-in remains unknown. But we do know that a good lockpicker could have changed history. The Watergate break-in was discovered when an alert security guard named Frank Wills noticed that a door to the parking garage had been suspiciously taped to stay open.[52]

Established by an 82–4 Senate vote, the bipartisan Church Committee held more than 100 hearings, conducted more than 800 interviews, reviewed more than 100,000 pages of documents, and released 14 volumes of hearings and reports—making it one of the most sweeping congressional investigations in history. It found the *New York Times* allegations to be the tip of the iceberg: the CIA, NSA, and FBI had been illegally spying on Americans for years.[53] Their activities included wiretapping phones; opening mail; intercepting millions of telegrams;[54] infiltrating and disrupting civil rights, women's rights, and anti-war groups; and conducting hundreds of warrantless black bag break-ins of offices and homes. "Intelligence agencies have undermined the constitutional rights of citizens," the final report concluded, "primarily because checks and balances designed by the framers of the Constitution to assure accountability have not been applied."[55] The committee recommended nearly 100 reforms.

Out of these recommendations emerged a signature change: the creation of dedicated intelligence oversight committees in both the House and Senate. The House Permanent Select Committee on Intelligence (HPSCI, or "Hipsee") and the Senate Select Committee on Intelligence (SSCI, or "Sissy") brought the Intelligence Community into the Madisonian framework of checks and balances for the first time. While executive branch officials still held the upper hand (more on that below), at least now they had to answer to Congress. The new committees created new expectations, new boundaries, new day-to-day staff work, and more rigorous budgetary and programmatic review of intelligence agencies and activities—all unheard of before.

The committees have been holding regular briefings and hearings, reviewing covert action and other sensitive programs, authorizing agency budgets, requiring reports, drafting legislation, confirming appointments to intelligence agency leadership positions, and conducting investigations ever since. Today, by law, the president is required to ensure that both committees are kept "fully and currently informed" of intelligence activities, though that requirement contains significant ambiguities.[56]

As NSA's former chief of legislative affairs William Nolte put it, "Oversight is the best thing that happened to American intelligence after 1975. It hasn't been perfect, but . . . they have saved the Intelligence Community from mistakes."[57]

The Era of Strategic Weakness: 1990s–Now

Routinizing oversight in the 1970s was a major step forward, but the 9/11 terrorist attacks revealed hidden weaknesses. In the 1990s, as the Cold War ended and the terrorist threat grew, intelligence agencies were struggling to adapt—and nobody on the intelligence oversight committees knew it.[58] Intelligence agencies were failing, and congressional oversight was, too.

The 9/11 Commission's postmortem called congressional oversight before the terrorist attacks "dysfunctional." Because Congress didn't reorganize itself when the Cold War ended and national security challenges shifted, new threats like terrorism fell between the cracks of fourteen different committees. Even on the intelligence committees, the commission found, members were spending much more time on scandals and investigations that provided media visibility rather than the "unglamorous but essential work of oversight."[59]

We now know that counterterrorism intelligence efforts in the 1990s were underfunded, underperforming, and uncoordinated. Congress kept passing budgets that poured money into electronic collection platforms ideal for counting Soviet warheads instead of human intelligence programs better suited for penetrating terrorist groups.[60] Although CIA Director George Tenet declared war on Osama bin Laden in a 1998 memo and urged that "no resources or people [be] spared" across the Intelligence Community to fight him, counterterrorism efforts were scattered across forty-six executive branch agencies without a central strategy, budget, or coordinating mechanism. Even Tenet's directive requiring that intelligence officials spend rotational postings in different agencies in order to be promoted was simply ignored.[61]

The FBI declared terrorism its top priority in 1998, but on 9/11 only 6 percent of personnel were working counterterrorism issues. New agents received more time for vacation than counterterrorism training. And just weeks before 9/11, an internal FBI counterterrorism review gave failing grades to every one of the FBI's fifty-six U.S. field offices.[62]

None of this was known to the House and Senate Intelligence Committees before 9/11. Nobody was asking big questions about emerging threats and how the Intelligence Community was adjusting to them. The 9/11 Commission concluded that "Congress gave little guidance to executive branch agencies, did not reform them in any significant way, and did not systematically perform oversight to identify, address, and attempt to resolve the many problems in national security and domestic agencies that became apparent in the aftermath of 9/11."[63] It was a scathing review.

Two decades after 9/11, almost none of the commission's recommendations to improve intelligence oversight have been adopted. The least reformed part of the U.S. intelligence enterprise isn't the CIA, FBI, or NSA. It's Congress.

Police Patrols, Fire Alarms, and the Limits of Congressional Intelligence Oversight

The history of intelligence oversight looks nothing like congressional oversight of domestic policy agencies. For years, political scientists have scoured data on agencies ranging from the Environmental Protection Agency to the Federal Communications Commission. They have found that Congress controls the bureaucracy—and in some surprisingly efficient ways.

Congress actually has considerable oversight powers, determining whether agencies live or die, who leads them, how much money they get, where they sit within the executive branch, and what they are allowed to do. Congress also has the power to investigate agency wrongdoing, hold hearings to demand answers and embarrass agency leaders, and pass new legislation to restrain agencies in new ways.

Over time, scholars have found, Congress has used these powers to oversee executive branch agencies in two basic models—referred to as police patrol[64] and fire alarm oversight.[65]

In police patrol oversight, legislators and their staffs are constantly on the lookout for hints of agency wrongdoing, inefficiency, or violations of legislative priorities. Oversight is done by holding hearings, summoning agency officials, making inquiries, and demanding changes. Congress cannot see everything all the time, but by sampling agency activities, oversight can catch some problems and deter the emergence of others.[66]

Notably, Congress's police patrols don't have to do much patrolling to be effective. Agency officials are not stupid. They know, as political scientist Mathew McCubbins put it, that "Congress holds the power of life or death in the most elemental terms" for their existence.[67] The mere anticipation of possible congressional punishment keeps bureaucrats in line.

Fire alarm oversight is less constant and direct. In this model, legislators set up rules and procedures that empower citizens, interest groups, and other third parties to monitor agency activities and sound the alarm if they see smoke. Legislators spring into action only when someone else is important enough and upset enough to ring the bell.[68] From Congress's perspective, the beauty of this system is efficiency. It provides oversight while freeing up legislators to pay more attention to activities—like district visits and constituent requests—that help them win re-election.

This research raises a puzzle: Why don't police patrols or fire alarms work in intelligence? The answer isn't that legislators get too partisan or don't care enough, though that happens and it certainly doesn't help. The root causes lie deeper, in the informational environment, incentive structure, and institutional dynamics that are unique to intelligence.

Information Asymmetry

If you've ever taken your car to a mechanic, you've experienced one of the biggest oversight challenges: information asymmetry.

Whenever one party relies on another to get something done, there's a risk that things go awry. The mechanic overcharges. The car still isn't fixed properly. Maybe the mechanic is dishonest, or careless, or overworked, or well intended but badly trained. Whatever the reason, you're disappointed.

Information asymmetry is a big part of the problem. One side knows much more than the other and can take advantage of the situation.[69] The mechanic knows you have no idea how to fix the car or what it should cost. He also knows his own capabilities better than you do.

Each party has different interests, too. The mechanic wants to charge the most he can while you want to pay the least. He wants to do the job fast. You want it done right. If only you knew more about cars and could monitor what he was doing under the hood, it wouldn't be a problem. Leveling the information playing field makes oversight work better.

Congressional oversight involves the same dynamic. The more congressional overseers know, the less government agencies can shirk, stumble, or behave in ways that serve their own interests. Information is key.

Executive branch agencies always know more about their own activities than legislators do. In the unclassified world, however, there are many ways for Congress to narrow the gap. Agencies churn out public reports, regulations, and information about their operations. Federal commissions like the Securities and Exchange Commission and Federal Communications Commission even have periods of public comment to inform their rulemaking processes. Interest groups like watchdog organizations and trade associations bombard legislators with up-to-the-minute information and analysis. Journalists, activists, academics, and bloggers abound. As former House Intelligence Committee chairman Lee Hamilton (D-IN) put it, "If you're the Chairman of a committee that works in the unclassified world, you get a lot of help."[70]

Importantly, legislators don't need any special rooms, classified briefings, or staffers with security clearances to find out what's going on. The easier it is to do oversight homework, the more likely it is that the homework gets done.

Intelligence is another story. "If you're on the outside world of intelligence, you know nothing about it other than what the executive branch decides to tell you," said Hamilton. "The Intelligence Committees are completely on their own."[71]

Even basic information about intelligence programs is secret, hindering both police patrol and fire alarm oversight in major ways. Interested citizens cannot just track intelligence personnel, budgets, or activities. They have to comb through declassified documents for clues or file a Freedom of Information Act request, which can take years and produce nothing.

Nor are there legions of interest groups cranking out reports and making donations to keep legislators informed and on their toes. In 2008, I actually counted them: I found more than twenty-five thousand interest groups registered in Washington, D.C. Even then, in the wake of 9/11 and the Iraq WMD intelligence failure, fewer than 1 percent of them focused on intelligence issues.[72] These groups, moreover, weren't lobbying behemoths like the AARP or the American Medical Association. They were small groups with tiny budgets and names you've never heard of.

In intelligence, getting information takes work. Legislators have to leave their offices and go to secure facilities to read classified materials, and often they aren't permitted to take notes. Only a small number of staff have the clearances to help.[73] "The Intelligence Committee is unlike any other Senate committee," said former committee chairman John D. Rockefeller IV (D-WV). "Our secure workspaces are windowless. Everything is enclosed in lead. We are guarded by the Capitol Police."[74] Because doing the homework is hard, it often doesn't get done. When I asked one former congressional staffer what her greatest frustration was, she immediately replied: "Getting Members to come down and read classified documents."[75]

In short, the executive branch has a sizable information advantage and knows it. Former House Intelligence Committee chair Lee Hamilton said the problem dated back "30 maybe 40 years" and that he battled the executive branch for information "every single week" as chairman in the 1980s. "I don't have any doubt in my mind the executive branch—not just this administration, but any administration—uses [classification] to their advantage time and time again . . . and there's not very much you can do about it," he said.[76]

For years, legislators have complained that meetings with intelligence officials can devolve into a frustrating game of twenty questions. "You have to ask precisely the right question of the intelligence briefer to get an answer that's useful," said former House Intelligence Committee ranking member Jane Harman (D-CA).[77]

One former intelligence official recounted briefing the congressional intelligence committees about the secret destruction of videotapes showing harsh interrogations at CIA black sites. "I went to the Hill and told them the tapes no longer existed," the official told me. "Now, I said they no longer exist; I did not say we crushed them up. It was up to them to figure out the rest."[78]

The briefing was truthful, but coy. The interrogation videotapes did not just disappear in a flood or get lost in the bureaucracy. Jose A. Rodriguez Jr., the head of the CIA's clandestine service, ordered that the tapes be pulverized by an industrial-strength shredder in a cable he sent with detailed instructions.[79] Though two agency lawyers told him they saw no legal obstacles,[80] Rodriguez sent the destruction order without the approvals and over the objections of the CIA director, the director of national intelligence, and the White House legal advisor.[81] "After scrutinizing the cable on my computer for a while, I thought about the decision," Rodriguez later wrote. "I took a deep breath of weary satisfaction and hit Send." Rodriguez was officially reprimanded by the CIA for violating the chain of command.[82] This was "the rest" that congressional overseers had to figure out by themselves.

Intelligence officials admit they parse language to reveal only what they must, especially in open, or unclassified, hearings. Not because they're bad people but because they're good intelligence officers who are trained to protect rather than disclose. "I readily concede that people like me can be too prone to keep too much hidden," wrote Michael Hayden.[83] Former DNI James Clapper agreed, writing, "As someone who had been in or around the intelligence business for the better part of seven decades, transparency felt 'genetically antithetical' to me."[84]

But keeping too many secrets from Congress can backfire, undermining trust and public accountability. Only the intelligence committees can say to the American people, "I don't have a dog in this fight. I'm not part of the executive branch. I've looked hard at overseeing the Intelligence Community's secret activities and I am satisfied they're doing a good job." Agencies must strike the right balance between secrecy and transparency. That's getting harder as information about everything becomes more available and public expectations of openness rise.

In March 2013, Director of National Intelligence James Clapper got into hot water when Senator Ron Wyden (D-OR) asked him whether the National Security Agency collected "any type of data at all on millions, or hundreds of millions, of Americans."[85] Clapper said no. But the correct answer was yes.

After 9/11, NSA began several new intelligence collection programs under the code name Stellarwind.[86] One involved the bulk collection of telephone metadata—the time, number, and duration of phone calls made by millions of Americans. The idea was to build an archive of who called whom that could be queried for possible connections to known terrorist phone numbers.[87] The program did not collect the identity of callers or the content of their calls. Still, it was massive. It targeted Americans, not foreigners. And it was a major departure from how NSA's authorities had been interpreted and used in the past. NSA, after all, was an organization that collected foreign intelligence, eavesdropping around the world.[88]

Some believed the terrorist threat demanded relaxing the divide between foreign and domestic intelligence collection. Congress's 9/11 Joint Inquiry found the government's weaknesses in monitoring communications between suspected terrorists when one party was already inside the United States left the country vulnerable to attack.[89] But others, including some inside the IC, were deeply uncomfortable with using NSA's vast surveillance capabilities on Americans. "The standard we grew up with was 'no U.S. persons,'" said a former intelligence official. "That made me squirm. I lost sleep over that. It wasn't illegal, but I lost sleep."[90] When Edward Snowden revealed details about NSA's metadata program, opposition grew. Congress eventually passed legislation effectively ending it.[91]

Clapper says he misspoke that day, thinking Senator Wyden was asking about a different Stellarwind program that targeted foreign communications content.[92] "I made a mistake; but I didn't lie," Clapper later reflected. "I've been to the Hill many times over 25 years; I've answered probably thousands of questions, either orally or in writing. It is incredulous for anyone who knows me to think that I would say, 'Gee, just for a change of pace, I think I'll lie on this one question in an open hearing.' Really?"[93]

Wyden, however, thought Clapper had been deliberately deceptive.[94] Clapper didn't help matters when he later told NBC's Andrea Mitchell that answering no was the "least untruthful" answer he could give. In some sense, this was technically accurate—the hearing was open, and answering yes would have publicly revealed a highly classified intelligence program that had already been briefed to Congress in private.[95] But the political damage was done.

After the Mitchell interview, all hell broke loose. Clapper offered to resign.[96] Misperceptions spread. Americans thought NSA's metadata program was eavesdropping on their phone calls with relatives and tracking their every move when it wasn't. NSA leaders tried to explain, but few believed them. In a national poll I conducted in October 2013, I found that more than half of Americans thought the NSA was lying about the metadata program, 30 percent weren't sure, and only 17 percent thought NSA was telling the truth.[97]

Had agency leaders leaned more toward openness earlier, the NSA might have avoided the distrust spiral. Michael Hayden, who came up with the Stellarwind programs when he was NSA director, later wrote that "we mishandled congressional notification—not constitutionally, but politically. We kept the circle small for noble reasons: to keep the secrets. But politically it was a mistake and strategically it led to a loss of political, and more important, popular support for what we were doing."[98] Another former senior intelligence official agreed that it was a major missed opportunity. "There would have been no outrage of 'Wow! What's NSA doing?!' if we had brought Congress into the tent," he told me. "We could have gotten anything we wanted after 9/11. We didn't have to do it in that semi-clandestine way."[99]

Electoral Incentives

Executive branch secrecy is a large part of the oversight story, but it's not the only part. Congress also ties its own hands—because voters reward them for it.

Let me explain. All of us respond to incentives. We pay more attention to some things than others depending on the rewards. If I told my

Stanford students they'd all receive A's in my course no matter how well they did on the final exam, chances are few would study very hard before taking it.

For legislators, the mother of all incentives is re-election. As Yale professor David Mayhew famously noted, electoral victory may not be a legislator's only goal, but it is always their primary one, "the goal that must be achieved over and over if other ends are to be entertained."[100] The electoral connection is a powerful motivator. It goes a long way toward explaining why legislators, regardless of party or era, typically behave in the ways they do.

Committee assignments in Congress illustrate the point. It should surprise no one that the Senate's Subcommittee on Science, Oceans, Fisheries, and Weather is filled with members from coastal states while the Senate Agriculture Committee has an abundance of members from places like Kansas, Iowa, and Nebraska. Because legislators prefer winning re-election to losing, they seek committee assignments that can best deliver benefits to voters back home.

The political calculations that drive oversight activities are less obvious but no different. Legislators engage in greater oversight the more they are rewarded for it by constituents and organized interest groups and the less costly those activities are—in terms of time demanded, activities forgone, and expertise required. Understanding oversight dynamics starts by getting inside a legislator's cost-benefit mindset, asking whether the political advantages of any particular action are worth the political costs.

It doesn't take much to see that intelligence oversight is an electoral loser. Voters don't care about it; even foreign policy writ large has never been the most important issue in a presidential election.[101] The intelligence committees cannot send jobs or benefits to the folks back home like most other committees can. Members cannot even talk about what they do because it's classified. As one staffer told me, "Legislators can't go home and hold intelligence awareness fundraisers in the district."[102]

Geography also hurts. Because intelligence is a national issue and not a regional one, citizens and groups who do care deeply are dispersed rather than concentrated in a handful of districts. Why do farmers receive huge subsidies each year despite being a tiny share of the U.S. population? Because they are geographically concentrated in farm states whose representatives work hard to get them.[103]

There is no farm-state equivalent for intelligence, no geographic center of industry or interests that encourages legislators to focus on intelligence oversight to win voter support. As Michael Hayden told me, "No member ever gets a bridge built or a road paved by serving on the intelligence committee. It's an act of patriotism."[104]

Savvy legislators know their time is better spent elsewhere. To be sure, some self-interested legislators harboring presidential ambitions serve on the committees to burnish their national security credentials. But even for them, the greatest benefits come from *joining* the committees, not actually working hard in them.

A few patriotic members do expend considerable effort on intelligence oversight, but they're rare. Most don't—because it's a thankless assignment. Good work remains silent, and public scandals can be politically costly. When intelligence controversies make the news, members often distance themselves by criticizing the very intelligence programs they may have privately supported and by summoning intelligence officials to hearings on Capitol Hill. For intelligence officials, this throw-them-under-the-bus dynamic can be infuriating.[105] As former CIA officer Cofer Black put it, "Over a 28-year career at CIA, I was never invited to testify before a congressional committee regarding a 'success.'"[106]

The electoral incentive problem is no secret. Legislators complain about each other almost as much as they complain about the executive branch. One member of a congressional intelligence committee called oversight "horrible" and gave Congress failing grades for being "an independent branch of government."[107] Another lamented, "There are a lot of Members, unfortunately, who just don't make that commitment" to do the work.[108] An intelligence committee staff member told me that in his experience, less than half of all committee members came into the secure office to read the classified committee materials.[109]

On one 2006 Sunday talk show, Senate Intelligence Committee chairman Pat Roberts (R-KS) shook a pill bottle and said he was going to prescribe "memory pills" for his colleagues who had never objected to a controversial NSA program in classified briefings but did when the program became public.[110]

In 2007, intelligence oversight was so bad, the Senate Select Committee on Intelligence held a hearing about itself. The committee asked me to testify. It's a bizarre experience, criticizing Congress to members of Congress. I tried to be tactful.

Former Congressman Lee Hamilton (D-IN) testified, too. I can still picture it. Hamilton was deeply respected across the aisle, having chaired the House Intelligence Committee from 1985 to 1987 and more recently serving as vice chairman of the 9/11 Commission. At the time, the commission had a huge media following. Its public hearings were riveting and nationally televised. Its 2004 final report became one of the bestselling government reports of all time and was even a finalist for the National Book Award.[111] During the fall 2004 presidential election, the commission and the 9/11 families received more national television news coverage than the war in Iraq.[112] The commission leveled some of its most blistering criticism at Congress.

Hamilton was blunt that day, too. Wagging his finger at the committee, he warned, "To me, the strong point is simply that the Senate of the United States and the House of the United States is [sic] not doing its job. And because you're not doing the job, the country is not as safe as it ought to be."[113] Around the room, Senators nodded in vigorous agreement.

And still, nothing changed.

Institutions

In addition to asymmetric information and electoral incentives, institutional features of Congress make oversight harder in intelligence than in other policy areas. In some ways, Congress is perfectly designed for poor intelligence oversight—with rules that prevent the development of expertise, committee jurisdictions that weaken Congress's budgetary power of the purse, and features that exacerbate partisanship in the House.

THE EXPERTISE PROBLEM

Congress has many more powdered milk experts than intelligence experts. Of the 535 members serving in the 116th Congress, only eighteen ever worked in an intelligence agency, but dozens of representatives came from dairy districts in New York, Wisconsin, Vermont, Texas, and elsewhere. That's better than it used to be. In 2009, only two members of Congress had prior intelligence careers.[114] The same year, the Congressional Dairy Farmers Caucus was founded with more than fifty members.[115]

As our earlier discussion suggests, expertise is essential for good oversight. The more a committee knows about an agency's domain, the more it can tackle information asymmetry by asking better questions and demanding better answers.

In most policy areas like dairy farming, expertise is homegrown. To get elected, legislators have to learn about the industries important to their districts. But not intelligence. Because of electoral incentives, few legislators walk in the door intelligence experts. They have to learn on the job. And yet, congressional rules prevent that, too.

From 1976 to 2005, Senate rules limited service on the intelligence committee to just eight years.[116] House rules still impose term limits for the intelligence committee[117] but almost no other committees.[118] The result: Just when legislators become experts, they are forced to stop overseeing the Intelligence Community.

Sounds crazy, I know. What's going on?

Many argue that term limits were originally designed to improve oversight by keeping legislators from getting too cozy with the spy agencies they were supposed to oversee. But by that rationale, all oversight committees should have term limits to foster greater independence from the executive branch.

A more likely explanation is that term limits help party leaders cajole legislators into doing the job. Most members do not consider the intelligence committees attractive assignments.[119] It's a duty, not a perk—sucking up time and delivering little in return. Term limits help solve the problem by enabling legislators to roll onto more attractive committees

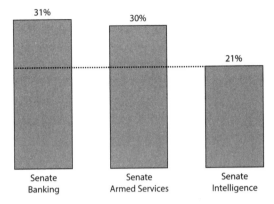

FIGURE 8.1 Longtermers* on Senate Committees, 1975–2020
Source: Official Congressional Directory, 94th–116th Congress
(Washington, D.C.: GPO).
Longtermers are defined as members serving on the committee
for five congressional sessions (ten years) or longer.

that offer greater constituent benefits after a few years of intelligence
service.

Not surprisingly, term limits have created expertise gaps between the
intelligence committees and Congress's other oversight committees.
Figure 8.1 shows the proportion of *longtermers*—defined as legislators
serving for five congressional sessions (ten years) or more—on the Senate Armed Services, Banking, and Intelligence Committees from 1975
to 2020. Longtermers constituted 31 percent of the banking committee
and 30 percent of the armed services committee but just 21 percent of
the intelligence committee.

As figure 8.2 illustrates, the experience gap is even more pronounced
in the House. The House Banking Committee had twice as many longtermers as the intelligence committee from 1975 to 2020. The armed
services committee had three times more.[120]

Fewer longtermers means more rookies. In the 103rd Congress
(1993–1995), one of the highest turnover periods, 11 of 19 House Intelligence Committee members and 7 of 17 Senate Intelligence Committee
members were serving for the first time.[121]

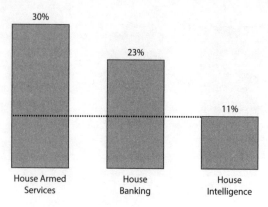

FIGURE 8.2 Longtermers on House Committees, 1975–2020
Source: Official Congressional Directory, 94th–116th Congress
(Washington, D.C.: GPO).

Although committee tenures have improved since the 1990s, the House Intelligence Committee still has a high proportion of newcomers. In the 114th Congress (2015–2017), for example, just as Congress was reforming NSA's telephone metadata program[122] and dealing with reports of Russia's interference in the 2016 presidential election,[123] 40 percent of House Intelligence Committee members were brand-new to the committee and just learning what the acronyms of all the intelligence agencies meant.

"Term limits are stupid," noted Michael Hayden. "I don't know why they still have them, but they are hanging themselves."[124]

BUDGET POWER

Budgetary authority is Congress's most powerful oversight weapon. As former House Intelligence Committee chairman Lee Hamilton noted, "All of us have to live by the golden rule, and the golden rule is that he who controls the gold makes the rules."[125] But the intelligence committees don't control intelligence agency budgets. The House and Senate Appropriations Committees do.

In most policy areas, this arrangement makes sense. In intelligence, it doesn't.

To understand why, we need a little background. Congress has two basic types of committees: authorizing committees, which examine agency activities, and appropriations committees, which fund them. Theoretically, this division of responsibilities ensures that authorizing committees develop policy expertise and examine policy issues in depth, while appropriations committees develop fiscal expertise and guard against excessive spending.

But this bifurcated system also means that an authorizing committee's power only goes so far. Authorizers can threaten to cut budgets, but appropriators must deliver on that threat. Wielding the power of the purse requires coordination across committees.

This is much easier to do in policy areas other than intelligence, for two reasons. First, secrecy rules make it hard for one committee to know what another is doing. Second, because intelligence is a small part of the behemoth $700 billion annual defense bill, intelligence committee members cannot object to a spending item without holding the entire defense budget hostage.

This budget system is ripe for gaming. Intelligence officials know they can easily bypass the intelligence committees and appeal to appropriators if there are funding decisions they don't like. It's the two-parent approach: if one says no, go to the other.

For years, Senate Intelligence Committee members voted to terminate several intelligence programs on a bipartisan basis, but appropriators kept putting them back in.[126] Senator John McCain grew so incensed by this pattern that in 2004 he took to the Senate floor and exhorted his colleagues to approve a resolution granting the intelligence committee appropriations power. "If we are going to have a truly effective Intelligence Committee oversight that can function with strength and power, we are going to have to give them appropriations authority," he said. "The appropriations process is what drives not only the money but also the policy."[127]

McCain's bill failed. Other reform efforts have, too. Today, the intelligence committees still don't have appropriations powers. Why? Because few things are as sacrosanct in Congress as turf, and few legislators are more powerful than appropriators. "In Congress, there are Democrats, Republicans, and Appropriators," joked one congressional staffer.[128]

So long as the intelligence committees cannot credibly threaten budgetary punishment, intelligence agencies will be less inclined to respond to their demands.

PARTISANSHIP IN THE HOUSE

So far, we've talked about Congress as a whole. There are important differences that make oversight more susceptible to partisanship in the House than in the Senate.

With a few notable exceptions, it's almost always been this way. In the 1970s, the Senate's Church Committee succeeded while its House counterpart collapsed under its own partisan weight. Half a century later, investigations into Russia's interference in the 2016 presidential election followed the same pattern: the Senate Intelligence Committee conducted a serious, bipartisan study while the House Intelligence Committee investigation became mired in partisan rancor.[129]

Here, too, institutional factors explain a lot. The House has shorter terms, four times more members, and different intelligence committee rules—all of which make the House naturally more unruly and more partisan than the Senate.

Jane Harman (D-CA), who served as the ranking member of the House Intelligence Committee, called the House a "perpetual election machine" where members are "out there all the time running for reelection."[130] Being in constant campaign mode amplifies the rancor. Size does, too. As one former House staffer told me, "The whole body is different." In the House, it's "majority rules. . . . You can shove anything down people's throats."[131]

The Senate is a different world. In the Senate, you have to compromise and build relationships across the aisle; the incentives for bipartisanship are greater. Senators know they have to work together to get anything done, and the Senate's slower campaign tempo enables them to do it. "You become friends," said Senator Saxby Chambliss (R-GA).[132] When Senator Bernie Sanders (I-VT) was asked who his favorite Republican was, his answer was surprising: conservative Oklahoma Senator Jim Inhofe. "Jim is a climate change denier. He is really, really conservative, but you know what, he is a decent guy and I like him," said Sanders, who joked that revealing their friendship might ruin Inhofe's career.[133]

Committee rules both reflect and reinforce these differences. Membership is just one example. In the Senate Intelligence Committee, the majority party always has just one more member than the minority. Even if there were eighty Democrats and twenty Republicans, the intelligence committee would still be split 8-7. This one-vote margin encourages members to work across party lines. House membership, by contrast, is more proportional, with the majority party getting a significantly greater number of committee seats. Of the committee's twenty-two members in 2020, thirteen were Democrats, nine were Republicans.[134] The House's membership rules make it easier for the majority to pass measures and conduct business along party lines.

In short, Congress isn't just at the mercy of the executive branch. It has tied its own oversight hands through rules that limit the development of expertise, turf protection that weakens the power of the purse, and features that reinforce partisanship in the House.

Old Weaknesses, New Tech

The problems of information, incentives, and institutions are coming to a head as technology advances at a breakneck pace. Information about intelligence is hard enough. Now, intelligence oversight committees also need to know more about emerging technologies transforming the intelligence landscape. A tough oversight problem is getting tougher.

In 2013, when I became co-director of Stanford's international security center, I went to Capitol Hill and asked, "How can our scholars work with you to improve policy?" The answer I kept hearing was, "Help Congress understand technology better." So my colleague Herb Lin and I started running cyber boot camps for congressional staff from all of the relevant oversight committees in the House and Senate. The staffers were smart, dedicated, nonpartisan—and really worried. Technology was fast outpacing policy, they told us. The divide between Washington and Silicon Valley was a national security risk. Technologists didn't understand the policy world and policymakers were struggling to understand technology.

Intelligence has always been a technical enterprise, with spy satellites, codebreaking, and engineering analysis of enemy weapons systems. Today's technological demands, though, are even greater because there are more breakthrough technologies. They're spreading faster and further. They're inherently hard to understand. They're driven by commercial companies seeking global markets, not governments seeking national security. And they are changing societies in ways that are difficult to imagine and impossible to contain.

Encryption is a good example. For a long time, encryption wasn't part of everyday life. In 2001, smart phones and social media didn't even exist. Now encryption is used to protect information in everything from classified networks to Internet protocols to cell phones and popular messaging apps like Signal and WhatsApp. Encryption algorithms and related security features are constantly improving.

Keeping current on this technical landscape is crucial for intelligence because encryption is a double-edged sword, protecting information for both the good guys and the bad.[135] Finding encryption weaknesses and other coding flaws before others do is vital to national security. So is deciding when to use these vulnerabilities for intelligence gathering or disclose them to the vendor to fix.[136]

NSA's work in this area is highly classified, but public accounts provide a glimpse at just how fast the technical terrain is shifting. In the 2000s, as encryption tools were spreading on the Internet, the agency spent billions on supercomputers and other measures to crack them. After Edward Snowden illegally revealed these highly classified programs in 2013, Apple, Google, Yahoo, and other companies raced to develop "strong crypto."[137] Companies saw both commercial and privacy benefits to better encryption.[138] New iPhones and Android devices suddenly had default encryption linked to passwords. Yahoo encrypted messages in Yahoo mail. Instant messaging apps like WhatsApp and Signal began using end-to-end encryption.[139]

By 2015, when Syed Rizwan Farook and his wife shot and killed fourteen people in San Bernardino, the FBI couldn't get into his phone. It was an iPhone 5C locked with a passcode that would delete all locally stored data after ten unsuccessful attempts to unlock it.[140] The FBI demanded that Apple write new software to undermine its own security features and unlock Farook's phone. Apple refused, a legal and media fight erupted, and according to press reports, the FBI eventually hired an Israeli forensics firm to successfully hack the phone.[141]

Encryption has continued to be a furious cat-and-mouse game, with companies developing new software to make products harder to crack and global intelligence services, forensics firms, and hackers hunting for new security flaws to exploit.[142] And that's just the beginning. Experts fear that within a decade, advances in quantum computing could make even today's most advanced encryption breakable. China is investing heavily to get there first, and Google, Microsoft, and IBM all have major quantum computing initiatives underway.[143]

There are plenty of other technological challenges for intelligence. As chapter 5 noted, artificial intelligence offers enormous opportunities, but it, too, requires technical know-how to understand the promise and pitfalls. And it, too, is developing at lightning speed. In 2014, the notion that AI could create fake images so real that you couldn't tell the difference was inconceivable. Now it's unavoidable. The code is open, available, and so simple, even a high schooler with no background in computer science can make deepfakes. And we haven't even talked about information warfare or synthetic biology.

The point is, good intelligence oversight requires much more technical knowledge than it used to—and Congress doesn't have it. In 2020, Congress had 210 lawyers but just 32 engineers.[144] There were only three engineers in the entire U.S. Senate.[145]

When Facebook CEO Mark Zuckerberg testified before a joint hearing of the Senate's Commerce and Judiciary Committees in April 2018 to discuss privacy issues and Russian disinformation, it was a jaw-dropping moment revealing just how little senators knew about the products and companies that are transforming global politics, commerce, and civil society.[146]

Senator Lindsey Graham (R-SC) asked whether Twitter was the same thing as Facebook. Senator Orrin Hatch (R-UT) asked Zuckerberg,

"How do you sustain a business model in which users don't pay for your service?" A dismayed Zuckerberg replied, "Senator, we run ads," grinning awkwardly. Even Senator Brian Schatz (D-HI), considered one of Congress's technology gurus, seemed not to know the difference between social media, email, and encrypted text messaging.

As former Secretary of Defense Ash Carter wrote, "All I can say is that I wish members had been as poorly prepared to question me on war and peace in the scores of testimonies I gave as they were when asking Facebook about the public duties of tech companies."[147]

The Senate Intelligence Committee has greater expertise than that; chairman Mark Warner (D-VA) led a successful tech company earlier in his career. But even here, only one other member has a technical background. They face a daunting task.

Remember how hard it is to get members to read classified materials? Now imagine they have to understand new technologies being developed in the private sector, too. And nobody rewards them for it. In short, information is getting harder to understand, congressional oversight incentives are not improving, and congressional institutions remain poorly equipped to oversee today's intelligence challenges.

While intelligence officials and legislators often do not see eye to eye on much, they do agree on one thing: congressional intelligence oversight needs help. Oversight has rarely worked well because the sources of dysfunction run deep—in information, incentives, and institutions.

It is always easier for spy agencies to hide than for Congress to seek. Electoral incentives are powerful things, affecting how legislators behave and the rules they create. Most members don't do the unheralded work of intelligence oversight precisely because it's unheralded: voters don't care and interest groups don't reward it. Congressional committees and procedures help members win re-election but reduce expertise, budgetary leverage, and, in the House, bipartisanship. In short, both old weaknesses and new technologies are combining to make oversight harder than ever.

9

INTELLIGENCE ISN'T JUST FOR GOVERNMENTS ANYMORE

NUCLEAR SLEUTHING IN A GOOGLE EARTH WORLD

The more classified something becomes, the less analysis you'll get.

—SIEGFRIED HECKER, FORMER DIRECTOR, LOS ALAMOS NATIONAL LABORATORY[1]

THE FIRE LOOKED suspicious. The flames were so bright, a weather satellite detected them from space around 2:00 A.M. on July 2, 2020. Iran's Atomic Energy Organization initially downplayed the news, calling the fire an "incident" involving an "industrial shed" under construction. The nuclear agency released a photograph of the damaged building, and Iranian state TV released a short video clip.[2]

David Albright got to work. A physicist who founded a nuclear nonproliferation nonprofit called the Institute for Science and International Security, Albright believed that scientists should play an active role in solving international security problems. His team had been closely tracking construction of the suspicious "shed" for years by analyzing commercial satellite imagery and Iranian official statements and photographs.[3]

Meanwhile, in California, a young researcher at the Center for Nonproliferation Studies named Fabian Hinz was tracking the fire, too.

Using images released by the Iranian government, commercial satellite imagery, and Google Earth, they geo-located the scorched building. On the basis of their nuclear and country expertise, each reached the same conclusion: the Iranians were lying. The shed was actually a nuclear centrifuge assembly building at Natanz, Iran's main uranium enrichment facility.[4] And the fire might have been an act of sabotage.[5]

Natanz was well known to United Nations weapons inspectors and American intelligence officials. Located about 125 miles south of Tehran, its vast underground facilities housed thousands of nuclear centrifuges, the advanced machines used to enrich uranium for both nuclear energy and nuclear weapons.[6] For years, the International Atomic Energy Agency (IAEA) had been locked in cat-and-mouse inspections there[7] to collect evidence about violations of the Nuclear Non-Proliferation Treaty[8] and to monitor Iran's compliance with the 2015 nuclear deal, which allowed only limited uranium enrichment for peaceful purposes.[9]

Natanz was also the site of the most sophisticated cyberattack ever conducted. Code-named "Olympic Games," the joint U.S.-Israeli cyber operation destroyed approximately one thousand[10] nuclear centrifuges by secretly injecting malware into their operating computers.[11] Experts believed "Olympic Games" slowed Iran's march to the bomb by a year or more.[12]

But Albright and Hinz weren't employees of the IAEA or the U.S. Intelligence Community. Armed only with open-source information and home computers, they were analyzing and shaping an unfolding international crisis. Within hours of the blaze, both were on Twitter and giving media interviews.[13] By 8:00 A.M., ABC News was running their analysis.[14] By mid-afternoon, the *New York Times* was, too.[15] By nightfall, Israeli Prime Minister Benjamin Netanyahu was asked whether Israeli sabotage was responsible. "I don't address these issues," he curtly replied.[16]

This is the new world of nuclear sleuthing.

Tracking nuclear threats used to be the province of secret agents and analysts at high-powered government intelligence agencies. Governments enjoyed a near-monopoly over collecting and analyzing threat information. Now, open-source information and connective technologies are enabling independent researchers and individual citizens to do it, too. This community is an eclectic mix straight out of the *Star Wars* bar scene—with hobbyists, journalists, activists, professors, students, profiteers, volunteers, former government officials, and more. Nearly all harbor an obsessive interest in nuclear secrets and finding creative ways to unlock them.

This chapter takes a deeper dive into this emerging world, examining how American intelligence agencies have estimated nuclear threats in the past, what factors are changing the game, and the benefits and risks of this non-governmental intelligence ecosystem.

Why focus on nuclear threats? Two reasons. First, no set of dangers is so often overlooked by the public but so important to intelligence officials and policymakers. To many, especially those who grew up after 9/11, nuclear weapons seem like Cold War relics.

But ask American foreign policy leaders what keeps them up at night, and you're sure to hear something from the nuclear list of horrors: proliferation to countries like Iran, North Korea, and Syria; the risk of conflict between India and Pakistan, two nuclear-armed neighbors; a Middle East war against nuclear-armed Israel; America's eroding nuclear deterrence in Europe and Asia; alarming nuclear modernization by Russia and China; nuclear terrorism; nuclear accidents; and the risk of miscalculation and accidental nuclear war by the United States and others.

Humans face three foreign policy challenges that are truly existential: global pandemics, climate change, and nuclear annihilation. Only the first two are top of mind for most people these days.

Second, nuclear threat intelligence constitutes a tough test for my argument that emerging technologies and open-source information are fundamentally challenging U.S. intelligence. Tough tests are analytically compelling. The idea is that if something seems true in the most unlikely conditions, then it's probably true in the likely conditions. Frank Sinatra's hit song "New York, New York" captures tough test reasoning beautifully: if you can make it here, you can make it anywhere.

Nuclear intelligence is a tough test because it is an area where we'd most expect secrets to matter and spy agencies to dominate. Estimating nuclear dangers has always been one of the most important intelligence missions, from Germany's race to develop an atomic bomb in World War II to North Korea's recent nuclear provocations.

It's also an area where clandestine tools really matter. Nuclear proliferators go to great lengths to hide their activities. Secret capabilities—from satellites in space to spies on the ground—are all the more important for discovering them. Yet, even here, I find that intelligence agencies are losing their advantage. David Albright and Fabian Hinz have company. More people in more countries are accessing open-source information and emerging technologies to track illicit nuclear activities. Intelligence isn't just for superpower governments anymore.

Hard Targets: Estimating Nuclear Dangers

Nuclear intelligence falls into four broad categories:

(1) Understanding the capabilities of known nuclear states like Russia, China, and North Korea;

(2) Understanding the spread of nuclear materials or know-how to non-nuclear states like Syria or terrorist groups;

(3) Understanding nuclear accident risks (such as the 1986 Chernobyl disaster); and

(4) Preventing strategic surprises like the 1962 Cuban missile crisis or the 1998 Indian nuclear test, which caught U.S. intelligence officials so off guard, they learned about it from an Indian press release.[17]

How well have U.S. intelligence agencies done? It's hard to say. Nuclear activities are especially challenging because countries work so hard to conceal them. During the Cold War, the Soviet Union built three plutonium production reactors underground, inside a mountain.[18] Khrushchev's secret operation to deploy nuclear missiles to Cuba in 1962 employed a deception operation so elaborate, planning documents were hand-carried to a tight inner circle and even ship captains carrying the missiles were not told their final destination until they reached the middle of the Atlantic Ocean. Saddam Hussein hid some of his facilities in a large date palm grove and buried telltale power line connections underground to obscure them from overhead reconnaissance.[19]

Assessing the record is also difficult because intelligence failures are public and well known, but successes are often silent or obscured by events. Everyone remembers the U.S. Intelligence Community's flawed Iraq WMD assessments. But almost nobody remembers how U.S. intelligence succeeded in getting Libya to relinquish its nuclear, chemical, and missile programs around the same time. "Intelligence was the key that opened the door to Libya's clandestine programs," noted CIA Director George Tenet in February 2004.[20]

He was right. In the fall of 2003, the CIA discovered that Pakistani scientist A. Q. Khan was planning to illegally ship uranium centrifuge parts to Libya as part of his worldwide nuclear smuggling operation. U.S. officials had the ship interdicted and, together with British intelligence, confronted Gaddafi with the evidence. American intelligence officials went on to play a major role in assessing whether Gaddafi's expressed desires to give up his WMD programs and rejoin the family of nations were sincere. By December 2003, they successfully engineered Gaddafi's abandonment of his nuclear ambitions and rollback of his missile program.

It was a success indeed, although eight years after Gaddafi came clean, the United States and its NATO allies became embroiled in Libya's civil war. Gaddafi was killed, order within the country unraveled, and the Libyan nuclear success story faded in the face of subsequent policy failures.[21]

Sometimes, even intelligence improvements look like failures. When a 2007 intelligence estimate[22] reversed earlier findings[23] and concluded Iran might not be marching toward the bomb as fast and furiously as analysts previously believed, criticism came from many directions. Some accused the Intelligence Community of sabotaging the administration as it sought a harder line, including international sanctions, against Iran.[24] President George W. Bush called the language "eye-popping."[25] Others questioned why the intelligence wasn't known earlier. Some wondered if the new judgments were compensation for the mistaken WMD assessment in Iraq. Almost nobody considered the possibility that the analysis changed because intelligence agencies got their hands on new and better information.[26]

In short, estimating nuclear threats is hard. Assessing the intelligence track record is, too.[27] Humility is in order.

The Scorecard: What Academic Analyses Find

Most studies of nuclear threat intelligence look at individual cases in isolation, examining what intelligence agencies got right or wrong about Country X or Event Y. The 1962 Cuban missile crisis is the granddaddy of them all. It is the most studied event of the nuclear age. Academics have written so much about that eyeball-to-eyeball moment, there's even an article about why we should stop writing articles about it.[28]

More recently, however, studies have started to look across cases and history. This research finds two important things. The first is that the Intelligence Community's track record is mixed. Using declassified archives and other sources, two leading scholars examined seventeen cases over sixty years in which countries tried to acquire nuclear weapons.[29] In three cases, U.S. intelligence agencies correctly identified what was happening and when. Intelligence officials underestimated foreign nuclear programs in five cases and overestimated in nine.[30]

This is a useful overview, but it has problems. The biggest is the study's demand for pinpoint accuracy—a standard that is often unhelpful and probably misleading in the real world. For example, the study labels a 1959 assessment of France's nuclear test an "overestimation" because the actual test came three months later than expected.[31] China's 1964 test was labeled an intelligence "underestimation" because the detonation came ten weeks earlier than anticipated, according to declassified documents from the time.[32]

These timing differences may not indicate intelligence failures at all. Sometimes other factors unknown even to foreign leaders themselves can change the timing of events. In World War II, for example, Eisenhower decided the allies would land at Normandy on June 5, 1944. Bad weather ended up delaying the invasion twenty-four hours. Had German intelligence analysts estimated that D-Day would be June 5, they would have been wrong, but not really. Intelligence estimates can look erroneous in hindsight even though they were correct at the time.

The second, and more interesting, finding is that intelligence agencies are prone to overcorrection: underestimation of one nuclear threat can lead to overestimation of the next. One study found that *overestimating* Iraq's nuclear weapons program in 2003 led American intelligence officials to approach Syria's suspected nuclear program with skepticism a few years later. Israeli intelligence, on the other hand, took the opposite approach, viewing intelligence about Syria with greater alarm. Why? Because the Israelis had been burned for *underestimating* Libya's nuclear program just a few years earlier. Each was overcorrecting for past analytic mistakes. In the Syria case, Israel's more "urgent judgment" lens paid off—leading to the discovery that Syria was secretly building a nuclear reactor after all.[33]

In short, research is moving toward a better understanding of how well American intelligence agencies have estimated nuclear dangers over time, and why.

The problem is that these retrospective studies are better suited to understanding the past than the future. Although intelligence agencies are still critical players in the nuclear threat assessment landscape, they are no longer the only critical players. Technological advances are democratizing the collection and analysis of intelligence, with potential far-reaching implications for American intelligence and the future assessment of nuclear dangers.

The Democratization of Intelligence

Three trends have democratized nuclear threat intelligence collection and analysis: rising commercial satellite quantities and capabilities; the explosion of connectivity and other open-source information on the Internet; and advances in automated analytics like machine learning.[34]

Low-Cost Eyes in the Sky

Governments of major powers used to corner the market in nuclear-related intelligence. In the early Cold War, the United States flew U-2 photoreconnaissance airplanes over the Soviet Union to try to ascertain how many nuclear missiles and bombers the Soviets had and where they were deployed. In 1960, America's CORONA satellite program ushered in the era of remote sensing from space. CORONA was essentially a large camera sent into orbit that photographed areas over the earth's surface and returned film in a parachuting capsule that had to be captured in midair over the Pacific Ocean to be developed. The first thirteen missions failed, but the fourteenth struck gold. CORONA's first success provided more coverage of the Soviet Union in a single mission than all previous U-2 flights combined.[35] Albert Wheelon, the CIA's first deputy director of science and technology, remarked that "it was as if an enormous floodlight had been turned on in a darkened warehouse."[36]

Satellite imagery quickly became the cornerstone of nuclear arms control verification, compensating for the lack of reliable on-the-ground intelligence inside the Soviet Union.[37] The Soviets soon followed, developing a CORONA counterpart named Zenit-2, which returned its first usable photographs (after several failed attempts) in 1962.[38] While imagery resolution improved and the first commercial satellite made imagery publicly available in 1972,[39] the U.S. and Soviet Union continued to dominate the space market, each operating a small number of large spy satellites that were the size of a bus, cost billions apiece to design and launch, used highly advanced technology, and produced classified information.[40]

In the early 2000s, technological advances and commercialization opportunities converged, giving rise to a dramatic increase in the capabilities, quality, and number of small satellites operated by private firms.

The first CORONA satellite had a resolution of twelve meters, which meant that the image could not distinguish between two adjacent objects on the ground unless they were at least twelve meters (or thirty-nine feet) apart. In the 1990s, the first commercial satellites offered sub-ten-meter electro-optical imagery. In 2000, one commercial satellite had sub-two-meter resolution. By 2019, there were twenty-five commercial satellites offering sub-two-meter resolutions. Most of them (19 of the 25) offered resolutions under one meter, and starting in 2014 with the WorldView-3 satellite, the sharpest commercial imagery available was thirty-one centimeters (or about one foot). According to Frank Pabian, one of the world's leading imagery analysts, thirty-one-centimeter resolution constitutes a 900 percent improvement over what was available just fifteen years earlier. With resolutions that sharp, an analyst can detect manhole covers, utility lines, building vents, and even different car models driving on a road—from space.[41]

Other improvements in satellite capabilities include video, which can facilitate observation of dynamic activities like vehicle movement, construction, and nuclear facility cooling plumes, and Synthetic Aperture Radar (SAR), which enables imaging even in cloudy weather, through dense vegetation, and at night.[42] SAR can also detect otherwise imperceptible micro changes of the earth's surface over time, enabling better detection of hidden nuclear activities such as underground tunnel construction.[43]

Satellites are not just getting better; they are getting more plentiful. According to then Director of National Intelligence Daniel Coats, the number of satellite launches more than doubled between 2016 and 2018.[44] In 2018 alone, 322 small satellites about the size of a shoebox were hurled into space. The Paris-based firm Euroconsult estimates that more than eight thousand small satellites will be launched between 2019 and 2028.[45] Although most of these small satellites are used for weather and communications, the number of imagery satellites is growing, too.[46]

For nuclear-related intelligence, increasing satellite quantity has a quality all its own. The more commercial satellites there are, the shorter the time lag between images captured of the same location. That allows for more finely tuned before-and-after comparisons of suspect facilities or geographic areas, potentially capturing on-the-ground activity that would not otherwise be observable.[47] Some companies are already moving into the high-revisit rate market, offering constellations of satellites that offer lower quality resolutions but higher frequency imaging. San Francisco startup Planet, which was founded by former NASA employees in 2010, has more than 150 satellites in orbit and offers imaging of any target up to two times a day, at three-meter and seventy-two-centimeter resolution.[48] Seattle-based startup BlackSky has four imagery satellites in orbit and plans to eventually build a sixty-satellite constellation capable of revisiting the same city every ten to fifteen minutes with sub-one-meter resolution.[49]

Perhaps the most revolutionary change in satellite imagery is that just about anyone can use it. The costs of acquiring satellite images have plummeted, from nearly $4,000 per frame to as little as $10.[50] Some high-resolution imagery is free: anyone with an Internet connection can access Google Earth, which has satellite and airplane overhead imagery with resolutions ranging from fifteen meters to less than half a centimeter. Google Earth also offers applications to conduct analysis, including 3D building modeling of facilities in its Earth maps and historical satellite image comparisons dating back thirty-five years.

In short, commercial satellites now offer low-cost eyes in the sky for anyone who wants them.

Connectivity: More Information
Available to More People

The second major trend democratizing nuclear threat intelligence is the Internet, which has powered an explosion in open-source information and the connectivity to make it widely available and sharable. In 2000, approximately 15 percent of the world's population was connected to the Internet.[51] Today, more than half the world is online, and more people are estimated to have mobile phones than access to running water.[52] Connectivity is turning everyday citizens into intelligence collectors, whether they know it or not. There's also metadata—such as the time, location, and equipment used to take a photograph posted online—downloadable 3D modeling applications, and community data sharing sites like OpenStreetMap, which allows users to post their GPS coordinates from their phones. All of these capabilities offer new clues and tools for nuclear sleuths.

As discussed more below, the online information ecosystem is making possible exciting new opportunities for societal verification or open crowdsourcing to assess nuclear threat information. But it is also making deception easier. In the new online ecosystem, information anywhere can go viral, regardless of its quality or credibility.

Automated Analytics: Machine Learning, Computer Modeling, and More

Large increases in computing power and training data over the past decade have spawned the creation of publicly available machine learning techniques that can analyze massive quantities of data at machine speed. Once algorithms are trained on a dataset to look for certain patterns, they can process thousands of images faster than humans by orders of magnitude.

For nuclear threat intelligence, machine learning techniques offer particular promise in analyzing satellite imagery of known missile sites or facilities to detect changes over time.[53] In 2017, for example, U.S. intelligence officials from the National Geospatial-Intelligence Agency (NGA) asked researchers at the University of Missouri to develop machine learning tools to see how fast and accurately they could identify surface-to-air missile sites over a huge area in Southwest China. The research team developed a deep learning neural network (essentially, a collection of algorithms working together) and used only commercially available satellite imagery with one-meter resolution.

Both the computer and the human team correctly identified 90 percent of the missile sites. But the computer completed the job eighty times faster than humans, taking just forty-two minutes to scan an area of approximately ninety thousand square kilometers (about three-fourths the size of North Korea).[54]

As noted in chapter 5, machine learning also holds promise for faster sifting of large quantities of written information—everything from trade documents that might suggest illicit financing schemes to the metadata of photos online—such as the date and time stamp on the picture, the type of camera used, the software that processed the image, and where the camera was placed when the picture was taken.[55]

In addition, computer modeling is enabling analysts to better understand the specifications and functions of structures already built.

Online crowdsourcing is offering promising new avenues, too. Already, thousands of citizen scientists have successfully sifted through massive quantities of data to help a Cal Tech and UC Santa Cruz team identify several new exoplanets[56] and an international team of physicists identify new gravitational lenses.[57] In 2016, Melissa Hanham at the Center for Nonproliferation Studies began a nuclear threat crowdsourcing initiative called Geo4Nonpro, which drew several hundred imagery experts together. They discovered the geolocation of North Korea's clandestine Kangson uranium enrichment facility.[58]

The New Nuclear Sleuths: Who's Who and What's Different

All of these developments have given rise to a cottage industry of nongovernmental nuclear intelligence collectors and analysts. Academic teams, like my colleagues at Stanford's Center for International Security and Cooperation, bring together researchers across disciplines and former government officials. Think tanks do, too.

Some organizations, like Janes and Maxar, provide commercial analysis for profit. There are advocacy groups, journalist organizations like Bellingcat, and even hobbyists. One of my favorites is Jacob Bogle, a coin dealer who lives in Tennessee and has a passion for developing detailed maps of North Korea using commercial imagery and making them available online.

Taken together, this nuclear sleuthing ecosystem looks very different from the classified world of intelligence agencies.[59] I summarize key differences in table 9.1.

For starters, the workforces differ dramatically. The non-governmental ecosystem is wide open to anyone with an Internet connection. It draws people with a grab-bag of backgrounds, capabilities, and incentives. Although many are former government officials, intelligence analysts, and experts from the United States and allied countries who take their responsibilities seriously, others are amateurs with little or no training. There are currently no formal open-source training programs or quality control processes.[60]

TABLE 9.1 Attributes of Non-Governmental vs. Government Ecosystems in Nuclear
Threat Analysis

	Non-Governmental	U.S. Government
Organizational objectives	Diverse: e.g., securing funding, informing public, pursuing hobby interests	Focused: informing U.S. government to provide decision advantage
Membership	Open. Anyone can join from anywhere	Closed. Strict hiring rules and security clearances
Analyst backgrounds	Broader	Narrower
Analyst formal training	None	Extensive
Product quality control	Peer review is voluntary and informal	Peer review is mandatory and formal
Quantity of technical collection assets	Large	Small*
Capability of technical collection assets	Limited but improving	Highly sophisticated
Ecosystem speed	Faster	Slower

*Collection platforms owned and operated by the U.S. government are few in number, but government agencies are increasingly purchasing commercial data.

Their motives run the gamut: informing the global public, securing non-profit grants, selling analysis for profit, advancing a political agenda, and having fun, to name a few. Members of this ecosystem can move quickly, publishing what they want, whenever they want, without bureaucratic approvals or required vetting. "I could take a random image of any land mass and say there was a 'unicorn training camp' and I promise you it would wind up in some form or another of publication," said Allison Puccioni, a former government imagery analyst who now works in the open-source community.[61]

Non-governmental actors have access only to commercial satellite sensors. These are more numerous than spy sensors but they offer lower quality and less capability.[62] That's no accident. U.S. laws currently restrict the resolutions of American commercial satellites so that government satellites still have an advantage.[63] As more foreign countries go into the commercial satellite business, however, these restrictions will confer less of an edge.

The classified world looks very different from the Wild West of the non-governmental sector. Participation requires security clearances and adherence to strict government hiring and information policies. Government analysts have access to the most sophisticated spy satellites and other collection platforms as well as commercial imagery.[64] Analysts come with a narrower set of backgrounds but a higher average skill level. They work inside bureaucracies with training programs, standards, and quality control mechanisms, but they move more slowly. While motives in the open-source world vary, in the government they don't. The mission is clear: giving U.S. policymakers decision advantage.[65]

In short, one ecosystem is more open, diffuse, diverse, and fast moving. The other is more closed, tailored, trained, and slower moving. Both offer advantages; neither is perfect.

Benefits: More Diverse Perspectives, More Hands on Deck, More Sharable Information

The non-governmental ecosystem offers three significant benefits. First, diverse backgrounds can improve analysis by bringing different perspectives to bear on problems and evidence.

Second, these groups provide more knowledgeable hands on deck, helping intelligence officials and policymakers identify false positives and fake claims, verify treaty compliance, monitor ongoing nuclear-related activities, and surface clandestine developments that might not otherwise be discovered. As MIT professor Vipin Narang noted, "Knowing the launch location for a test or one that failed used to be the monopoly of intelligence agencies."[66] That's no longer true.

Non-governmental intelligence collectors and analysts have also played a major role in correcting mistakes and debunking misinformation. In 2013, a post to *Wired* magazine by someone claiming to be an ex-CIA analyst that China may have built a "mystery complex" sparked a furor. To stop the non-story from going viral, geospatial blogger Stefan Greens posted evidence online that the complex was nothing more than an industrial park. Similar efforts revealed that a suspected gas centrifuge facility in Syria was actually a cotton textile plant, that a cylindrical foundation in Iran that could have indicated the beginnings of a nuclear reactor was actually the foundation of a hotel being built near a shopping mall, and that an Israeli television report showing a satellite image of an Iranian missile launch pad big enough to send a nuclear weapon to the United States was just a massive elevator that resembled a rocket in a blurry image.[67]

One of the most high-profile debunking successes involved international efforts to freeze Iran's nuclear program and one Iranian dissident group's effort to sandbag them. On February 24, 2015, a group calling itself the National Council for the Resistance of Iran (NCRI) tried to derail international negotiations by claiming that a company named Matiran was housing a secret nuclear facility in its Tehran office basement. NCRI's evidence included satellite imagery of the secret facility as well as photographs of its hallways and a large lead-lined door to prevent radiation leakage.

Within a week, Jeffrey Lewis's team at the Center for Nonproliferation Studies showed conclusively that all of NCRI's so-called evidence was fabricated. Lewis's team found that Matiran was a real company all right; it even had employees on LinkedIn. But Matiran had nothing to do with nuclear enrichment. It specialized in making secure documents like national identification cards. Analyzing commercial satellite imagery, Lewis's team found no unusual construction activity at the site during the alleged construction timeframe or obvious signatures of nuclear enrichment activities found at other known Iranian sites—such as ventilation systems or an electrical substation to power nuclear centrifuges.

Using 3D modeling, they showed how the photos and description of the claimed facility looked too small to fit the machines and infrastructure required. They noted that none of Iran's known enrichment facilities used lead doors because they didn't need them; radiation leakage had never been a concern. Lewis's team also found that the lead door photograph had actually been copied from a promotional photograph used on a commercial Iranian website. Metadata from the photograph suggested the actual door was from a different company's warehouse elsewhere in Iran that had nothing to do with any illicit nuclear activities.

The team used crowdsourcing and social media to find someone whose self-posted GPS coordinates from his cell phone showed he had actually been to the Maritan facility. They contacted the visitor via email and verified through social media that he really did work in the secure documents business and was who he claimed to be. They found information about his marital status, his volunteer activities and hobbies, and even obtained his photograph. The source confirmed that Maritan really did make secure documents and that many foreign contractors routinely visited its location—making it highly unlikely that Maritan would put a secret nuclear enrichment facility in the basement.[68]

Non-governmental nuclear sleuths have also uncovered important new information about clandestine nuclear activities that have aided intelligence agencies and influenced policy.[69] In 2012, Stanford's Siegfried Hecker and Frank Pabian determined the locations and supporting tunnels of North Korea's first two nuclear tests using commercial imagery and publicly available seismological information[70]—assessments that proved highly accurate when North Korea revealed the actual test locations six years later.[71]

Hecker and colleagues also utilized commercial satellite imagery and Google Sketchup, a 3D modeling program, to track the construction of a new nuclear reactor at North Korea's Yongbyon complex in 2012 and model the uranium centrifuge facility they were shown. No foreigners are known to have been allowed into the Yongbyon facilities after Hecker and his Stanford colleagues visited in November 2010. But by tracking the facility using overhead photography combined with what they learned during their visit, they concluded that the reactor was still a long way from operations and that North Korea must also have an undisclosed pilot centrifuge plant.[72]

Third and finally, these non-governmental actors offer more than just the benefits of information; they offer information that can be shared. Because they operate in the unclassified world, their findings can be publicized, alerting the general public and generating policy attention to an issue. Many already have extensive relationship networks with senior American officials, international inspectors, and journalists.

Just as important, their information can be more easily shared *across* the U.S. government, as well as with allies, international organizations, and even adversaries—without jeopardizing classified intelligence sources and methods.[73] Particularly because nuclear threats are so dangerous, intelligence about them is often highly classified. And the more classified something becomes, the less analysis it gets because so few people have access; going black runs the risk of going dark.

Indeed, evidence suggests that U.S. intelligence officials are already well aware of these challenges and benefits of sharing non-governmental unclassified intelligence. While current information sharing is informal and discretionary, in 2018, the Center for Strategic and International Studies, a Washington-based think tank, and the National Geospatial-Intelligence Agency, one of the eighteen agencies of the Intelligence Community, took a step toward more formalized arrangements, announcing a partnership to "produce unclassified reporting on issues of importance in North Korea."[74]

Risks: When Information Is Wrong, When Information Is Right

This non-governmental ecosystem also generates risks. Some arise when information is wrong. Others arise when information is right.

First and most obviously, non-governmental nuclear sleuths can inject errors in the policymaking world. While the examples above highlight the best of non-governmental nuclear intelligence, the landscape is filled with questionable data, shoddy analyses, pet theories, and political agendas. Many amateur imagery analysts are well intentioned but poorly trained. As Pabian notes, there's a common misperception that "anyone can look at pictures." In reality, imagery analysis requires considerable skill and training to know how shapes, shadows, sizes, scales, textures, perspectives, and contexts can obscure or delineate different objects seen from space, viewed from directly overhead, which is generally an unfamiliar vantage point.[75] And nuclear imagery requires understanding the nuclear fuel cycle so that the analyst knows what to look for in the first place—like signs of ventilation and air conditioning systems necessary for underground gas centrifuge facilities or large open halls required for autoclaves and other machinery.[76] The real value of satellite imagery lies in the analysis of what it means.[77] Pictures may be commoditizing, but analysis is not.

David Sandalow, who served in senior positions at the Department of Energy, Department of State, and White House warned that mistakes can be easily made and rapidly spread. "Without strong experience and training, it can be relatively easy to see proof of sinister intent in a benign image, or to miss details that would be conclusive to a knowledgeable photo interpreter."[78]

That's exactly what happened in 2011, when a former Pentagon strategist teaching at Georgetown University led his students on a Chinese nuclear missile hunt. Phillip Karber asked his students to study China's underground tunnel system known as the "underground great wall." The tunnel's existence was well known—it had even been reported on China's state-run television—but debate swirled about its purpose. To get answers, Karber's students turned to commercial imagery, blogs, military journals, even a fictional Chinese television drama about the military. They concluded the tunnels were probably being used to hide nuclear weapons—lots of them: three thousand, to be exact. It was an astronomical number, more than ten times higher than declassified intelligence estimates or international forecasts.[79]

Karber's Georgetown study produced headlines and heartburn. The *Washington Post* reported that it had "sparked a congressional hearing and been circulated among top officials in the Pentagon, including the Air Force vice chief of staff." As one Defense Department official commented, "It's not quite a bombshell, but those thoughts and estimates are being checked against what people think they know based on classified information."[80]

Experts found egregious errors. A Harvard researcher found that Karber's students based their three thousand weapons number on an American intelligence projection from the 1960s; assuming it was accurate, they just kept adding weapons at a constant rate of growth. Apparently, they did not take seriously any of the other declassified intelligence estimates forecasting that China probably had only two hundred warheads, not three thousand.[81]

The math concerning plutonium did not make sense, either. On the basis of the plutonium used in China's nuclear tests, Jeffrey Lewis, director of the East Asia Nonproliferation Project at Middlebury Institute's Center for Nonproliferation Studies, concluded that China did not have enough to produce anywhere near three thousand weapons. It turns out Karber's plutonium estimates were based on Chinese blog posts discussing a single anonymous 1995 Usenet post that was then plagiarized by a Singapore college student. The sourcing was "so wildly incompetent as to invite laugher," wrote Lewis.[82]

So why did China build the underground great wall? Most likely to protect its small, vulnerable land-based nuclear arsenal from a crippling first strike. Because China had a stated doctrine of "no first use" of nuclear weapons, survivable forces were essential for deterrence. And since China lacked reliable sea- and air-based nuclear forces, the logical solution to ensure China retained a survivable second-strike force was to move its missiles deeper underground.[83]

Karber's claims were distracting, taking precious time and resources away from real issues, but they were debunked before any serious international harm resulted. That may not always be the case. As Sandalow noted, "Satellite images have the potential, if interpreted incorrectly, to increase tensions among nations and create confusion during periods of crisis, rather than to promote stability."[84] Given how fast information and misinformation can go viral online, the price of shoddy analysis could be high.

And that's just the honest mistakes. The non-governmental intelligence ecosystem also increases the likelihood of deliberate deception. Thanks to the rise of social media and advances in artificial intelligence, spreading lies and confusing the truth have never been easier. Russia's interference in the 2016 American presidential election was the first warning sign of the coming deception revolution.[85]

Russia's deception playbook isn't just for Russia anymore. In October 2019, Facebook publicly acknowledged its discovery of foreign influence campaigns waged by Iran and China on its platform.[86] As the COVID-19 pandemic spread in 2020, China orchestrated an aggressive global social media campaign spreading false information along with it—including that the United States created COVID-19 as a bioweapon.[87]

Advances in artificial intelligence have given rise to deepfakes, digitally manipulated audio, photographs, and videos that are highly realistic and difficult to authenticate. Deepfake application tools are now widely available online and so simple to use that high school students with no coding background can create convincing forgeries. In May 2019, anonymous users doctored a video to make House Speaker Nancy Pelosi appear drunk, which went viral on Facebook. When the social media giant refused to take it down, two artists and a small tech-nology startup created a deepfake of Mark Zuckerberg and posted it on Instagram. In August, the *Wall Street Journal* reported the first known use of deepfake audio to impersonate a voice in a cyber heist. Believing he was talking to his boss, an energy executive transferred $243,000. The voice turned out to be an AI-based imitation that was so real, it even had the boss's slight German accent and lilt.

The Nuclear Bombshell That Backfired

One night in northern Iraq, a mysterious visitor appeared at the hotel room of British journalist Gwynne Roberts. The visitor called himself Leone. He arrived shivering and afraid. He said he was one of Saddam Hussein's nuclear scientists and he had proof that Saddam had secretly tested a nuclear bomb, hoodwinking the West. It was January 1998—just as tensions between United Nations weapons inspectors and the Iraqi regime were escalating.

Leone worked through the night providing Roberts with evidence. He sketched nuclear bomb designs. He described organizational details of Saddam's WMD program. He showed a photograph of a warhead allegedly bought from Russia. And he gave the exact time and location of Saddam's alleged nuclear test: September 19, 1989, at 10:30 a.m., at an underground site 150 kilometers southwest of Baghdad.

Roberts was a well-regarded journalist, and he did not just take Leone's word for it. He spent the next three years investigating the Iraqi's claims. He even went high-tech, buying commercial satellite images of the test site Leone described before and after the claimed test date and had them analyzed by Professor Bhupendra Jasani of King's College London.

Jasani's imagery analysis found all sorts of evidence confirming the test site, including the existence of a wide tunnel stretching under a lake—exactly as Leone had described. There was also a railway line with roads leading to a shaft entrance, which was a huge rectangular structure. And Jasani found evidence of an "unusually sensitive military zone," an army base with forty buildings. "If you wanted to hide something, I guess this is exactly what you would do," said Jasani.

In February 2001, Roberts' bombshell story ran in the London *Sunday Times*.[88]

All of it turned out to be wrong, even the "smoking gun" satellite imagery.[89]

Jasani was mistaken. Frank Pabian, the former nuclear chief inspector for the UN's International Atomic Energy Agency in Iraq and a leading satellite imagery expert, reviewed the same images and found absolutely no evidence the area had ever been used to conduct an underground nuclear test. Jasani had misinterpreted the satellite photos. The tunnel was actually an agricultural area served by a natural spring. The rail lines were a dual-lane paved highway. The huge rectangular structure was an irrigated field. The unusually sensitive military zone with forty buildings really had just two conventional ammunitions storage facilities with a number of typical storage bunkers nearby. And if the tunnel's dimensions were what Jasani believed them to be from the satellite imagery, excavation would have required the removal of enormous volumes of earth that would be impossible to conceal. Yet there was nothing in any imagery showing the removal, storage, or replacement of massive quantities of earth when the alleged underground testing facility was constructed and used.[90]

Pabian and Terry Wallace, then a geophysics professor and forensic seismologist and now director emeritus at Los Alamos National Laboratory, later also debunked the *Sunday Times* story using seismological evidence and sent their information to the International Atomic Energy Agency. Still, Gwynne Roberts's investigation appeared on BBC in March 2001, where it could still be found online, uncorrected, in 2021—years after additional evidence showed conclusively that Saddam tried but never succeeded in developing a nuclear bomb.[91]

Roberts's story and its undoing were an early example of the benefits and risks of non-governmental nuclear sleuths. Claims were first reported by a British journalist, reinforced by a British professor, and discredited by an American former weapons inspector with the help of an American future national nuclear lab director. All of them drew only from publicly available unclassified sources.

It does not take much to realize the manipulative potential these technologies hold for nuclear-related issues. In a world of cheap satellite imagery, deepfakes, and the weaponization of social media, foreign governments, their proxies, and third party organizations and individuals will all be able to inject convincing, false information and narratives into the public domain at speed and scale. If their goal is to confuse rather than convince, a little deception can go a long way. Imagine a deepfake video depicting a foreign leader secretly discussing a clandestine nuclear program with his inner circle. Although the leader issues vehement denials, doubt lingers—because seeing has always been believing and nobody can be completely sure whether the video is real or fake.

This ecosystem can also generate significant policy risks even when the information it uncovers is accurate. The key here is transparency— and what happens when secret information becomes public.

Particularly in crises and sensitive diplomatic negotiations, policymakers rely on useful fictions to buy time and save face, giving one or both sides a way out. As we saw in chapter 7, when the Soviet Union invaded Afghanistan, the CIA began arming Afghan Mujahidin. The Soviets knew it, and the Americans knew the Soviets knew. But the fiction kept a proxy war from becoming a superpower war with the potential for nuclear escalation.[92] Fig leaves can be useful.[93]

Even accurate information, if revealed, can make these situations more dangerous—by forcing action too soon and narrowing the range of face-saving political outcomes for each side. Imagine what would have happened during the Cuban missile crisis if non-governmental nuclear sleuths had discovered the secret deal between President Kennedy and Soviet leader Nikita Khrushchev to remove U.S. Jupiter missiles from Turkey in exchange for dismantling Soviet nuclear weapons from Cuba. With congressional midterm elections just days away, Kennedy was under intense pressure to stand tough against the Soviets. Real-time fact-checking could have derailed that agreement, escalating a superpower standoff already teetering on the brink of global nuclear war.

In this emerging world, U.S. intelligence agencies may increasingly have to serve as verifiers of last resort. As one expert nuclear panel noted, "Only governments can satisfactorily validate the results of open-source analysis using classified sources and methods, and only governments can make verification judgments."[94] This, too, poses significant challenges for effective nuclear intelligence: the more time government intelligence agencies spend debunking, validating, or adjudicating the work of others, the less time they have to advance their own intelligence collection and analysis priorities. One consequence is that net production of reliable, verified nuclear threat intelligence could go down, not up.

In the Karber case alone, the poorly researched claims of a few Georgetown students ended up sending the offices of several senior Pentagon officials and at least one congressional committee on a wild goose chase that took time, resources, and attention away from everything else. Accurate reports can burn time, too. Each time a nongovernmental organization publishes something that makes headlines, intelligence officials have to spend time going over the history of "what we already know about Subject X" with policymakers and explain why the news is not really new.

This, too, is not a hypothetical problem. It became an actual one in January 2019 when the prominent think tank, the Center for Strategic and International Studies, announced the discovery of an undeclared missile site in North Korea and estimated that there may be nineteen more.[95] Even though many of the undeclared missile sites were already known,[96] the story made *New York Times* and *Washington Post* headlines and national television news.[97] "The Intelligence Community, I am sure, had to do a lot of explaining with the DC government community," said one former official.[98]

Then there's the countermeasure risk: clever nuclear sleuthing in the public domain can alert adversaries about weaknesses in their own camouflage, concealment, and deception techniques that they did not know existed. Militaries are always thinking about how to overcome vulnerabilities and negate the other side's advantage. The invention of submarines led to sonar, bombers led to radar, tanks led to anti-tank missiles. Today, evidence suggests that the advent of Google Earth has prompted new Chinese efforts to conceal military facilities from more frequent satellite shooting intervals,[99] and Western media reports using open-source imagery led North Korea to conceal a hot-water cooling line from one of its nuclear reactors so analysts could no longer use it to tell whether the reactor was making weapons-grade plutonium.[100]

In 2016, Dave Schmerler, a researcher at the Center for Nonproliferation Studies, was able to measure the size of North Korea's first nuclear device (called a disco ball) and locate the building where it was photographed by using objects in the room as telltale markers. The next North Korean photo of a warhead was taken in a completely white room with nothing to measure.[101] Whether Schmerler's research prompted the change is impossible to know. But the dynamics are well known: any time new indicators or monitoring methods are revealed, countermeasures are likely to follow, making future monitoring even more difficult. The upshot is that short-term intelligence gains could unwittingly generate far greater long-term intelligence losses.[102]

The Future Is Unlikely to Look Like the Present

Estimating nuclear dangers is not just for governments anymore. Thanks to the small satellite revolution, the rise of online information and connectivity, and advances in automated analytics, individuals and organizations outside of governments are playing new and important roles. Leading non-governmental nuclear intelligence organizations have already become essential partners to American intelligence agencies and international nonproliferation organizations, enabling faster and better intelligence assessments of illicit nuclear activities in North Korea, Iran, and elsewhere. Non-governmental nuclear intelligence organizations are also playing pivotal roles in monitoring treaty compliance, identifying false positives, and debunking false claims.

Several of these non-governmental nuclear intelligence groups have amassed a breadth of expertise that rivals or, in some cases, exceeds the capabilities of the U.S. Intelligence Community—harnessing the talents of former international weapons inspectors, nuclear physicists, senior government officials, imagery analysts, geolocation specialists, and scholars using emerging and advanced technological tools. Because their work is all unclassified, it provides new avenues for information sharing both within and between governments. Their work also makes it more difficult for policymakers to misuse intelligence by cherry-picking, mischaracterizing, mistakenly interpreting, or selectively publicizing information that advances a particular policy position.

But this ecosystem also brings risks, particularly as technological tools spread and more individuals and organizations use them. In the unclassified world, there is no legal or bureaucratic firewall preventing information from getting "into the wild." Consequently, erroneous analyses can go viral before they can be verified and deception can flourish. As this world evolves, U.S. intelligence agencies may suffer degraded effectiveness as they spend more time validating the work of others rather than doing their own. Even good open-source information can backfire, escalating crises, derailing sensitive negotiations, and leading adversaries to take countermeasures that make future nuclear intelligence collection more difficult for everyone.

These are early days. Much about the effects of open-source nuclear threat intelligence on American policymaking remains unknown. When, where, and how is open-source intelligence likely to be redundant? Additive? Clarifying? Confirming or disconfirming? Under what circumstances does information transparency help, and when does it hurt? As nuclear seeking becomes more sophisticated and pervasive, how will nuclear hiding change? Will open-source nuclear threat intelligence increase costs to proliferators—adding more security burdens that slow their programs down? As these questions suggest, there is much more academic and policy work to be done.

Looking ahead, maximizing the benefits and mitigating the risks of the evolving open-source nuclear intelligence landscape will be essential. That process starts by recognizing that the future may not look like the present and that the present system has weaknesses.

Today, open-source nuclear threat intelligence is dominated by Americans and Western democratic allies. Many of the leading organizations are filled with experts who are driven by a sense of responsibility to the nonproliferation mission, who have exacting quality standards, and who work closely with U.S. and allied government officials. All of this, however, is informal. There is no official governmental tasking of priorities to these organizations; each decides for itself what to collect and analyze, and how—on the basis of what individuals personally think is important or interesting or necessary to keep their organizations going. There is also no formalized or standardized quality control handbook for open-source nuclear threat intelligence. While today's standards are often very high, they are entirely self-determined.

This informal, American-led ecosystem serves American national interests well. But the future is likely to bring more players from more countries and organizations with different values, less expertise, less responsibility, and less connectivity to American and allied intelligence officials and policymakers. China already operates commercial satellites, and the internationalization of the commercial satellite business is expected to grow significantly in the next several years.[103] It is important to ask now, "What would the future look like in a more crowded, less benign open-source world?"

Doing so suggests that finding ways to codify and institutionalize current best practices, norms, and networks among leading nongovernmental nuclear intelligence collectors and analysts is an important first step. The good news is that nascent efforts are underway to establish standards, develop shared norms, and improve skills. In July 2019, the Stanley Center for Peace and Security, a nonprofit, began a series of international stakeholder workshops to examine ethical challenges in the open-source community and develop recommendations for addressing them.[104] The bad news is that such initiatives cut in two directions, improving standards and tradecraft for well-meaning nongovernmental actors as well as for potential adversaries.

10

DECODING CYBER THREATS

We don't have the luxury of shaking our fists at the cosmos and
longing for a simpler time.

—SUSAN M. GORDON, PRINCIPAL DEPUTY DIRECTOR OF
NATIONAL INTELLIGENCE, 2017–2019[1]

SHOUTS ERUPTED AND TEMPERS flared.[2] At noon on May 21, 2016,
Houston's Islamic Da'wah Center became the site of two dueling protests.[3] On one side of the street, a group called Heart of Texas rallied to
"stop Islamization of Texas,"[4] with protestors carrying Confederate flags
and wearing "White lives matter" T-shirts. On the other side, United
Muslims of America staged a counter-protest to "save Islamic knowledge" with homemade placards declaring "no hate" and "peace on
earth."[5]

Real Americans. Real divisions. Real anger. All taking place on a
Texas street.[6] The entire scene was instigated by the Kremlin—but none
of the protesters knew it.[7]

Heart of Texas and United Muslims of America were Facebook groups
created by a shadowy Kremlin-backed organization called the Internet
Research Agency (IRA).[8] Inside nondescript offices in St. Petersburg,
Russia, hundreds of trolls masqueraded as Americans in around-the-
clock shifts—tweeting, liking, friending, and sharing in English to attract American followers.[9]

This was no fly-by-night outfit. Russia's online influence operation[10]
was described by the Senate Intelligence Committee as "painstaking

FIGURE 10.1 Russia's Facebook Deception in Action, 2016
Source: Exhibits used by Senator Richard Burr (R-NC), Senate Select Committee
on Intelligence Hearing, November 1, 2017.

and deliberate."[11] In 2014, two Russian operatives even traveled to the United States on an intelligence gathering mission, meeting with American political activists—all to make their social media deception more realistic and effective.[12]

It worked. To thousands of Americans, the Facebook groups seemed genuine. As figure 10.1 shows, Heart of Texas's page featured a heart-shaped Texas flag emblazoned with the words "Time to secede" and a tagline that read "Texas—homeland of guns, BBQ and ur heart!" It attracted more than 250,000 followers, all advocating for anti-immigrant and anti-Muslim policies.[13]

United Muslims of America's page also looked real, drawing more than 320,000 Facebook followers promoting what it said were pro-Islamic themes. The group's Arabic and English tagline was "I'm a Muslim and I'm proud."[14]

Russian trolls organized the dueling Houston rallies for the same day, time, and place on Facebook. They also bought Facebook ads for Heart of Texas and United Muslims of America—together seen by nearly fifteen thousand people—to draw bigger crowds.[15] The goal: stoking conflict between Americans in the virtual and physical worlds.[16]

Heart of Texas and United Muslims of America were just two among thousands of fake social media accounts on Facebook,[17] Twitter,[18] Instagram, and YouTube[19] impersonating Americans to spew incendiary views, generate political discord, and interfere in the 2016 presidential election.[20] Kremlin-instigated content on Facebook platforms is estimated to have reached more than 126 million Americans in the run-up to the election—more than a third of the U.S. population.[21]

Weaponizing social media was just one facet of Russian President Vladimir Putin's information warfare campaign.[22] Kremlin-backed operations included hacking into the systems of the Democratic National Committee and Democratic presidential candidate Hillary Clinton's campaign; releasing stolen information on WikiLeaks; spreading propaganda through state-run Russian media organizations such as RT America (formerly called Russia Today); and infiltrating state and local election infrastructures that included voter registration databases.[23]

The U.S. Intelligence Community concluded, and a bipartisan Senate Intelligence Committee investigation agreed, that Putin's aim was to undermine American democracy and tilt the 2016 presidential election in favor of Republican candidate Donald Trump.[24] Or as former CIA Deputy Director David Cohen more colorfully put it, "They wanted Donald Trump to win, they wanted Hillary to lose, but most of all they just wanted to fuck with us."[25]

American intelligence agencies quickly detected many parts of Russia's unfolding election interference efforts and warned President Obama,[26] but they never saw the social media operation coming.[27] A month before the election, Secretary of Homeland Security Jeh Johnson and Director of National Intelligence James Clapper issued a rare public warning. Social media was not even mentioned.[28]

Johnson later said that Russia's social media operation "was something . . . that we were just beginning to see."[29] Clapper wrote in his memoir that "in the summer of 2015, it would never have occurred to us that low-level Russian intelligence officers might be posing as Americans on social media."[30] The Intelligence Community would not understand the full magnitude of Russia's social media operation until much later.[31]

Russia's interference in the 2016 presidential election marked the dawn of a new era in cyber warfare and a moment of reckoning for

American intelligence agencies. Without firing a shot, Putin had discovered a powerful new lever to weaken American democracy from within—manipulating what Americans believed and how they behaved. And he did it by using social media platforms exactly as they were intended: to engage likeminded people at scale. Social media turned out to be the easiest and cheapest weapon in his arsenal.

This chapter examines how we got here—why and how cyber threats have evolved, what they look like today, what they mean for intelligence, and the key challenges they raise. As we'll see, no global threat has been more wide-ranging and fast-changing than cyber. And no set of security challenges places more demands on intelligence.

A Different Kind of Battleground

Cyberattacks are defined as "deliberate actions to alter, disrupt, deceive, degrade, or destroy computer systems or networks or the information and/or programs resident in or transiting these systems or networks."[32] Put more simply, cyberattacks involve any activity that alters the *confidentiality*, *integrity*, or *availability* of information on digital systems.

Beneath that definition lie profound changes in the power of data and the contours of today's battleground.

Information has always been important in geopolitics, but for most of history physical resources mattered more. Whoever had better farmland, healthier livestock, bigger armies, sturdier fortresses, better weapons, and faster ships prospered. Tangible assets generated trade, transformed societies, and won wars.

Today, by contrast, data has become much more essential for power—whether it's the market power of firms, the domestic political power of governments, or the military power of nations. Nearly two-thirds of today's global economy is based on intangible services,[33] not tangible goods, and some experts estimate that up to 40 percent of the world's jobs could be automated in the next fifteen to twenty-five years.[34] Authoritarian regimes increasingly rely on continuous data streams that track citizen activities, locations, and relationships to control their domestic populations. Modern warfare relies on assured command, control, and communications from space. As former senior intelligence official Susan Gordon noted, with the exception of weapons of mass destruction, "all the really vexing threats are to and through data."[35]

The skyrocketing rise in the number and magnitude of cyberattacks is not a coincidence. Data is coming under attack like never before because data has never been more prized. Many have called data "the new oil"—a precious resource that fuels geopolitical competition.[36]

In many ways, it's a poor analogy. The differences between oil and data are stark, and they offer insight into just how much the world is changing. Oil is valuable because it is scarce; data is valuable because it isn't. Data is essentially infinite and everyone can get it—creating network effects. Oil is captive to geography, making some countries more powerful than others. Data is unbound by geography, making even powerful countries vulnerable to attack (more on that below). Adversaries cannot turn oil into water or make it look like something it isn't. But they can with data, corrupting it or generating so much uncertainty that nobody trusts it. Data is simultaneously mighty and weak.

As the discussion above suggests, cyberspace is unlike any other battleground. The military's traditional air, land, and sea domains are all natural, not manmade. Nature provides geographic advantages for some and vulnerabilities for others. Portugal's empire, for example, stemmed in no small part from its isolated location on the edge of the Atlantic, which served as a springboard for fifteenth-century maritime expeditions—and its slavery business—along the West African coast. For centuries, America's two oceans have protected against the ravages of foreign invasion. The last time a foreign army marched on Washington was the War of 1812.

Cyberspace, by contrast, is manmade and inherently insecure. The Internet was never designed with security in mind. It was created in 1969 to link a handful of academic researchers who already knew and trusted each other. In cyberspace, there are no mountains or oceans to protect people or their assets from others. Good neighborhoods and dangerous ones are unavoidably connected. We are all geographically unlucky.

In the physical world, countries with the most powerful militaries are more secure. Navies with better ships are more likely to rule the seas. Armies with bigger and better land forces will dominate ground warfare. Air forces with greater range, stealth, and maneuverability will gain air supremacy.

In the cyber world, that's not true. There, power and vulnerability go hand in hand because the most powerful countries are often the most digitally connected. Advanced capitalist democracies like the United States rely on computer networks and systems for everything—working, learning, socializing, governing, shopping, conversing, transacting, traveling, spying, and warfighting. Reliance on digital technology brings both strength and weakness.

To see this in action, consider North Korea's 2014 cyberattack against Sony Pictures.[37] The Hermit Kingdom crippled one of the world's most powerful entertainment companies; toppled its co-chairman, Amy Pascal; directly threatened violence in movie theaters if the studio went ahead with its planned release of a comedy depicting the assassination of North Korean leader Kim Jong-Un; held freedom of speech hostage inside the United States; and caused a major national security incident involving the president of the United States.[38]

Yet when North Korea's Internet went down in what looked like U.S. retaliation,[39] the effects weren't noticeable because North Korea had only twenty-eight websites.[40] In a country where just 10 percent of the population owned a cell phone, shutting off the Internet did not shut down much.[41]

The Evolution of Cyber Threats:
What a Difference a Decade Makes

Cyber threats have evolved with dizzying speed.

It's hard to imagine now, but as late as 2007, the Intelligence Community's annual threat assessment did not include the word *cyber* once.[42] In 2009, cyber threats still ranked so low on the priority list, they were buried on page 38 of the forty-five-page threat assessment, just below drug trafficking in West Africa.[43]

Fast forward five years and the world looked very different, with cyber vaulting to the top tier of the 2012 intelligence threat list.[44] In 2013, the director of national intelligence named cyber the number one threat to the United States, ranking it ahead of terrorism for the first time since 9/11.[45]

At the time, policymakers were chiefly concerned about the potential for physical destruction. In 2012, Secretary of Defense Leon Panetta warned of a "cyber Pearl Harbor" in a major public speech. Standing on the deck of the USS Intrepid, an aircraft-carrier-turned-museum, to send the Pearl Harbor point home, Panetta ran down the list of cyber scenarios he worried most about: attacks shutting down the grid, derailing passenger trains, contaminating water supplies, disabling military communications networks, or multiple simultaneous strikes against critical infrastructure causing physical damage, loss of life, and national panic.[46] "Panetta Warns of Dire Threat of Cyberattack on U.S.," blared the ensuing New York Times headline.[47]

Panetta's remarks reflected the prevailing view that cyber acts of war would look a lot like physical acts of war: they would be large, visible, and damaging. The challenge was deterring and defending against them beforehand.

In April 2015, I invited Secretary of Defense Ash Carter to Stanford, where he unveiled a new Pentagon cyber strategy in an auditorium packed with faculty, students, and Silicon Valley tech leaders. A few months earlier, Carter had just started a fellowship in the center I co-directed at Stanford. He was learning how to navigate the campus's "circle of death" with undergraduates whizzing by on bicycles when he was tapped for the Pentagon's top job. In April, he returned to campus to honor his longtime mentor, Stanford nuclear physicist Sidney Drell.

But Carter had also traveled to Silicon Valley to make a point: the government needed help. New threats demanded urgent new collaborations between American tech and political leaders. His message was even more prescient than he realized. At that very moment, Russia was already using Facebook and other social media platforms to wage information warfare, even though nobody sitting in the auditorium knew it.[48]

Carter's cyber strategy took a major step forward, articulating a vision of the emerging threat landscape and how the Pentagon planned to confront it. The Defense Department, Carter said, had three core cyber missions: protecting military systems, networks, and information from attack; providing cyber capabilities to support military operations and contingency plans when needed; and defending the United States and its interests against "cyberattacks of significant consequence."[49]

What exactly were "cyberattacks of significant consequence"? That was the question.[50] While the Pentagon had responsibility for defending the .mil domain in cyberspace, it was less clear when or how the Defense Department was responsible for defending everything else—including the companies, organizations, and digital security of everyday Americans. When was an attack significant enough to trigger government protection, deterrence, or response?

Understanding that threshold was hard and urgent work. For the time being, the president and his national security team would determine significant consequence "on a case-by-case and fact-specific basis," though the 2015 cyber strategy noted that "significant consequences may include loss of life, significant damage to property, serious adverse U.S. foreign policy consequences, or serious economic impact on the United States."[51]

In other words, national security leaders might not be able to delineate the cyber threshold of war in advance, but they believed a threshold existed. It probably involved observable, near-term damage. And it would be clear when the line had been crossed.

No one knows whether this strategy ever deterred anybody. But we do know the idea of a cyber threshold of war quickly became irrelevant. Instead, cyber warfare looked a lot more like covert action, operating in the gray zone between war and peace without official government acknowledgment.[52] By 2017—just a decade after the DNI threat assessment didn't mention *cyber*—cyber war was occurring every day, and it didn't resemble any war anyone had seen before.

While physical warfare involved major mobilizations and strategic strikes—German troops marching into Poland, American atomic bombs dropping in Japan, Iraqi tanks rolling into Kuwait—cyber warfare was more of a bleed-every-minute insidious campaign in which attackers influenced outcomes one hack or Tweet at a time. In isolation, each might be too small for deterrence or retaliation. But cumulatively the damage could be devastating, stealing billions of dollars of intellectual property and cutting-edge innovations, sabotaging weapons systems, blowing entire spy networks, threatening massive disruption, and more.[53] The character of war looked entirely different in cyberspace.

Uncertainty played a much bigger role. Victims might not know they had been attacked for months, even years. And even if they did, quickly figuring out who was responsible with enough certainty to publicly attribute responsibility was difficult. Attacks could be traced to a computer, but discovering who was typing on the keyboard and the nature of their relationship with a foreign government or group was murky business.[54]

The "attribution problem," as experts called it, was particularly vexing because it struck at the heart of deterrence. Scholars have written tomes on the logic of deterrence theory, but the essence is making credible threats to stop bad things from occurring in the first place. Deterrence entails warning an adversary, "If you do that, you'll regret it." All parents are deterrence experts, threatening punishment to shape behavior: "If you hit your brother, you'll lose your dessert / television time / phone."

Successful deterrence has three requirements: (1) clear redlines delineating what behavior is unacceptable; (2) a credible capacity and willingness to punish violators (otherwise threats become hollow); and (3) the ability to identify the culprit quickly.[55]

Notice the word *quickly*. Identifying an offender *eventually* isn't good enough. Imagine I came home one day to find the kitchen a mess, and my three kids are pointing fingers at each other. To deter them from making future messes, I threaten: "It will take me six months or longer, but if I can figure out which one of you is behind this, you'll be punished someday!"

The longer attribution takes, the weaker my threat of punishment becomes—and the more deterrence unravels. Fast attribution matters, and it is far more elusive in cyberspace than anywhere else.

The 2016 presidential election revealed something else: cyber warfare could hack minds, not just machines, spreading disinformation to degrade societies from within. "The immediate threat is more corrosive than explosive," noted former Undersecretary of Defense for Policy Michèle Flournoy and Defense Department cyber advisor Michael Sulmeyer in 2018.[56]

With an evolving cyber threat came an evolving cyber strategy. In 2018, the Pentagon moved from hunkering down and defending American computer systems against incoming attacks to embracing a proactive, take-the-fight-to-them-every-day strategy called Defend Forward.[57] Restraint wasn't working. It was time to do more. Instead of waiting for a cyber Pearl Harbor that might never come, United States Cyber Command would compete all the time, combatting cyber enemies even outside American computer systems and networks. "We realized that Cyber Command needs to do more than prepare for a crisis in the future; it must compete with adversaries today," wrote Gen. Paul Nakasone, the nation's top cyberwarrior, in 2020.[58]

That's a lot of change in just a decade.

Cyber Threats Today: Four Main Adversaries, Five Types of Attacks

The cyber landscape today seems bewildering, with threats coming from everywhere and everyone—criminals, hackers, activists, terrorists, spies, militaries, even devious teens operating out of their parents' basements. In 2018, about two billion people, or two-thirds of the online population, had their personal information stolen or compromised.[59]

Former FBI Director Robert Mueller likes to tell the story of Mafiaboy. In 2000, a distributed denial of service attack hit eBay, e*TRADE, Yahoo! (which at the time was the world's largest search engine), CNN, and others. The FBI began an investigation, which led them to a fifteen-year old Canadian who went by the handle Mafiaboy. When the police finally arrested him, he was having a sleepover at a friend's house, staying up late, eating junk food, and watching the movie *Goodfellas*.[60]

Twenty years later, when a hack took over dozens of high-profile Twitter accounts, including those of former President Barack Obama, former Vice President Joseph Biden, and business leaders Elon Musk and Bill Gates, the culprit was a seventeen-year-old named Graham Ivan Clark who lived in Tampa and wanted to sell user names.[61]

Stories like Mafiaboy and Clark's Twitter takeover generate headlines that often confuse as much as they clarify. The truth is, not every nefarious actor in cyberspace poses a national security threat. Often, breaches are more the result of weak defenses than mastermind-level offensive operations. There are cyber threats and then there are cyber threats.

The most serious threats from a national security perspective don't come from Cheeto-eating teens. They come from well-trained operatives and proxies operating at the behest of four countries: China, Russia, Iran, and North Korea.[62] Together, these four nations are behind 77 percent of all suspected state-sponsored cyberattacks since 2005.[63] As Director of National Intelligence Dan Coats testified in 2019, "China, Russia, Iran, and North Korea increasingly use cyber operations to threaten both minds and machines in an expanding number of ways." Coats went on to suggest that Russia's 2016 election interference was only the beginning, with new tactics emerging as adversaries learn from experience.[64]

While running a wide range, the cyberattacks perpetrated by China Russia, Iran, and North Korea come in five basic types: *stealing, spying, disrupting, destroying,* and *deceiving.* Some countries specialize in certain attack types more than others. Sometimes, countries use multiple types simultaneously. But each seeks to achieve different effects.

Stealing in cyberspace is big business and instrumental to geopolitical competition. In 2018 cyber theft cost an estimated $600 billion globally. That's about as much as the global illicit drug trade.[65] If cybercrime were a country, it would rank in the top twenty-five in terms of annual GDP.

Many nations steal online, but North Korea is particularly aggressive, targeting financial institutions and cryptocurrency exchanges to steal billions to fund its illicit nuclear weapons program.[66]

China's cyber theft of intellectual property is even more consequential because it is designed to secure national advantage. China is believed to have stolen trillions of dollars of intellectual property,[67] including terabytes of data and schematics for the F-35 and F-22 stealth fighter jet programs, two of the most sophisticated aircraft in the U.S. arsenal.[68] Targeting industries at the forefront of innovation and commerce, China's intellectual property theft strikes at the heart of economic power. It was considered so serious, Gen. Keith Alexander, once the nation's top cyberwarrior, called it "the greatest transfer of wealth in history."[69] The Justice Department indicted five Chinese officials[70] for cyber espionage against U.S. companies and in 2015 President Obama held a summit with Chinese leader Xi Jinping to try to rein it in.[71]

Hacking has become an indispensable part of twenty-first-century espionage, whether it's infiltrating communications systems to obtain secret documents and eavesdrop on adversaries,[72] accessing foreign weapons systems,[73] or identifying potential spies.[74] Many countries, including the United States, do it, some more effectively than others.[75] In 2015, the top cyber advisor to the secretary of defense testified that external actors were probing U.S. Defense Department networks for vulnerabilities "millions of times each day" and that more than 100 foreign intelligence agencies were "continually" trying to infiltrate defense networks.[76]

China tops this list, too, acquiring more than 21 million security clearance records from the U.S. Office of Personnel Management (OPM) in 2015 that revealed personal information about individuals in sensitive positions—including their financial debts, foreign friends, relatives, medical problems, substance abuse history, and psychiatric care.[77] China is also believed to be behind hacks of Anthem insurance (80 million records), Marriott (400 million records), and Equifax's 146 million credit records covering nearly every adult in America.[78] All of this information can be used to blow intelligence covers and identify and pressure vulnerable targets to betray the United States.[79] It's an intelligence bonanza for Beijing and a nightmare for Washington—the largest and most sophisticated intelligence database ever collected against an adversary. "You have to kind of salute the Chinese for what they did," noted Director of National Intelligence James Clapper after the OPM breach.[80] From an intelligence perspective, it was a masterstroke.

Russia is aggressive on this front, too. In December 2020, the cybersecurity firm FireEye reported that it had been penetrated by sophisticated hackers who got in by corrupting the software of a widely used network-monitoring vendor called SolarWinds.[81] The SolarWinds breach turned out to be massive, unfolding like a scene from a horror movie: victims frantically barricaded the doors, only to discover the enemy had been hiding inside the house the whole time. For months, hackers had been roaming wild, undetected, inside the nation's government networks (including nuclear labs and the Departments of Commerce, Defense, Homeland Security, Justice, State, and Treasury), as well as nearly all of the *Fortune* 500 companies and thousands of other organizations.[82] Intelligence agency leaders publicly announced that Russia was "likely" behind SolarWinds.[83] So far, the breach appears to have been an intelligence-gathering effort rather than a cyberattack meant to disrupt, corrupt, or destroy, though investigations are ongoing. What's already clear, however, is that the damage is immense and America's cyberwarriors and spies never detected a thing until FireEye sounded the alarm.[84]

Disruptive cyberattacks have already targeted power grids, communications networks, and other critical infrastructure. Russia has been using its neighbors as testbeds—cutting Estonia's Internet in 2007,[85] waging cyberattacks on Georgia during the 2008 invasion, and shutting down Ukrainian websites during its 2014 invasion.[86] Russia was almost certainly behind the 2015 and 2016 cyberattacks shutting off Ukrainian power to millions of customers[87] and the 2017 NotPetya cyberattack targeting Ukrainian banks, agencies, and companies that spread worldwide, causing more than $10 billion in damage.[88]

Destroying is less common but still of great concern. To many, the watershed moment occurred in 2010, when a computer worm designed to sabotage Iran's nuclear weapons program got "into the wild"[89] (see box). Security researchers later determined, and public reports in the *New York Times* indicate, that the worm was the work of a joint U.S.-Israeli covert operation.[90]

Iran's offensive cyber operations have focused on destructive attacks, including a 2012 attack that destroyed thirty thousand Saudi Arabian computers[91] and a 2014 attack that wiped hard drives at the Sands Casino in Las Vegas.[92] That same year, North Korea's bizarre attack on Sony Pictures destroyed thousands of computers and servers and sent the company reeling—all in retaliation for a Seth Rogen comedy called *The Interview*.[93]

Crossing the Cyber Rubicon: Stuxnet

President George W. Bush was worried about Iran.[94] Iranian leader Mahmoud Ahmadinejad told reporters he wanted to install up to fifty thousand nuclear centrifuges—the delicate machines needed to enrich uranium—inside an underground facility at Natanz. Uranium could be used for power or weapons, but Iran had just one nuclear power plant. Nobody needed that many centrifuges just for energy.[95]

In the spring of 2006, aides debated options. Some wanted to attack Iran. Others believed the United States was already stretched thin in Iraq and Afghanistan and any military strike would backfire, unifying Iran, prompting retaliation, and entrenching the country's desire for the bomb. Some wanted sanctions. The CIA's past sabotage efforts hadn't done much.[96] Israel started requesting U.S. military assistance to significantly enhance its ability to strike unilaterally.[97] It was time to get creative.

Gen. James E. Cartwright had an idea. Cartwright, who was then in charge of American nuclear deterrence, had been thinking about new technologies. What if the United States attacked Iran's centrifuges with a cyberweapon?[98]

The result was Stuxnet, the most sophisticated cyber weapon in the world, with code fifty times larger than typical malware.[99] The CIA, the NSA, and Israel's elite cyber Unit 8200 reportedly joined forces.[100] Forensics revealed that Stuxnet used four rare and valuable "zero day" vulnerabilities (coding flaws unknown to security researchers or software vendors) to find the precise software operating Iran's centrifuges, spread inside, hide, and destroy without a trace.[101]

Still, the operation needed humans. The Natanz computers were "air gapped"—they weren't connected to the Internet. The U.S.-Israeli team somehow got Iranians inside Natanz to infect the machines with USB drives. Apparently, only some knew they were accomplices.[102]

Stuxnet would lie in wait and then suddenly spring into action, speeding up or slowing down the spinning centrifuges for a few minutes before hiding again and repeating the operation until the centrifuges tore themselves apart. "The idea was to string it out as long as possible," said one of the officials in the operation. "If you had wholesale destruction right away . . . it doesn't look like incompetence."[103]

All the while, Stuxnet transmitted false data showing centrifuge operations looking normal—like a fake videotape reassuring security guards standing watch that nothing was amiss.

Experts believe that one thousand of Iran's six thousand centrifuges were destroyed, though they dispute how much of Iran's nuclear progress was delayed.[104]

A new type of weapon had been born—a cyberattack, in peacetime, that destroyed another nation's critical infrastructure. "This has the whiff of August 1945," said former NSA and CIA Director Michael Hayden, referring to the emergence of the atomic bomb. "That's a big deal."[105]

Cyberattacks meant to deceive are newest on the scene. Deception, of course, has been around forever. In 480 B.C.E. an Athenian general named Themistocles used a double agent to lure the Persian navy into the narrow Strait of Salamis, where it was ambushed and defeated by a smaller fleet of more maneuverable Greek ships. During the American Revolution, George Washington's sand-filled gunpowder barrels, letters to phantom troops, and falsely positioned French bake ovens helped win the war.

But cyber deception is different—operating with far greater reach, speed, sophistication, and availability.

Before now, deception was an elite affair in which leaders tried to trick each other and left the rest of us out of it. Washington only needed to fool a handful of British generals to win the Revolutionary War. The allies' surprise D-Day landing hinged on convincing Hitler and his commanders—by using phantom troops, dummy landing craft, false communications, and double agents—that Pas-de-Calais was the invasion site, not Normandy. The Soviets' 1962 nuclear gambit in Cuba required lying to President Kennedy and hiding the deployment of nuclear missiles from most Soviet military leaders, including the ship captains carrying them.[106]

Today, cyber-enabled deception operations seek to trick us all, shaping mass opinions across borders. Connective technologies, especially in democratic societies with freedom of speech, are enabling false messages to go viral at scales and speeds previously unimaginable.

During the Cold War, the Soviets launched "active measures" campaigns to conjure false narratives that spread slowly, if at all. One suggested that the CIA was involved in the Kennedy assassination.[107] The most well known narrative peddled a conspiracy theory in an obscure Indian newspaper that the AIDS virus had been created by the U.S. military. It took years to gain international attention.[108]

Now, Russian disinformation is designed to flood the zone, reaching millions within hours across every format (text, video, audio, photos) and information channel imaginable—social media, Internet websites, satellite television, and traditional radio and television.[109]

Volume is key. Twitter now estimates that Russia used more than fifty thousand automated accounts or bots to Tweet election-related content during the 2016 presidential campaign. Twitter and Facebook are the best-known disinformation superhighways, but there are many others. Russian officers have infiltrated everything from 4chan to Pinterest.[110]

Overt state-funded media outlets are used to amplify false messages. In 2019, for example, RT (formerly called Russia Today)[111] had a $300 million annual budget, video programming that looked like legitimate news in multiple languages,[112] and more than three million YouTube subscribers—more than Fox News, CBS News, or NBC News.[113]

The aim is to overwhelm, divide, and breed distrust in information itself, undermining democratic discourse. One expert study called Russia's information warfare approach a "firehose of falsehood."[114]

Russia was the first to embrace cyber weapons of mass deception, but it's not alone anymore. China's operations grew more sophisticated during the COVID-19 pandemic, which began in Wuhan in late 2019. Within months, China's disinformation campaigns to shift blame for the virus had grown so widespread, the European Union called it an "info-demic."[115] At the same time, the U.S. National Counterintelligence and Security Center warned that foreign countries—led by Russia, but now also including China and Iran—were using online disinformation to "sway U.S. voters' preferences and perspectives, to shift U.S. policies, to increase discord, and to undermine confidence in our democratic process" before the 2020 presidential election.[116]

Companies are also providing spying-for-hire services that use false identities and wage information warfare, spreading messages with the intent of influencing what people believe, even if the information isn't true.

Psy-Group was one of them. Staffed by former Israeli intelligence officers, the company went defunct after its activities were revealed in the *New Yorker* and reports surfaced that the company was being investigated by Special Counsel Robert Mueller as part of his 2016 election interference inquiry.[117] Psy-Group's business brochure featured a goldfish with a shark fin on its back below the tagline, "Reality is a matter of perception." The company's alleged activities included everything from creating a sham European think tank that churned out reports favoring the parliamentary election campaign of a client to creating websites making false claims disparaging the opponent of a client running for the local hospital board in Tulare, California, a town of just sixty thousand people.[118]

As former senior Israeli intelligence official Uzi Shaya put it, "Social media allows you to reach virtually anyone and to play with their minds. . . . You can do whatever you want. You can be whoever you want. It's a place where wars are fought, elections are won, and terror is promoted. There are no regulations. It's a no-man's land."[119]

What's more, new technologies are making cyber deception tools more effective and accessible to everyone. Manipulated photographs and video are getting better and spreading rapidly. In November 2018, White House Press Secretary Sarah Huckabee Sanders tweeted a video that had been doctored to make it look like CNN reporter Jim Acosta was aggressively grabbing a microphone from a White House intern when in fact he wasn't. The White House suspended Acosta's press credential, prompting outcries.[120] A few months later, a video of House Speaker Nancy Pelosi was distorted to make her sound drunk and posted on social media, where it was viewed two million times and made headline news.[121] When Facebook refused to remove the fake Pelosi video, two British artists posted their own doctored video of Facebook CEO Mark Zuckerberg claiming he wanted to "control billions of people's stolen data, all their secrets" and thanking Spectre, the fictional evil organization from James Bond stories.[122]

These "cheapfakes" used rudimentary technology that was relatively easy to spot. Deception is going to get much worse, thanks to advances in artificial intelligence fueling the development of deepfake digital impersonation technology. Already, deepfake technology has created remarkably lifelike photographs of non-existent celebrities,[123] audios so real they duped an employee into letting criminals steal hundreds of thousands of dollars,[124] and videos of leaders saying things they never uttered.[125]

Deepfakes are growing more convincing and nearly impossible to detect, thanks to a breakthrough AI technique invented by Google engineer Ian Goodfellow in 2014.[126] Called "generative adversarial networks," the approach essentially pits two computer algorithms against each other. One learns to generate a realistic image of something while the other learns to decide whether the image is real or fake. Because these algorithms are designed to learn by competing, deepfake countermeasures are unlikely to work for long. "We are outgunned," said Hany Farid, a computer science professor at the University of California at Berkeley.[127]

Deepfake code is open and spreading fast. In the past few years, anonymous GitHub user "torzdf" and Reddit user "deepfakeapp" have vastly simplified the code and interface required to generate deepfakes, creating programs called "faceswap" and "FakeApp," which are easy enough for a high school student with no coding background to use. The two other key ingredients for making deepfakes—computing power and large libraries of training data—are also becoming widely available.[128]

The impact of deepfakes could be profound, and policymakers know it. In 2019, deepfakes were a leading point of discussion at Congress's Worldwide Threat Hearings, and the House Intelligence Committee held a separate hearing dedicated entirely to deepfakes for the first time.[129] "One does not need any great imagination to envision . . . nightmarish scenarios that would leave the government, the media, and the public struggling to discern what is real and what is fake," said House Intelligence Committee chairman Adam Schiff (D-CA).

Schiff proceeded to describe three possible nightmares: A malign actor creates a deepfake video of a political candidate accepting a bribe to influence an election. A hacker claims to have stolen audio of a conversation between two world leaders that never occurred. A troll farm uses text generating algorithms to write false news stories at scale, flooding social media platforms and overwhelming journalists' ability to verify and citizens' ability to trust what they are seeing.[130]

Deception has always been part of statecraft, espionage, and warfare, but not like this.

What Does Intelligence Have to Do with Cyber?

Four features of the evolving cyber landscape are placing unprecedented demands on intelligence.

First, cyberattacks, whether they are successful or not, compromise trust in information and computer systems. In the physical world of tanks and troops, countries know immediately when they are being attacked. In cyberspace, they may not. Cyberattacks operate in the shadows, burrowing into systems to corrupt, degrade, destroy, deceive, and deny information to rightful users in hidden ways. Attackers can operate anonymously or make it look like they're somebody else. They can strike without warning or lie in wait for years. Cyberspace is an ideal battleground for secret action. That's what makes it so attractive in the first place.

Iranian leaders may not have realized that their nuclear centrifuges were being destroyed by a cyber operation for months, possibly years.[131] When North Korean rockets suddenly started exploding and veering off course in 2016,[132] Kim Jong-Un wasn't sure whether the problem was faulty engineering or a secret American cyber operation. (Americans weren't sure, either. A cyber operation was reportedly underway, but nobody knew for certain whether it was working.)[133] Russia's social media operation wasn't known until after the 2016 election, and understanding its full scope remains a work in progress. The SolarWinds hackers went undetected for nine months, possibly longer.[134]

When cyberattacks take so long to uncover, uncertainty grows. Leaders start wondering: Are Americans clashing because they want to exercise their First Amendment freedoms or because they are unwitting Russian pawns undermining American democracy? Is the missile failing because of designed flaws or sabotage? Are our computers working properly or have they been compromised? Cyber operations can generate tremendous doubt about the credibility of information and whether systems are functioning as intended.[135]

Trusting computer systems to work is a big deal. Back in 1994, an obscure bug in Intel's Pentium micro-processing chip produced calculation errors in extremely rare types of high-precision division operations.[136] Because the bug affected so few users, Intel did not think it was a problem. Customers thought otherwise. The company ended up having to fix every chip, taking a $475 million loss.[137] When it comes to trusting computers, even the remote possibility of an unexpected error can be too high. As my Stanford cyber colleague Herb Lin put it, "If you had a calculator that gave you the wrong answer once every ten thousand times, and you knew it, would you use the calculator at all or throw it away?"[138]

For an adversary, generating this kind of uncertainty is one of the benefits of cyber warfare. For intelligence agencies, it's a growing problem. Remember, intelligence is the business of collecting, protecting, verifying, and understanding information for national advantage. Knowing whether citizens have been misled by foreign influence operations, or whether weapons systems have been secretly sabotaged by malware, or whether a foreign intelligence service has penetrated American spy networks, or whether information about an ally or adversary is credible—all of these questions are becoming more pervasive, immediate, and important for intelligence agencies to answer.

Second, in cyberspace it's hard to know when a weapon is actually a weapon: breaches used to inflict damage are often indistinguishable from intrusions to gather intelligence.

From a technical perspective, the first 90 percent of any cyber operation looks the same, whether the intention is defending, attacking, or just surveilling someone else's computer network. As former NSA Deputy Director Chris Inglis wrote, every intrusion starts by "finding and fixing a target of interest in cyberspace."[139] It's the final 10 percent of any cyber weapon—the payload that gets unleashed—that determines what happens once an attacker gets inside.

When spying and warfare are hard to distinguish, understanding the bigger picture becomes even more important. Policymakers need to know: Is the attacker inside a network to watch? Steal information? Disrupt operations? Delete files? Corrupt them? Is the intrusion laying the groundwork for a distant future action or something imminent? When attacks can look like intelligence operations and intelligence operations can look like attacks, the risks of miscalculation are high and intelligence about context and adversary intentions matters more.[140]

Third, offensive cyber operations require ubiquitous, exquisite, real-time intelligence. That's even harder than it sounds. The attack surface in cyberspace is huge, growing, and changing every millisecond. The scale and dynamism are hard to fathom. Over half the world is already connected to the Internet, using more than 20 billion smart devices—including baby monitors, fitness trackers, bird feeders, medical devices, home appliances, cars, and even children's toys like Hello Barbie.[141]

The first cyberattack using a refrigerator occurred in 2013.[142] Two years later, Chrysler had to recall more than a million Jeep Cherokees after two researchers demonstrated they could remotely cut off the engine and the brakes by wirelessly accessing the car's entertainment system.[143] In 2016, an attack using home appliances shut down the Internet on much of the East Coast.[144] In 2018, Princeton engineers showed how a "botnet" or army of smart air conditioners and heaters could be used to launch large-scale attacks on the power grid.[145]

Technologists estimate that in every 2,500 lines of code there's roughly one coding weakness—some kind of vulnerability that software engineers did not anticipate or catch when they were writing it.[146] One in 2,500 may sound reassuring. It shouldn't be. A typical Android phone runs on twelve million lines of code. Microsoft Windows has forty million lines. That's thousands of hidden weaknesses waiting to be exploited by malign actors.

Anything running on code and connected to the Internet is a potential cyberattack vector. This global battlespace changes every time anyone on earth downloads an app, installs a patch, inserts a thumb drive, connects to airport Wi-Fi, or plugs in a smart toaster. Targets and vulnerabilities are all constantly appearing and disappearing. Intelligence has to keep up with these changes, finding the right vulnerabilities to exploit in the right targets at the right time or else offensive cyber operations won't work. As the Pentagon's Cyber Command put it, "No target remains static; no offensive or defensive capability remains indefinitely effective; and no advantage is permanent."[147]

When tiny changes in a target can spell the difference between success and failure, intelligence is more than an input. It's an essential requirement for any mission.[148]

In the physical world, military planners can draw up target lists that last for years because things like buildings and missile silos are hard to move. Any bomb with a high enough yield will destroy a structure regardless of whether it's made of wood or concrete, whether it gets remodeled or stays exactly the same. In cyberspace, that's not true. Cyber intelligence has to be precise and up-to-the-minute to be useful. Getting inside a target network often requires painstaking knowledge. Even slight modifications like installing a Microsoft update can make a target suddenly impenetrable and a "cyber bomb" against it useless.

What's more, intelligence about potential cyber targets has to be global to be useful. Why? Because you never know where you need to attack next; cyberwarriors need to be prepared to attack anywhere at any time.

Military leaders have often lamented the terrible prediction record of where wars would occur. As Secretary of Defense Robert Gates told West Point cadets in 2011, "When it comes to predicting the nature and location of our next military engagements, since Vietnam, our record has been perfect. We have never once gotten it right, from the Mayaguez to Grenada, Panama, Somalia, the Balkans, Haiti, Kuwait, Iraq, and more—we had no idea a year before any of these missions that we would be so engaged."[149] Before 9/11, the Clinton administration's national security priority list rated transnational terrorism and Afghanistan in the lowest tier. The military had not ordered a new map of Afghanistan in years.[150]

In the physical world, there's time to adjust. Even in crises, military mobilization takes time. Iraqi leader Saddam Hussein watched for five months as coalition forces gathered and developed war plans to expel him from Kuwait in 1991.

Cyberspace doesn't afford that kind of time. There, preventing and responding to attacks requires mobilization in milliseconds. As Inglis wrote, intelligence in cyberspace has to enable "the command to go from a standing start to a precise and responsive engagement in the shortest possible time."[151] That kind of instant response requires groundwork years in advance. Everywhere.

Fourth and finally, there's the quantity versus variety problem of cyber weapons.[152] In the physical world of warfare, quantities matter: two fighter jets are always better than one. But in cyberspace, more of the same weapon is just the same: two copies of the same piece of malware don't get you anything more than one. In cyberspace, weapons variety wins the day—and that requires identifying different vulnerabilities and ways to exploit them. The intelligence demands are high.

Silent but Deadly Organizational Challenges

Looking ahead, meeting these demands is more than a technical challenge of zeroes and ones. It is an organizational challenge involving the balance between warriors and spies and a new understanding of who counts as a decisionmaker in the cyber age.

To spy or not to spy has always been a question. Spies naturally prefer surveilling to attacking. Their job is acquiring information that yields advantage. Access to valuable information, whether it comes from a human or inside a computer network, is hard-won and fiercely guarded. When in doubt, spies will always elect to keep listening rather than lose a collection stream.

Warfighters, by contrast, want to use the information advantages they have. Their job is fighting and winning. They want to protect their soldiers in harm's way. Access to valuable information may be fleeting. If they don't use it, they could lose it.

The *Washington Post* provided a rare glimpse into this spy-versus-attack dilemma when it reported on a 2008 debate involving an online forum for Islamist extremists. According to the *Post*, the site was actually a "honey pot" set up by the Saudis and the CIA to gather intelligence on potential terrorists and catch them. U.S. military leaders believed the online forum was being used by extremists to attack allied forces in Iraq. Gen. Raymond Odierno, the top U.S. commander in Iraq, considered the threat to his forces to be so serious, he reportedly asked that the site be shut down. CIA officials believed they would lose intelligence, damage relationships with Saudi intelligence officials, and encourage extremists to migrate to other sites where they wouldn't be so easily monitored. In this case, Defense Department arguments won the day, resulting in a bizarre outcome: a U.S. military cyber operation to cripple a CIA-run website.[153]

Intelligence-military frictions are especially salient in cyberspace today because intelligence is so integral to effective offensive cyber operations. It's no coincidence that the nation's top cyberwarrior also runs the National Security Agency. The four-star military leader in charge of American Cyber Command has been "dual hatted" ever since Cyber Command was created in 2009.

This arrangement usefully consolidates cyber expertise but tips the balance toward spying, not attacking. Cyber Command is the junior partner in this relationship. NSA has been penetrating foreign communications systems for over half a century. It has the highest concentration of the best cyber expertise in government, employing more mathematicians than any organization in the United States.[154] As former NSA Director Michael Hayden wrote, cyber weapons descend from an NSA bloodline.[155]

The United States "needs to break through the conceptual block of looking at its own cyber-capabilities primarily as instruments of foreign surveillance," wrote two Defense Department officials in 2018.[156] Even Hayden agreed, writing that spy agencies have retarded the development of "digital combat power."[157]

Cyberspace also raises new questions about who counts as a decisionmaker—and how the Intelligence Community should interact with them. Before the 2016 election, the first organization to notice suspicious Russian activity on Facebook was Facebook. The company contacted U.S. law enforcement officials, but information sharing between them was rudimentary. Twitter's general counsel testified that as far as the company knew, nobody from the U.S. government told the company anything before the 2016 election about state-sponsored information operations. While intelligence about information warfare and intelligence sharing relationships has improved since then, intelligence agencies are still focused on producing classified products for Washington policymakers.[158] Their organizational structures and cultures, career promotion incentives, analytic tradecraft, and written products are all oriented to a closed, classified world.

Susan Gordon spent forty years inside the Intelligence Community, including serving as the number two intelligence official from 2017 to 2019. She's convinced that intelligence must be fundamentally reformed to produce for private sector leaders and the broader public. "Our business isn't secrecy," she noted in a 2020 interview. "Our business is national security. And if the people who are affecting national security are either the populace—they're being influenced—or the private sector, they're making decisions that affect security."[159]

The Intelligence Community needs to inform a much broader set of decisionmakers. "That's not a casual change," she reflected. It's not just handing reports to new people. It requires a wholesale reimagining of how intelligence operates and who it operates for.[160]

It's also a revolutionary shift for American tech companies, many of whom resist the idea that they have any responsibility for American national security. Just as tech leaders have been stunned by hearings showing Congress's poor understanding of technology, policymakers have been stunned by Silicon Valley's cavalier view of how their products are being used by malign actors.

When Facebook CEO Mark Zuckerberg testified before Congress in April 2018, it was a jaw-dropping moment showing just how much naïveté and profits were driving Facebook's decisions and just how little Zuckerberg and his team had considered the possibility that anyone could use their platform to undermine democracy and inflict damage across borders. In his opening statement, Zuckerberg admitted, "Facebook is an idealistic and optimistic company. For most of our existence, we focused on all of the good that connecting people can do." Zuckerberg added, "But it's clear now that we didn't do enough to prevent these tools from being used for harm."[161] While Facebook executives have been apologizing to Congress in public, they have been waging a campaign in private to deny, delay, and deflect regulation and stifle critics.[162]

Google executives, citing ethical concerns, canceled an artificial intelligence project with the Pentagon and refused to even bid on the Defense Department's Project JEDI, a desperately needed $10 billion program to modernize the military's cloud computing systems.[163] At the same time, Google agreed to help the Chinese government develop a more effective censored search engine until outcries from human-rights groups,

American politicians, and its own employees became overwhelming.[164] In 2019 congressional hearings, Google's vice president of public policy, Karan Bhatia, would not commit the company to refusing Chinese business that involved censoring information to Chinese citizens.[165]

Many in tech companies harbor deep ethical concerns about helping warfighters, while many in the defense community harbor deep ethical concerns about what they view as the erosion of patriotism and national service in the tech industry. Each side is left wondering, *How can anyone possibly think that way?* In 2018, when Chairman of the Joint Chiefs of Staff Gen. Joseph Dunford was asked what he would tell engineers at companies like Google and Amazon, he replied, "Hey, we're the good guys. . . . It's inexplicable to me that we wouldn't have a cooperative relationship with the private sector."[166]

It's hard to overstate just how foreign the worlds of Washington and Silicon Valley are to each other. At the exact moment when great-power conflict is making a comeback and harnessing technology is the key to success, Silicon Valley and Washington are still working on working together.[167]

Closing this divide is nothing short of a national security imperative.

Intelligence Has Never Been More Important or Challenging

Cyber threats are vastly different from traditional national security threats, with profound implications for intelligence. In cyberspace, everyone is vulnerable. Adversaries steal, spy, disrupt, destroy, and deceive at speeds and scales unthinkable even a few years ago. Uncertainty abounds. Espionage, defense, and attack are hard to differentiate. Cyber weapons require global, persistent, real-time intelligence to work. It's a tall order.

And that's not all. Increasingly, key cyber decisionmakers sit in board rooms and living rooms, not just in the White House Situation Room. Cyber threats directly involve technology companies and everyday citizens whether they like it or not. In this emerging world, intelligence has never been more important, or more challenging.

ACKNOWLEDGMENTS

I BEGAN STUDYING INTELLIGENCE by accident. I had just finished a summer stint working on Asia policy on President Clinton's National Security Council (NSC) staff and had returned to Stanford to start my political science doctoral dissertation. It was 1993. The Cold War was over and the talk was of peace dividends, the inexorable spread of democracy, and the "end of history." But as I searched for a topic, I saw uncertainty, not closure. I kept thinking about what I had experienced on the NSC staff: decisionmakers grappling with how to understand the end of one era and the unknowns of another. I became fascinated by information and institutions—and how the machinery of government made sense of the world beyond.

Camping out in the darkened basement of Green Library, I began poring through government documents about the institutions created at the dawn of the Cold War. I soon discovered the National Security Act of 1947, which reorganized the military, created the National Security Council, and established an organization that received almost no attention in the bitter congressional debates of the time: the Central Intelligence Agency. I have been hooked on intelligence ever since.

This book draws on nearly thirty years of research about the evolution, operation, and challenges of American intelligence agencies as well as my personal experiences advising policymakers, interviewing intelligence officers, and teaching undergraduates about this secret world at UCLA and Stanford. Authors often say there are too many people to thank properly. With a book so long in the making, this time it's really true.

I owe an enduring debt to all of the intelligence officers and policymakers who have generously shared their thoughts in personal interviews over many years. While several are attributed by name in these pages, most have asked to remain anonymous.

A talented crew of undergraduate and graduate student research assistants contributed invaluably to this project. I am particularly indebted to Sebastian Alarcon, Philip Clark, Matt Clawson, Gabby Conforti, Alexa Corse, Ravi Doshi, Stacy Edgar, Kyle Fendorf, Matt Ferraro, Katie Frost, Cole Griffiths, Taylor Grossman, Rachel Hirshman, Katherine Irajpanah, Dylan Junkin, Katharine Leede, Ryan Likes, Melinda McVay, Greg Midgette, Andrew Milich, Eric Min, Josh Mukhopadhyay, Avanika Narayan, Jaclyn Nelson, Avery Rogers, Jean Schindler, Tien Vo, Margaret Fairtree Williams, Antigone Xenopolous, Chris Yeh, and Corinne Zanolli.

I am deeply grateful for the vibrant and generous intellectual community at Stanford University's Center for International Security and Cooperation (CISAC), the Freeman Spogli Institute for International Studies (FSI), the Hoover Institution, the Institute for Human-Centered Artificial Intelligence (HAI), and the Department of Political Science. For their leadership and partnership, I'd especially like to thank Rod Ewing, Colin Kahl, and Harold Trinkunas at CISAC; Michael Mc-Faul and Kathryn Stoner at FSI; Condi Rice and Dan Kessler at Hoover; Fei-Fei Li, John Etchemendy, and Michael Sellitto at HAI; and political science chair Mike Tomz.

Bob and Marion Oster, Lew and Pilar Davies, Rod and Laurie Shepard, and Shirley Cox Matteson and her late husband, Duncan, have been unwavering champions of Hoover's National Security Affairs Fellows program and our national security endeavors. I am honored beyond words to be the Morris Arnold and Nona Jean Cox Senior Fellow at Hoover—and to have the names of Shirley's parents next to my own.

I would also like to thank the Hoover and FSI staff who make everything possible, especially Carmen Allison, Christina Ansel, Chris Dauer, Kelly Doran, Andrea Gray, Stephanie James, Rick Jara, Karen Weiss Mulder, Nga-My Nguyen, Emilie Silva, Jules Porter Thompson, and Shannon York.

I have benefitted tremendously from the research, seminars, discussions, questions, advice, and assistance of Michael Allen, Elisabeth Allison, Matt Atkins, Jim Baker, Nora Bensahel, Tom Berson, Coit

Blacker, Brad Boyd, David Brady, Michael Brown, Robert Cardillo, Al Carnesale, Bobby Chesney, Kevin Childs, Matt Cordova, Martha Crenshaw, Mariano-Florentino Cuellar, Matt Daniels, Eric DeMarco, Larry Diamond, Whit Diffie, Dan Drezner, Kristen Eichensehr, Niall Ferguson, Jack Goldsmith, Andy Grotto, Rosanna Guadagno, Anna Grzymala-Busse, Jim Fearon, Joe Felter, Frank Fukuyama, Steve Haber, Leon Hall, Jeff Hancock, Marty Hellman, Toomas Hendrik Ilves, Chris Inglis, Bobby Inman, Jamil Jaffer, Bob Jervis, Loch Johnson, David Kennedy, Michal Kosinski, Steve Krasner, Paul Krattiger, Sarah Kreps, Todd Mahar, Matteo Martemucci, Mark Mazzetti, H. R. McMaster, Greg Mendenhall, Keren Yahri-Milo, Asfandyar Mir, Barry "Papa" Murphy, Dutch Murray, Paul Narain, Anne Neuberger, the late and great Janne Nolan, Joe Nye, Martin Oppus, Enrique Oti, Bill Perry, Mark "Zulu" Pye, Julie Quinn, Jay Raymond, Eric Reid, Mike Robinson, Lee Ross, Gary Roughead, David Sanger, Marietje Schaake, Jackie Schneider, Adam Segal, Raj Shah, Scott Shane, the late George Shultz, Jennifer Smith-Heys, Abe Sofaer, Alex Stamos, Eli Sugarman, John Taylor, Phil Taubman, Phil Tetlock, John Villasenor, and Janine Zacharia.

Other institutions hosted initiatives and discussions that helped improve particular chapters and ideas. Thanks to my fellow commissioners on the Center for Strategic and International Security (CSIS) Technology and Intelligence Task Force and the leaders of our band: Avril Haines, Stephanie O'Sullivan, Kath Hicks, and Brian Katz. The American Academy of Arts & Sciences project on "Meeting the Challenges of the New Nuclear Age" led by Vipin Narang and Scott Sagan took me into the fascinating world of open-source nuclear threat intelligence and brought scary workshops on all things nuclear to my desktop during the pandemic. The *Atlantic* asked me to write about my research for a broader audience, and I couldn't have done it without the support and editorial magic of Kathy Gilsinan, Dante Ramos, and Yoni Applebaum. My deep thanks also to the Strauss Center at the University of Texas at Austin and Harvard's Belfer Center for giving me opportunities to discuss all things cyber.

A virtual "murder board" of experts read early chapters and offered priceless feedback: Stephen Aftergood, Tom Fingar, Joe Gartin, Rose Gottemoeller, Sig Hecker, Rick Ledgett, John McLaughlin, Frank

Pabian, Allison Puccioni, Josh Rovner, Steve Slick, Michael Sulmeyer, Jeff Vanak, and Matt Waxman. A special thanks to Herb Lin and Michael Morell, dream co-authors, whose collaborations on technology, cyber challenges, and intelligence sharpened my thinking and got this ball rolling.

My talented literary agent, Christy Fletcher, has been giving me great guidance for over a decade. Chuck Myers, Eric Crahan, Bridget Flannery-McCoy, and their wonderful team at Princeton University Press showed far more patience than I deserve, sticking with this project and improving it every step of the way. Thanks also to Jane Fransson, who helped make my prose sing.

This book would never have been written without the keen minds, kind hearts, and dedication of my research director, Taylor Johnson McLamb, and my former chief of staff and research associate Russell Wald.

Condi Rice started me on this journey in graduate school. The only experience more rewarding than having her as a doctoral advisor is coming back to Stanford and working with her as a dear colleague.

My thanks to the extended Mallery and Zegart clans, two incredible families.

The COVID-19 pandemic brought unexpected lockdown with my kids, Alexander, Jack, and Kate Mallery. Experiencing daily life in close quarters with two displaced college students and a teen daughter has been a rare gift—from our serious national security dinner conversations to the daily ribbing about my office wall notes looking like Carrie Mathison in her craziest moments. Each brought different rays of sunshine to a dark time and made this book immeasurably better. Alexander gave me new insight into computer science and how engineers think. Jack read and offered feedback on every chapter. Kate helped me test drive ideas in her high school foreign policy class. Nothing says love more than letting your embarrassing mother teach your sixteen-year-old friends.

My husband, Craig Mallery, brought his writer's flair and lawyerly mind to every page and made me think hard and laugh harder. Six moves, six books, five careers, three kids, and seven high-maintenance pets later, the evidence is in: I won the lottery when I met him.

NOTES

Chapter 1: Intelligence Challenges in the Digital Age

1. Brandon Griggs, "The CIA Sends Its First Tweet (or Not)," CNN, June 6, 2014, https://www.cnn.com/2014/06/06/tech/social-media/cia-first-tweet/index.html#:~:text=At%201%3A49%20pm%20ET,Internet%20immediately%20erupted%20with%20delight.

2. I am grateful to Michael Morell for developing these ideas. An earlier version of the argument can be found in Amy Zegart and Michael Morell, "Spies, lies, and algorithms," *Foreign Affairs* 98, no. 3 (May/June 2019): 85–96.

3. Scott Pelley, "Facial and Emotional Recognition: How One Man Is Advancing Artificial Intelligence," CBS News, January 13, 2019, https://www.cbsnews.com/news/60-minutes-ai-facial-and-emotional-recognition-how-one-man-is-advancing-artificial-intelligence/ (accessed September 24, 2020); Kai-Fu Lee, *AI Superpowers: China, Silicon Valley, and the New World Order* (New York: Houghton Mifflin, 2018).

4. As the National Security Commission on Artificial Intelligence noted in its October 2020 report, the U.S. military has already tested an AI-powered command and control system that successfully shot down a cruise missile with a "smart bullet" and demonstrated that an AI-operated fighter jet could defeat a human pilot in a dogfight simulation. National Security Commission on Artificial Intelligence, "Interim Report and Third Quarter Recommendations," October 2020, 6.

5. Letter from commission co-chairs, National Security Commission on Artificial Intelligence, "Interim Report and Third Quarter Recommendations."

6. Quoted in James Vincent, "Putin says the nation that leads in AI 'will be the ruler of the world,'" *Verge*, September 4, 2017, https://www.theverge.com/2017/9/4/16251226/russia-ai-putin-rule-the-world (accessed November 22, 2020).

7. People's Republic of China, State Council Notice on the Issuance of the Next Generation Artificial Intelligence Development Plan, "A Next Generation Artificial Intelligence Development Plan," released July 20, 2017, translated by Graham Webster, Rogier Creemers, Paul Triolo, and Elsa Kania (August 1, 2017), https://www.newamerica.org/cybersecurity-initiative/digichina/blog/full-translation-chinas-new-generation-artificial-intelligence-development-plan-2017/.

8. National Security Commission on Artificial Intelligence, "Interim Report," November 2019, https://science.house.gov/imo/media/doc/Schmidt%20Testimony%20Attachment.pdf (accessed September 26, 2020), 6.

9. Fredrik Dahlqvist, Mark Patel, Alexander Rajko, and Jonathan Shulman, "Growing Opportunities in the Internet of Things," *McKinsey & Company*, July 22, 2019, https://www.mckinsey.com/industries/private-equity-and-principal-investors/our-insights/growing-opportunities-in-the-internet-of-things# (accessed September 24, 2020).

10. Cade Metz, "Google Claims a Quantum Breakthrough That Could Change Computing," *New York Times*, October 23, 2019, https://www.nytimes.com/2019/10/23/technology/quantum-computing-google.html (accessed September 24, 2020).

11. McKinsey Global Institute, "The Bio Revolution," May 2020, https://www.mckinsey.com/~/media/McKinsey/Industries/Pharmaceuticals%20and%20Medical%20Products/Our%20Insights/The%20Bio%20Revolution%20Innovations%20transforming%20economies%20societies%20and%20our%20lives/May_2020_MGI_Bio_Revolution_Report.pdf (accessed September 24, 2020); National Academies of Sciences, Engineering, and Medicine, *Biodefense in the Age of Synthetic Biology* (Washington, D.C.: National Academies Press, 2018).

12. Author discussions with three leading synthetic biologists, May 8, 2020.

13. Elsa B. Kania and Wilson Vorndick, "Weaponizing biotech: How China's military is preparing for a 'new domain of warfare,'" *Defense One*, August 14, 2019.

14. Ben Cohen, "Why Every NBA Player Is Getting a Ring," *Wall Street Journal*, June 22, 2020, https://www.wsj.com/articles/nba-oura-ring-disney-bubble-11592809399 (accessed September 24, 2020).

15. Mark Zastrow, "South Korea is reporting intimate details of COVID-19 cases: Has it helped?" *Nature*, March 18, 2020, https://www.nature.com/articles/d41586-020-00740-y (accessed September 24, 2020).

16. Cyberspace Solarium Commission, "Cyberspace Solarium Commission Report," March 2020, https://drive.google.com/file/d/1ryMCIL_dZ3oQyjFqFkkf1oMxIXJGT4yv/view (accessed September 24, 2020), 9–11.

17. Defense Intelligence Agency, "Challenges to Security in Space," January 2019, https://www.dia.mil/Portals/27/Documents/News/Military%20Power%20Publications/Space_Threat_V14_020119_sm.pdf (accessed September 25, 2020), 13–22.

18. U.S. Senate Select Committee on Intelligence, "Report on the Investigation into Russian Interference in the 2016 Presidential Election," Vol. 2, March 2019, https://www.justice.gov/storage/report_volume2.pdf (accessed September 24, 2020); "Cyberspace Solarium Commission Report," 11–12.

19. Countries that have used drones in combat are the United States, the United Kingdom, Israel, Pakistan, Iraq, Nigeria, Iran, and Turkey. Peter Bergen, Melissa Salyk-Virk, David Sterman, "World of drones: Who has what: Countries that have conducted drone strikes," New America Foundation, July 30, 2020, https://www.newamerica.org/international-security/reports/world-drones/who-has-what-countries-that-have-conducted-drone-strikes (accessed September 9, 2020).

20. Maeghin Alarid, "Recruitment and radicalization: The role of social media and new technology," *PRISM: The Journal of Complex Operations*, May 24, 2016, https://cco.ndu.edu/News/Article/780274/chapter-13-recruitment-and-radicalization-the-role-of-social-media-and-new-tech/ (accessed September 25, 2020).

21. Allison Puccioni, "Double-edged sword: Satellite imagery offers new tools to militants," *IHS Jane's Intelligence Review*, July 2016, 28.

22. Paul Mozur, Jonah M. Kessel, and Melissa Chan, "Made in China, Exported to the World: The Surveillance State," *New York Times*, April 24, 2019, https://www.nytimes.com/2019/04/24/technology/ecuador-surveillance-cameras-police-government.html (accessed September 24, 2020).

23. Zegart and Morell, "Spies, lies, and algorithms."

24. Amy Zegart, "The Cuban missile crisis as intelligence failure," *Policy Review*, Hoover Institution, October 2, 2012, https://www.hoover.org/research/cuban-missile-crisis-intelligence-failure (accessed September 20, 2020).

25. Jeff Jardins, "How much data is generated each day?" World Economic Forum, April 17, 2019, https://www.weforum.org/agenda/2019/04/how-much-data-is-generated-each-day-cf4bddf29f/ (accessed September 24, 2020).

26. Domo, "Data Never Sleeps 7.0," https://web-assets.domo.com/blog/wp-content/uploads/2019/07/data-never-sleeps-7-896kb.jpg (accessed January 17, 2021).

27. Zegart and Morell, "Spies, lies, and algorithms."

28. Jason Murdock, "What is Faces of the Riot? Website features people at Capitol siege seen in Parler videos," *Newsweek*, January 25, 2021.

29. Jardins, "How much data is generated each day?"

30. Editorial Team, "The exponential growth of data," *insideBigData*, February 16, 2020, https://insidebigdata.com/2017/02/16/the-exponential-growth-of-data/ (accessed September 25, 2020).

31. Zegart and Morell, "Spies, lies, and algorithms," 90–91.

32. Zegart and Morell, 90.

33. Daniel R. Coats, "Statement for the Record: Worldwide Threat Assessment of the US Intelligence Community," Senate Select Committee on Intelligence, January 29, 2019, 17; Maxime Puteaux and Alexandre Najar, "Are Smallsats Entering the Maturity Stage?" Space News, August 6, 2019, https://spacenews.com/analysis-are-smallsats-entering-the-maturity-stage/ (accessed September 24, 2020). Not all small satellites collect imagery. Most are used for communications and weather. Nevertheless, the number of commercial imagery satellites has increased dramatically in recent years, too. See Allison Puccioni and Neil Ashdown, "Raising standards," *IHS Jane's Intelligence Review*, December 2019, 8.

34. Although U.S. laws restrict the resolution of images collected by American commercial satellite sensors and designate which foreign entities may purchase their products, the internationalization of the small satellite business is reducing these legal protections. In 2019, there were nearly fifty commercial imagery satellites in orbit, including those operated by companies in China, France, Italy, South Korea, Spain, and the United Kingdom. Puccioni and Ashdown, "Raising standards," 8.

35. Frank Pabian, "Commercial Satellite Imagery as an Evolving Open-Source Verification Technology," Joint Research Centre, European Commission, 2015, 11; satellite launch dates and resolution data from "Satellite Sensors," Satellite Imaging Corporation, https://www.satimagingcorp.com/satellite-sensors/ (accessed September 24, 2020).

36. For more on Synthetic Aperture Radar (SAR) technology, see Pabian, "Commercial Satellite Imagery"; Allison Puccioni, "Penetrating vision," *IHS Jane's Intelligence Review*, May 2016, 55–57.

37. Allison Puccione and Sulgiye Park, "Remote Sensing for Environmental Security in North Korea," research seminar, Center for International Security and Cooperation, Stanford University, January 27, 2021.

38. Sandra Erwin, "Analysts: NRO's Commercial Imagery Purchases Could Reach $400 Million by 2023," Space News, June 29, 2020, https://spacenews.com/analysts-nros-commercial -imagery-purchases-could-reach-400-million-by-2023/ (accessed September 24, 2020).

39. See *Phillippi v. CIA*, 546 F.2d 1009, 1013 (D.C. Cir. 1976), raising the issue of whether the CIA could refuse to confirm or deny its ties to Howard Hughes's submarine retrieval ship, the *Glomar Explorer*. The court ruled that "the fact of the existence or non-existence of the records you request would relate to information pertaining to intelligence sources and methods which the Director of Central Intelligence has the responsibility to protect from unauthorized disclosure in accordance with section 102(d)(3) of the National Security Act of 1947 [50 U.S.C. § 403(d)(3) (1970)]."

40. Paul H. B. Shin, "The CIA's Secret History of the Phrase 'Can Neither Confirm Nor Deny," ABC News, June 6, 2014, https://abcnews.go.com/US/cias-secret-history-phrase -confirm-deny/story?id=24033629 (accessed September 24, 2020); National Security Archive, "Project Azorian: The CIA's Declassified History of the *Glomar Explorer*," edited by Matthew Aid with William Burr and Thomas Blanton, February 12, 2010, https://nsarchive2.gwu.edu/nukevault /ebb305/index.htm; Radiolab, "Neither Confirm nor Deny," podcast, June 4, 2019, https://www .wnycstudios.org/podcasts/radiolab/articles/confirm-nor-deny (accessed September 26, 2020).

41. William Farr and Jerry Cohen, "Sunken Ship Deal by CIA, Hughes Told," *Los Angeles Times*, February 7, 1975.

42. David H. Sharp, director of recovery systems in AZORIAN, wrote a declassified book about it: *The CIA's Greatest Covert Operation* (Lawrence, Kan.: University Press of Kansas, 2012), noting that the submarine carried three nuclear missiles and two nuclear torpedoes (1); Central Intelligence Agency, "Project AZORIAN," https://www.cia.gov/legacy/museum/exhibit /project-azorian/ (accessed January 25, 2021).

43. Sharp, *CIA's Greatest Covert Operation*, 33–37; Central Intelligence Agency, "Project AZORIAN."

44. Sharp, *CIA's Greatest Covert Operation*, 1.

45. Sharp, 5–6. Sharp writes that Adm. Thomas H. Moorer, the chief of naval operations, said the value to the country could be immense and that "other key members of the intelligence community felt the same way. The potential intelligence coup was too valuable to just forget" (6). A classified CIA summary of the operation that was redacted, declassified, and released in 2010 notes that CIA Director Richard Helms "stated that the ad hoc committee of the U.S. Intelligence Board (USIB) had completed a detailed review of the value of the AZORIAN target on which they had placed the highest priority, and he concurred in their assessment." Central Intelligence Agency, "Project AZORIAN: The Story of the *Hughes Glomar Explorer*," originally published in *Studies of Intelligence* (1985), redacted, declassified, and released January 4, 2010, https://www.cia.gov/readingroom/docs/DOC_0005301269.pdf, 4, 12 (accessed September 26, 2020); Central Intelligence Agency, "Project AZORIAN."

46. Sharp, *CIA's Greatest Covert Operation*, 190–98; 211; 223–24.

47. Central Intelligence Agency, "Project AZORIAN: The Story of the *Hughes Glomar Explorer*," 2; National Security Archive, "Project Azorian: The CIA's Declassified History of the *Glomar Explore*"; Sharp, 252–53; Central Intelligence Agency, "Project AZORIAN."

48. Radiolab, "Neither Confirm nor Deny."

49. Count as of 2019. Ian Shapira, "A Suicide Sparks Hard Questions about the Agency's Memorial Wall," *Washington Post*, May 21, 2019, https://www.washingtonpost.com/local/a-cia -suicide-sparks-hard-questions-about-the-agencys-memorial-wall/2019/05/18/20c8c284-7687 -11e9-bd25-c989555e7766_story.html (accessed September 24, 2020).

50. Central Intelligence Agency, "Ask Molly: March 22, 2019," https://www.cia.gov/stories /story/ask-molly-march-22-2019/ (accessed September 26, 2020); Central Intelligence Agency, "CIA Book of Honor," https://www.cia.gov/legacy/headquarters/cia-book-of-honor/ (accessed January 25, 2021).

51. "Artificial Intelligence at Google: Our Principles," https://ai.google/principles (accessed November 23, 2020).

52. National Security Commission on Artificial Intelligence, "First Quarter Recommendations," March 2020, https://drive.google.com/file/d/1wkPh8Gb5drBrKBg6OhGu5oNaTEER bKss/view (accessed September 26, 2020), 22.

53. Cade Metz, "When the A.I. Professor Leaves, Students Suffer, Study Says," *New York Times*, September 6, 2019, https://www.nytimes.com/2019/09/06/technology/when-the-ai-professor -leaves-students-suffer-study-says.html (accessed September 24, 2020); Brooke Sutherland, "GM and Nikola are a match made in Tesla hell," *Bloomberg*, September 8, 2020, https://www.bloomberg .com/opinion/articles/2020-09-08/gm-nikola-electric-truck-partnership-creates-formidable -tesla-rival (accessed September 24, 2020); National Security Commission on Artificial Intelligence, "Interim Report," 25; Michael Gofman and Zhao Jin, "Artificial Intelligence, Human Capital, and Innovation," University of Rochester, August 20, 2019.

54. Hani Shawna, "The CIA Joins Twitter and Facebook," CBS News, June 6, 2014, https:// www.cbsnews.com/news/cia-joins-twitter-and-facebook/ (accessed September 24, 2020).

55. Aris Pappas, "Ryszard Kuklinski: A Case Officer's View," incidental paper, Seminar on Intelligence, Command, and Control, Center for Information Policy Research, Harvard University, April 29, 2004, 5.

56. U.S. Department of Homeland Security Press Office, "Joint Statement from the Department of Homeland Security and the Office of the Director of National Intelligence on Election Security," October 7, 2016, https://www.dhs.gov/news/2016/10/07/joint-statement-department -homeland-security-and-office-director-national (accessed November 3, 2020).

57. Amy Zegart, "Intelligence isn't just for government anymore," *Foreign Affairs*, November 2, 2020.

58. Federal Bureau of Investigation, *Safeguarding Your Vote: A Joint Message on Election Security*, YouTube, October 6, 2020, https://www.youtube.com/watch?v=H-3Ek14eO70 (accessed November 3, 2020).

59. *Safeguarding Your Vote.*

60. Subscriber count as of November 3, 2020. RT America, Youtube, https://www.youtube .com/user/RTAmerica.

61. Roberta Wohlstetter, *Pearl Harbor: Warning and Decision* (Palo Alto, Calif.: Stanford University Press, 1962).

62. Amy B. Zegart, *Spying Blind: The CIA, the FBI, and the Origins of 9/11* (Princeton, N.J.: Princeton University Press, 2007); National Commission on Terrorist Attacks Upon the United States, *The 9/11 Commission Report, Authorized Version* (New York: W. W. Norton, 2004).

63. Zegart and Morell, "Spies, lies, and algorithms."

64. Leon E. Panetta with Jim Newton, *Worthy Fights: A Memoir of Leadership in War and Peace* (New York: Penguin, 2014), 390.

Chapter 2: The Education Crisis

1. Quoted in *Quotable Quotes*, edited by Deborah DeFord (Pleasantville, N.Y.: Reader's Digest, 1997), 140. Clancy adapted the original quote from Mark Twain (Samuel Clemens), *Following the Equator: A Journey Around the World*, chap. 15 (Hartford, Conn.: The American Publishing Company, 1898): "Truth is stranger than fiction, but it is because fiction is obliged to stick to possibilities, truth isn't."

2. Author visit to CIA, November 2019.

3. Amy B. Zegart, "Spytainment: The real influence of fake spies," *International Journal of Intelligence and Counterintelligence* 23, no. 4 (2010): 599–622, https://doi.org/10.1080/08850607.2010.501635.

4. Classified materials must be carefully secured at all times from anyone without the necessary clearances. Executive Order 13526, December 29, 2009, https://www.archives.gov/isoo/policy-documents/cnsi-eo.html#four (accessed April 28, 2020); Office of the Director of National Intelligence, "Implementation Plan of Executive Order 13526," December 31, 2010, https://fas.org/sgp/othergov/intel/plan.pdf (accessed April 28, 2020); Letter from Michael G. Vickers, Under Secretary of Defense for Intelligence, "DoD Information Security Program: Protection of Classified Information," accompanying *Department of Defense Manual* 5200.01, Vol. 3, February 24, 2012, https://www.esd.whs.mil/Portals/54/Documents/DD/issuances/dodm/520001_vol3.pdf (accessed April 28, 2020).

5. Executive Order 13526. For examples of approved methods for disposing of classified information, see https://www.nsa.gov/Resources/NSA-Classified-Materiel-Conversion-CMC/ (accessed April 16, 2021), and *Defense Department Manual*, 42.

6. Nada Bakos, *The Targeter* (New York: Little, Brown, 2019), 14.

7. Office of the Director of National Intelligence, "History," https://www.dni.gov/index.php/nctc-who-we-are/history (accessed April 21, 2020).

8. See, for example, this video of the NCTC featured in 2020 on its website: Office of the Director of National Intelligence, *The National Counterterrorism Center*, December 13, 2018, YouTube https://www.youtube.com/channel/UChGV6oLYpVFgOWs7aeLrdEQ (accessed April 30, 2020).

9. Lawrence Wright, *The Terror Years: From Al-Qaeda to the Islamic State* (New York: Penguin, 2016), 211–12.

10. Intelligence Science Board, "Educing Information: Interrogation: Science and Art Foundations for the Future, Phase I Report" (Washington, D.C.: National Defense Intelligence College, 2006), ix.

11. Scott Horton, "How Hollywood learned to stop worrying and love the (ticking) bomb," *Harper's*, March 1, 2008, https://harpers.org/blog/2008/03/how-hollywood-learned-to-stop-worrying-and-love-the-ticking-bomb/ (accessed August 31, 2017); Jane Mayer, "Whatever it takes: The politics behind the man behind '24,'" *New Yorker*, February 11, 2007, http://www.newyorker.com/magazine/2007/02/19/whatever-it-takes (accessed June 15, 2020).

12. Jim Mattis and Kori N. Schake, eds., *Warriors & Citizens: American Views of Our Military* (Stanford, Calif.: Hoover Institution Press, 2016).

13. Amy Zegart and Kevin Childs, "The divide between Silicon Valley and Washington is a national-security threat," *Atlantic*, December 13, 2018, https://www.theatlantic.com/ideas/archive/2018/12/growing-gulf-between-silicon-valley-and-washington/577963/ (accessed June 15, 2020).

14. Michael Hayden, remarks at George Washington University, February 19, 2013.

15. My analysis is based on examination of the 116th Congress member bios posted on bioguide.congress.gov and information from members' websites, campaign websites, or online news sources. Intelligence experience is defined broadly to include (1) service in an element of the U.S. Intelligence Community, (2) service as an intelligence officer as part of the armed forces, or (3) participation in military intelligence collection other than HUMINT (for example, flying surveillance aircraft). Fifteen members of the House and three Senators (Thomas Carper, Daniel Sullivan, and Todd Young) had prior intelligence experience.

16. Council on Foreign Relations, "The Iraq War," https://www.cfr.org/timeline/iraq-war; Commission on the Intelligence Capabilities of the United States Regarding Weapons of Mass Destruction (Silberman-Robb Commission or WMD Commission), "Report to the President," March 31, 2005, https://fas.org/irp/offdocs/wmd_report.pdf.

17. Council on Foreign Relations, "U.S. Domestic Surveillance," last modified December 18, 2013, https://www.cfr.org/backgrounder/us-domestic-surveillance (accessed June 15, 2020); U.S. Department of Justice, "The NSA Program to Detect and Prevent Terrorist Attacks: Myth v. Reality," January 27, 2006, https://www.justice.gov/sites/default/files/opa/legacy/2006/02/02/nsa_myth_v_reality.pdf (accessed June 16, 2020); U.S. Library of Congress Congressional Research Service, John W. Rollins and Edward C. Liu, "NSA Surveillance Leaks: Background and Issues for Congress," R43134, September 4, 2013, https://fas.org/sgp/crs/intel/R43134.pdf. The revelation of the wiretapping program was a bombshell: James Risen and Eric Lichtblau, "Bush Lets U.S. Spy on Callers without Courts," *New York Times*, December 16, 2005, https://www.nytimes.com/2005/12/16/politics/bush-lets-us-spy-on-callers-without-courts.html (accessed June 15, 2020).

18. Julie Vitkovskaya, "What Are 'Black Sites'? 6 Key Things to Know about the CIA's Secret Prisons Overseas," *Washington Post*, January 1, 2017, https://www.washingtonpost.com/news/checkpoint/wp/2017/01/25/what-are-black-sites-6-key-things-to-know-about-the-cias-secret-prisons-overseas/ (accessed June 15, 2020); U.S. Senate Select Committee on Intelligence, "Committee Study of the Central Intelligence Agency's Detention and Interrogation Program,"

113th Cong., 2nd sess., December 9, 2014, https://www.intelligence.senate.gov/sites/default /files/documents/CRPT-113srpt288.pdf.

19. Student survey, Political Science M120C: U.S. Intelligence Agencies in Theory and Practice, UCLA, Winter 2009. Content analysis of 24 by the nonpartisan Parents Television Council finds that the show depicted torture frequently (averaging one torture scene every other episode) and always favorably; in Jack Bauer's world, harsh methods are what the good guys use, and they work. Parents Television Council data cited in Mayer, "Whatever it takes"; "Parents Beware of 24," *Weekly Wrap*, Parents Television Council, November 21, 2008.

20. Amy B. Zegart, "Real Spies, Fake Spies, NSA, and More: What My 2012 and 2013 National Polls Reveal," Lawfare, November 7, 2013, https://www.lawfareblog.com/real-spies-fake-spies -nsa-and-more-what-my-2012-and-2013-national-polls-reveal (accessed August 31, 2017). The 2012 poll was conducted August 24–30, 2012, had a sample of one thousand general population respondents, and had a margin of error of +/– 4 percent. The 2013 poll was conducted October 5–7, 2013, had a sample of one thousand general population respondents, and had a margin of error of +/– 4.3 percent.

21. Allen Dulles, who served as CIA director from 1953 to 1962, estimated in 1947 that more than 80 percent of intelligence collected during peacetime came from open sources. "Memorandum Respecting Section 202 (Central Intelligence Agency) of the Bill to Provide for a National Defense Establishment, Submitted by Allen W. Dulles, April 25, 1947," reprinted in *National Defense Establishment (Unification of the Armed Services)*, 80th Cong., 1st sess., U.S. Senate Armed Services Committee Hearings Part 3, 525. Since the Cold War's end, the percent of open-source intelligence has increased. In 1997, former Defense Intelligence Agency Director Lt. Gen. Samuel V. Wilson estimated that "ninety percent of intelligence comes from open sources. The other ten percent, the clandestine work, is just more dramatic. The real intelligence hero is Sherlock Holmes, not James Bond." Quoted in Richard S. Friedman, "Open source intelligence: A review essay," *Parameters* 28, no. 2 (Summer 1998): 159. Notably, the percentage of secret information in intelligence reports varies substantially by subject. *Hard targets*, or adversaries that are largely closed to the outside world (such as North Korea), have a higher concentration of secret information because the United States cannot get information in any other way.

22. 2012 YouGov National Security Poll.

23. "Transcript: Senate Intelligence Hearing on National Security Threats," January 29, 2014, https://www.washingtonpost.com/world/national-security/transcript-senate-intelligence -hearing-on-national-security-threats/2014/01/29/b5913184-8912-11e3-833c-33098f9e5267_story .html (accessed June 15, 2020); Jack Goldsmith, "Three Years Later: How Snowden Helped the U.S. Intelligence Community," Lawfare, June 6, 2016, https://www.lawfareblog.com/three-years -later-how-snowden-helped-us-intelligence-community (accessed June 15, 2020); David E. Sanger and Eric Schmitt, "Snowden Used Low-Cost Tool to Best N.S.A.," *New York Times*, February 8, 2014, https://www.nytimes.com/2014/02/09/us/snowden-used-low-cost-tool-to -best-nsa.html (accessed April 21, 2020).

24. Steve Holland, Mark Hosenball, and Jeff Mason, "Obama Bans Spying on Leaders of U.S. Allies, Scales back NSA Program," Reuters, January 17, 2014, https://www.reuters.com /article/us-usa-security-obama/obama-bans-spying-on-leaders-of-u-s-allies-scales-back-nsa -program-idUSBREA0G0JI20140117 (accessed May 13, 2020).

25. President's Review Group on Intelligence and Communications Technologies, "Liberty and Security in a Changing World: Report and Recommendations of the President's Review Group on Intelligence and Communications Technologies," December 12, 2013, 94–108.

26. Barton Gellman and Ashkan Soltani, "NSA Infiltrates Links to Yahoo, Google Data Centers Worldwide, Snowden Documents Say," *Washington Post*, October 30, 2013, https://www.washingtonpost.com/world/national-security/nsa-infiltrates-links-to-yahoo-google-data-centers-worldwide-snowden-documents-say/2013/10/30/e51d661e-4166-11e3-8b74-d89d714ca4dd_story.html (accessed June 15, 2020); Amy Davidson Sorkin, "Tech companies slap back at the N.S.A.'s smiley face," *New Yorker*, November 1, 2013, https://www.newyorker.com/news/amy-davidson/tech-companies-slap-back-at-the-n-s-a-s-smiley-face (accessed June 15, 2020); Claire Cain Miller, "Angry Over U.S. Surveillance, Tech Giants Bolster Defenses," *New York Times*, October 31, 2013, https://www.nytimes.com/2013/11/01/technology/angry-over-us-surveillance-tech-giants-bolster-defenses.html?hp (accessed August 19, 2020).

27. Kennedy Elliott and Terri Rupar, "Six Months of Revelations on NSA," *Washington Post*, December 23, 2013, https://www.washingtonpost.com/wp-srv/special/national/nsa-timeline/ (accessed June 15, 2020).

28. The *New York Times* article archives were searched from June 5, 2013, through December 5, 2013, excluding opinion editorials, blog posts, corrections, and articles in the magazine. Because the *Guardian* does not offer similar search capabilities, LexisNexis searches were used with keywords "Edward Snowden" and the same date ranges.

29. Peter Finn and Sari Horwitz, "U.S. Charges Snowden with Espionage," *Washington Post*, June 21, 2013, https://www.washingtonpost.com/world/national-security/us-charges-snowden-with-espionage/2013/06/21/507497d8-dab1-11e2-a016-92547bf094cc_story.html (accessed June 15, 2020).

30. "U.S. Revokes Snowden's Passport: Official Source," Reuters, June 23, 2013, https://www.reuters.com/article/us-usa-security-passport-idUSBRE95M0CW20130623 (accessed April 21, 2020).

31. President's Review Group on Intelligence and Communications Technologies, "Liberty and Security," 76.

32. The 2015 USA Freedom Act required phone providers to hold telephone metadata rather than giving it to the government. This revamped system appears to have been ended entirely by the NSA a few years later. See USA Freedom Act, 2014, H.R.3361, 113th Cong., 2nd sess., https://www.congress.gov/bill/113th-congress/house-bill/3361. In 2020, a three-judge panel of the 9th Circuit Court of Appeals ruled that the NSA's telephone metadata program violated the Foreign Intelligence Surveillance Act and may have been unconstitutional. *United States v. Moalin*, 973 F.3d 977 (9th Cir. 2020).

33. "Edward Snowden did this country a great service. Let him come home," *Guardian*, September 14, 2016, https://www.theguardian.com/us-news/2016/sep/14/edward-snowden-pardon-bernie-sanders-daniel-ellsberg (accessed April 22, 2020); Michael German, "Edward Snowden Is a Whistleblower," ACLU, August 2, 2013, https://www.aclu.org/blog/national-security/secrecy/edward-snowden-whistleblower (accessed April 22, 2020).

34. PBS NewsHour, *Former Def. Sec. Gates Says Edward Snowden Is a Traitor*, January 14, 2014, https://www.youtube.com/watch?v=sQKUe96TAh4; ABC News, *Edward Snowden NSA*

Leaker: Boehner Says "He's a Traitor," June 11, 2013, https://www.youtube.com/watch?v=GIgUVExgDeo.

35. Author interview with Michael V. Hayden, *Inside the NSA: An Evening with General Michael Hayden*, Stanford University, October 28, 2014, YouTube, https://www.youtube.com/watch?v=_ESGBPmfomc at 53:40.

36. Adm. Michael Rogers, NSA Director, testimony before the U.S. Senate Select Committee on Intelligence, National Security Agency Activities and Its Ability to Meet Its Diverse Mission Requirements, S. Hrg. 114-772, September 24, 2015, https://www.intelligence.senate.gov/hearings/open-hearing-national-security-agency-activities-and-its-ability-meet-its-diverse-mission# (accessed April 27, 2020); Cheryl Pellerin, "Rogers Discusses NSA Reorganization, National Security Threats," DOD News, September 25, 2015, https://www.defense.gov/Explore/News/Article/Article/620617/rogers-discusses-nsa-reorganization-national-security-threats/ (accessed April 27, 2020).

37. Office of the Director of National Intelligence, "Members of the IC," https://www.dni.gov/index.php/what-we-do/members-of-the-ic#nsa (accessed May 13, 2020); "Statement for the Record by Lt. Gen. Michael V. Hayden, Director of the National Security Agency, before the House Permanent Select Committee on Intelligence," April 12, 2000, https://www.nsa.gov/news-features/speeches-testimonies/Article/1620510/statement-for-the-record-by-lt-gen-michael-v-hayden-usaf-director-before-the-ho/ (accessed June 15, 2020); Michael V. Hayden, *Playing to the Edge: American Intelligence in the Age of Terror* (New York: Penguin, 2016), 8–26; Nicole Perlroth, Jeff Larson, and Scott Shane, "N.S.A. Able to Foil Basic Safeguards of Privacy on Web," *New York Times*, September 5, 2013, https://www.nytimes.com/2013/09/06/us/nsa-foils-much-internet-encryption.html (accessed June 15, 2020).

38. National Security Agency, "About Us," http://www.nsa.gov/about/index.shtml (accessed May 29, 2012).

39. Pew Research Center News Release, September 3, 2009.

40. The death of Ryan Dunn, star of the television program *Jackass*, did, ranking nineteenth. "Most Shared Articles on Facebook in 2011," Facebook, November 29, 2011, https://www.facebook.com/notes/facebook-media/most-shared-articles-on-facebook-in-2011/283221585046671 (accessed August 31, 2017); Andrew Hough, "Facebook's most popular 'shared' news stories for 2011 revealed," *Telegraph*, November 30, 2011, http://www.telegraph.co.uk/technology/facebook/8924835/Facebooks-most-popular-shared-news-stories-for-2011-revealed.html (accessed August 31, 2017).

41. 2013 YouGov National Security Poll.

42. Notably, the CIA's own inspector general came to a different conclusion about interrogation methods than the general public. He found the effectiveness of harsh techniques more questionable. Office of the Inspector General, Central Intelligence Agency, "Special Review: Counterterrorism Detention and Interrogation Activities (September 2001–October 2003)," 2003-7123-IG, May 7, 2004, declassified and redacted August 24, 2009, https://fas.org/irp/cia/product/ig-interrog.pdf (accessed July 26, 2017); Intelligence Science Board, "Educing Information."

43. Alan Abrahamson, "Applications Hit Record Highs for U.S. Law Schools: Increase Attributed to Impact of Television Hit 'L.A. Law,'" *Los Angeles Times*, August 20, 1989, https://www.latimes.com/archives/la-xpm-1989-08-20-me-1216-story.html (accessed April 22, 2020).

44. Arun Rath, "Is the 'CSI Effect' Influencing Courtrooms?" *Weekend Edition Sunday*, NPR, February 5, 2011, https://www.npr.org/2011/02/06/133497696/is-the-csi-effect-influencing -courtrooms (accessed April 22, 2020).

45. Mark Evje, "'Top Gun' Boosting Service Sign-Ups," *Los Angeles Times*, July 5, 1986, https://www.latimes.com/archives/la-xpm-1986-07-05-ca-20403-story.html (accessed April 22, 2020); Carl Forsling, "The original 'Top Gun' was a recruiter's dream. The sequel will be anything but," *Task and Purpose*, August 2, 2019, https://taskandpurpose.com/vultures-row/top -gun-maverick-military-recruitment (accessed June 15, 2020); David Sorota, "25 Years Later, How 'Top Gun' Made America Love War," *Washington Post*, August 26, 2011, https://www .washingtonpost.com/opinions/25-years-later-remembering-how-top-gun-changed-americas -feelings-about-war/2011/08/15/gIQAU6qJgJ_story.html (accessed June 15, 2020).

46. Christopher Andrew, *For the President's Eyes Only: Secret Intelligence and the American Presidency from Washington to Bush* (New York: Harper Perennial, 1996), 12. The author, James Fenimore Cooper, is known today for writing *The Last of the Mohicans*, but *The Spy* is what made him famous in his lifetime, becoming an international bestseller.

47. Ludlum has sold over 290 million copies worldwide, while Clancy has sold more than 100 million. BBC News, "Gaming World Set for Ludlum Books," August 11, 2005, http://news .bbc.co.uk/1/hi/entertainment/4142130.stm (accessed April 7, 2020); Julie Bosman, "Tom Clancy, Best-Selling Master of Military Thrillers, Dies at 66," *New York Times*, October 2, 2013, https://www.nytimes.com/2013/10/03/books/tom-clancy-best-selling-novelist-of-military -thrillers-dies-at-66.html?_r=0 (accessed April 7, 2020).

48. CNN.com Transcripts, "America Under Attack: Israeli Prime Minister, Foreign Minister Offer Condolences to the American People," September 11, 2001, 16:58 EST, http://transcripts .cnn.com/TRANSCRIPTS/0109/11/bn.74.html (accessed August 31, 2017).

49. CNN.com Transcripts, "Bin Laden Plotted New Attack; Bin Laden's Wife Questioned; A Private Moment with the President," May 5, 2011, 20:00 EST, http://transcripts.cnn.com /TRANSCRIPTS/1105/05/ita.01.html (accessed March 25, 2020).

50. Alex Rider, http://www.alexrider.com (accessed March 25, 2020).

51. Entertainment Software Association, "U.S. Video Game Sales Reach Record-Breaking $43.4 Billion in 2018," press release, January 22, 2019, https://www.theesa.com/press-releases/u -s-video-game-sales-reach-record-breaking-43-4-billion-in-2018/ (accessed April 7, 2020). In comparison, the global recorded music industry generated $19.1 billion in revenue during 2018. "IFPI Global Music Report 2019," April 2, 2019, https://www.ifpi.org/news/IFPI-GLOBAL -MUSIC-REPORT-2019 (accessed April 7, 2020). In 2015, the Pew Research Center reported that nearly half of all adults and 72 percent of teens played video games, and over eighty million American households owned at least one gaming console. Amanda Lenhart, "Video Games Are Key Elements in Friendships for Many Boys," Pew Research Center, August 6, 2015, http://www .pewinternet.org/2015/08/06/chapter-3-video-games-are-key-elements-in-friendships-for -many-boys/ (accessed July 24, 2017); Maeve Duggan, "Gaming and Gamers," Pew Research Center, December 15, 2015, http://www.pewinternet.org/2015/12/15/gaming-and-gamers/ (accessed July 24, 2017). According to the Entertainment Software Association's 2016 Report on the Computer and Gaming Industry, 65 percent of U.S. households owned at least one device used to play video games in 2015. In 2015, the U.S. Census Bureau reported there were 124.59

million households. See Erin Duffin, "Number of Households in the U.S. from 1960 to 2016 (in millions)," Statista: The Statistics Portal, November 28, 2019, https://www.statista.com/statistics /183635/number-of-households-in-the-us/ (accessed July 26, 2017).

52. Tim Brooks and Earle Marsh, *The Complete Directory to Prime Time Network TV Shows*, 9th ed. (New York: Ballantine, 2007).

53. Author's analysis of U.S. box office receipts for movies released in each year. Box Office Mojo, "Domestic Yearly Box Office," http://www.boxofficemojo.com/yearly/chart/ (accessed May 28, 2020).

54. Caroline Kitchenner, Karen Yuan, and Abdallah Fayyad, "Pay no attention to the G-man behind the curtain," *Atlantic*, March 16, 2018, https://www.theatlantic.com/membership /archive/2018/03/pay-no-attention-to-the-g-man-behind-the-curtain/555839/ (accessed April 22, 2020).

55. Ronald Kessler, *The Bureau: The Secret History of the FBI* (New York: St. Martin's, 2003), 44–46.

56. PBS, "The Era of Gangster Films," *The American Experience*, www.pbs.org/wgbh/amex /dillinger/peopleevents/e_hollywood.html (accessed April 28, 2020).

57. Kessler, *Bureau*, 44–46.

58. PBS, "Era of Gangster Films."

59. Mark Riffee, "CIA pitches scripts to Hollywood," *Wired*, September 15, 2011, http://www .wired.com/dangerroom/2011/09/cia-pitches-hollywood/ (accessed August 2, 2012); Office of Inspector General, Central Intelligence Agency, "Report of Audit: CIA Processes for Engaging with the Entertainment Industry," Report. No. 2012-0013-AS, Issued December 31, 2012, approved for release July 20, 2015, 2-3; John Ohab, "Pentagon's Entertainment Office Brings Military Science to Hollywood," Armed with Science: Research and Applications for the Modern Military, U.S. Department of Defense, http://science.dodlive.mil/2010/05/20 /pentagons-entertainment-office-brings-military-science-to-hollywood/ (accessed August 3, 2012); Central Intelligence Agency, "Offices of CIA," last updated March 27, 2015, https:// www.cia.gov/about/organization/public-affairs/#entertainment-inquiries (accessed January 25, 2021).

60. Federal Bureau of Investigation, "From Fact to Fiction: Giving Writers an Inside Look at the FBI," October 6, 2008, https://archives.fbi.gov/archives/news/stories/2008/october /writers_100608 (accessed April 28, 2020).

61. Central Intelligence Agency Entertainment Industry Liaison, last updated March 27, 2015, https://www.cia.gov/offices-of-cia/public-affairs/entertainment-industry-liaison/index.html (accessed August 3, 2012).

62. U.S. Department of Defense, "U.S. Military Assistance in Producing Motion Pictures, Television Shows, Music Videos," https://archive.defense.gov/faq/pis/PC12FILM.aspx (accessed August 20, 2020).

63. Author's visit to CIA, November 2019.

64. Associated Press, "New C.I.A. Recruiting Video Features 'Alias' Star," *New York Times*, March 10, 2004, http://www.nytimes.com/2004/03/10/politics/new-cia-recruiting-video -features-alias-star.html?_r=0 (accessed August 30, 2017).

65. CIA Kids Page, https://www.cia.gov/kids-page/index.html (accessed May 22, 2017). The current website which no longer includes Ava Shoephone, is https://www.cia.gov/spy-kids/ (accessed April 16, 2021).

66. Jeffrey Smith, "In-Q-Tel: The CIA's Tax-Funded Player in Silicon Valley," interview by Robert Siegel, *All Tech Considered*, NPR, July 16, 2012, http://www.npr.org/transcripts/156839153 (accessed March 25, 2020).

67. Nicholas Dujmovic, "Hollywood, don't you go disrespectin' my culture: *The Good Shepherd* versus real CIA history," *Intelligence and National Security* 23, no. 1: 25–41; see also unclassified segments of roundtable discussion on *The Good Shepherd* by David Robarge, Gary McCollim, Nicholas Dujmovic, and Thomas Coffee, *Studies in Intelligence* 51, no. 1 (2007): 47–54, https://www.tandfonline.com/doi/full/10.1080/02684520701798080 (accessed January 23, 2021). A transcript of the roundtable is in *Studies in Intelligence* 51, no. 1 (January 8, 2007), https://www.cia.gov/static/5e897e8297cc9446cc7a884703bcf6ef/Review-The-Good-Shepherd .pdf (accessed April 16, 2021).

68. *Zero Dark Thirty* was nominated for five Academy Awards and was considered an Oscar favorite for best picture until controversy erupted over the filmmakers' access to intelligence and its depiction of the efficacy of interrogation methods. Tim Reid and Jill Serjeant, "'Zero Dark Thirty' Fails at Oscars amid Political Fallout," Reuters, February 24, 2013, https://www .reuters.com/article/entertainment-us-oscars-zero/zero-dark-thirty-fails-at-oscars-amid -political-fallout-idUSBRE91O07S20130225 (accessed June 16, 2020).

69. Declassified documents detailing discussions between U.S. Defense Department officials and the movie team can be found at "Judicial Watch Bin Laden Movie—DoD," Scribd, http://www.scribd.com/doc/94447718/Judicial-Watch-Bin-Laden-Movie-DoD#page=140 (accessed August 3, 2012). Declassified documents about CIA assistance can be found at Jason Leopold and Ky Henderson, "Tequila, Painted Pearls, and Prada—How the CIA Helped Produce 'Zero Dark Thirty,'" Vice News, https://www.vice.com/en/article/xw3ypa/tequila -painted-pearls-and-prada-how-the-cia-helped-produce-zero-dark-thirty (accessed April 16, 2021).

70. Office of Inspector General, Central Intelligence Agency, "Report of Investigation: Potential Ethics Violations Involving Film Producers," September 16, 2013, approved for release August 8, 2015, 67–69.

71. "Message from the Acting Director: 'Zero Dark Thirty,'" December 21, 2012, https://cja .org/cja/downloads/Message%20from%20the%20Acting%20Director.pdf (accessed April 16, 2021).

72. "Message from the Acting Director." Policy wonks also blasted the film's claims to reportage and its sympathetic depiction of the efficacy of harsh interrogation methods. See Letter from Senators Dianne Feinstein, Carl Levin, and John McCain to Acting CIA Director Michael Morell, December 19, 2012, http://www.feinstein.senate.gov/public/index.cfm/files/serve /?File_id=d5bcc8f1-4ac5-4d25-9371-4f748c225597 (accessed June 23, 2014). Real reporters of facts were especially rankled. Pulitzer Prize–winning journalist Steve Coll called the movie "shoddy reporting" in "'Disturbing' & 'Misleading,'" *New York Review of Books*, February 7, 2013, https://www.nybooks.com/articles/2013/02/07/disturbing-misleading-zero-dark-thirty/

(accessed June 16, 2020). The *New Yorker*'s Jane Mayer, who spent years covering the CIA's detention and interrogation program, wrote, "Knowing the real facts . . . I had trouble enjoying the movie." Mayer, "Zero conscience in 'Zero Dark Thirty,'" *New Yorker*, December 14, 2012.

73. For more on this debate, see U.S. Senate Select Committee on Intelligence, "Report on the Central Intelligence Agency's Detention and Interrogation Program," December 8, 2014, https://www.intelligence.senate.gov/sites/default/files/publications/CRPT-113srpt288.pdf (accessed January 23, 2021); Michael Morell with Bill Harlow, *The Great War of Our Time: The CIA's Fight against Terrorism—From al Qa'ida to ISIS* (New York: Twelve, 2015), 269–79; Leon Panetta with Jim Newton, *Worthy Fights: A Memoir of Leadership in War and Peace* (New York: Penguin, 2014), 222–24; Hayden, *Playing to the Edge*, 396–402.

74. Ann Horaday, "'Zero Dark Thirty' and the New Reality of Reported Filmmaking," *Washington Post*, December 13, 2012, https://www.washingtonpost.com/entertainment/movies/zero-dark-thirty-and-the-new-reality-of-reported-filmmaking/2012/12/13/3630ce2c-4548-11e2-8e70-e1993528222d_story.html (accessed November 18, 2020).

75. F.S., "Taking on terror: Q&A with Kathryn Bigelow," *Economist*, https://www.economist.com/prospero/2013/01/24/taking-on-terror; Michael Cieply and Brooks Barnes, "Bin Laden Film's Focus Is Facts, Not Flash," *New York Times*, November 23, 2012, https://www.nytimes.com/2012/11/24/movies/zero-dark-thirty-by-kathryn-bigelow-focuses-on-facts.html; David Gritten, "Kathryn Bigelow Interview for Zero Dark Thirty: The Director on the Trail of Terrorism, *Telegraph*, January 18, 2013, https://www.telegraph.co.uk/culture/film/9809355/Kathryn-Bigelow-interview-for-Zero-Dark-Thirty-The-director-on-the-trail-of-terrorism.html.

76. *The Colbert Report*, Comedy Central, January 22, 2013.

77. Kathryn Bigelow, "Kathryn Bigelow Addresses 'Zero Dark Thirty' Torture Criticism," *Los Angeles Times*, January 15, 2013, http://articles.latimes.com/2013/jan/15/entertainment/la-et-mn-0116-bigelow-zero-dark-thirty-20130116 (accessed June 23, 2014).

78. Importantly, in 2015 the Office of the Director of National Intelligence produced "Principles of Transparency for the Intelligence Community," available at https://www.odni.gov/index.php/how-we-work/transparency (accessed November 18, 2020). General background on the IC is at https://intelligence.gov; the Foreign Intelligence Surveillance Court's website is https://fisc.uscourts.gov/.

79. Section 1.2 of Executive Order 13526; Office of the Director of National Intelligence, *Classification Guide*, Version 2.1, September 30, 2014, https://www.dni.gov/files/documents/FOIA/DF-2015-00044%20(Doc1).pdf (accessed April 28, 2020), 10.

80. Defense Department Commission on Classified Information, "Report to the Secretary of Defense by the Committee on Classified Information," November 8, 1956, Availability of Information from Federal Departments and Agencies, Part 5, Hearings before a Subcommittee of the Committee on Government Operations, U.S. House of Representatives, 84th Cong., 2nd sess., July 9, 10, 12, 1956, Appendix, https://books.google.com/books?id=NE4iAAAAMAAJ&pg=PA2133&lpg=PA2133&dq=Report+to+the+Secretary+of+Defense+by+the+Committee+on+Classified+Information,%E2%80%9D+November+8,+1956&source=bl&ots=J_cISy9bLf&sig=ACfU3U3Njv-CcAosTnPkYW059HXZdYc7qw&hl=en&sa=X&ved=2ahUKEwjDr6fVi_3vAhXKHTQIHT_XAPMQ6AEwBHoECAUQAw#v=onepage&q=Report%20to%20

the%20Secretary%20of%20Defense%20by%20the%20Committee%20on%20Classified%20 Information%2C%E2%80%9D%20November%208%2C%201956&f=false (accessed April 16, 2021), 2136. Major secrecy reform efforts and studies have appeared just about every decade since. These include Defense Science Board, "Report of the Defense Science Board Task Force on Secrecy" (Washington, D.C.: GPO, 1970), https://fas.org/sgp/othergov/dsbrep.html (accessed April 16, 2021); Commission to Review the Department of Defense Security Policy and Practices (Stilwell Commission), "Keeping the Nation's Secrets: A Report to the Secretary of Defense," November 19, 1985, https://fas.org/sgp/library/stilwell.html (accessed April 16, 2021); Joint Security Commission, "Redefining Security: A Report to the Secretary of Defense and the Director of Central Intelligence," February 28, 1994, https://fas.org/sgp/library/jsc/ (accessed April 16, 2021); Commission on Protecting and Reducing Government Secrecy (Moynihan Commission), "Report of the Commission on Protecting and Reducing Government Secrecy," 103rd Cong., March 3, 1997 (Washington, D.C.: GPO, 1997), https://fas.org/sgp/library /moynihan/title.html (accessed April 16, 2021); National Commission on Terrorist Attacks Upon the United States, *The 9/11 Commission Report, Authorized Version* (New York: W. W. Norton, 2004).

81. Moynihan Commission, Summary of Findings and Recommendations, "Report of the Commission on Protecting and Reducing Government Secrecy," xxii.

82. Moynihan Commission, Chairman's Forward, xxxi.

83. Donald Rumsfeld, "War of the Words," *Wall Street Journal*, July 18, 2005, A12.

84. U.S. House Committee on Government Reform, Hearing before the Subcommittee on National Security, Emerging Threats, and International Relations, 108th Cong., 2nd sess., August 24, 2004, Serial No. 108-263, https://fas.org/sgp/congress/2004/082404transcript.pdf (accessed April 16, 2021), 82.

85. Quoted in Aaron Mehta, "'Unbelievably Ridiculous': Four-Star General Seeks to Clean Up Pentagon's Classification Process," *Defense News*, January 29, 2020.

86. Office of the Director of National Intelligence, "2017 Annual Report on Security Clearance Determinations," https://www.dni.gov/files/NCSC/documents/features/20180827 -security-clearance-determinations.pdf (accessed May 14, 2020), 5.

87. Population estimate as of July 2019 from United States Census Bureau, "Los Angeles city, California," QuickFacts, https://www.census.gov/quickfacts/losangelescitycalifornia (accessed November 18, 2020).

88. Information Security Oversight Office, "2013 Report to the President," National Archives and Records Administration, https://www.archives.gov/files/isoo/reports/2013-annual-report .pdf, 6.

89. Information Security Oversight Office, "2016 Report to the President," National Archives and Records Administration, https://www.archives.gov/files/isoo/reports/2016-annual-report .pdf, 4. Each time anyone with a clearance uses secret materials in another document format (like an email), that subsequent work product must also be classified in a process called a "derivative classification." For new formats, see Mark A. Bradley, "Letter to the President," August 16, 2019, https://www.archives.gov/files/isoo/images/2018-isoo-annual-report.pdf (accessed June 16, 2020).

90. From 1995 to 1999, the federal government declassified an average of 157 million pages annually. Information Security Oversight Office, "2009 Report to the President," National Archives and Records Administration, March 31, 2010, https://www.archives.gov/files/isoo/reports/2009-annual-report.pdf (accessed June 16, 2020), 11. In 2017, by contrast, 46 million pages were declassified. Information Security Oversight Office, "2017 Report to the President," National Archives and Records Administration, May 31, 2018, https://www.archives.gov/files/isoo/reports/2017-annual-report.pdf (accessed April 8, 2020), 14–15. Figures exclude mandatory declassification review, which "provides for direct, specific review for declassification of information when requested." Information Security Oversight Office, "2009 Report to the President," 11.

91. Information Security Oversight Office, "2017 Report to the President," 15.

92. Herbert Lin and Amy Zegart, "Introduction," in *Bytes, Bombs, and Spies* (Washington, D.C.: Brookings Institution Press, 2019), 5. My Stanford colleague Herb Lin and I were so concerned that classification was impeding the development of strategic thinking in cyber, we asked United States Cyber Command to partner with us and hold a workshop bringing academics and policymakers together to examine the strategic dimensions of offensive cyber operations. To Cyber Command's credit, they agreed. The workshop was the first of its kind, and it produced new research that is still being used by Cyber Command, other Defense Department officials, and congressional committees.

93. White House Office of the Press Secretary, "Remarks by the President at the 'Change of Office' Chairman of the Joint Chiefs of Staff Ceremony," September 30, 2011, https://obamawhitehouse.archives.gov/the-press-office/2011/09/30/remarks-president-change-office-chairman-joint-chiefs-staff-ceremony; Tim Mak and Josh Gerstein, "Al Qaeda 'key leader' killed in Yemen," *Politico*, September 30, 2011, https://www.politico.com/story/2011/09/al-qaeda-key-leader-killed-in-yemen-064790.

94. In response to a November 2011 ACLU Freedom of Information Act request for records related to the legal authority and factual basis for the targeted killing on Anwar al-Awlaki, the government replied, "The Office of Legal Counsel neither confirms nor denies the existence of the documents described. . . . We cannot do so because the very fact of the existence or nonexistence of such documents is itself classified, protected from disclosure by statues, and privileged." https://www.aclu.org/doj-office-legal-counsel-response-al-awlaki-foia-request?redirect=national-security/doj-office-legal-counsel-response-al-awlaki-foia-request.

95. *Politico*, for example, noted that "Obama provided no details on Awlaki's demise, which reportedly was caused by missiles fired from U.S. military-run drones in an operation overseen by the Central Intelligence Agency." Mak and Gerstein, "Al Qaeda 'key leader' killed in Yemen." More examples of press articles referencing the CIA drone activity/program pre–September 30, 2011: David S. Cloud, "CIA Drones Have Broader List of Targets," *Los Angeles Times,* May 5, 2010, https://www.latimes.com/world/la-xpm-2010-may-05-la-fg-drone-targets-20100506-story.html (accessed April 16, 2021); David S. Cloud, "U.N. Report Faults Prolific Use of Drone Strikes by U.S.," *Los Angeles Times,* June 3, 2010, https://www.latimes.com/archives/la-xpm-2010-jun-03-la-fg-cia-drones-20100603-story.html (accessed April 16, 2021); "The C.I.A. and Drone Strikes," *New York Times*, August 13, 2011, https://www.nytimes.com/2011/08/14/opinion/sunday/the-cia-and-drone-strikes.html?searchResultPosition=3https://www.nytimes.com

/2009/08/21/us/21intel.html?searchResultPosition=15 (accessed April 16, 2021); Mark Maz-zetti, "C.I.A. Takes on Bigger and Riskier Role on Front Lines," *New York Times,* December 31, 2009, https://www.nytimes.com/2010/01/01/world/asia/01khost.html?searchResultPosition =24 (accessed April 16, 2021); Bob Woodward, "Secret CIA Units Playing a Central Combat Role," *Washington Post,* November 18, 2001, https://www.washingtonpost.com/wp-dyn/content /article/2007/11/18/AR2007111800675.html (accessed April 16, 2021); Scott Shane, "A Close-Mouthed Policy Even on Open Secrets," *New York Times,* October 4, 2011.

96. Thom Shanker, "Loophole May Have Aided Theft of Classified Data," *New York Times,* July 8, 2010, https://www.nytimes.com/2010/07/09/world/09breach.html (accessed March 26, 2020); Matthew Shaer, "The Long, Lonely Road of Chelsea Manning," *New York Times,* June 12, 2017, https://www.nytimes.com/2017/06/12/magazine/the-long-lonely-road-of-chelsea -manning.html?searchResultPosition=3 (accessed August 20, 2020).

97. Stephanie Gaskell, "How badly did Manning hurt the United States," *Defense One,* Au-gust 22, 2013, https://www.defenseone.com/ideas/2013/08/how-badly-did-manning-hurt -united-states/69218/.

98. Julie Tate, "Bradley Manning Sentenced to 35 Years in WikiLeaks Case," *Washington Post,* August 21, 2013, https://www.washingtonpost.com/world/national-security/judge-to -sentence-bradley-manning-today/2013/08/20/85bee184-09d0-11e3-b87c-476db8ac34cd _story.html (accessed August 20, 2020); Reuters, "Leaked U.S. Video Shows Deaths of Reuters' Iraqi Staffers," April 5, 2010, https://www.reuters.com/article/us-iraq-usa-journalists/leaked -u-s-video-shows-deaths-of-reuters-iraqi-staffers-idUSTRE6344FW20100406 (accessed August 20, 2020).

99. Memorandum from the Undersecretary of Defense, "Notice to DoD Employees and Contractors on Protecting Classification Information and the Integrity of Unclassified Govern-ment Information Technology (IT) Systems," January 11, 2011, https://fas.org/sgp/othergov /dod/wl-notice.pdf (accessed May 5, 2020); Eric Schmitt, "Air Force Blocks Sites That Posted Secret Cables," *New York Times,* December 15, 2010, https://www.nytimes.com/2010/12/15/us /15wiki.html; Spencer Ackerman, "Airmen, it's illegal for your kids to read Wikileaks," *Wired,* February 7, 2011, https://www.wired.com/2011/02/air-force-its-illegal-for-your-kids-to-read -wikileaks/ (accessed June 16, 2020); John Cook, "State Department Bars Employees from Reading Wikileaks on 'Personal Time,'" *Gawker,* December 15, 2010, https://gawker.com /5713964/state-department-bars-employees-from-reading-wikileaks-on-personal-time?skyline =true&s=i (accessed April 10, 2020).

100. Ackerman, "Airmen, it's illegal"; Schmitt, "Air Force Blocks Sites."

101. Cook, "State Department Bars Employees"; Memorandum from the Undersecretary of Defense, "Notice to DoD Employees and Contractors."

102. Information Security Oversight Office, "Audit Report, Withdrawal of Records from Public Access at the National Archives and Records Administration for Classification Pur-poses," National Archives and Records Administration, April 26, 2006, http://www.fas.org/sgp /news/2006/04/nara042606.html (accessed Oct. 5, 2009), 1. In a sample survey of the with-drawn records, the ISOO found "that even trained classifiers, with ready access to the latest classification and declassification guides, and trained in their use, got it clearly right only 64% of the time in making determinations as to the appropriateness of continued classification." The

director concluded, "This is emblematic of the daily challenges confronting agencies when ensuring that the 3 million plus cleared individuals with at least theoretical ability to derivatively classify information get it right each and every time." J. William Leonard, "ISOO Director's Message" (Attachment A to ISOO Audit), Information Security Oversight Office, National Archives and Records Administration, April 26, 2006, https://www.fas.org/sgp/isoo/isoo042606.pdf (accessed August 9, 2012).

103. William Burr, ed., *National Security Archive Electronic Briefing Book No. 197*, August 18, 2006, http://www.gwu.edu/~nsarchiv/NSAEBB/NSAEBB197/index.htm (accessed October 5, 2009).

104. Burr, ed.

105. Quoted in Robert Fahs, "Gen. Hyten Finds Over-Classification of Space Information Undermines National Security, Promises Reform," Public Interest Declassification Board blog, National Archives, December 1, 2020, https://transforming-classification.blogs.archives.gov/2020/12/01/gen-hyten-finds-over-classification-of-space-information-undermines-national-security-promises-reform/ (accessed December 7, 2020).

106. James Bamford, *The Puzzle Palace* (New York: Penguin, 1982), 15–16.

107. Author's visit to NSA, September 23, 2013.

108. Amy B. Zegart, "Cloaks, Daggers, and Ivory Towers: Why Academics Don't Study U.S. Intelligence," in *Strategic Intelligence: Understanding the Hidden State of Government*, Vol. 1, edited by Loch K. Johnson (Westport, Conn.: Praeger Publishers, 2007), 26.

109. Federal Bureau of Investigation, "Keeping Tomorrow Safe: Draft FBI Strategic Plan, 1998–2003," unclassified version, May 8, 1998.

110. Zegart, "Cloaks, Daggers, and Ivory Towers," 26.

111. The document is Federal Bureau of Investigation, "Keeping Tomorrow Safe: Draft FBI Strategic Plan, 1998–2003," unclassified version, May 8, 1998.

112. Amy Zegart, *Spying Blind: The CIA, the FBI, and the Origins of 9/11* (Princeton, N.J.: Princeton University Press, 2007), 141. See also Office of the Inspector General, Department of Justice, "A Review of the Federal Bureau of Investigation's Counterterrorism Program: Threat Assessment, Strategic Planning, and Resource Management," Audit Report 02-38, executive summary declassified and redacted September 2002.

113. Library of Congress, "Historical Supreme Court Cases Now Online," March 13, 2018, https://www.loc.gov/item/prn-18-026/historical-supreme-court-cases-now-online/2018-03-13/ (accessed June 13, 2020).

114. Zegart, "Cloaks, Daggers, and Ivory Towers," 25.

115. There are "unusual circumstances" exceptions. For example, the Office of the Director of National Intelligence notes that "every attempt to respond within the 20 day timeframe established by the FOIA will be made. However, because of the complexity of records maintained by the ODNI, it will not always be possible for this agency to meet that requirement." Office of the Director of National Intelligence, *ODNI FOIA Handbook*, https://www.dni.gov/files/documents/FOIA/odni_foia_handbook.pdf (accessed June 13, 2020). See also U.S. Department of Justice, "Responding to Requests," last updated October 30, 2018, https://www.justice.gov/archives/open/responding-requests (accessed April 27, 2020).

116. Zegart, "Cloaks, Daggers, and Ivory Towers," 25.

117. As of May 5, 2020. Reports can be generated at U.S. Department of Justice, https://www
.foia.gov/data.html. According to the FAQ section of the FOIA website, "simple requests are
typically more targeted and seek fewer pages of records. Complex requests typically seek a high
volume of material or require additional steps to process such as the need to search for records
in multiple locations."

118. At NSA, the average processing time for simple requests was 367 days, 826 days for
complex requests, and nine to thirteen years for the ten oldest requests (as of May 5, 2020).

119. For an expanded discussion, see Zegart, "Cloaks, Daggers, and Ivory Towers."

120. Polling of political scientists reveals substantial consensus about the top three general
disciplinary journals. For more, see James C. Garrand and Micheal W. Giles, "Journals in the
discipline: A report on a new survey of American political scientists," *PS: Political Science and
Politics* (April 2003): 293–308.

121. Author analysis of abstracts from January 2001 through December 2016. The five
intelligence-related articles were Darren W. Davis and Brian D. Silver, "Civil liberties vs. Security: Public opinion in the context of the terrorist attacks on America," *American Journal of Political Science* 48, no. 1 (January 2004): 28–46; Robert Powell, "Defending against terrorist attacks with limited resources," *American Political Science Review* 101 (2007): 527–41; Tiberiu
Dragu, "Is there a trade-off between security and liberty? Executive bias, privacy protections,
and terrorism prevention," *American Political Science Review* 105 (2011): 64–78; Tiberiu Dragu
and Mattias Polborn, "The rule of law in the fight against terrorism," *American Journal of Political
Science* 58, no. 2 (April 2014): 511–25; Jennifer L. Selin, "What makes an agency independent?"
American Journal of Political Science 59, no. 4 (October 2015): 971–87.

122. "Best national universities," *U.S. News & World Report* 139, no. 7 (August 29, 2005): 80.

123. The four were Duke, Georgetown, Massachusetts Institute of Technology, and University of Virginia, based on analysis of online university course catalogs conducted March 24–31,
2006. See Zegart, "Cloaks, Daggers, and Ivory Towers."

124. Data from 2016–2017 *U.S. News & World Report* rankings and author search of online
university undergraduate course catalogs, June–August 2017. Data do not include summer or
inter-term courses. Twenty-six colleges comprised the top twenty-four schools due to tied
rankings.

125. The Intelligence Community has an Academic Centers for Excellence program that
provides grants to colleges and universities to support the development of intelligence-related
curricula and programs. Its goal, however, is to attract and train a diverse pool of aspiring practitioners, not to provide educational programs for everyone else about the role of intelligence
in American foreign policymaking. Courses are geared toward the detailed professional aspects
of intelligence (like the methods of covert action or dealing with congressional liaison). See
Loch K. Johnson, "Spies and scholars in the United States: Winds of ambivalence in the groves
of academe," *Intelligence and National Security* 34, no. 1 (2019): 14–15; U.S. Government Accountability Office, "Intelligence Community: Actions Needed to Improve Planning and Oversight
of the Centers for Academic Excellence Program" (GAO-19-529), August 2019, https://www
.gao.gov/assets/710/700713.pdf. Thirty colleges and universities have received grants during the

last fifteen years. Five were ranked in the top 100 institutions ranked by *U.S. News & World Report* in 2020 (analysis by author).

126. Lev Grossman, "Why the 9/11 conspiracy theories won't go away," *Time*, September 3, 2006, http://content.time.com/time/magazine/article/0,9171,1531304,00.html (accessed May 26, 2020).

127. See, for example, David Ray Griffin, *The New Pearl Harbor Revisited: 9/11, the Cover-Up, and the Exposé* (Northampton, Mass.: Olive Branch Press, 2008).

128. Grossman, "Why the 9/11 conspiracy theories won't go away."

129. "*Economist*/YouGov Poll," December 17–20, 2016, https://d25d2506sfb94s.cloudfront.net/cumulus_uploads/document/ljv2ohxmzj/econTabReport.pdf (accessed July 26, 2017).

130. In 2016, one popular conspiracy theory claimed that Democratic presidential candidate Hillary Clinton was running a pedophile ring from the basement of a Washington pizzeria. "Pizzagate: From Rumor, to Hashtag, to Gunfire in D.C.," *Washington Post*, December 6, 2016, https://www.washingtonpost.com/local/pizzagate-from-rumor-to-hashtag-to-gunfire-in-dc/2016/12/06/4c7def50-bbd4-11e6-94ac-3d324840106c_story.html (accessed June 16, 2020). As the COVID-19 virus spread from Wuhan, China, across the globe, Chinese officials began pushing anti-American conspiracy theories on Twitter and YouTube that the U.S. Army may have originated the virus and brought it to Wuhan. Edward Wong, Matthew Rosenberg, and Julian E. Barnes, "Chinese Agents Helped Spread Messages That Sowed Virus Panic in U.S., Officials Say," *New York Times*, April 23, 2020, https://www.nytimes.com/2020/04/22/us/politics/coronavirus-china-disinformation.html (accessed June 16, 2020). "When did patient zero begin in US?" wrote Zhao Lijian, a Ministry of Foreign Affairs spokesman, on Twitter in English and Chinese. "How many people are infected. What are the names of the hospitals? It might be US army who brought the epidemic to Wuhan. Be transparent! Make public your date! US owe us an explanation." Mr. Zhao's hashtag, #ZhaoLijianPostedFiveTweetsinaRowQuestioning-America, was viewed on Weibo, China's popular social media platform, more than 160 million times. Steven Lee Myers, "China Spins Tale That the U.S. Army Started the Coronavirus Epidemic," *New York Times*, March 17, 2020, https://www.nytimes.com/2020/03/13/world/asia/coronavirus-china-conspiracy-theory.html (accessed June 16, 2020).

131. Shortly after the 2016 election, an anonymous columnist named Virgil posted a lengthy screed on the conservative site Breitbart.com introducing the idea of the anti-Trump Deep State: "Virgil: The Deep State vs. Donald Trump," Breitbart, December 12, 2016, https://www.breitbart.com/politics/2016/12/12/virgil-the-deep-state-vs-donald-trump/ (accessed June 16, 2020). See also Evan Osnos, "Trump vs. The Deep State," *New Yorker*, May 14, 2018, https://www.newyorker.com/magazine/2018/05/21/trump-vs-the-deep-state (accessed June 16, 2020); David Rohde, *In Deep: The FBI, the CIA, and the Truth about America's "Deep State"* (New York: W. W. Norton, 2020).

132. Peter Baker, Lara Jakes, Julian E. Barnes, Sharon LaFraniere, and Edward Wong, "Trump's War on the 'Deep State' Turns Against Him," *New York Times*, December 23, 2019, https://www.nytimes.com/2019/10/23/us/politics/trump-deep-state-impeachment.html (accessed June 16, 2020).

133. Amy Zegart, "The next director of national intelligence," *Foreign Affairs*, August 9, 2019, https://www.foreignaffairs.com/articles/2019-08-09/next-director-national-intelligence (accessed June 16, 2020).

134. Amy Zegart, "Trump says Russia isn't still targeting the U.S.—but he's wrong," *Atlantic*, July 18, 2018, https://www.theatlantic.com/ideas/archive/2018/07/the-russians-are-coming/565478/ (accessed June 16, 2020); Rohde, *In Deep*, 158–59, 164.

135. Zachary Cohen and Nicole Gaouette, "Trump Says Ratcliffe Will 'Rein in' US Intelligence Agencies as Spy Chief," CNN, July 30, 2019, https://www.cnn.com/2019/07/30/politics/trump-ratcliffe-rein-in-us-intelligence-agencies/index.html (accessed June 16, 2020); Justin Coleman, "Trump Formally Sends Ratcliffe Nomination for DNI to Senate," *Hill*, March 2, 2020, https://thehill.com/homenews/administration/485618-trump-formally-sends-ratcliffe-nomination-for-dni-to-senate (accessed June 16, 2020).

136. Joe Sommerlad, "Trump News: President Smears Vaccine Whistleblower as Coronavirus Shutdown Sees US Unemployment Claims Soar to 36m," *Independent*, May 14, 2020, https://www.independent.co.uk/news/world/americas/us-politics/trump-news-live-coronavirus-twitter-white-house-press-briefing-us-obama-latest-a9508101.html (accessed June 16, 2020).

137. Aaron Rupar, "Trump's Latest Coronavirus Meltdown Features QAnon, Accidental Self-Owns, and a Lot of "OBAMAGATE," *Vox*, May 11, 2020, https://www.vox.com/2020/5/11/21254398/trump-tweets-mothers-day-obamagate-coronavirus (accessed June 16, 2020).

138. John Bowden, "Trump Lashes Out at Obama in Mother's Day Tweetstorm," *Hill*, May 10, 2020, https://thehill.com/homenews/administration/497057-trump-lashes-out-at-obama-in-mothers-day-tweetstorm (accessed June 16, 2020).

139. The video of this exchange during President Trump's press conference is available on Aaron Rupar's Twitter feed, May 11, 2020, https://twitter.com/i/status/1259954909467869184.

140. Nicholas Dujmovic, "Reflections on the deep state myth," *Intelligence and National Security Special Forum* 35, no. 1 (2020): 5, https://doi.org/10.1080/02684527.2019.1691138 (accessed June 14, 2020).

141. Aaron Blake, "The 'Deep State' Is President Trump's Most Compelling Conspiracy Theory," *Washington Post*, April 27, 2017, https://www.washingtonpost.com/news/the-fix/wp/2017/04/27/the-deep-state-is-president-trumps-most-compelling-conspiracy-theory/ (accessed June 16, 2020).

142. Kathy Frankovic, "How Americans View the 'Deep State,'" YouGov, October 31, 2019, https://today.yougov.com/topics/politics/articles-reports/2019/10/31/how-americans-view-deep-state-poll (accessed June 16, 2020).

143. Associated Press, "Transcript of Trump's Speech at Rally Before US Capitol Riot," January 13, 2021, https://www.usnews.com/news/politics/articles/2021-01-13/transcript-of-trumps-speech-at-rally-before-us-capitol-riot (accessed January 29, 2021).

144. Alison Durkee, "52% of Republicans think Trump 'rightfully won' election, poll finds," *Forbes*, November 18, 2020. For a summary of Biden's margin of victory in historical perspective and failed lawsuits in the 2020 election, see William Cummings, Joey Garrison, and Jim Sergent, "By the Numbers: President Donald Trump's Failed Efforts to Overturn the Election," *USA Today*, January 6, 2021, https://www.usatoday.com/in-depth/news/politics/elections/2021/01/06/trumps-failed-efforts-overturn-election-numbers/4130307001/ (accessed January 29, 2021).

145. U.S. Senate Select Committee on Intelligence, Worldwide Threats, 117th Cong., 1st sess., April 14, 2021.

146. Greg Miller, "Muslim Cleric Aulaqi Is 1st U.S. Citizen on List of Those CIA Is Allowed to Kill," *Washington Post*, April 7, 2010, https://www.washingtonpost.com/wp-dyn/content/article/2010/04/06/AR2010040604121.html (accessed June 16, 2020); ACLU, "Al-Aulaqi v. Panetta—Constitutional Challenge to Killing Three U.S. Citizens," updated June 4, 2014, https://www.aclu.org/cases/al-aulaqi-v-panetta-constitutional-challenge-killing-three-us-citizens (accessed June 16, 2020).

147. Philippe Sands, *Torture Team: Rumsfeld's Memo and the Betrayal of American Values* (London: Palgrave Macmillan, 2008), 61–62.

148. U.S. Senate Committee on Armed Services, "Inquiry into the Treatment of Detainees in U.S. Custody: Report," 110th Cong., 2nd sess., November 20, 2008; Dahlia Lithwick, "The fiction behind torture policy," *Newsweek*, August 4, 2008, 11.

149. Mayer, "Whatever it takes."

150. The video is no longer available on the Human Rights First website; a copy can be viewed on their Facebook page at https://www.facebook.com/humanrightsfirst/videos/19724238167/.

151. See, for example, U.S. House Committee on the Judiciary, "Torture and the Cruel, Inhuman and Degrading Treatment of Detainees: The Effectiveness and Consequences of 'Enhanced' Interrogation," Hearing before the Subcommittee on the Constitution, Civil Rights, and Civil Liberties, 110th Cong., 1st sess., November 8, 2007, Serial No. 110-94; Philip Zelikow, "Legal Policy for a Twilight War," annual lecture, *Houston Journal of International Law*, April 26, 2007, in U.S. Senate Committee on Foreign Relations, Extraordinary Rendition, Extraterritorial Detention and Treatment of Detainees Hearing, 110th Cong., 1st sess., July 26, 2007; Sanford Levinson and Juliette Kayyem, "Is Torture Ever Justified?" *Frontline*, PBS, October 18, 2005, http://www.pbs.org/wgbh/pages/frontline/torture/justify/ (accessed July 26, 2017); U.S. House Committee on the Judiciary, "Department of Justice to Guantanamo Bay: Administration Lawyers and Administration Interrogation Rules (Part I)," Hearing before the Subcommittee on the Constitution, Civil Rights, and Civil Liberties, 110th Cong., 2nd sess., May 6, 2008, Serial No. 110-97.

152. *Foreign Policy* interview of Jack Cloonan, *Three Torture Myths*, March 9, 2008, https://www.youtube.com/watch?v=lvsvO9kvSdo (accessed April 16, 2021). See also "The Jack Bauer Exception: Obama's Executive Order Wants It Both Ways on Interrogation," Opinion, *Wall Street Journal*, January 23, 2009, http://online.wsj.com/article/SB123267082704308361.html (accessed October 9, 2009); "The Jack Bauer Exception II," Opinion, *Wall Street Journal*, February 7, 2009, http://online.wsj.com/article/SB123396474404658733.html (accessed October 9, 2009).

153. U.S. Senate Committee on the Judiciary, Confirmation Hearing on the Nomination of Alberto R. Gonzales to be Attorney General of the United States, 109th Cong., 1st sess., January 6, 2005, Serial No. J-109, 155–62.

154. Heritage Foundation, *"24" and America's Image in Fighting Terrorism: Fact, Fiction, or Does It Matter?* June 23, 2006.

155. John Yoo, *War by Other Means: An Insider's Account of the War on Terror* (New York: Atlantic Monthly Press, 2006), 172.

156. *Meet the Press*, NBC News, September 30, 2007.

157. U.S. Senate Select Committee on Intelligence, Hearing on the Nomination of Leon Panetta to be Director of Central Intelligence Agency, 111th Cong., 1st sess., February 5, 2009.

158. "Jack Bauer Exception," Opinion, *Wall Street Journal*; "Jack Bauer Exception II," Opinion, *Wall Street Journal*.

159. Colin Freeze, "What Would Jack Bauer Do? Canadian Jurist Promotes International Justice Panel to Debate TV Drama 24's Use of Torture," *Globe and Mail*, June 16, 2007; Horton, "How Hollywood learned to stop worrying and love the (ticking) bomb."

160. BBC News, "US Judge Steps into Torture Row," February 12, 2008, http://news.bbc.co.uk/1/hi/world/americas/7239748.stm (accessed August 31, 2017); Debra Cassens Weiss, "Scalia: Torture Not an Easy Constitutional Issue," American Bar Association, February 12, 2008, https://www.abajournal.com/news/article/scalia_torture_not_an_easy_constitutional_issue (accessed August 12, 2020).

161. Lisa Belkin, "Quayle Discards His Script on Military Issues and Raises Eyebrows," *New York Times*, September 8, 1988, http://www.nytimes.com/1988/09/09/us/quayle-discards-his-script-on-military-issues-and-raises-eyebrows.html (accessed July 21, 2017).

162. Peter Travers, "The Hunt for Red October," *Rolling Stone*, March 2, 1990, http://www.rollingstone.com/movies/reviews/the-hunt-for-red-october-19900302 (accessed July 21, 2017).

163. Justin George, "FBI Files Show Details of Background Checks on Author Tom Clancy," *Baltimore Sun*, September 27, 2017, http://www.baltimoresun.com/news/maryland/sun-investigates/bs-md-sun-investigates-tom-clancy-fbi-20140927-story.html (accessed July 21, 2017).

164. Michael Schaub, "Spy Novels Get Shout-out during Jeff Sessions' Testimony on the Russia Probe," *Los Angeles Times*, June 14, 2017, http://www.latimes.com/books/jacketcopy/la-ca-jc-sessions-spy-20170614-story.html (accessed July 21, 2017).

165. Michael Hayden, address of October 19, 2000, quoted in James Bamford's preface to *Body of Secrets: Anatomy of the Ultra-Secret National Security Agency* (New York: Doubleday, 2001).

Chapter 3: American Intelligence History at a Glance

1. Letter from George Washington to Robert Hunter Morris, Winchester, January 5, 1756, in *The Writings of George Washington from the Original Manuscript Sources: Vol. 1, 1745–1799*, edited by John Clement Fitzpatrick. This version is available on the Hathi Trust Digital Library from the University of Michigan, https://babel.hathitrust.org/cgi/pt?id=mdp.39015011819060&view=1up&seq=27.

2. Richard M. Ketchum, *Victory at Yorktown: The Campaign that Won the Revolution* (New York: Henry Holt and Company, 2004); Nathanial Philbrick, *In the Hurricane's Eye: The Genius of George Washington and the Victory at Yorktown* (New York: Penguin, 2018), xii.

3. "From George Washington to Noah Webster, 31 July 1788," Founders Online, National Archives, https://founders.archives.gov/documents/Washington/04-06-02-0376.

4. The Papers of George Washington, Library of Congress, Washington, D.C. (Charlottesville: University Press of Virginia, 1976–1979), 3:409; De Grasse to Rochambeau et al., July 28, 1781, in Henri Doniol, *Histoire de la participation de la France a l'establissement des Etats-Unis d'Amerique* (Paris: Imprimerie Nationale, 1886–1892), 4:650–51.

5. In a letter to Noah Webster years later, Washington recalled, "That much trouble was taken and finesse used to misguide & bewilder Sir Henry Clinton in regard to the real object, by fictitious communications, as well as by making a deceptive provision of Ovens, Forage & Boats in his Neighborhood, is certain." Washington to Webster, July 31, 1788.

6. The Papers of George Washington, Library of Congress, Washington, D.C., 3:413; John A. Nagy, *George Washington's Secret Spy War: The Making of America's First Spymaster* (New York: St. Martin's Press, 2016), 237–38; Thomas Schactman, "The French Bread Connection," *Journal of the American Revolution* (September 12, 2017).

7. Schactman, "French Bread Connection"; Morris County Tourism board, https://www.morristourism.org/historic-highlight-of-our-39-towns/; Borough of Chatham https://www.chathamborough.org/chatham/Living%20in%20Chatham/Explore%20Chatham/History/.

8. "From George Washington to Samuel Miles, 27 August 1781," Founders Online, National Archives http://founders.archives.gov/documents/Washington/99-01-02-06801.

9. *The Art of War* was written between 544–496 B.C.E. Sun Tzu, *The Art of War*, translated by Lionel Giles (New York: Barnes & Noble, 2003).

10. Christopher Andrew, *The Secret World: A History of Intelligence* (New Haven, Conn.: Yale University Press, 2018), 118–40.

11. Sir Francis Walsingham served as the queen's intelligence chief and her foreign secretary, the first time both posts were held by the same person. Records show that Walsingham had daily access to the queen, and on one occasion in 1586, he so angered Elizabeth during a discussion that she took off her shoe and threw it at his head. Andrew, *Secret World*, 160.

12. The two other instances when codebreaking penetrated invasion plans were against Philip II's Spanish Armada in 1588 and Napoleon at the start of the nineteenth century. Andrew, *Secret World*.

13. The one partial exception to this trend was the Cipher Bureau—more commonly called the Black Chamber, a peacetime codebreaking agency that was created after World War I and operated within the State Department until it was eliminated in 1929 by Secretary of State Henry Stimson. Christopher Andrew, *For the President's Eyes Only: Secret Intelligence and the American Presidency from Washington to Bush* (New York: Harper Perennial, 1996), 62; David Kahn, *The Codebreakers: The Comprehensive History of Secret Communication from Ancient Times to the Internet* (New York: Scribner, 1996), 355–60.

14. National Security Act of 1947, Public Law 235, July 26, 1947, https://www.dni.gov/index.php/ic-legal-reference-book/national-security-act-of-1947.

15. Estimate by Stephen Aftergood, Federation of American Scientists. Justin Brown "The 'Top Secret' at CIA: Its Own Budget," *Christian Science Monitor*, May 26, 2000, https://www.csmonitor.com/2000/0526/p2s1.html.

16. Yet, European powers did not institutionalize intelligence during this period, leaving intelligence in some capitals weaker than it had been earlier. Andrew, *Secret World*.

17. Thomas Jefferson, "First Inaugural Address," March 4, 1801, The Avalon Project at Yale Law School, https://avalon.law.yale.edu/19th_century/jefinau1.asp.

18. John Quincy Adams, "July 4, 1821: Speech to the U.S. House of Representatives on Foreign Policy," University of Virginia Miller Center, https://millercenter.org/the-presidency/presidential-speeches/july-4-1821-speech-us-house-representatives-foreign-policy.

19. David M. Kennedy, "Thinking Historically about Grand Strategy," in *Grand Strategy: Ideas and Challenges in a Complex World* (Stanford, Calif.: Hoover Institution, 2014), http://www .hoover.org/research/thinking-historically-about-grand-strategy (accessed July 7, 2014).

20. Julian E. Zelizer, *Arsenal of Democracy* (New York: Basic Books 2010), 9.

21. Estimate is based on twenty million dead in World War I (*Encyclopedia Britannica*) and sixty million in World War II (National World War II museum.)

22. For a detailed discussion of the international order, see Michael J. Mazarr and Ashley L. Rhoades, "Testing the Value of the Postwar International Order," RAND Report, 2018.

23. Winston Churchill, "'Iron Curtain' speech," Westminster College, Fulton, Mo., March 5, 1946, National Archives, https://www.nationalarchives.gov.uk/education/resources/cold-war -on-file/iron-curtain-speech/.

24. Henry M. Jackson, "How Shall We Forge a Strategy for Survival?" Address before the National War College, April 16, 1959, Washington, D.C., in *Decisions of the Highest Order: Perspectives on the National Security Council*, edited by Karl F. Inderfurth and Loch K. Johnson (Pacific Grove, Calif.: Brooks/Cole, 1988), 78–81.

25. Office of the Director of National Intelligence, National Counterintelligence and Security Center, "Fiscal Year 2017 Annual Report on Security Clearance Determinations," https:// www.dni.gov/files/NCSC/documents/features/20180827-security-clearance-determinations .pdf (accessed September 26, 2020), 4.

26. When the names of all the special access programs were printed for the armed services committees, the list was three hundred pages long. See Dana Priest and William M. Arkin, *Top Secret America: The Rise of the New American Security State* (New York: Little, Brown, 2011).

27. Quote from Priest and Arkin, 27.

28. Benjamin Wittes and Ritika Singh, "Madison's Vacillations—And Ours: Seeing a Founder, an Opposition Leader, a Muddle-Through Executive, and a Wartime President in Ourselves," Lawfare, November 28, 2013, https://www.lawfareblog.com/madisons-vacillations%E2%80%94 and-ours-seeing-founder-opposition-leader-muddle-through-executive-and-wartime.

29. This section is taken from Amy Zegart, "George Washington Was a Master of Deception," as first published in *The Atlantic*, November 25, 2018.

30. Alexander Rose, *Washington's Spies: The Story of America's First Spy Ring* (New York: Bantam, 2007), 121.

31. Kenneth A. Daigler, *Spies, Patriots, and Traitors: American Intelligence in the Revolutionary War* (Washington, D.C.: Georgetown University Press, 2014), 99.

32. Andrew, *Secret World*, 303.

33. Daigler, *Spies, Patriots, and Traitors*, 99–101.

34. James Hutson, "Nathan Hale Revisited: A Tory's Account of the Arrest of the First American Spy," *Library of Congress Information Bulletin* 62, no. 7 (July/August 2003), http:// www.loc.gov/loc/lcib/0307-8/hale.html (accessed June 26, 2014); E. R. Thompson, *Secret New England: Spies of the American Revolution* (New England Chapter, Association of Former Intelligence Officers, 1991).

35. Hutson, "Nathan Hale Revisited." See also G. J. A. O'Toole, *Encyclopedia of American Intelligence and Espionage* (New York and Oxford: Facts on File, 1988).

36. Streeter Bass, "Nathan Hale's Mission," CIA Historical Review Program, July 2, 1996, https://www.cia.gov/static/d709cbec73f51410da657b2bafc90466/Nathan-Hales-Mission.pdf (accessed January 29, 2021).

37. The Culper ring, which consisted of a small group of friends in Setauket, Long Island, used dead drops, signals, codes, and smugglers to convey vital information about British fortifications and troop movements in the New York area between 1778 until the war's end in 1783. It is believed to have been the most successful spy network on either side of the Revolutionary War. See Rose, *Washington's Spies*; "The Culper Gang," William L. Clements Library, University of Michigan, https://clements.umich.edu/exhibit/spy-letters-of-the-american-revolution /stories-of-spies/culper-gang/.

38. Andrew, *Secret World*, 9–10.

39. Thomas Fleming, "George Washington, General," in *Experience of War*, edited by Robert Cowley (New York: W. W. Norton, 1992), 140–50. Fleming's article by the same name originally appeared in *Quarterly Journal of Military History* 2, no. 2 (Winter 1990): 38–47.

40. Daigler, *Spies, Patriots, and Traitors*, 78.

41. P. K. Rose, "The Founding Fathers of American Intelligence," Central Intelligence Agency, https://www.cia.gov/static/4c28451b90165b446ac948e3dd47c972/The-Founding -Fathers-of-American-Intelligence-.pdf (accessed January 29 2021).

42. "Draft Text for CIA Pamphlet 'Intelligence in the War of Independence,'" Historical Intelligence Collection, Central Reference Section DD/I, June 28, 1976, in collection of Marsh Papers, Ford Library, https://www.fordlibrarymuseum.gov/library/document/0067/1563276 .pdf (accessed April 18, 2019), 23; Charles Burr Todd, *Life of Colonel Aaron Burr: Vice President of the United States* (New York: S. W. Green, 1879), 83.

43. James Jay, brother of the future chief justice of the U.S. Supreme Court John Jay, crafted an invisible ink for Washington to use for his Culper spy ring. Washington became so desperate for more ink that Jay eventually created a laboratory where he could make it in larger quantities. See Glenn P. Hastedt, *Spies, Wiretaps and Secret Operations: An Encyclopedia of American Espionage*, Vol. 1 (Santa Barbara: ABC-CLIO, 2011), 417.

44. "From George Washington to Nathaniel Sackett, 8 April 1777," Founders Online, National Archives, http://founders.archives.gov/documents/Washington/03-09-02-0096 (source: *The Papers of George Washington*, Revolutionary War Series, Vol. 9: 28 March 1777–10 June 1777, edited by Philander D. Chase [Charlottesville: University Press of Virginia, 1999], 95).

45. Edward F. Sayle, "The historical underpinnings of the U.S. Intelligence Community," *International Journal of Intelligence and CounterIntelligence* 1, no. 1 (1986): 6.

46. Andrew, *For the President's Eyes Only*, 9.

47. Michael J. Sulick, *Spying in America: Espionage from the Revolutionary War to the Dawn of the Cold War* (Washington, D.C.: Georgetown University Press, 2012), 3; Nathaniel Philbrook, "Why Benedict Arnold turned traitor against the American Revolution," *Smithsonian Magazine*, May 2016, https://www.smithsonianmag.com/history/benedict-arnold-turned-traitor -american-revolution-180958786/.

48. Walter Isaacson, *Benjamin Franklin: An American Life* (New York: Simon & Schuster, 2008), 333; Thomas Schaeper, *Edward Bancroft: Scientist, Author, Spy* (New Haven, Conn.: Yale

University Press, 2011); National Counterintelligence Center, *A Counterintelligence Reader*, Vol. 1: American Revolution to World War II, https://fas.org/irp/ops/ci/docs/ci1/ch1c.htm.

49. Sayle, "Historical Underpinnings of the U.S. Intelligence Community," 9, citing National Archives and Records Administration, "From George Washington to Gouverneur Morris, 13 October 1789."

50. Sayle, 9. The fund was used for a variety of activities that included but were not limited to intelligence. Figures for the 2019 total intelligence budget are from Federation of American Scientists, "Intelligence Budget Data," https://fas.org/irp/budget/.

51. Andrew, *For the President's Eyes Only*, 11.

52. For important exceptions, see Stephen F. Knott, *Secret and Sanctioned: Covert Operations and the American Presidency* (Oxford, U.K.: Oxford University Press, 1996).

53. Donald R. Hickey, *War of 1812: A Forgotten Conflict* (Champaign: University of Illinois Press, 2012), 207; Thomas Fleming, "When Dolley Madison took command of the White House," *Smithsonian Magazine* (March 2010), https://www.smithsonianmag.com/history/how-dolley-madison-saved-the-day-7465218/.

54. Edwin C. Fishel, *The Secret War for the Union: The Untold Story of Military Intelligence in the Civil War* (New York: Houghton Mifflin Harcourt, 1996), 40.

55. Fishel, 39–40; Rebecca Robbins Raines, *Getting the Message Through: A Branch History of the U.S. Army Signal Corps*, Army Historical Series (Washington, D.C.: Center of Military History, United States Army, 2011), 3–16; David L. Woods, *A History of Tactical Communication Techniques* (Orlando, Fla.: Martin-Marietta Corp., 1965).

56. Fishel, *Secret War for the Union*, 6.

57. Andrew, *For the President's Eyes Only*, 20.

58. Andrew, 21.

59. During the 1860s, *secret service* was a term that generally denoted intelligence activities as well as non-military detective work. Though both Pinkerton and Baker called their organizations secret services, these were not the same as the modern-day Secret Service that protects the president. The national secret service of the United States was formed after the Civil War. Fishel, *Secret War for the Union*, 8. See also United States Secret Service, "History," https://www.secretservice.gov/about/history/ (accessed June 24, 2020).

60. CIA Office of Public Affairs, "Intelligence in the Civil War," https://fas.org/irp/cia/product/civilwar.pdf (accessed April 16, 2021); Fishel, *Secret War for the Union*, 55.

61. CIA Office of Public Affairs, "Intelligence in the Civil War," 17.

62. Fishel, *Secret War for the Union*, 298–300.

63. Quoted in CIA Office of Public Affairs, "Intelligence in the Civil War."

64. Andrew, *For the President's Eyes Only*, 25.

65. Sayle, "Historical Underpinnings of the U.S. Intelligence Community," 20.

66. Andrew, *For the President's Eyes Only*, 53, 68.

67. Sharad Chauhan, *Inside CIA: Lessons in Intelligence* (New Delhi: APH Publishing, 2004), 342–43.

68. Howard Blum, *Dark Invasion: 1915: Germany's Secret War and the Hunt for the First Terrorist Cell in America* (New York: Harper, 2014); David Pfeiffer, "Tony's lab," *Prologue Magazine*

(U.S. National Archives) 49, no. 3 (Fall 2017), https://www.archives.gov/publications/prologue/2017/fall/tonys-lab.

69. Tim Weiner, *Enemies: A History of the FBI* (New York: Random House, 2012), 3; FBI History, "Black Tom 1916 Bombing," FBI History, https://www.fbi.gov/history/famous-cases/black-tom-1916-bombing.

70. "Liberty State Park: Black Tom Explosion," New Jersey Department of Environmental Protection, updated January 26, 2005, http://www.state.nj.us/dep/parksandforests/parks/liberty_state_park/liberty_blacktomexplosion.html (accessed July 9, 2014); FBI History, "Black Tom 1916 Bombing"; Chad Millman, *The Detonators: The Secret Plot to Destroy America and an Epic Hunt for Justice* (New York: Little, Brown, 2006).

71. The FBI was at the time called the Bureau of Investigation. See Federal Bureau of Investigation, "A Brief History: The Nation Calls, 1908–1923," https://www.fbi.gov/history/brief-history (accessed January 30, 2021).

72. U.S. Secret Service, "History," https://www.secretservice.gov/about/history/events/.

73. In those early years, the FBI didn't amount to much. The Bureau's own history notes, "During its first 15 years, the Bureau was a shadow of its future self. It was not yet strong enough to withstand the sometimes corrupting influence of patronage politics on hiring, promotions, and transfers. New agents received limited training and were sometimes undisciplined and poorly managed." One special agent split his time between conducting investigations and overseeing his cranberry bog. Federal Bureau of Investigation, "Brief History."

74. Andrew, *For the President's Eyes Only*, 54; John F. Fox Jr., "Bureaucratic wrangling over counterintelligence, 1917–18," *Studies in Intelligence* 49, no. 1 (1985).

75. Weiner, *Enemies*, 13–25; Andrew, *For the President's Eyes Only*, 54–71.

76. Letter from William MacAdoo to Woodrow Wilson, June 2, 1917. See Fox Jr., "Bureaucratic wrangling over counterintelligence."

77. Quoted in Andrew, *For the President's Eyes Only*, 56 (original source: Arthur S. Link, ed., *The Papers of Woodrow Wilson*, Vol. 45 [Princeton: Princeton University Press, 1966–1992], 75).

78. Federal Bureau of Investigation, "Brief History"; Ronald Kessler, *Inside the FBI: The World's Most Powerful Law Enforcement Agency* (New York: Pocket, 1994); Weiner, *Enemies*.

79. Andrew, *For the President's Eyes Only*, 69–70; Jeffrey T. Richelson, *A Century of Spies: Intelligence in the Twentieth Century* (New York: Oxford University Press, 1995), 69–77.

80. Henry L. Stimson and McGeorge Bundy, *On Active Service in Peace and War* (New York: Harper & Brothers, 1947), 188.

81. "Speech by Franklin D. Roosevelt, New York (Transcript)," Address to Congress, December 8, 1941, Library of Congress, https://www.loc.gov/resource/afc1986022.afc1986022_ms2201/?st=text (accessed November 30, 2020).

82. Technically, the very first such agency was the Coordinator of Information (COI), which was also led by Bill Donovan and became the OSS. See Michael Warner, "COI Came First," *The Office of Strategic Services: America's First Intelligence Agency* (Washington, D.C.: Central Intelligence Agency, 2008), https://www.cia.gov/static/7851e16f9e100b6f9cc4ef002028ce2f/Office-of-Strategic-Services.pdf.

83. Amy Zegart, *Flawed by Design: The Evolution of the CIA, JCS, and NSC* (Palo Alto, Calif.: Stanford University Press, 1999), 166.

84. Tim Weiner, *Legacy of Ashes: The History of the CIA* (New York: Anchor Books, 2008), 3–5.

85. The clandestine service is called the Directorate of Operations. Central Intelligence Agency, "About CIA—Organization," https://www.cia.gov/about/organization/#directorate -of-operations (accessed January 30, 2021).

86. These were the Roberts Commission (established by executive order and chaired by Supreme Court Justice Owen Roberts), the Navy Department's Hart inquiry, the Army Pearl Harbor Board, the Naval Court of Inquiry, the Clauson investigation (directed by the Secretary of War to supplement the Army Board's investigation), the Hewitt Inquiry (directed by the Secretary of the Navy), the Clarke Investigation (led by Colonel Carter Clarke, head of the Military Intelligence Division), and the Joint Congressional Committee Investigation which produced forty volumes of findings.

87. Roberta Wohlstetter, *Pearl Harbor: Warning and Decision* (Palo Alto, Calif.: Stanford University Press, 1962).

88. U.S. Senate, "Report of the Joint Committee on the Investigation of the Pearl Harbor Attack," 79th Cong., 2nd sess., July 20, 1946, Document 244 (Washington, D.C.: GPO, 1946), 257.

89. National Archives, "Office of Strategic Services Personnel Files from World War II," https://www.archives.gov/research/military/ww2/oss/personnel-files.html (accessed November 30, 2020); "24,000 WWII-Era Spies Revealed in U.S. Documents," *New York Times*, August 14, 2008, https://www.nytimes.com/2008/08/14/world/americas/14iht-spies.4 .15302307.html (accessed September 26, 2020); Central Intelligence Agency, "Julia Child and the OSS Recipe for Shark Repellent," posted July 9, 2015, updated June 14, 2017, https://www .cia.gov/stories/story/julia-child-and-the-oss-recipe-for-shark-repellent/ (accessed January 29, 2021).

90. Central Intelligence Agency, "Stories—Julia Child: Cooking Up Spy Ops for OSS," March 30, 2020, https://www.cia.gov/stories/story/julia-child-cooking-up-spy-ops-for-oss/ (accessed April 16, 2021).

91. U.S. Senate, "Report of the Joint Committee," 253.

92. The term *rogue elephant* was first applied to the CIA by Sen. Frank Church in his 1976 review of the agency's history and activities. See U.S. Senate Select Committee to Study Governmental Operations with Respect to Intelligence Activities of the United States (Church Committee), "Final Report," 94th Cong., 2nd sess., April 26, 1976, S. Rept. 940-775, Serial 13133–3–3.

93. William M. Leary, ed., *The Central Intelligence Agency: History and Documents* (Tuscaloosa: University of Alabama Press, 1984), 6.

94. Zegart, *Flawed by Design*, 163.

95. Zegart.

96. "From the Desk of Harry S. Truman," December 1, 1963, Document 94, Papers of David M. Noyes, Truman Library.

97. National Security Act of 1947, Public Law 235, July 26, 1947, https://www.dni.gov/index .php/ic-legal-reference-book/national-security-act-of-1947.

98. Quoted in Amy Zegart, "The legend of a democracy promoter," *National Interest*, September 16, 2008, https://nationalinterest.org/article/the-legend-of-a-democracy-promoter -2839.

99. U.S. Department of State, Office of the Historian, "National Security Council Directive to Director of Central Intelligence Hillenkoetter," attachment to "Memorandum from the Executive Secretary of the National Security Council (Souers) to Director of Central Intelligence Hillenkoetter," December 17, 1947, "Foreign Relations of the United States, 1945–1950, Emergence of the Intelligence Establishment," Document #257, https://history.state.gov/historicaldocuments/frus1945-50Intel/d257.

100. Anne Karalekas, "History of the Central Intelligence Agency," in Leary, *Central Intelligence Agency*, 43; Zegart, *Flawed by Design*, 189.

101. Church Committee, "Final Report," 445. For recent work examining the strategic uses of covert operations, see Austin Carson, *Secret Wars: Covert Conflict in International Politics* (Princeton, N.J.: Princeton University Press, 2018); Lindsey O'Rourke, *Covert Regime Change* (Ithaca, N.Y.: Cornell University Press, 2018); Michael Poznansky, *In the Shadow of International Law* (New York: Oxford University Press, 2020).

102. To make their cover story believable, the agency set up a fake production company called Studio Six Productions in offices previously used by film star Michael Douglas. They also produced phony movie posters and ads for trade magazines, used an actual science-fiction movie script, and brought disguises for the diplomats that made them look more like hip Hollywood moviemakers. Antonio J. Mendez, "A Class Case of Deception: CIA Goes Hollywood," https://www.cia.gov/library/center-for-the-study-of-intelligence/csi-publications/csi-studies/studies/winter99-00/art1.html.

103. Marcus Rosenbaum, "'Argo': What Really Happened in Tehran? A CIA Agent Remembers," *Weekend Edition Saturday*, NPR, February 16, 2013, https://www.npr.org/2013/02/16/172098605/argo-what-really-happened-in-tehran-a-cia-agent-remembers; Mark Lijek, "I Was Rescued from Iran: It Wasn't Like the Movie," *Slate*, October 18, 2012, https://slate.com/culture/2012/10/argo-hostage-story-mark-lijeks-true-account-of-fleeing-iran.html (accessed September 26, 2020).

104. Thomas F. Troy, *Donovan and the CIA: A History of the Establishment of the Central Intelligence Agency* (Frederick, Md.: University Publications of America, 1981), 278.

105. Zegart, *Flawed by Design*.

106. John Ranelagh, *The Agency: The Rise and Decline of the CIA* (New York: Simon & Schuster, 1986), 113.

107. Zegart, *Flawed by Design*, 189–90.

108. Zegart, 192.

109. Andrew, *For the President's Eyes Only*, 216.

110. Zegart, *Flawed by Design*, 192.

111. Seymour Hersh, "Huge CIA Operation Reported in U.S. against Antiwar Forces, Other Dissidents in Nixon Years," *New York Times*, December 22, 1974, https://www.nytimes.com/1974/12/22/archives/huge-cia-operation-reported-in-u-s-against-antiwar-forces-other.html.

112. Amy Zegart, *Spying Blind: The CIA, the FBI, and the Origins of 9/11* (Princeton, N.J.: Princeton University Press, 2007), 71; James R. Clapper with Trey Brown, *Facts and Fears: Hard Truths from a Life in Intelligence* (New York: Penguin, 2018), 87.

113. Michael Morell with Bill Harlow, *The Great War of Our Time: The CIA's Fight against Terrorism—From Al-Qa'ida to ISIS* (New York: Twelve, 2015), 74.

114. William G. Hyland, op-ed [no title], *New York Times*, May 20, 1991, A15.

115. Zegart, *Spying Blind*, 71.

116. Zegart, 65–66, 82.

117. Interview by author, December 2004; Zegart, *Spying Blind*, 82–83.

118. Zegart, 27–41.

119. Zegart, 27–41.

120. Zegart, 3–4, 78–82.

121. Zegart. For a debate about alternative views, see "Correspondence: How intelligent is intelligence reform?" *International Security* 30, no. 4 (Spring 2006): 196–208.

122. Zegart, *Spying Blind*, 1–3, 104–106.

123. Brent Scowcroft, testimony before the U.S. House Permanent Select Committee on Intelligence and U.S. Senate Select Committee on Intelligence, "Joint Inquiry into Intelligence Community Activities before and after the Terrorist Attacks of September 11, 2001," 107th Cong., 2nd sess., September 19, 2002.

124. National Intelligence Estimate 2002-16HC, "Iraq's Continuing Programs for Weapons of Mass Destruction," October 2002, redacted and declassified April 2004, https://fas.org/irp/cia/product/iraq-wmd-nie.pdf.

125. Commission on the Intelligence Capabilities of the United States Regarding Weapons of Mass Destruction (Silberman-Robb Commission or WMD Commission), "Report to the President," March 31, 2005, https://fas.org/irp/offdocs/wmd_report.pdf.

126. Silberman-Robb Commission, 45–196. Others found that political pressure added to existing weaknesses, causing worst-case assumptions to become mainstream. Joshua Rovner, *Fixing the Facts: National Security and the Politics of Intelligence* (Ithaca, N.Y.: Cornell University Press, 2011), 137–84.

127. Silberman-Robb Commission, "Report to the President," 47.

128. Quoted in Chris Whipple, *The Spymasters: How the CIA Directors Shape History and the Future* (New York: Scribner, 2020), 205.

129. For a summary of the legislative reform process, see Michael Allen, *Blinking Red: Crisis and Compromise in American Intelligence after 9/11* (Dulles, Va.: Potomac Books, 2013).

130. There are six top tier intelligence agencies: the CIA, which is independent; the FBI, which is part of the Justice Department; and four agencies inside the Department of Defense—the National Security Agency, National Reconnaissance Office, Defense Intelligence Agency, and National Geospatial-Intelligence Agency. Michael Hayden, *Playing to the Edge: American Intelligence in the Age of Terror* (New York: Penguin, 2016), 166–67.

131. Quoted in Philip Shenon and Douglas Jehl, "House Proposal Puts Less Power in New Spy Post," *New York Times*, September 25, 2004.

132. Jane Harman, Intelligence Reauthorization News conference with members of the House Permanent Select Committee on Intelligence, March 30, 2006. Harman went on to say that she believed the law had overcome Pentagon objections and provided adequate statutory authority to the DNI but needed more vigorous leadership to be effective.

133. Clapper, *Facts and Fears*, 106–7; "Robert Gates Oral History (Transcript)," interview by Mike Nelson and Jeffrey Engel, July 8, 2013, Presidential Oral Histories, University of Virginia Miller Center, https://millercenter.org/the-presidency/presidential-oral-histories/robert-gates-oral-history.

134. Clapper, *Facts and Fears*, 128. In January 2021, the Intelligence Community grew from seventeen to eighteen agencies with the addition of Space Force intelligence.

135. Clapper, 137.

136. Mark Lowenthal, *Intelligence: From Secrets to Policy*, 7th ed. (Thousand Oaks, Calif.: CQ Press, 2017), 40.

137. Clapper, *Facts and Fears*, 117; U.S. Library of Congress Congressional Research Service, Richard A. Best Jr., "The National Intelligence Council (NIC): Issues and Options for Congress," R40505, https://fas.org/sgp/crs/intel/R40505.pdf.

138. Lowenthal, *Intelligence: From Secrets to Policy*, 43.

139. Leon Panetta with Jim Newton, *Worthy Fights: A Memoir of Leadership in War and Peace* (New York: Penguin, 2014), 228.

140. The CIA is also the only agency outside the Office of the Director of National Intelligence that is independent. The sixteen other intelligence agencies are part of cabinet departments (nine are in the Defense Department).

141. Clapper, *Facts and Fears*, 117.

142. U.S. Senate Committee on Intelligence, *Global Threats and National Security*, C-Span, January 29, 2019, https://www.c-span.org/video/?457211-1/national-security-officials-testify-threats-us.

143. Lowenthal, *Intelligence: From Secrets to Policy*, 51–52; Steve Slick, "Intelligence Studies Essay: 'After you, Alphonse,' or Why Two Different Intelligence Agencies Now Attend National Security Council Meetings, Whether It Matters, and How to Mitigate the Potential Hazards," *Lawfare*, July 27, 2017, https://www.lawfareblog.com/intelligence-studies-essay-after-you-alphonse-or-why-two-different-intelligence-agencies-now-attend#:~:text=President%20Trump's%20revised%20executive%20order,HSC%20and%20that%20both%20agencies. Initially President Trump demoted the DNI and the chairman of the Joint Chiefs of Staff to "invitation only" members of the National Security Council and left the CIA director out entirely. In April 2017, he reversed course and added all three to NSC meetings.

144. Hayden, *Playing to the Edge*, 166–167.

145. Office of the Director of National Intelligence, "Members of the IC," https://www.dni.gov/index.php/what-we-do/members-of-the-ic#nsa.

146. National Geospatial-Intelligence Agency, "About NGA," https://www.nga.mil/About/Pages/Default.aspx.

147. Lowenthal, *Intelligence: From Secrets to Policy*, 111.

148. Susan M. Gordon, keynote address, GEOINT 2018 Symposium, April 24, 2018, https://trajectorymagazine.com/building-to-scale-and-creating-anew/ (accessed September 24, 2020).

Chapter 4: Intelligence Basics

1. Interview by author, September 24, 2020.

2. They were Vice President Joe Biden, Secretary of Defense Bob Gates, Secretary of State Hillary Clinton, Chairman of the Joint Chiefs of Staff Adm. Mike Mullen, Vice Chairman of the Joint Chiefs of Staff Gen. James "Hoss" Cartwright, White House intelligence advisor John Brennan, National Security Advisor Tom Donilon, Director of National Intelligence James

Clapper, CIA Director Leon Panetta, Deputy CIA Director Michael Morell, and National Counterterrorism Center Director Michael Leiter.

3. Michael Morell with Bill Harlow, *The Great War of Our Time: The CIA's Fight against Terrorism—From al Qa'ida to ISIS* (New York: Twelve, 2015), 150. The official NSC calendar listed the bin Laden meetings only as "Mickey Mouse meetings" to preserve operational security. John O. Brennan, *Undaunted: My Fight against America's Enemies, at Home and Abroad* (New York: Celadon Books, 2020), 230–31.

4. Amy Zegart and Michael Morell, "Spies, lies, and algorithms," *Foreign Affairs* 98, no. 3 (May/June 2019): 90–91.

5. Leon Panetta with Jim Newton, *Worthy Fights: A Memoir of Leadership in War and Peace* (New York: Penguin, 2014), 294–97; Morell, *Great War of Our Time*, 146–47, 150–71.

6. Mark Mazzetti and Helene Cooper, "Detective Work on Courier Led to Breakthrough on Bin Laden," *New York Times*, May 2, 2011, https://www.nytimes.com/2011/05/02/world/asia/02reconstruct-capture-osama-bin-laden.html.

7. Leon E. Panetta and Jeremy Bash, "The former head of the CIA on managing the hunt for Bin Laden," *Harvard Business Review*, May 2, 2016, https://hbr.org/2016/05/leadership-lessons-from-the-bin-laden-manhunt.

8. Mazzetti and Cooper, "Detective Work."

9. Morell, *Great War of Our Time*, 148, 152.

10. Nicholas Schmidle, "Getting Bin Laden," *New Yorker*, August 8, 2011, https://www.newyorker.com/magazine/2011/08/08/getting-bin-laden.

11. Peter Bergen, "The 'Manhunt' to Capture Osama Bin Laden (Transcript)," interview by Dave Davies, *Fresh Air*, NPR, May 1, 2012, https://www.npr.org/transcripts/151766454.

12. Mark Bowden, "The hunt for 'Geronimo,'" *Vanity Fair*, October 12, 2012, https://www.vanityfair.com/news/politics/2012/11/inside-osama-bin-laden-assassination-plot.

13. Bob Woodward, "Death of Osama Bin Laden: Phone Call Pointed US to Compound—and to 'the Pacer,'" *Washington Post*, May 6, 2011, https://www.washingtonpost.com/world/national-security/death-of-osama-bin-laden-phone-call-pointed-us-to-compound--and-to-the-pacer/2011/05/06/AFnSVaCG_story.html.

14. Panetta, *Worthy Fights*, 294–300.

15. Morell, *Great War of Our Time*, 157–58.

16. Panetta, *Worthy Fights*, 313–28.

17. The Office of the Director of National Intelligence has declassified and released three tranches of materials seized from bin Laden's Abbottabad compound. See "Bin Laden's Bookshelf," https://www.dni.gov/index.php/features/bin-laden-s-bookshelf?start=1 (accessed September 25, 2020).

18. James Clapper with Trey Brown, *Facts and Fears: Hard Truths from a Life in Intelligence* (New York: Penguin, 2018), 156; Barack Obama, "Remarks by the President on Osama Bin Laden," East Room, Washington, D.C., May 2, 2011, https://obamawhitehouse.archives.gov/the-press-office/2011/05/02/remarks-president-osama-bin-laden.

19. Clapper, *Facts and Fears*, 153.

20. "The cost of being Osama bin Laden," *Forbes*, September 14, 2001, https://www.forbes.com/2001/09/14/0914ladenmoney.html#4e9cec6c32a3 (accessed September 25, 2020).

21. The term *intelligence* is often confusing because it is used to denote a *product* (information), a *process* (the manner in which information is collected, analyzed, and disseminated to policymakers), and a *set of organizations* (eighteen federal agencies that perform these functions). This chapter focuses on the intelligence product and how it differs from other types of information available to policymakers.

22. Sun Tzu, *The Art of War*, translated by Lionel Giles (New York: Barnes & Noble, 2003), 17.

23. "The Poetry of Donald Rumsfeld, Set to Music," *Morning Edition*, NPR, March 12, 2004, https://www.npr.org/templates/story/story.php?storyId=1761585.

24. Secretary of Defense Donald Rumsfeld and Gen. Richard Myers, DOD News Briefing, transcript, U.S. Department of Defense, February 12, 2002, https://fas.org/irp/news/2002/02/dod021202.html.

25. David A. Graham, "Rumsfeld's knowns and unknowns: The intellectual history of a quip," *Atlantic*, March 27, 2014, https://www.theatlantic.com/politics/archive/2014/03/rumsfelds-knowns-and-unknowns-the-intellectual-history-of-a-quip/359719/.

26. James R. Holmes, "The long, strange trip of China's first aircraft carrier," *Foreign Policy*, February 3, 2015, https://foreignpolicy.com/2015/02/03/the-long-strange-trip-of-chinas-first-aircraft-carrier-liaoning/.

27. Sherman Kent, "A Crucial Estimate Relived," *Studies in Intelligence* (Spring 1964), https://www.cia.gov/static/f547ed3bcd5793ff5456dc381c2df789/A-Crucial-Estimate-Relived.pdf.

28. Thomas Fingar, "Analysis in the U.S. Intelligence Community: Missions, Masters, and Methods," in National Research Council, *Intelligence Analysis for Tomorrow: Advances from the Behavioral and Social Sciences* (Washington, D.C.: National Academies Press, 2011), 3.

29. Dana Priest and William M. Arkin, "Top Secret America: A Hidden World, Growing Beyond Control," *Washington Post*, July 19, 2010, https://live.washingtonpost.com/topsecret-0719.html.

30. For decades, intelligence budgets were classified. That changed in 2007 when Congress required disclosure of the total intelligence budget. This estimate is a combination of the budget request for the National Intelligence Program and the Military Intelligence Program. "Intelligence Budget Data," Federation of American Scientists, Intelligence Resource Program, https://fas.org/irp/budget/#:~:text=The%20Fiscal%20Year%202020%20budget,for%20the%20Military%20Intelligence%20Program (accessed September 6, 2020).

31. National Geospatial Intelligence Agency, "NGA's Mission," https://www.nga.mil/about/1596052185524_Mission.html (accessed September 6, 2020).

32. Defense Intelligence Agency, "Human Intelligence," https://www.dia.mil/Careers-Internships/Career-Fields/Human-Intelligence/#operations-support (accessed September 6, 2020).

33. Zegart and Morell, "Spies, lies, and algorithms."

34. Josh Chin, "China Spends More on Domestic Security as Xi's Powers Grow," *Wall Street Journal*, March 6, 2018, https://www.wsj.com/articles/china-spends-more-on-domestic-security-as-xis-powers-grow-1520358522?mod=mktw&adobe_mc=MCMID%3D3370608410963891126350136059869841598 4%7CMCORGID%3DCB68E4BA55144CAA0A4C98A5%2540AdobeOrg%7CTS%3D1600534321.

35. Vladimir Kara-Murza, "Putin's Dark Cult of the Secret Police," *Washington Post*, December 28, 2017, https://www.washingtonpost.com/news/democracy-post/wp/2017/12/28/putins-dark-cult-of-the-secret-police/.

36. The Department of Homeland Security does not collect intelligence but it does have a domestic intelligence mandate that includes two-way intelligence sharing between the federal government and state, local, tribal, and territorial governments to protect the homeland. U.S. Department of Homeland Security, Office of Intelligence and Analysis, "Mission," https://www.dhs.gov/office-intelligence-and-analysis-mission#:~:text=The%20mission%20of%20the%20Intelligence,safe%2C%20secure%2C%20and%20resilient (accessed January 17, 2021).

37. National Security Act of 1947, Public Law 235, July 26, 1947, https://www.dni.gov/index.php/ic-legal-reference-book/national-security-act-of-1947.

38. U.S. Senate Select Committee to Study Governmental Operations with Respect to Intelligence Activities (Church Committee), "Supplementary Detailed Staff Reports on Intelligence Activities and the Rights of Americans, Book 3: Final Report" (Washington, D.C.: GPO, 1976), 765–77; James M. Olson, *Fair Play: The Moral Dilemmas of Spying* (Dulles, Va.: Potomac Books, 2006), 40.

39. Church Committee, "Supplementary Detailed Staff Reports," 3, 559–636.

40. This 80 percent estimation originated from former CIA Director Allen Dulles in testimony to the Senate in 1947. See Peter Grose, *Gentleman Spy: The Life of Allen Dulles* (Boston: Houghton Mifflin, 1994), 525–28. Some scholars and intelligence officials now estimate that intelligence found in publicly available sources could be as high as 90 percent. See Loch Johnson, *Bombs, Bugs, Drugs and Thugs* (New York: NYU Press, 2002), 185–86. For a broader discussion on estimates of open-source intelligence, see Stevyn D. Gibson, "Exploring the Role and Value of Open Source Intelligence," in Christopher Hobbs, Matthew Moran, and Daniel Salisbury, eds., *Open Source Intelligence in the Twenty-First Century: New Approaches and Opportunities* (New York: Springer, 2014).

41. Michael D. Shear, Maggie Haberman, Nicholas Confessore, Karen Yourish, Larry Buchanan, and Keith Collins, "How Trump Reshaped the Presidency in Over 11,000 Tweets," *New York Times*, November 2, 2019.

42. Robert Draper, "The Man Behind the President's Tweets," *New York Times*, April 16, 2018, https://www.nytimes.com/2018/04/16/magazine/dan-scavino-the-secretary-of-offense.html.

43. "Intelligence Budget Data." This estimate is a combination of the budget request for the National Intelligence Program and the Military Intelligence Program.

44. Interview by author, August 28, 2020.

45. Interview by author, August 13, 2020.

46. Interview by author, September 25, 2020.

47. David E. Sanger and Julian E. Barnes, "On North Korea and Iran, Intelligence Chiefs Contradict Trump," *New York Times*, January 29, 2019, https://www.nytimes.com/2019/01/29/us/politics/kim-jong-trump.html.

48. Zegart and Morell, "Spies, lies, and algorithms," 91.

49. Woodward, "Death of Osama Bin Laden."

50. "George Tenet Pt. 2," *The Daily Show*, Comedy Central, May 8, 2007, http://www.cc.com/video-clips/xdh025/the-daily-show-with-jon-stewart-george-tenet-pt-2, at 2:30.

51. Clapper, *Facts and Fears*, 143.

52. Former Director of National Intelligence Dennis Blair, for example, frequently engaged in policy discussions. Clapper attributes this aberrational behavior to the fact that Blair was not a career intelligence officer. He was a Navy admiral who had spent thirty-four years consuming intelligence, not providing it. See Clapper, *Facts and Fears*, 127. Blair had a tumultuous and short tenure as DNI.

53. Robert Gates, *From the Shadows: The Ultimate Insider's Story of Five Presidents and How They Won the Cold War* (New York: Simon & Schuster, 1996), 375.

54. "Former Top DNI Official Sue Gordon Discusses Circumstances of Her Departure from ODNI—Transcript," interview by Michael Morell, *Intelligence Matters*, CBS, February 14, 2020, https://www.cbsnews.com/news/former-top-dni-official-sue-gordon-discusses-circumstances -of-her-departure-from-odni-transcript/.

55. "Oral History Transcript, John A. McCone, Interview 1," interview by Joe B. Frantz, August 19, 1970, LBJ Library Oral Histories, LBJ Presidential Library, https://www.discoverlbj .org/item/oh-mcconej-19700819-1-74-150.

56. Christopher R. Moran and Richard J. Aldrich, "Trump and the CIA," *Foreign Affairs*, April 24, 2017, https://www.foreignaffairs.com/articles/2017-04-24/trump-and-cia.

57. R. James Woolsey Oral History (Transcript), interview by Russell L. Riley, January 13, 2010, William J. Clinton Presidential History Project, University of Virginia Miller Center, https://millercenter.org/the-presidency/presidential-oral-histories/r-james-woolsey-oral -history-director-central.

58. Gates, *From the Shadows*, 567.

59. Mark Landler, "Trump under Fire for Invoking Nazis in Criticism of U.S. Intelligence," *New York Times*, January 11, 2017, https://www.nytimes.com/2017/01/11/us/donald-trump-nazi -comparison.html.

60. Caitlin Oprysko, "Trump tells intel chiefs to 'go back to school' after they break with him," *Politico*, January 30, 2019, https://www.politico.com/story/2019/01/30/trump-national -security-1136433.

61. Zachary Cohen and Nicole Gaouette, "Trump Says Ratcliffe Will 'Rein In' U.S. Intelligence Agencies as Spy Chief," CNN, July 30, 2019, https://www.cnn.com/2019/07/30/politics /trump-ratcliffe-rein-in-us-intelligence-agencies/index.html.

62. Alison Durkee, "Rep. John Ratcliffe is already out as Trump's DNI pick," *Vanity Fair*, August 2, 2019, https://www.vanityfair.com/news/2019/08/john-ratcliffe-dni-nominee -withdraw-trump.

63. Shane Harris, "Senate Confirms John Ratcliffe as Next Director of National Intelligence in Sharply Divided Vote," *Washington Post*, May 21, 2020.

64. Julian E. Barnes and Mark Mazzetti, "For Spies Emerging from the Shadows, a War with Trump Carries Risks," *New York Times*, July 24, 2018, https://www.nytimes.com/2018/07/24 /us/politics/trump-security-clearances.html. See also John Gentry, "An INS special forum: US intelligence officers' involvement in political activities in the Trump era," *Intelligence and National Security* 35, no. 1: 1–19.

65. Michael V. Hayden, "The End of Intelligence," *New York Times*, April 28, 2018, https:// www.nytimes.com/2018/04/28/opinion/sunday/the-end-of-intelligence.html.

66. Amy Zegart, "Politicization of intelligence," in Gentry, "INS special forum."

67. John O. Brennan (@JohnBrennan), Twitter, October 2, 2019, 12:59 P.M., https://twitter
.com/JohnBrennan/status/1179485989854744576.

68. Dylan Scott, "Former CIA director: Trump-Putin press conference 'nothing short of
treasonous,'" *Vox*, July 16, 2018, https://www.vox.com/world/2018/7/16/17576804/trump-putin
-meeting-john-brennan-tweet-treasonous.

69. Sophie Tatum, "Former CIA Chief to Trump on McCabe Firing: 'America Will Triumph
Over You,'" CNN, March 17, 2018, https://www.cnn.com/2018/03/17/politics/john-brennan
-donald-trump-mccabe-firing/index.html; author's analysis of Brennan's Tweets from January 2019 to October 10, 2019.

70. Interview by author, July 30, 2020.

71. Interview by author.

72. Interview by author.

73. Morell, *Great War of Our Time*, 3.

74. Clapper, *Facts and Fears*, 9–11.

75. Interview by author, July 21, 2020.

76. Robert Baer, *See No Evil: The True Story of a Ground Soldier in the CIA's War on Terrorism*
(New York: Crown, 2002), 12–13.

77. Nevertheless, significant racial and gender diversity challenges remain. See Central Intel-
ligence Agency, "Director's Diversity in Leadership Study," June 30, 2015, https://www.cia.gov
/static/d8681a6dc20446042a8c3020459ca1d4/Directors-Diversity-in-Leadership-Study
-Overcoming-Barriers-to-Advancement.pdf (accessed December 15, 2020); Central Intelligence
Agency, "Director's Advisory Group on Women in Leadership" (chaired by Madeleine K.
Albright), March 2013, https://permanent.fdlp.gov/gpo38506/CIA-Women-In-Leadership
-March2013.pdf (accessed April 16, 2021).

78. Interview by author, August 10, 2020.

79. Interview by author, July 30, 2020.

80. Josh Meyer, "McLaughlin Has Long Resume Up His Sleeve," *Los Angeles Times*, June 4,
2004, https://www.latimes.com/archives/la-xpm-2004-jun-04-na-mclaughlin4-story.html; Joel
Brinkley, "Resignation from the C.I.A.: Man in the News; A Quiet Man Takes Charge—John
Edward McLaughlin," *New York Times*, June 4, 2004, https://www.nytimes.com/2004/06/04
/world/resignation-cia-man-quiet-man-takes-charge-john-edward-mclaughlin.html.

81. Interview by author, July 30, 2020.

82. Interview by author, August 19, 2020.

83. Interview by author, October 7, 2020; Morrell is quoting former Defense Department
official John Hamre.

84. Interview by author, July 21, 2020.

85. Olson, *Fair Play*, 8–9.

86. Morell, *Great War of Our Time*, 167. Secrecy creates stresses at home but also bonds at
the office. "There's a strong sense of family that pervades the whole place that comes from not
being able to talk about your work to your real family and friends," Morell told me. Interview
by author, October 7, 2020.

87. Olson, *Fair Play*, 8.

88. Gina M. Bennett, *National Security Mom* (Deadwood, Ore.: Wyatt-MacKenzie, 2008), 15–16.

89. Interview by author, July 31, 2020.

90. Olson, *Fair Play*, 8.

91. Interview by author, August 19, 2020.

92. Interview by author, October 13, 2020.

93. Interview by author, August 26, 2020.

94. Interview by author, July 21, 2020.

95. Interview by author, August 17, 2020.

96. Interview by author, July 30, 2020.

97. Olson, *Fair Play*, 45.

98. Interview by author, October 7, 2020.

99. Panetta, *Worthy Fights*, 318–19.

100. Interview by author, July 21, 2020; Bennett is quoting a former boss.

101. Interview by author, August 19, 2020.

102. Interview by author, September 24, 2020.

103. Interview by author, August 26, 2020.

104. Michael Hayden, *Playing to the Edge: American Intelligence in the Age of Terror* (New York: Penguin, 2016), 218.

105. U.S. Senate Committee on Foreign Relations, "Tora Bora Revisited: How We Failed to Get Bin Laden and Why It Matters Today," 111th Cong., 1st sess., November 30, 2009, S. Prt. 111-35, https://www.govinfo.gov/content/pkg/CPRT-111SPRT53709/html/CPRT-111SPRT53709.htm.

106. Annie Lowrey, "How Osama Bin Laden escaped," *Foreign Policy*, December 11, 2009, https://foreignpolicy.com/2009/12/11/how-osama-bin-laden-escaped-2/; Senate Committee on Foreign Relations, "Tora Bora Revisited."

107. Gary Bernsten and Ralph Pezzullo, *Jawbreaker* (New York: Crown Publishers, 2005), 185–89; Tom Shroder, "The Long Hunt for Osama Bin Laden: Tom Shroder Answers Your Questions," *Washington Post*, June 30, 2011, https://live.washingtonpost.com/tom-shroder-hunt-for-osama-bin-laden.html.

108. Peter Finn, "Bin Laden Used Ruse to Flee," *Washington Post*, January 21, 2003, https://www.washingtonpost.com/archive/politics/2003/01/21/bin-laden-used-ruse-to-flee/028759f9-153f-48fd-a6fc-a6c3edob8c8e/; Shroder, "Long Hunt." Shroder put together the book *The Hunt for Bin Laden*, a compilation of fifteen years of reporting by *Post* journalists.

109. Jane Mayer, "The search for Osama," *New Yorker*, July 28, 2003, https://www.newyorker.com/magazine/2003/08/04/the-search-for-osama.

110. Dana Priest and Ann Tyson wrote in 2006 that bin Laden had released twenty-three audio- and videotapes in the previous five years: "Bin Laden Trail 'Stone Cold' U.S. Steps Up Efforts, But Good Intelligence on Ground Is Lacking," *Washington Post*, September 20, 2006, https://www.washingtonpost.com/archive/politics/2006/09/10/bin-laden-trail-stone-cold-span-classbankheadus-steps-up-efforts-but-good-intelligence-on-ground-is-lackingspan/f637c785-25ac-4646-99b4-e321864b86a9/; Mayer, "Search for Osama"; see also Morell, *Great*

War of Our Time, 145; Douglas Jehl and David Johnston, "In Video Message, Bin Laden Issues Warning to U.S.," *New York Times*, October 30, 2004, https://www.nytimes.com/2004/10/30/world/middleeast/in-video-message-bin-laden-issues-warning-to-us.html.

111. Greg Miller, "Bin Laden Tapes Raked for Inadvertent Leads," *Los Angeles Times*, December 28, 2004, https://www.latimes.com/archives/la-xpm-2004-dec-28-fg-verify28-story.html.

112. Dana Priest and William M. Arkin, *Top Secret America: The Rise of the New American Security State* (New York: Little, Brown, 2011), 71.

113. Peter Bergen, "Will We Ever Find Bin Laden? Don't Count on It," *Washington Post*, January 28, 2011, https://www.washingtonpost.com/wp-dyn/content/article/2011/01/28/AR2011012803001.html.

114. Peter Bergen, *The Longest War: The Enduring Conflict between America and Al Qaeda* (New York: Free Press, 2011), 345.

115. Priest and Tyson, "Bin Laden Trail."

116. Panetta, *Worthy Fights*, 290.

117. Mayer, "Search for Osama."

118. Mark Memmott, "What Panetta Told McCain about Bin Laden and 'Enhanced Interrogation,'" NPR, May 16, 2011, https://www.npr.org/sections/thetwo-way/2011/05/16/136366360/what-panetta-told-mccain-about-bin-laden-and-enhanced-interrogation.

119. Mayer, "Search for Osama."

120. Memmott, "What Panetta Told McCain."

121. U.S. Senate Select Committee on Intelligence, "Committee Study of the Central Intelligence Agency's Detention and Interrogation Program," 113th Cong., 2nd sess., December 9, 2014, S. Report 113-288, https://www.intelligence.senate.gov/sites/default/files/publications/CRPT-113srpt288.pdf, 541.

122. Bergen, "'Manhunt' to Capture Osama Bin Laden"; Mark Mazzetti, Helene Cooper, and Peter Baker, "Behind the Hunt for Bin Laden," *New York Times*, May 2, 2011, https://www.nytimes.com/2011/05/03/world/asia/03intel.html; Peter Bergen, *Manhunt: The Ten-Year Search for Bin Laden from 9/11 to Abbottabad* (New York: Broadway Books, 2013), 95–107; Morell, *Great War of Our Time*, 145–46.

123. Bowden, "Hunt for 'Geronimo'"; Mazzetti and Cooper, "Detective Work."

124. Woodward, "Death of Osama Bin Laden."

125. Schmidle, "Getting Bin Laden."

126. Marc Ambinder, "The little-known agency that helped kill Bin Laden," *Atlantic*, May 5, 2011, https://www.theatlantic.com/politics/archive/2011/05/the-little-known-agency-that-helped-kill-bin-laden/238454/.

127. Morell, *Great War of Our Time*, 151.

128. Greg Miller, "CIA Spied on Bin Laden from Safe House," *Washington Post*, May 6, 2011, https://www.washingtonpost.com/world/cia-spied-on-bin-laden-from-safe-house/2011/05/05/AFXbG31F_story.html.

129. Bergen, "'Manhunt' to Capture Osama Bin Laden."

130. Panetta and Bash, "Former head of the CIA"; Morell, *Great War of Our Time*, 152.

131. Mark Mazzetti, "Vaccination Ruse Used in Pursuit of Bin Laden," *New York Times*, July 11, 2011; see also M. Ilyas Khan, "Shakil Afridi: The Doctor Who Helped the CIA Find Bin Laden," BBC News, October 9, 2019, https://www.bbc.com/news/world-asia-49960979, which notes that in 2012, U.S. government officials publicly acknowledged that Afridi had worked for U.S. intelligence but did not acknowledge his involvement in the vaccine program.

132. Woodward, "Death of Osama Bin Laden."

133. Miller, "CIA Spied on Bin Laden."

134. Morell, *Great War of Our Time*, 145.

135. Peter Bergen, "The long hunt for Osama," *Atlantic*, October 2004, https://www.theatlantic.com/magazine/archive/2004/10/the-long-hunt-for-osama/303508/.

136. Panetta, *Worthy Fights*, 291.

137. Steve Coll, "Notes on the death of Osama Bin Laden," *New Yorker*, May 2, 2011, https://www.newyorker.com/news/news-desk/notes-on-the-death-of-osama-bin-laden.

138. Panetta and Bash, "Former head of the CIA."

139. Miller, "CIA Spied on Bin Laden."

140. Peter Bergen, "A Visit to Osama Bin Laden's Lair," CNN, May 3, 2012, https://www.cnn.com/2012/05/03/opinion/bergen-bin-laden-lair/index.html; Bergen, *Manhunt: The Ten-Year Search*, 12.

141. For assumptions, see Panetta and Bash, "Former head of the CIA"; Bergen, "Visit to Osama Bin Laden's Lair"; Joshua Keating, "Bin Laden apparently not on dialysis," *Foreign Policy*, May 4, 2011.

142. Bergen, *Manhunt: The Ten-Year Search*, 4.

143. Bergen, "Long hunt for Osama."

144. Panetta and Bash, "Former head of the CIA."

145. Panetta, *Worthy Fights*, 294.

146. Morell, *Great War of Our Time*, 163–64.

147. Morell, 159–60.

148. Woodward, "Death of Osama Bin Laden."

149. Morell, *Great War of Our Time*, 161.

150. Woodward, "Death of Osama Bin Laden"; Bowden, "Hunt for 'Geronimo.'"

151. Bowden, "Hunt for 'Geronimo.'"

152. Morell, *Great War of Our Time*, 161.

153. Interview by author, October 27, 2020.

154. National Security Act of 1947, Public Law 235, July 26, 1947, https://www.dni.gov/index.php/ic-legal-reference-book/national-security-act-of-1947.

155. Clapper, *Facts and Fears*, 151–54.

156. Panetta, *Worthy Fights*, 311.

157. Bergen, "'Manhunt' to Capture Osama Bin Laden."

158. Clapper, *Facts and Fears*, 152.

159. Morell, *Great War of Our Time*, 157. The CIA's covert operation to get bin Laden did not have to use Navy SEALS; the CIA has its own paramilitary capabilities, and Panetta writes that he considered a CIA-led ground raid. But he and other agency leaders believed that an operation that complex deep inside a foreign country would be better conducted by special operations forces. *Worthy Fights*, 299.

160. Schmidle, "Getting Bin Laden."

161. Eric Schmitt and Thom Shanker, *Counterstrike: The Untold Story of America's Secret Campaign against Al Qaeda* (New York: Times Books, 2011), 264.

162. Schmidle, "Getting Bin Laden."

163. Miller, "CIA Spied on Bin Laden."

164. Bergen, *Manhunt: The Ten-Year Search*, 227.

165. Schmidle, "Getting Bin Laden."

166. Schmitt and Shanker, *Counterstrike*, 265.

167. Mazzetti, Cooper, and Baker, "Behind the Hunt."

Chapter 5: Why Analysis Is So Hard

1. George Tenet with Bill Harlow, *At the Center of the Storm: My Years at the CIA* (New York: HarperCollins, 2007), 499.

2. David Halberstam, *The Coldest Winter: America and the Korean War* (Great Britain: Macmillan, 2008), 395, 398.

3. Joint Strategic Plans Committee, "Courses of Action in Korea," August 23, 1950, Folder CCS383.21 Korea (3-19-45), Record Group 218, "Joint Chiefs of Staff, Geographic File 1948-50," Modern Military Records, National Archives; Memorandum by the Central Intelligence Agency in *Foreign Relations of the United States, 1950, Korea*, Vol. 7, "Threat of Full-Scale Chinese Communist Intervention in Korea," October 12, 1950, 933. Yet by late October, State Department analysts, especially Edmund O. Clubb, director of the Office of Chinese Affairs, argued that large-scale Chinese intervention was likely. See Eliot A. Cohen, "The Chinese intervention in Korea," *Studies in Intelligence* 32, no. 3 (Fall 1988, approved for release September 22, 1993): 56–57, https://www.cia.gov/readingroom/docs/1988-11-01.pdf; Alexander Ovodenko, "(Mis)interpeting threats: A case study of the Korean War," *Security Studies* 16, no. 2 (2007): 254–86.

4. U.S. Department of State, Office of the Historian, "Substance of Statements Made at Wake Island Conference on 15 October 1950," in *Foreign Relations of the United States, 1950, Korea*, Vol. 7, Executive Secretariat Files: Lot 59D-95 (Wake Island Conference, October 1950), https://history.state.gov/historicaldocuments/frus1950v07/d680; Halberstam, *Coldest Winter*, 367.

5. David Halberstam, "MacArthur's grand delusion," *Vanity Fair*, October 2007 (printing an excerpt from Halberstam, *Coldest Winter*), https://www.vanityfair.com/news/2007/10/halberstam200710.

6. James Wright, "What we learned from the Korean War," *Atlantic*, July 23, 2013, https://www.theatlantic.com/international/archive/2013/07/what-we-learned-from-the-korean-war/278016/.

7. Cohen, "Chinese intervention in Korea," 54–55.

8. "North Korea: How Many Political Prisoners Are Detained in Prison?" BBC News, May 10, 2018, https://www.bbc.com/news/world-asia-44069749.

9. Estimated GDP per capita from 2015 (most recent year offered) in *The CIA World Factbook*, https://www.cia.gov/the-world-factbook/countries/korea-north/#economy.

10. Eleanor Albert, "North Korea's Military Capabilities," December 2019, Council on Foreign Relations, https://www.cfr.org/backgrounder/north-koreas-military-capabilities.

11. There is wide consensus that the Korean War intelligence failure did not stem from insufficient intelligence collection. See Allen Whiting and Harvey de Weerd, *China Crosses the Yalu: The Decision to Enter the Korean War* (Palo Alto, Calif.: Stanford University Press, 1960); Ovodenko, "(Mis)interpreting threats," 254–86.

12. CIA wartime documents show that agency analysts better estimated Chinese capabilities than MacArthur's Far East Command but misread Chinese intent, believing that the Soviet Union controlled the major foreign policy decisions of other Communist countries and that Soviet leaders were unwilling to risk global war with the United States. Cohen, "Chinese intervention in Korea"; P. K. Rose, "Two Strategic Intelligence Mistakes in Korea, 1950," Defense Technical Information Center, https://apps.dtic.mil/dtic/tr/fulltext/u2/a529658.pdf; Woodrow J. Kuhns, *Assessing the Soviet Threat: The Early Cold War Years* (Washington, D.C.: Center for the Study of Intelligence, 1997); Ovodenko, "(Mis)interpreting threats," 254–86.

13. William Stueck, *Rethinking the Korean War: A New Diplomatic and Strategic History* (Princeton, N.J.: Princeton University Press, 2002), 113.

14. Elizabeth Mix, "Dewey Defeats Truman Election Headline Gaffe," History, November 1, 2018, (updated November 4, 2019), https://www.history.com/news/dewey-defeats-truman-election-headline-gaffe.

15. Nate Silver, "Why FiveThirtyEight Gave Trump a Better Chance Than Almost Anyone Else," FiveThirtyEight, November 11, 2016, https://fivethirtyeight.com/features/why-fivethirtyeight-gave-trump-a-better-chance-than-almost-anyone-else/.

16. "Baseball Stats and History," Baseball Reference, https://www.baseball-reference.com/.

17. Eight countries currently possess nuclear weapons: the United States, United Kingdom, France, Russia, China, India, Pakistan, and North Korea. Experts agree that Israel has a nuclear arsenal, although the country has never declared it.

18. Choe Sang-Hun and Martin Fackler, "North Korea's Heir Apparent Remains a Mystery," *New York Times*, June 14, 2009, https://www.nytimes.com/2009/06/15/world/asia/15kim.html?ref=kimjongun.

19. "South Africa," Nuclear Threat Initiative, https://www.nti.org/learn/countries/south-africa/nuclear/.

20. MacArthur's quote, from declassified notes of a Wake Island meeting taken by MacArthur's aide, Colonel Laurence Bunker, appears in Stanley Weintraub, *MacArthur's War: Korea and the Undoing of an American Hero* (New York: Free Press, 2000), 191.

21. Weintraub, 197–198.

22. The CIA had no representative at the Far East Command headquarters in Japan and did not participate in preparing intelligence for MacArthur's army. Bruce Riedel, "Catastrophe on the Yalu: America's Intelligence Failure in Korea," Brookings, September 13, 2017, https://www.brookings.edu/blog/order-from-chaos/2017/09/13/catastrophe-on-the-yalu-americas-intelligence-failure-in-korea/.

23. Amy Zegart, *Spying Blind: The CIA, the FBI, and the Origins of 9/11* (Princeton, N.J.: Princeton University Press, 2007).

24. Janet Reno, former attorney general of the United States, testimony before the National Commission on Terrorist Attacks Upon the United States (the 9/11 Commission), April 13, 2004, 6.

25. Interview by author, 2004, in *Spying Blind*, 114. For an alternative view of the CIA's willingness to share with the FBI before 9/11, see Tenet, *At the Center of the Storm*.

26. See also Daniel Kahneman, *Thinking, Fast and Slow* (New York: Farrar, Straus and Giroux, 2011), 241–42.

27. Philip E. Tetlock and Dan Gardner, *Superforecasting: The Art and Science of Prediction* (New York: Crown Publishing Group, 2015), 181.

28. Tetlock and Gardner, 13–14.

29. Interview by author, October 27, 2020.

30. Tetlock's own study asked questions with shorter time horizons and more discrete answers, like "Will there be a nonviolent end to Apartheid in South Africa?" rather than questions closer to what intelligence officers confront, like "What will South Africa's domestic political landscape look like in a decade?"

31. See James B. Bruce and Michael Bennett, "Foreign Denial and Deception: Analytical Imperatives," in *Analyzing Intelligence: Origins, Obstacles, and Innovations*, edited by Roger Z. George and James B. Bruce (Washington, D.C.: Georgetown University Press, 2008), 122–37.

32. "Chairman Khrushchev's Letter to President Kennedy, October 23, 1962," John F. Kennedy Presidential Library and Museum, https://microsites.jfklibrary.org/cmc/oct23/doc6.html.

33. Weintraub, *MacArthur's War*, 197.

34. Kahneman, *Thinking, Fast and Slow*.

35. Amos Tversky and Daniel Kahneman, "Extensional versus Intuitive reasoning: The conjunction fallacy in probability judgement," *Psychological Review* 90, no. 4 (October 1983): 293–315.

36. "List of cognitive biases," Wikipedia, https://en.wikipedia.org/wiki/List_of_cognitive_biases (accessed April 26, 2021).

37. Charles G. Lord, Lee Ross, and Mark R. Lepper, "Biased assimilation and attitude polarization: The effects of prior theories on subsequently considered evidence," *Journal of Personality and Social Psychology* 37, no. 11 (1979): 2098–109.

38. Quoted in Druin Burch, *Taking the Medicine: A Short History of Medicine's Beautiful Idea, and Our Difficulty Swallowing It* (London: Vintage, 2010), 37.

39. Francis Bacon, *Novum Organon*, standard translation of James Spedding, Robert Leslie Ellis, and Douglas Denon Heath in *The Works*, Vol. 8 (Boston: Taggard and Thompson, 1863), 79, reprinted at https://archive.org/details/worksfrancisbaco08bacoiala/page/78/mode/2up?q=The+human+understanding (accessed April 17, 2021).

40. Rose McDermott and Uri Bar-Joseph describe Willoughby as an "officer who monopolized the intelligence process, estimated the enemy according to his own logic, and exhibited the symptoms of a high need for closure and an unshakable faith that MacArthur could not be wrong." McDermott and Bar-Joseph, "The Second Dyad," *Intelligence Success and Failure: The Human Factor* (New York: Oxford University Press, 2017), 59.

41. Halberstam, "McArthur's grand delusion."

42. National Intelligence Estimate 2002-16HC, "Iraq's Continuing Programs for Weapons of Mass Destruction," October 2002, redacted and declassified April 2004, https://fas.org/irp/cia/product/iraq-wmd-nie.pdf. For more on the substance of the NIE, see Commission on the Intelligence Capabilities of the United States Regarding Weapons of Mass Destruction

(Silberman-Robb Commission), "Report to the President of the United States," March 31, 2005, https://fas.org/irp/offdocs/wmd_report.pdf.

43. Silberman-Robb Commission, "Report to the President," 2 (letter transmitting final report), report pages 8–9.

44. Central Intelligence Agency, "Iraq Survey Group Nuclear Report," September 30, 2004, https://www.govinfo.gov/app/details/GPO-DUELFERREPORT/context, chap. 4.

45. Iraq Survey Group Chemical Warfare Report, September 30, 2004, https://www.govinfo .gov/app/details/GPO-DUELFERREPORT/context, chap. 5.

46. Silberman-Robb Commission, "Report to the President," 80–110; Iraq Survey Group Biological Warfare Report, September 30, 2004.

47. Silberman-Robb Commission, "Report to the President," 87. The Iraq Survey Group concluded that the trailers captured by coalition forces in 2003 were almost certainly used for keeping hydrogen, not bioweapons. See also U.S. Senate Select Committee on Intelligence, "Postwar Findings about Iraq's WMD Programs and Links to Terrorism and How They Compare with Prewar Assessments, together with Additional and Minority Views," 109th Cong., 2nd sess., September 8, 2006; Robert Jervis, "Reports, politics, and intelligence failures: The case of Iraq," *Journal of Strategic Studies* 29, no. 1 (2006): 3–52.

48. John O. Brennan, *Undaunted: My Fight Against America's Enemies, at Home and Abroad* (New York: Celadon Books, 2020), 128.

49. Silberman-Robb Commission, "Report to the President," 168–69.

50. Neil D. Weinstein, "Optimistic biases about personal risks," *Science* 246 (December 8, 1989): 1232–33; Manju Puri and David Robinson, "Optimism and Economic Choice," National Bureau of Economic Research, May 2005, https://www.nber.org/papers/w11361.pdf; Tali Sharot, *Optimism Bias* (New York: Vintage Books, 2012).

51. Albesh B. Patel, *Investing Unplugged: Secrets from the Inside* (New York: Springer, 2005); H. Kent Baker and John R. Nofsinger, "Psychological biases of investors," *Financial Services Review* 11 (2002): 97–116.

52. Joseph P. Simmons and Cade Massey, "Is optimism real?" *Journal of Experimental Psychology* 141, no. 4 (2012): 630–34.

53. Donald Granberg and Edward Brent, "When prophecy bends: The preference-expectation link in U.S. presidential elections, 1952–1980," *Journal of Personality and Social Psychology* 45 (1983): 477–81; Zlatan Krizan, Jeffrey C. Miller, and Omesh Johar, "Wishful thinking in the 2008 presidential election," *Psychological Science* 2, no. 1 (2010): 140–46; Samuel P. Hayes Jr., "The predictive ability of voters," *Journal of Social Psychology* 7 (1936): 183–91.

54. Daniel Kahneman and Jonathan Renshon, "Why hawks win," *Foreign Policy*, October 13, 2009, https://foreignpolicy.com/2009/10/13/why-hawks-win/.

55. Kahneman and Renshon.

56. "Casualties of World War I," Facing History and Ourselves, https://www.facinghistory .org/weimar-republic-fragility-democracy/politics/casualties-world-war-i-country-politics -world-war-i.

57. Cohen, "Chinese intervention in Korea," 56–58. Analysts at the CIA and Joint Chiefs of Staff also discounted the likelihood of large-scale Chinese intervention. The State Department was a notable exception, concluding that a large-scale Chinese intervention was likely.

58. Chris Whipple, *The Spymasters: How the CIA Directors Shape History and the Future* (New York: Scribner, 2020), 1.

59. Condoleezza Rice and Amy Zegart, *Political Risk* (Twelve: New York, 2018), 86–87.

60. Paul Slovic, Baruch Fischhoff, and Sarah Lichtenstein, "Facts versus Fears: Understanding Perceived Risk," in *Societal Risk Assessment*, edited by Richard C. Schwing and Walter A. Albers, Jr. (New York: Plenum Press, 1980), 181–211.

61. Mark Bowden, "The hunt for 'Geronimo,'" *Vanity Fair*, November 2012, http://www .vanityfair.com/news/politics/2012/11/inside-osama-bin-laden-assassination-plot; Bob Woodward, "Death of Osama bin Laden: Phone Call Pointed U.S. to Compound—and to 'the Pacer,'" *Washington Post*, May 6, 2011, https://www.washingtonpost.com/world/national-security /death-of-osama-bin-laden-phone-call-pointed-us-to-compound--and-to-the-pacer/2011/05 /06/AFnSVaCG_story.html.

62. See also Cullen G. Nutt, "Proof of the bomb: The influence of previous failure on intelligence judgments of nuclear programs," *Security Studies* 28, no. 2 (2019): 321–59.

63. Kahneman and Renshon, "Why hawks win."

64. For more about misperception and foreign policy, see Robert Jervis, "Hypotheses on misperception," *World Politics* 20, no. 3 (April 1968): 454–79.

65. Charles A. Duelfer and Stephen Benedict Dyson, "Chronic misperception and international conflict: The U.S.-Iraq experience," *International Security* 36, no. 1 (Summer 2011): 73–100.

66. Cohen, "Chinese intervention in Korea," 59.

67. Quoted in John W. Spanier, *The Truman-MacArthur Controversy* (New York: W. W. Norton, 1965), 97.

68. For the basis of mirror imaging in social psychology experiments, see Lee Ross, David Greene, and Pamela House, "The 'false consensus effect': An egocentric bias in social perception and attribution processes," *Journal of Experimental Social Psychology* 13 no. 3 (1977).

69. Frank Watanabe, "Fifteen axioms for intelligence analysis," *Studies in Intelligence* 1, no. 1 (1997): 7.

70. R. Jeffrey Smith, "CIA Missed Signs of India's Tests, U.S. Officials Say," *Washington Post*, May 13, 1998.

71. Central Intelligence Agency, "Jeremiah News Conference," June 2, 1998, https:// nsarchive2.gwu.edu/NSAEBB/NSAEBB187/IN39.pdf (accessed January 7, 2021).

72. Mary "Polly" Nayak, former CIA South Asia issue manager, remarks at Dwight D. Eisenhower National Security Conference, September 25–26, 2003; James Risen, Steven Lee Myers, and Tim Weiner, "U.S. May Have Helped India Hide Its Nuclear Activity," *New York Times*, May 25, 1998, https://www.nytimes.com/1998/05/25/world/us-may-have-helped-india-hide -its-nuclear-activity.html (accessed January 7, 2021).

73. The review is known as the Jeremiah Commission, after its chair, retired Adm. David E. Jeremiah. Walter Pincus, "Spy Agencies Faulted for Missing Indian Tests," *Washington Post*, June 3, 1998.

74. Central Intelligence Agency, "Jeremiah News Conference."

75. Ovodenko, "(Mis)interpreting threats," 277.

76. Amy Zegart, "The Cuban missile crisis as intelligence failure," *Policy Review*, Hoover Institution, October 2, 2012, https://www.hoover.org/research/cuban-missile-crisis-intelligence -failure (accessed September 20, 2020); U.S. Department of State, Office of the Historian, "SNIE 80-62: The Threat to U.S. Security Interests in the Caribbean Area," January 17, 1962, in *Foreign Relations of the United States, 1961–1963 [FRUS]*, Vol. 12: American Republics, https://history .state.gov/historicaldocuments/frus1961-63v12/d91 (accessed September 2, 2020); U.S. Depart- ment of State, Office of the Historian, "NIE 85-62: The Situation and Prospects in Cuba," March 21, 1962, in *FRUS*, Vol. 10: Cuba, January 1961–September 1962, https://history.state.gov /historicaldocuments/frus1961-63v10/d315 (accessed September 2, 2020); U.S. Department of State, Office of the Historian, "NIE 85-2-62: The Situation and Prospects in Cuba," August 1, 1962, in *FRUS*, Vol. 10: Cuba, January 1961–September 1962, https://history.state.gov /historicaldocuments/frus1961-63v10/d363 (accessed September 2, 2020); U.S. Department of State, Office of the Historian, "SNIE 85-3-62: The Military Buildup in Cuba," September 19, 1962, in *FRUS*, Vol. 10: Cuba, January 1961–September 1962, https://history.state.gov /historicaldocuments/frus1961-63v10/d433 (accessed September 2, 2020).

77. Department of State, "NIE 85-62." These judgments persisted even when intelligence reports came pouring in showing a dramatic uptick in military shipments arriving on the island that were being unloaded under tight security and the cover of darkness. "Soviet policy remains fundamentally unaltered," concluded the September 19, 1962, Special National Intelligence Es- timate, noting that the Soviets "almost certainly" knew that placing offensive nuclear weapons in Cuba would provoke "a dangerous U.S. reaction." See "SNIE 85-3-62."

78. Graham Allison and Philip Zelikow, *Essence of Decision: Explaining the Cuban Missile Crisis*, 2nd ed. (New York: Longman Press, 1999); Jonathan Renshon, "Mirroring risk: The Cuban missile crisis estimation," *Intelligence and National Security* 24, no. 3 (June 2009): 315–38.

79. Aleksandr Fursenko and Timothy Naftali were the first two scholars with extensive ac- cess to the KGB and GRU documents on the crisis. They found that Khrushchev functioned largely as his own intelligence analyst, and there was no evidence that he even asked for an intel- ligence assessment of how Kennedy might react to his fait accompli. Fursenko and Naftali, "Soviet intelligence and the Cuban missile crisis," *Intelligence and National Security* 13, no. 3 (2008): 64–87.

80. Fursenko and Naftali; Renshon, "Mirroring risk"; James G. Blight and David A. Welch, eds., *Intelligence and the Cuban Missile Crisis* (London: Frank Cass, 1999); Allison and Zelikow, *Essence of Decision*.

81. Raymond L. Garthoff, "U.S. intelligence in the Cuban missile crisis," *Intelligence and National Security* 13, no. 3 (1998): 47.

82. Quoted in Theodore Sorenson, *Kennedy* (New York: Harper & Row, 1965), 705.

83. Arthur Schlesinger, remarks at "On the Brink: The Cuban Missile Crisis," John F. Ken- nedy Library Forum, October 20, 2002, https://www.jfklibrary.org/events-and-awards/forums /past-forums/transcripts/on-the-brink-the-cuban-missile-crisis#:~:text=ARTHUR%20 SCHLESINGER%2C%20JR.%3A%20Well,to%20blow%20up%20the%20world.

84. Rice and Zegart, *Political Risk*, 100–101.

85. Tetlock and Gardner, *Superforecasting*, 55–56.

86. Jack Davis, "Sherman Kent and the profession of intelligence analysis," *Sherman Kent Center for the Study of Intelligence* 1, no. 5 (November 2002): 55.

87. Tetlock and Gardner, *Superforecasting*, 56–57. More recent research finds that quantitative probability estimates improve accuracy. See Jeffrey A. Friedman, Joshua D. Baker, Barbara A. Mellers, Philip E. Tetlock, and Richard Zeckhauser, "The value of precision in probability assessment: Evidence from a large-scale geopolitical forecasting tournament," *International Studies Quarterly* 62, no. 2 (June 2018): 410–22.

88. Intelligence Community Directive 203 (ICD 203), "Analytic Standards," June 21, 2007, https://www.dni.gov/files/documents/ICD/ICD%20203%20Analytic%20Standards%20pdf -unclassified.pdf.

89. There's a vast literature examining group decisionmaking, why groups so often perform better than individuals, and what makes some groups more accurate than others. For a useful review, see Michael Horowitz, Brandon M. Stewart, Dustin Tingley, Michael Bishop, Laura Resnick Samotin, Margaret Roberts, Welton Chang, Barbara Mellers, and Philip Tetlock, "What makes foreign policy teams tick: Explaining variation in group performance at geopolitical forecasting," *Journal of Politics* 81, no. 4 (2019).

90. Irving Janis, *Groupthink: Psychological Studies of Policy Decisions and Fiascoes* (Boston: Houghton Mifflin, 1982), 12.

91. For a different view, see Robert Jervis, "'Groupthink' Isn't the CIA's Problem," *Los Angeles Times*, July 11, 2004, https://www.latimes.com/archives/la-xpm-2004-jul-11-oe-jervis11-story .html.

92. "Key Judgments from October 2002 NIE: Iraq's Continuing Programs for Weapons of Mass Destruction," Federation of American Scientists, https://fas.org/irp/cia/product/iraq -wmd.html.

93. See Silberman-Robb Commission, "Report to the President," 169; Iraq Survey Group Biological Warfare Report; Senate Select Committee on Intelligence, "Postwar Findings about Iraq's WMD Programs."

94. Michael Morell with Bill Harlow, *The Great War of Our Time: The CIA's Fight against Terrorism—From al Qa'ida to ISIS* (New York: Twelve, 2015), 89.

95. Jervis, "Reports, politics, and intelligence failures," 15–16.

96. Silberman-Robb Commission, "Report to the President," 155–156. Groupthink extended beyond the Intelligence Community. Kenneth M. Pollack writes that in the spring of 2002, a group of nearly twenty former United Nations Iraqi weapons inspectors was asked whether Iraqi leader Saddam Hussein was secretly enriching uranium. Everyone thought he was. Pollack, "Spies, lies, and weapons: What went wrong," *Atlantic*, Jan/Feb 2004.

97. For research on the ineffectiveness of information-based debiasing strategies, see Hal Arkes, "Costs and benefits of judgment errors: Implications for debiasing," *Psychological Bulletin* 110, no. 3 (1991): 486–98; M. L. Graber, "Metacognitive training to reduce diagnostic errors: Ready for prime time?" *Academic Medicine* 78, no. 8 (2003); Helen L. Neilens, Simon J. Handley, and Stephen E. Newstead, "Effects of training and instruction on analytic and belief-based reasoning processes," *Thinking & Reasoning* 15, no. 1 (2009): 37–68; Duane T. Wegener and Richard E. Petty, "The Flexible Correction Model: The Role of Naïve Theories of Bias in Bias Correction," in *Advances in Experimental Social Psychology*, edited by M. P. Zanna (Mahwah,

N.J.: Erlbaum, 1997), 141–208; Welton Chang, Eva Chen, Barbara Mellers, and Philip Tetlock, "Developing expert political judgment: The impact of training and practice on judgmental accuracy in geopolitical forecasting tournaments," *Judgment and Decision Making* 11, no. 5 (September 2016): 509–26.

98. Rice and Zegart, *Political Risk*, 175–76; Pierre Wack, "Shooting the rapids," *Harvard Business Review*, November 1985; Peter Schwartz, *The Art of the Long View* (New York: Doubleday, 1991); Peter Schwartz, *Learnings from the Long View* (San Francisco: Global Business Network, 2011); Pierre Wack: "Scenarios: Uncharted waters ahead," *Harvard Business Review*, September 1985.

99. Darrell Rigby and Barbara Bilodeau, "Management Tools and Trends 2015," Bain & Company, June 10, 2015, https://www.bain.com/insights/management-tools-and-trends-2015/.

100. Schwartz, *Art of the Long View*, 9; Pierre Wack, "Scenarios: The gentle art of reperceiving," Shell International Petroleum Company, 1985. For more, see Rice and Zegart, *Political Risk*, 153–187.

101. Rice and Zegart, 179.

102. Quoted in Micah Zenko, "Inside the CIA Red Cell," *Foreign Policy*, October 30, 2015.

103. Micah Zenko, *Red Team: How to Succeed by Thinking Like the Enemy* (New York: Basic Books, 2015); Rachel Martin and Ben Zimmer, "Who Is the Devil's Advocate," NPR, March 3, 2013.

104. For more about the use of these and other process-based methods in business settings and intelligence analysis, see Rice and Zegart, *Political Risk*, 177–181. For academic analyses of the efficacy of process-based approaches, see Gideon Keren, "Cognitive aids and debasing methods: Can cognitive pills cure cognitive ills," *Advances in Psychology* 68 (1990): 523–52; Fei-Fei Cheng and Chin-Shan Wu, "Debiasing the framing effect: The effect of warning and involvement," *Computer Science* 49, no. 3 (June 2010): 328–34; Lee Ross, Mark R. Lepper, and Michael Hubbard, "Perseverance in self-perception and social perception: Biased attributional processes in the debriefing paradigm," *Journal of Personality and Social Psychology* 32, no. 5 (1975): 880–92; Richard P. Larrick, James N. Morgan, and Richard E. Nisbett, "Teaching the use of cost-benefit reasoning in everyday life," *Psychological Science* 1, no. 6 (November 1990): 362–70; Stefan M. Herzog and Ralph Hertwig, "The wisdom of many in one mind: Improving individual judgements with dialectical bootstrapping," *Psychological Science* 20, no. 2 (2009): 231–37; Baruch Fischhoff and Maya Bar-Hillel, "Diagnosticity and the base-rate effect," *Memory & Cognition* 12, no. 4 (1984): 402–10.

105. Richards J. Heuer Jr. pioneered efforts to harness the insights of psychology to improve intelligence analysis starting in the 1970s. Over time, his approach was modified and renamed Structured Analytic Techniques (SATs). SATs are still widely used in intelligence analyst training. Heuer, *Psychology of Intelligence Analysis* (Center for the Study of Intelligence, Central Intelligence Agency, 1999); Richards J. Heuer and Randolph H. Pherson, *Structured Analytic Techniques for Intelligence Analysis* (Washington, D.C.: CQ Press, 2010); Central Intelligence Agency, *A Tradecraft Primer: Structured Analytic Techniques for Improving Intelligence Analysis* (March 2009).

106. Central Intelligence Agency, *Tradecraft Primer*.

107. For criticism of SATs, see Welton Chang, Elissabeth Berdini, David R. Mandel, and Philip E. Tetlock, "Restructuring structured analytic techniques in intelligence," *Intelligence and National Security* 33, no. 3 (2018): 337–56.

108. Gerd Gigerenzer and Ulrich Hoffrage, "How to improve Bayesian reasoning without instruction: Frequency formats," *Psychological Review* 102, no. 4 (1995): 685.

109. Ward Casscells, Arno Schoenberger, and Thomas Grayboys, "Interpretation by physicians of clinical laboratory results," *New England Journal of Medicine* 299 (1978): 999–1000; David M. Eddy, "Probabilistic Reasoning in Clinical Medicine: Problems and Opportunities," in *Judgment Under Uncertainty: Heuristics and Biases*, edited by Dan Kahneman, Paul Slovic, and Amos Tversky (Cambridge, U.K.: Cambridge University Press, 1982), 249–67.

110. Gigerenzer and Hoffrage, "How to improve Bayesian reasoning," 684–704.

111. This section draws from Chang et al., "Developing expert political judgment."

112. Another initiative was the creation of the Intelligence Advanced Research Projects Activity (IARPA). Like its Defense Department counterpart, DARPA, IARPA lives on the frontiers of technology and social science, harnessing the most "out there" ideas to improve intelligence analysis.

113. National Research Council, *Intelligence Analysis for Tomorrow: Advances from the Behavioral and Social Sciences* (Washington, D.C.: National Academies Press, 2011).

114. Thomas Fingar, "Analysis in the U.S. Intelligence Community: Missions, Masters, and Methods," in *Intelligence Analysis: Behavioral and Social Scientific Foundations*, edited by Baruch Fischhoff and Cherie Chauvin, National Research Council of the National Academies (Washington, D.C.: National Academies Press, 2011), 3.

115. Tetlock and Gardner, *Superforecasting*, 4.

116. Tetlock and Gardner, 16.

117. Tetlock and Gardner, 18.

118. Tetlock and Gardner, 3.

119. Tetlock and Gardner, 18.

120. Jeff Desjardins, "How Much Data Is Generated Each Day?" World Economic Forum and Visual Capitalist, April 7, 2019 https://www.weforum.org/agenda/2019/04/how-much-data-is-generated-each-day-cf4bddf29f/ (accessed January 17, 2021).

121. Domo, "Data Never Sleeps 7.0," https://web-assets.domo.com/blog/wp-content/uploads/2019/07/data-never-sleeps-7-896kb.jpg (accessed January 17, 2021).

122. Sandra Erwin, "With Commercial Satellite Imagery, Computer Learns to Quickly Find Missile Sites in China," Space News, October 19, 2017.

123. Center for Strategic and International Studies (CSIS), "Maintaining the Intelligence Edge: Reimagining and Reinventing Intelligence through Innovation," A Report of the CSIS Technology and Intelligence Task Force, January 2021, https://www.csis.org/analysis/maintaining-intelligence-edge-reimagining-and-reinventing-intelligence-through-innovation (accessed January 17, 2021), 13–14.

124. CSIS, 13–14.

125. Pedro A. Ortega, Vishal Maini, and the Deepmind Safety Team, "Building Safe Artificial Intelligence: Specification, Robustness, and Assurance," Medium, September 27, 2018, https://medium.com/@deepmindsafetyresearch/building-safe-artificial-intelligence-52f5f75058f1.

126. U.S. Census Bureau, *Statistical Abstract of the United States: 2012* (Washington, D.C.: Government Printing Office, 2012), 506. Note: Annual firm death estimate is the average of firm

deaths from 2000 to 2007. This estimate is likely conservative because it pre-dates the 2008 economic crisis.

127. National Security Commission on Artificial Intelligence, "Interim Report," July 2019. https://drive.google.com/file/d/153OrxnuGEjsUvlxWsFYauslwNeCEkvUb/view.

128. Interview by author, August 26, 2020.

129. Richard P. Feynman, "Cargo Cult Science," commencement address, California Institute of Technology, June 14, 1974, http://calteches.library.caltech.edu/51/2/CargoCult.htm.

Chapter 6: Counterintelligence

1. "Robert M. Gates Oral History (Transcript)," July 23–24, 2000, University of Virginia Miller Center, https://millercenter.org/the-presidency/presidential-oral-histories/robert-m -gates-deputy-director-central (accessed August 22, 2020), quoting former CIA Director Richard Helms (personal conversation).

2. Hanssen affidavit, U.S. District Court for the Eastern District of Virginia, 2001, 11–12, www .fbi.gov/file-repository/hanssen-affidavit.pdf/view (accessed August 22, 2020).

3. Quote in Brooke A. Masters, "Hanssen Admits Spying, Avoids Death Penalty," *Washington Post*, July 7, 2001, https://www.washingtonpost.com/archive/politics/2001/07/07/hanssen -admits-spying-avoids-death-penalty/148284b5-6671-41aa-bcc8-fd52a783f8ee/ (accessed August 20, 2020).

4. Office of the Inspector General, "A Review of the FBI's Performance in Deterring, Detecting, and Investigating the Espionage Activities of Robert Philip Hanssen," August 14, 2013, https://fas.org/irp/agency/doj/oig/hanssen.html.

5. Johanna McGeary, "The FBI spy it took 15 years to discover," *Time*, March 5, 2001, http:// content.time.com/time/world/article/0,8599,2047748,00.html.

6. James Olson, *To Catch a Spy: The Art of Counterintelligence* (Washington D.C.: Georgetown University Press, 2019), xiii; Masters, "Hanssen Admits Spying, Avoids Death Penalty"; Eric Lichtblau, "Report Details FBI's Security Failings and Missed Spy Signals," *Los Angeles Times*, April 5, 2002, https://www.latimes.com/archives/la-xpm-2002-apr-05-mn-36370-story .html (accessed August 22, 2020).

7. Federal Bureau of Investigation, "Robert Hanssen," History, https://www.fbi.gov/history /famous-cases/robert-hanssen (accessed August 23, 2020).

8. Olson, *To Catch a Spy*, 23.

9. Olson, xiii.

10. Central Intelligence Agency, "About CIA—Organization," https://www.cia.gov/about /organization/#directorate-of-operations (accessed February 1, 2021).

11. Olson, *To Catch a Spy*, xi.

12. Olson, 100.

13. Peter Baker and Judi Rudoron, "Jonathan Pollard, American Who Spied for Israel, Released after 30 Years," *New York Times*, November 20, 2015, https://www.nytimes.com/2015/11 /21/world/jonathan-pollard-released.html (accessed August 22, 2020).

14. Olson, *To Catch a Spy*, 168. For the CIA's declassified damage assessment, see Jeffrey Richelson, ed., "The Jonathan Pollard Spy Case: The CIA's 1987 Damage Assessment

Declassified," National Security Archive, December 14, 2012https://nsarchive2.gwu.edu
/NSAEBB/NSAEBB407/.

15. Matthew S. Schwartz, "Jonathan Pollard, Who Sold Cold War Secrets to Israel, Completes Parole," NPR, November 21, 2020.

16. Ellen Nakashima, "Parole Ended for Jonathan Pollard, Who Spied for Israel, Freeing Him to Leave the United States," *Washington Post*, November 20, 2020.

17. J. J. Green, "The Fog of Espionage Part I," WTOP News, September 23, 2019, https://wtop
.com/j-j-green-national/2019/09/the-fog-of-espionage-part-1-an-existential-threat/ (accessed December 1, 2020).

18. Daniel R. Coats, "Statement for the Record: Worldwide Threat Assessment of the US Intelligence Community," Senate Select Committee on Intelligence, January 29, 2019, 13.

19. Olson, *To Catch a Spy*, 7–8.

20. Christopher Wray, FBI director, remarks at Hudson Institute video event "China's Attempt to Influence U.S. Institutions," Washington, D.C., July 7, 2020, https://www.fbi.gov
/news/speeches/the-threat-posed-by-the-chinese-government-and-the-chinese-communist
-party-to-the-economic-and-national-security-of-the-united-states (accessed December 1, 2020).

21. Christopher Wray, remarks at Hudson Institute; Colleen Shalby, "UCLA Professor Faces 219 Years in Prison for Conspiring to Send U.S. Missile Chips to China," *Los Angeles Times*, July 11, 2019, https://www.latimes.com/local/lanow/la-me-ucla-professor-military-china
-20190711-story.html (accessed December 1, 2020).

22. Daniel R. Coats, "Statement for the Record: Worldwide Threat Assessment of the US Intelligence Community," Senate Select Committee on Intelligence, January 29, 2019, 12–13.

23. Office of the Director of National Intelligence, National Counterintelligence and Security Center, "National Counterintelligence Strategy of the United States of America 2016," https://www.dni.gov/files/NCSC/documents/Regulations/National_CI_Strategy_2016.pdf (accessed August 22, 2020), 5.

24. James Bamford, *The Shadow Factory: The Ultra-Secret NSA from 9/11 to the Eavesdropping on America* (New York: Anchor Books, 2008), 13.

25. Executive Order 13526, December 29, 2009, https://www.archives.gov/isoo/policy
-documents/cnsi-eo.html#four (accessed April 28, 2020).

26. David Axe, "Coastie Cutter's risky secret room," *Wired*, November 14, 2008, https://www
.wired.com/2008/11/coastie-cutters-2/.

27. Andrew Rafferty, "What Is a SCIF and Who Uses It?" NBC News, April 7, 2017, https://
www.nbcnews.com/politics/politics-news/what-scif-who-uses-it-n743991.

28. Rajini Vaidyanathan, "Barack Obama's Top Secret Tent," BBC, March 22, 2011, https://
www.bbc.com/news/world-us-canada-12810675.

29. Bamford, *Shadow Factory*, 14.

30. Office of the Director of National Intelligence, National Counterintelligence and Security Center, "Fiscal Year 2017 Annual Report on Security Clearance Determinations," https://
www.dni.gov/files/NCSC/documents/features/20180827-security-clearance-determinations
.pdf, 4.

31. Lindy Kyzer, "Progress Is Finally Being Made on Security Clearance Backlog," Government Executive, April 23, 2019, https://www.govexec.com/management/2019/04/progress-finally-being-made-security-clearance-backlog/156481/ (accessed August 22, 2020); Nicole Ogrysko, "As NBIB Shrinks the Security Clearance Backlog, Other Personnel Vetting Agencies Feel the Pressure," Federal News Network, March 13, 2019, https://federalnewsnetwork.com/other-dod-agencies/2019/03/as-nbib-shrinks-the-security-clearance-backlog-other-personnel-vetting-agencies-feel-the-pressure/ (accessed August 22, 2020).

32. Mark Harris, "The lie generator: Inside the black mirror world of polygraph job screenings," Wired, December 1, 2018, https://www.wired.com/story/inside-polygraph-job-screening-black-mirror/ (accessed August 22, 2020).

33. U.S. Senate Select Committee on Intelligence, "An Assessment of the Aldrich H. Ames Espionage Case and Its Implications for U.S. Intelligence: Report," 1994, S. Rep. 84-046, 44–45.

34. Mark Zaid, "Failure of the Polygraph," Washington Post, April 16, 2002. https://www.washingtonpost.com/archive/opinions/2002/04/16/failure-of-the-polygraph/07c406a5-0aa3-4e20-8dcc-89781162aaa8/?utm_term=.2fbaf95ac00b (accessed August 22, 2020).

35. National Research Council Committee to Review the Scientific Evidence on the Polygraph, Division of Behavioral and Social Sciences and Education, The Polygraph and Lie Detection (Washington, D.C.: National Academies Press, 2003), https://doi.org/10.17226/10420, 2.

36. National Research Council, 5–6.

37. National Research Council, 6.

38. Office of the Director of National Intelligence, "Intelligence Community Policy Guidance 704.6: Conduct of Polygraph Examinations for Personnel Security Vetting," February 4, 2015, https://www.odni.gov/files/documents/ICPG/ICPG%20704.6.pdf; Central Intelligence Agency, "Applying to CIA: Introduction," https://www.cia.gov/careers/how-we-hire/hiring-process/application-process/ (accessed February 1, 2021).

39. Eric Schmitt, "Security Move Means 500 at FBI Face Lie Detector," New York Times, March 25, 2001.

40. Quoted in "A conversation with former DCI William Colby: Spymaster during the 'year of the intelligence wars,'" conducted January 22, 1991, published by Loch Johnson, Intelligence and National Security 22, no. 2 (April 2007): 263.

41. Michael V. Hayden, Playing to the Edge: American Intelligence in the Age of Terror (New York: Penguin, 2016), 278.

42. Michael Sulick, Spying in America: Espionage from the Revolutionary War to the Dawn of the Cold War (Washington D.C.: Georgetown University Press, 2012), 8.

43. One Cold War dead drop the United States used to communicate with Alexander Ogorodnik, a key U.S. asset working inside the Soviet Ministry of Foreign Affairs, was a crushed cigarette package that hid messages and a miniature camera inside. The package was placed under a specific light pole in Moscow. David E. Hoffman, The Billion Dollar Spy: A True Story of Cold War Espionage and Betrayal (New York: Anchor Books, 2016), 35.

44. Hanssen affidavit, U.S. District Court for the Eastern District of Virginia, 8.

45. Olson, To Catch a Spy, 47.

NOTES TO CHAPTER 6 333

46. Emily Langer, "Tennent H. 'Pete' Bagley, Noted CIA Officer, Dies at 88," *Washington Post*, February 24, 2014, https://www.washingtonpost.com/national/tennent-h-pete-bagley -noted-cia-officer-dies-at-88/2014/02/24/b2880bf2-9d6c-11e3-a050-dc3322a94fa7_story.html (accessed December 1, 2020).

47. David Wise, *Spy: The Inside Story of How the FBI's Robert Hanssen Betrayed America* (New York: Random House, 2002), 219–30.

48. Wise, 225–28; Olson, *To Catch a Spy*, 24. See also Loch Johnson, "Deadly Interval," manuscript based on interviews 1992–2008 with intelligence officials (November 2008).

49. Scott Shane, "A Spy's Motivation: For Love of Another Country," *New York Times*, April 20, 2008; Henry A. Crumpton, *The Art of Intelligence: Lessons from a Life in the CIA's Clandestine Service* (New York: Penguin, 2012), 35.

50. Sulick, *Spying in America*, 7; John A. Nagy, *Dr. Benjamin Church, Spy: A Case of Espionage on the Eve of the American Revolution* (Yardley, Pa.: Westholme Publishing, 2013).

51. U.S. Department of Defense, Katherine Herbig, "The Expanding Spectrum of Espionage by Americans, 1947–2015," Defense Personnel and Security Research Center (PERSEREC), Office of People Analytics, 2017.

52. *United States v. Kevin Patrick Mallory*, affidavit, Case 1:17-cr-00154-TSE, U.S. District Court for the Eastern District of Virginia, June 21, 2017, http://assets.documentcloud.org /documents/4489860/Mallory-affadavit-in-support-of-criminal-complaint.pdf, 12.

53. S. J. Hamrick, *Deceiving the Deceivers: Kim Philby, Donald Maclean, and Guy Burgess* (New Haven, Conn.: Yale University Press, 2004).

54. Rachel Weiner and Shane Harris, "Former CIA Officer Jerry Lee Admits Conspiracy to Spy for China," *Washington Post*, May 1, 2019, https://www.washingtonpost.com/local/public -safety/former-cia-officer-jerry-lee-admits-conspiracy-to-spy-for-china/2019/05/01/aed1bddc -6b89-11e9-8f44-e8d8bb1df986_story.html?utm_term=.83b83f6a147e (accessed August 22, 2020).

55. Herbig, "Expanding Spectrum of Espionage."

56. Pete Earley, *Confessions of a Spy: The Real Story of Aldrich Ames* (New York: Berkley Books, 1997), 252.

57. Herbig, "Expanding Spectrum of Espionage," 45-49.

58. Herbig, 8–9, 29.

59. U.S. Senate Select Committee on Intelligence, "An Assessment of the Aldrich H. Ames Espionage Case and Its Implications for U.S. Intelligence," 103rd Cong., 2nd sess., November 1, 1994, S. Prt 103-90, https://www.intelligence.senate.gov/sites/default/files/publications/10390 .pdf, 53; Tim Weiner, David Johnston, and Neil A. Lewis, *Betrayal: The Story of Aldrich Ames, an American Spy* (New York: Random House, 1995), 98–99.

60. Weiner, Johnston, and Lewis, 39–40.

61. Senate Select Committee on Intelligence, "Assessment of the Aldrich H. Ames Espionage Case," 53.

62. Senate Select Committee on Intelligence, 59.

63. Elaine Shannon, "Death of the Perfect Spy," *Time*, June 24, 2001 http://content.time.com/time /magazine/article/0,9171,164863,00.html; Weiner and Harris, "Former CIA Officer Jerry Lee," 23.

64. Shannon, "Death of the Perfect Spy."

65. Senate Select Committee on Intelligence, "Assessment of the Aldrich H. Ames Espionage Case," 53.

66. Weiner, Johnston, and Lewis, *Betrayal*, 15–16.

67. Senate Select Committee on Intelligence, "Assessment of the Aldrich H. Ames Espionage Case," 24.

68. Weiner, Johnston, and Lewis, *Betrayal*, 130–31.

69. Senate Select Committee on Intelligence, "Assessment of the Aldrich H. Ames Espionage Case," 58–59.

70. Weiner, Johnston, and Lewis, *Betrayal*, 130.

71. Senate Select Committee on Intelligence, "Assessment of the Aldrich H. Ames Espionage Case," 53, 57, 59.

72. Weiner, Johnston, and Lewis, *Betrayal*, 133.

73. Senate Select Committee on Intelligence, "Assessment of the Aldrich H. Ames Espionage Case," 23–24.

74. Weiner, Johnston, and Lewis, *Betrayal*, 144–49, 279–80.

75. Weiner, Johnston, and Lewis, 42.

76. Senate Select Committee on Intelligence, "Assessment of the Aldrich H. Ames Espionage Case," 53, 59. CIA Director James Woolsey agreed. In a stunning forty-five-minute public speech given a few months after Ames's arrest, Woolsey declared, "There are elements in the culture of the CIA that must be changed, especially in the field of counterintelligence." Woolsey took unprecedented and direct aim at the brotherhood. "Neither the Directorate of Operations [where Ames worked], nor for that matter any other part of the CIA can function as a fraternity." Woolsey, "The Future Direction of Intelligence," speech at the Center for Strategic and International Studies, Washington, D.C., July 18, 1994.

77. Interview by author, October 13, 2020.

78. Bill Phillips email to author, September 11, 2019.

79. David Robarge, "Moles, defectors, and deceptions: James Angleton and CIA counterintelligence," *Journal of Intelligence History* (Winter 2003): 26–27.

80. David Robarge, "James J. Angleton, Anatoliy Golitsyn, and the 'Monster Plot': Their impact on CIA personnel and operations," *Studies in Intelligence* 55, no. 4 (December 2011), declassified and approved for release April 5, 2013.

81. Robarge, "Moles, defectors, and deceptions," 28–29; Robarge, "James J. Angleton," 40–41.

82. Robarge, "Moles, defectors, and deceptions," 34.

83. Anthony Cave Brown, *Treason in the Blood: H. St. John Philby, Kim Philby, and the Spy Case of the Century* (Boston: Houghton Mifflin, 1994), 551.

84. Robarge, "James J. Angleton," 42.

85. David Stout, "Yuri Nosenko, Soviet Spy Who Defected, Dies at 81," *New York Times*, August 27, 2008, https://www.nytimes.com/2008/08/28/us/28nosenko.html (accessed August 22, 2020).

86. Stout.

87. Robarge, "Moles, defectors, and deceptions," 39.

88. Robert M. Gates, *From the Shadows: The Ultimate Insider's Story of Five Presidents and How They Won the Cold War* (New York: Simon & Schuster, 1996), 34.

89. David Johnston, "CIA Dug for Moles but Buried the Loyal," *New York Times*, March 8, 1992, https://www.nytimes.com/1992/03/08/us/cia-dug-for-moles-but-buried-the-loyal.html (accessed August 22, 2020); Adam Bernstein, "CIA Officer Richard Kovich Obituary,"

Washington Post, February 27, 2006, https://www.washingtonpost.com/archive/local/2006/02/27/cia-officer-richard-kovich/d2869c00-e26b-432e-84d1-5798cb20e467/ (accessed August 22, 2020); Michael R. Beschloss, "Fools or Traitors?" *New York Times*, March 15, 1992, https://www.nytimes.com/1992/03/15/books/fools-or-traitors.html (accessed August 22, 2020).

90. Johnston, "CIA Dug for Moles."

91. Gates, *From the Shadows*, 34.

92. David Robarge, "The James Angleton phenomenon: 'Cunning Passages, Contrived Corridors': Wandering in the Angletonian wilderness," *Studies in Intelligence* 53, no. 4, December 2009: 49–61, https://apps.dtic.mil/sti/pdfs/ADA514366.pdf (accessed February 1, 2021).

93. Interview by author, October 13, 2020.

94. U.S. House Permanent Select Committee on Intelligence, "Review of the Unauthorized Disclosures of Former National Security Agency Contractor Edward Snowden," 114th Cong., 2nd sess., December 23, 2016, H. Rep. 114-891, https://www.congress.gov/114/crpt/hrpt891/CRPT-114hrpt891.pdf, 14–16.

95. House Permanent Select Committee on Intelligence, 21, citing "Testimony of Mr. Scott Liard, Deputy Director for Counterintelligence, Defense Intelligence Agency, HPSCI Hearing (Jan. 27, 2014)," 7–8, https://fas.org/irp/congress/2016_rpt/hpsci-snowden.pdf.

96. House Permanent Select Committee on Intelligence, i.

97. David E. Sanger and Eric Schmitt, "Snowden Used Low-Cost Tool to Best N.S.A," *New York Times*, February 8, 2014, https://www.nytimes.com/2014/02/09/us/snowden-used-low-cost-tool-to-best-nsa.html (accessed August 22, 2020); Amy B. Zegart, "NSA Confronts a Problem of Its Own Making," *Atlantic*, June 29, 2017, https://www.theatlantic.com/international/archive/2017/06/nsa-wannacry-eternal-blue/532146/ (accessed August 22, 2020).

98. "Ex-CIA officer Kevin Mallory sentenced to 20 years for spying for China," *Guardian*, May 18, 2019, https://www.theguardian.com/us-news/2019/may/18/ex-cia-officer-kevin-mallory-sentenced-to-20-years-for-spying-for-china (accessed August 22, 2020).

99. Scott Shane, "N.S.A. Contractor Arrested in Biggest Breach of U.S. Secrets Pleads Guilty," *New York Times*, March 28, 2019, https://www.nytimes.com/2019/03/28/us/politics/hal-martin-nsa-guilty-plea.html (accessed August 22, 2020); Josh Gerstein, "Ex-NSA contractor accused of hoarding classified info to plead guilty," *Politico*, January 1, 2013, https://www.politico.com/story/2018/01/03/nsa-harold-martin-guilty-plea-322113 (accessed August 22, 2020). It's not yet known whether Martin attempted to release any of the classified information he took to others.

100. Ellen Nakashima and Phillip Rucker, "U.S. Declares that North Korea Carried Out Massive WannaCry Cyber Attack," *Washington Post*, December 18, 2017, https://www.washingtonpost.com/world/national-security/us-set-to-declare-north-korea-carried-out-massive-wannacry-cyber-attack/2017/12/18/509deb1c-e446-11e7-a65d-1acofd7f097e_story.html?utm_term=.9e258fd09db7 (accessed August 22, 2020); Zack Whittaker "Two years after WannaCry, a million computers at risk, " *TechCrunch*, May 12, 2019, https://techcrunch.com/2019/05/12/wannacry-two-years-on/ (accessed August 22,2020).

101. Zegart, "NSA Confronts a Problem."

102. Quoted in Shane Harris and Ellen Nakashima, "Spies Fear Former CIA Officer May Not Face Justice for Suspected Role in Exposure of Sources in China," *Washington Post*, January 17, 2018.

103. Tom Winter, Ken Dilanian, and Jonathan Dienst, "Alleged CIA China Turncoat Lee May Have Compromised U.S. Spies in Russia Too," NBC News, January 19, 2018, https://www .nbcnews.com/news/china/cia-china-turncoat-lee-may-have-compromised-u-s-spies-n839316 (accessed August 22, 2020); Zach Dorfman, "Botched CIA communications system helped blow cover of Chinese agents," *Foreign Policy*, August 15, 2018, https://foreignpolicy.com/2018 /08/15/botched-cia-communications-system-helped-blow-cover-chinese-agents-intelligence/ (accessed August 22, 2020); Mark Mazzetti, Adam Goldman, Michael S. Schmidt, and Matt Apuzzo, "Killing CIA Informants, China Crippled U.S. Spying Operations," *New York Times*, May 20, 2017, https://www.nytimes.com/2017/05/20/world/asia/china-cia-spies-espionage .html (accessed August 22, 2020).

104. David Ignatius, "The Saga of the Chinese Mole Reads like a Spy Thriller," *Washington Post*, May 8, 2019, https://www.washingtonpost.com/opinions/global-opinions/the-saga-of -the-chinese-mole-reads-like-a-spy-thriller/2019/05/08/3952392c-71da-11e9-9f06-5fc2ee80027a _story.html?utm_term=.fd0997be1ce0 (August 22, 2020).

105. Winter, Dilanian, and Dienst, "Alleged CIA China Turncoat."

106. *United States of America v. Jerry Chun Shing Lee*, indictment, Criminal No. 1:15-cr-89 TSE, U.S. District Court for the Eastern District of Virginia, May 8, 2018, https://www.justice.gov /opa/press-release/file/1061631/download (accessed September 26, 2020).

107. Mathew Kahn, "Documents: Jerry Chun Shing Lee Plea Documents," Lawfare, May 8, 2018, https://www.lawfareblog.com/documents-jerry-chun-shing-lee-plea-documents (accessed August 22, 2020); Amy B. Zegart, "The specter of a Chinese mole in America," *Atlantic*, January 17, 2018, https://www.theatlantic.com/international/archive/2018/01/jerry-chun-shing -lee-cia-mole-china/550658/ (accessed August 22, 2020).

108. Notably, this count did not charge Lee with actually passing classified materials to the Chinese. In August 2020, another former CIA officer, Alexander Yuk Ching Ma, was arrested and charged with giving classified information to the Chinese government. Julian E. Barnes, "Ex-CIA Officer Is Accused of Spying for China," *New York Times*, August 17, 2020, https://www .nytimes.com/2020/08/17/us/politics/china-spying-alexander-yuk-ching-ma.html (accessed September 21, 2020).

109. Dorfman, "Botched CIA communications system."

110. Dorfman; Mazzetti et al., "Killing CIA Informants."

111. Weiner and Harris, "Former CIA Officer Jerry Lee"; Zach Dorman and Jenna McLaughlin, "The CIA's Communications Suffered a Catastrophic Compromise. It Started in Iran," Yahoo! News, November 2, 2018, https://news.yahoo.com/cias-communications-suffered -catastrophic-compromise-started-iran-090018710.html (accessed August 22, 2020).

Chapter 7: Covert Action

1. Interview by author, October 7, 2020.

2. Sources for the narrative of this drone strike on Anwar al-Awlaki are as follows: Scott Shane, *Objective Troy: A Terrorist, a President, and the Rise of the Drone* (New York: Tim Duggan Books, 2015), 61, 82–107, 283, 290–91, 386; Mark Mazzetti, *The Way of the Knife: The CIA, a Secret Army, and a War at the Ends of the Earth* (New York: Penguin, 2013), 302, 309–10, 321; Leon E.

Panetta with Jim Newton, *Worthy Fights: A Memoir of Leadership in War and Peace* (New York: Penguin, 2014), 386; "Behind the Scenes of the Air Force's Anti-Terrorism Drone Program," CBS News, July 23, 2019, https://www.cbsnews.com/news/air-force-anti-terrorism-drone -program-behind-the-scenes/; "The US Air Force's Commuter Drone Warriors," BBC News, January 8, 2017, https://www.bbc.com/news/magazine-38506932; Scott Shane, "The Lessons of Anwar al-Awlaki," *New York Times*, August 27, 2015, https://www.nytimes.com/2015/08/30 /magazine/the-lessons-of-anwar-al-awlaki.html; Robert Chesney, "Who May Be Killed? Anwar Al-Awlaki as a Case Study in the International Legal Regulation of Lethal Force," in *Yearbook of International Humanitarian Law* 13, edited by M. N. Schmitt et al. (August 2010), 6–8, doi:10.1007/978-90-6704-811-8_1.

3. For a description of what it's like to watch a drone strike, see Jane Mayer, "The predator war: What are the risks of the C.I.A.'s covert drone program?" *New Yorker*, October 19, 2009, https://www.newyorker.com/magazine/2009/10/26/the-predator-war#ixzz2Be8WuX2V.

4. Mazzetti, *Way of the Knife*, 310; Shane, *Objective Troy*, 290-91.

5. Mazzetti, *Way of the Knife*, 321. "Behind the scenes of the Air Force's anti-terrorism drone program," CBS News, July 23, 2019, https://www.cbsnews.com/news/air-force-anti-terrorism -drone-program-behind-the-scenes/; "The US Air Force's commuter drone warriors," *BBC News*, January 8, 2017, https://www.bbc.com/news/magazine-38506932

6. Lauren Goodstein, "American Muslims; Influential American Muslims Temper Their Tone," *New York Times*, October 19, 2001, https://www.nytimes.com/2001/10/19/us/nation -challenged-american-muslims-influential-american-muslims-temper-their.html.

7. U.S. Senate Committee on Homeland Security and Governmental Affairs, "A Ticking Time Bomb: Counterterrorism Lessons from the U.S. Government's Failure to Prevent the Fort Hood Attack, A Special Report by Joseph I. Lieberman, Chairman and Susan M. Collins, Ranking Member," 112th Cong., 1st sess., February 3, 2011, 20–21.

8. Shane, *Objective Troy*, 107–8, 224; Panetta, *Worthy Fights*, 386; James R. Clapper, "Declaration in Support of Formal Claim of State Secrets Privilege," in United States District Court for the District of Columbia, *Nasser al-Aulaqi v. Barack Obama, Robert Gates, and Leon Panetta*, Civ. A. No. 10-cv-1469, September 24, 2010, https://fas.org/sgp/jud/statesec/aulaqi-clapper-092510 .pdf; Amy Zegart, "The Fort Hood Terrorist Attack: An Organizational Postmortem of Army and FBI Deficiencies," in *Insider Threats*, edited by Matthew Bunn and Scott Sagan (Ithaca, N.Y.: Cornell University Press, 2017), 42–73.

9. Clapper, "Declaration in Support," 8. See also Chesney, "Who May Be Killed?" 6–8.

10. Al-Awlaki was known to be a "virtual spiritual sanctioner" of terrorism, someone who provides religious justification for violent political extremism of individuals who are radicalizing. In years past, spiritual sanctioners exercised their influence in person. Over time, however, the Internet made it possible for virtual spiritual sanctioners to serve this same role from a distance. See Mitchell D. Silber and Arvin Bhatt, *Radicalization in the West: The Homegrown Threat*, New York Police Department, 2007; Mitchell D. Silber, director of intelligence analysis, New York City Police Department, Statement before the U.S. Senate Homeland Security and Governmental Affairs Committee, 111th Cong., 1st sess., November 19, 2009; Senate Committee on Homeland Security and Governmental Affairs, "Ticking Time Bomb," 20–21. See also Alexander Meleagrou-Hitchens, "Voice of terror," *Foreign Policy*, January 18, 2011, http://www

.foreignpolicy.com/articles/2011/01/18/voice_of_terror (arguing that al-Awlaki has become the most significant English-language propagandist of jihad in terms of Western audiences in particular).

11. "Anwar al-Awlaki," Times Topics, *New York Times*, updated January 23, 2020, at http://topics.nytimes.com/topics/reference/timestopics/people/a/anwar_al_awlaki/index.html (accessed September 25, 2020); Tim Lister and Paul Cruickshank, "Anwar al-Awlaki: Al Qaeda's Rock Star No More," CNN, September 30, 2011 (accessed September 25, 2020) http://www.cnn.com/2011/09/30/world/meast/analysis-anwar-al-awlaki/index.html; William H. Webster Commission, "The Federal Bureau of Investigation, Counterterrorism Intelligence, and the Events at Fort Hood, Texas, on November 5, 2009, Final Report," redacted version released July 19, 2012 (accessed September 25, 2020), https://www.hsdl.org/?view&did=717443, 33; "Make a Bomb in the Kitchen of Your Mom" was published in the summer 2010 issue of *Inspire*.

12. Clapper, "Declaration in Support," 7–9; Mark Hosenhall, "Secret Panel Can Put Americans on Kill List," Reuters, October 5, 2011, https://www.reuters.com/article/us-cia-killlist/secret-panel-can-put-americans-on-kill-list-idUSTRE79475C20111005; Chesney, "Who May Be Killed?" 9.

13. Scott Shane, "The enduring influence of Anwar al-Awlaki in the age of the Islamic State," *CTC Sentinel* 9, no. 7 (July 2016) https://www.ctc.usma.edu/the-enduring-influence-of-anwar-al-awlaki-in-the-age-of-the-islamic-state/; Mazzetti, *Way of the Knife*, 305; Nasser al-Awlaki, "The Drone That Killed My Grandson," *New York Times*, July 17, 2013, https://www.nytimes.com/2013/07/18/opinion/the-drone-that-killed-my-grandson.html.

14. Scott Shane, "U.S. Approves Targeted Killing of American Cleric," *New York Times*, April 6, 2010, https://www.nytimes.com/2010/04/07/world/middleeast/07yemen.html.

15. John O. Brennan, *Undaunted: My Fight against America's Enemies, at Home and Abroad* (New York: Celadon Books, 2020), 222; Dana Priest, "Inside the CIA's 'Kill List,'" PBS, September 6, 2011, https://www.pbs.org/wgbh/frontline/article/inside-the-cias-kill-list/; Shane, *Objective Troy*, 285–93. For an overview of legal justifications for drone strikes targeting American citizens, see Chesney, "Who May be Killed?" 3–60.

16. Michael Hayden, cited in Mark M. Lowenthal, *Intelligence: From Secrets to Policy*, 7th ed. (Thousand Oaks, Calif.: CQ Press, 2017), 271.

17. Shane, *Objective Troy*, 290.

18. Panetta, *Worthy Fights*, 385–86; Shane, "US Approves Targeted Killing"; Priest, "Inside the CIA's 'Kill List,'" quoted in Dana Priest and William Arkin, *Top Secret America: The Rise of the New American Security State* (New York: Little, Brown, 2011). For drone strike approval by President Obama, see his remarks at National Defense University, May 23, 2013, https://obamawhitehouse.archives.gov/the-press-office/2013/05/23/remarks-president-national-defense-university; https://www.washingtonpost.com/news/worldviews/wp/2015/04/23/the-u-s-keeps-killing-americans-in-drone-strikes-mostly-by-accident/.

19. Mazzetti, *Way of the Knife*, 302; Shane, *Objective Troy*, 51–52.

20. *Al-Aulaqi v. Obama*, 727 F. Supp.2d1 (D.D.C. 2010), Civil Action No. 10-1469, decided December 7, 2010. Aulaqi was killed in September 2011. Shane, "Lessons of Anwar al-Awlaki."

21. Mark Mazzetti, Eric Schmitt, and Robert F. Worth, "Two-Year Manhunt Led to Killing of Awlaki in Yemen," *New York Times*, September 30, 2011, https://www.nytimes.com/2011/10/01/world/middleeast/anwar-al-awlaki-is-killed-in-yemen.html.

22. Across all polls conducted in the United States between 2011 and 2015 about drone strikes, American support averaged 62 percent. See polls in Amy Zegart, "The value of cheap fights: Drones and the future of coercion," *Journal of Strategic Studies* 43, no. 1 (February 2018): 6–46.

23. Panetta, *Worthy Fights*, 390.

24. U.S. Senate Select Committee to Study Governmental Operations with Respect to Intelligence Activities (Church Committee) 1975–1976, "Interim Report, Alleged Assassination Plots Involving Foreign Leaders," S. Rep. No. 94-465, "Staff Report, Covert Action in Chile, 1963–1973," "Final Report," S. Rep. No. 94-755 (Books 1–6); Greg Treverton, *Covert Action* (New York: Basic Books, 1987), 13; L. Britt Snider, *The Agency and the Hill: The CIA's Relationship with Congress, 1946–2004* (Washington, D.C.: Center for the Study of Intelligence, 2008), 299–300; R. Jeffrey Smith and David B. Ottaway, "Anti-Saddam Operation Cost CIA $100 Million," *Washington Post*, September 15, 1996, https://www.washingtonpost.com/wp-srv/inatl/longterm/iraq/stories/cia091596.htm; Tim Weiner, "Iraqi Offensive into Kurdish Zone Disrupts U.S. Plot to Oust Hussein," *New York Times*, https://www.nytimes.com/1996/09/07/world/iraqi-offensive-into-kurdish-zone-disrupts-us-plot-to-oust-hussein.html. One of the most documented covert operations now declassified is the overthrow of the Guatemalan government in 1954. In May 2003 the State Department published a supplemental volume of *Foreign Relations of the United States, 1952–1954, Guatemala*, examining the event: https://history.state.gov/historicaldocuments/frus1952-54Guat.

25. Church Committee, "Alleged Assassination Plots Involving Foreign Leaders," 1975 U.S. Senate Report on CIA Covert Operations to Kill Fidel Castro, Ngo Dinh Diem, and Others, November 1975, https://www.intelligence.senate.gov/sites/default/files/94465.pdf, 71–85.

26. Gary C. Schroen, *First In: An Insider's Account of How the CIA Spearheaded the War on Terror in Afghanistan* (New York: Random House, 2005), 38.

27. Quoted in Bob Woodward, *Bush at War* (New York: Simon & Schuster, 2002), 52.

28. Mazzetti, *Way of the Knife*, 12.

29. Loch K. Johnson, "Covert action and accountability," *International Studies Quarterly* 33, no. 1 (March 1989), 84.

30. National Security Act of 1947, Public Law 235, July 26, 1947, https://www.dni.gov/index.php/ic-legal-reference-book/national-security-act-of-1947.

31. The Intelligence Authorization Act of 1991 is Public Law 102-88, 102nd Cong., August 14, 1991, now 50 U.S.C. section 3093e (2018), https://www.congress.gov/bill/102nd-congress/house-bill/1455.

32. Treverton, *Covert Action*, 14–17.

33. Lowenthal, *Intelligence: From Secrets to Policy*, 252.

34. David Sanger, *The Perfect Weapon: War, Sabotage, and Fear in the Cyber Age* (New York: Crown, 2018), 7–36.

35. Covert action is often confused with secret or clandestine activities. They are not the same. The U.S. military does many things in secret—for example, refusing to say when or where

they are operating. Covert action goes further, seeking to hide the hand of the United States government entirely, not just the operational details of an activity.

36. Title 50 of the U.S. Code states, "No covert action may be conducted which is intended to influence United States political processes, public opinion, policies, or media." See 50 U.S.C. section 3093a (2018); U.S. Library of Congress Congressional Research Service, Michael E. DeVine, "Covert Action and Clandestine Activities of the Intelligence Community: Selected Definitions in Brief," R45175, June 14, 2019.

37. Lowenthal, *Intelligence: From Secrets to Policy*, 256; Kevin O'Brien, "The Quiet Option," in *Strategic Intelligence: Understanding the Hidden State of Government*, Vol. 3: Covert Action, edited by Loch K. Johnson (Westport, Conn.: Praeger Publishers, 2007), 33. See also Philip M. Taylor, *Munitions of the Mind: A History of Propaganda from the Ancient World to the Present Day*, 3rd ed. (Manchester, U.K.: Manchester University Press, 2003).

38. Church Committee, "Report 1976, History of the Central Intelligence Agency, Supplementary Detailed Staff Reports on Foreign and Military Intelligence," Book 4, April 23, 1976, 29.

39. Quoted in David Shimer, *Rigged: America, Russia and One Hundred Years of Covert Electoral Interference* (New York: Knopf, 2020), 120.

40. Treverton, *Covert Action*, 13.

41. Amy Zegart, *Flawed by Design: The Evolution of the CIA, JCS, and NSC* (Palo Alto, Calif.: Stanford University Press, 1999), 188.

42. Christopher Andrew, *For the President's Eyes Only: Secret Intelligence and the American Presidency from Washington to Bush* (New York: Harper Perennial, 1996), 172; Bruce D. Berkowitz and Allan E. Goodman, *Best Truth: Intelligence in the Information Age* (New Haven, Conn.: Yale University Press, 2000), 127.

43. Shimer, *Rigged*, 40.

44. See quote by CIA historian David Robarge in Shimer, *Rigged*, 44.

45. Shimer, 9, 109–115. For CIA covert action against Milosevic in the 1990s, see James M. Scott and Jerel A. Rosati, "Such Other Functions and Duties," in *Strategic Intelligence: Understanding the Hidden State of Government*, Vol. 3: Covert Action, edited by Loch K. Johnson (Westport, Conn.: Praeger Publishers, 2007), 96.

46. Treverton, *Covert Action*, 13.

47. Smith and Ottaway, "Anti-Saddam Operation Cost CIA $100 Million"; Weiner, "Iraqi Offensive into Kurdish Zone."

48. O'Brien, "Quiet Option," 2–43.

49. The Reagan administration authorized the mining of Nicaraguan harbors to reduce commercial shipping there. Loch K. Johnson, *America's Secret Power: The CIA in a Democratic Society* (New York: Oxford University Press, 1989), 26; O'Brien, "Quiet Option," 42–43.

50. Treverton, *Covert Action*, 25–28.

51. The countries were Afghanistan, Albania, Angola, Bolivia, China, Cuba, Dominican Republic, Greece, Guatemala, Haiti, Hungary, Indonesia, Iraq, Malaysia, Nicaragua, North Korea, Oman, Poland, Thailand, Turkey, Venezuela, Vietnam, and Ukraine. Johnson, "Covert action and accountability," 86.

52. Jack Pfeiffer, *Official History of the Bay of Pigs Operation*, Central Intelligence Agency, https://www.cia.gov/readingroom/docs/C01254908.pdf (accessed January 31, 2021).

53. Joshua E. Keating, "Don't try to convince yourself that you're in control: Afghan lessons for arming the Syrian rebels from the CIA's Mujahideen point man," *Foreign Policy*, June 14, 2013, https://foreignpolicy.com/2013/06/14/dont-try-to-convince-yourself-that-youre-in-control/; Austin Carson, *Secret Wars: Covert Conflict in International Politics* (Princeton, N.J.: Princeton University Press, 2018), 238–82.

54. President's Special Review Board, "Tower Commission Report," February 26, 1987, https://archive.org/stream/TowerCommission/President%27s%20Special%20Review%20Board%20%28%22Tower%20Commission%22%29#page/n1/mode/2up.

55. Executive Order 11905 was signed by President Gerald Ford. For a full text see https://fas.org/irp/offdocs/eo11905.htm.

56. Church Committee, "Alleged Assassination Plots Involving Foreign Leaders," 13–67.

57. Tim Weiner, *Legacy of Ashes: The History of the CIA* (New York: Anchor Books, 2008), 162–63; Church Committee, "Alleged Assassination Plots Involving Foreign Leaders," 13–67; "The C.I.A and Lumumba," *New York Times*, August 2, 1981, https://www.nytimes.com/1981/08/02/magazine/the-cia-and-lumumba.html.

58. Lowenthal, *Intelligence: From Secrets to Policy*, 259. Rendition includes any extrajudicial, involuntary, secret movement of a terror suspect from one jurisdiction to another.

59. For a primer on drones, see Sarah E. Kreps, *Drones: What Everyone Needs to Know* (New York: Oxford University Press, 2016).

60. See, for example, Greg Miller, "Why CIA Drone Strikes Have Plummeted," *Washington Post*, June 16, 2016, https://www.washingtonpost.com/world/national-security/cia-drone-strikes-plummet-as-white-house-shifts-authority-to-pentagon/2016/06/16/e0b28e90-335f-11e6-8ff7-7b6c1998b7a0_story.html; Priest, "Inside the CIA 'Kill List'"; Greg Miller, "U.S. Launches Secret Drone Campaign to Hunt Islamic State Leaders in Syria," *Washington Post*, September 1, 2015, https://www.washingtonpost.com/world/national-security/us-launches-secret-drone-campaign-to-hunt-islamic-state-leaders-in-syria/2015/09/01/723b3e04-5033-11e5-933e-7d06c647a395_story.html.

61. Micah Zenko, "Obama's Embrace of Drone Strikes Will Be a Lasting Legacy," *New York Times*, January 16, 2016, https://www.nytimes.com/roomfordebate/2016/01/12/reflecting-on-obamas-presidency/obamas-embrace-of-drone-strikes-will-be-a-lasting-legacy. Casualty figures vary widely. For more on how to understand differences in casualty estimates, see "Civilians and Collateral Damage," Lawfare, https://www.lawfareblog.com/civilian-casualties-collateral-damage.

62. Zenko, "Obama's Embrace of Drone Strikes."

63. Nicholas Grossman, "Trump Cancels Drone Strike Civilian Casualty Report: Does It Matter?" War on the Rocks, April 2, 2019, https://warontherocks.com/2019/04/trump-cancels-drone-strike-civilian-casualty-report-does-it-matter/.

64. Bruce D. Berkowitz and Allan E. Goodman originally made this important point in "The logic of covert action," *National Interest*, March 1, 1998, https://nationalinterest.org/article/the-logic-of-covert-action-333.

65. Even when the CIA's cover was blown on its broadcasting efforts, Radio Free Europe and Radio Liberty continued overtly.

66. "The VOA Charter: Telling America's Story," Editorials, VOA, July 12, 2016, https://editorials.voa.gov/a/the-voa-charter-telling-americas-story/3414626.html.

67. Public Law 105–338, October 31, 1998, 112 Stat. 3179, https://www.congress.gov/105/plaws /publ338/PLAW-105publ338.pdf.

68. Andrew Glass, "U.S. planes bomb Libya, April 15, 1986," *Politico*, April 15, 2019, https:// www.politico.com/story/2019/04/15/reagan-bomb-libya-april-15-1986-1272788.

69. *President Reagan's Address to the Nation on the Bombing on Libya, April 14, 1986*, Reagan Library, Youtube, https://www.youtube.com/watch?v=pjYMVSA6xM8.

70. Sanger, *Perfect Weapon*; Kim Zetter, *Countdown to Zero Day: Stuxnet and the Launch of the World's First Digital Weapon* (New York: Crown Publishers, 2014).

71. Greg Miller, "Under Obama, An Emerging Global Apparatus for Drone Killing," *Washington Post*, December 27, 2011, https://www.washingtonpost.com/national/national-security /under-obama-an-emerging-global-apparatus-for-drone-killing/2011/12/13/gIQANPdILP _story.html.

72. Statement by the Department of Defense, January 2, 2020, https://www.defense.gov /Newsroom/Releases/Release/Article/2049534/statement-by-the-department-of-defense/.

73. Remarks by President Trump on the Killing of Qasem Soleimani, Palm Beach, Florida, January 3, 2020, https://www.iranwatch.org/library/governments/united-states/executive-branch /white-house/remarks-president-trump-killing-qasem-soleimani (accessed April 16, 2021).

74. Treverton, *Covert Action*, 14; Snider, *Agency and the Hill*, 27–99; President's Special Review Board, "Tower Commission Report."

75. Quoted in Andrew, *For the President's Eyes Only*, 425–26.

76. Treverton, *Covert Action*, 14; Johnson, *America's Secret Power*, 103; Andrew, *For the President's Eyes Only*.

77. "Tie a Yellow Ribbon—The Iran Hostage Crisis as Seen from the Home Front," Association for Diplomatic Studies & Training, https://adst.org/2012/10/tie-a-yellow-ribbon-the-iran -hostage-crisis-as-seen-from-the-home-front/.

78. Stansfield Turner, *Secrecy and Democracy: The CIA in Transition* (Boston: Houghton Mifflin, 1985), 87.

79. Mark Bowen, "The Desert One debacle," *Atlantic*, May 2006, https://www.theatlantic .com/magazine/archive/2006/05/the-desert-one-debacle/304803/; Charlie A. Beckwith with Donald Knox, *Delta Force* (San Diego: Harcourt Brace Jovanovich, 1983). Operation EAGLE CLAW was not legally a covert action activity carried out under CIA authorities.

80. President Jimmy Carter, State of the Union Address, January 23, 1980, https://www .jimmycarterlibrary.gov/assets/documents/speeches/su80jec.phtml.

81. U.S. Department of State, *Foreign Relations of the United States, 1977–1980*, Vol. 12, Afghanistan (Washington, D.C.: GPO, 2018), ix.

82. "Memorandum from the President's Assistant for National Security Affairs (Brzezinski) to Secretary of State Vance," January 2, 1980, *Foreign Relations of the United States, 1977–1980, Vol. 12, Afghanistan,* 351.

83. President Reagan dramatically expanded the effort. See Tim Weiner, "History to Trump: CIA Was Aiding Afghan Rebels before the Soviets Invaded in '79," *Washington Post*, January 7, 2019, https://www.washingtonpost.com/outlook/2019/01/07/history-trump-cia-was-arming -afghan-rebels-before-soviets-invaded/.

84. Keating, "Don't try to convince yourself."

85. Eric Rosenbach and Aki J. Peritz, "Covert action: Memo in report 'Confrontation or Collaboration? Congress and the Intelligence Community,'" Belfer Center for Science and International Affairs, Harvard Kennedy School, July 2009, https://www.belfercenter.org/publication/covert-action.

86. Weiner, *Legacy of Ashes*, 357; Andrew, *For the President's Eyes Only*, 455.

87. Turner, *Secrecy and Democracy*, 87.

88. Bill Adair and Angie Drobnic Holan, "Several ratings rank Obama lower," Politifact, September 26, 2008, https://www.politifact.com/factchecks/2008/sep/26/john-mccain/several-ratings-rank-obama-lower/.

89. Amy Zegart, "Legend of a democracy promoter," *National Interest*, September 16, 2008, https://nationalinterest.org/article/the-legend-of-a-democracy-promoter-2839.

90. "Obama's Speech on Drone Policy," *New York Times*, May 23, 2013, https://www.nytimes.com/2013/05/24/us/politics/transcript-of-obamas-speech-on-drone-policy.html.

91. Zenko, "Obama's Embrace of Drone Strikes." Zenko takes the average estimates of three non-governmental organizations and finds that President George W. Bush authorized approximately 50 drone strikes that killed 296 terrorists and 195 civilians in Yemen, Pakistan and Somalia, while Obama authorized 506 strikes that killed 3,040 terrorists and 391 civilians.

92. Scholars also find that presidents opt for covert action when international law would prohibit overt engagement. See Michael Poznansky, *In the Shadow of International Law: Secrecy and Regime Change in the Postwar World* (New York: Oxford University Press, 2020).

93. Church Committee, "Final Report, Foreign and Military Intelligence," Book 1, 564, https://www.intelligence.senate.gov/sites/default/files/94755_I.pdf.

94. Berkowitz and Goodman, "Logic of covert action."

95. For details, see Antonio J. Mendez, "A classic case of deception: CIA goes Hollywood," *Studies in Intelligence* (Winter 1999/2000), https://www.cia.gov/static/48176093196e51d95219f3e3e762f038/Classic-Case-of-Deception.pdf (accessed January 30, 2021).

96. Andrew, *For the President's Eyes Only*, 450.

97. Carson, *Secret Wars*, 1–2.

98. Carson, 1–2, 241, 264, 268–70; Treverton, *Covert Action*, 27.

99. Gregory F. Treverton, "Forward to the Past?" in *Strategic Intelligence: Understanding the Hidden State of Government*, Vol. 3: Covert Action, edited by Loch K. Johnson (Westport, Conn.: Praeger Publishers, 2007), 8; Carson, *Secret Wars*, 264–70; Steve Coll, *Ghost Wars: The Secret History of the CIA, Afghanistan, and Bin Laden, from the Soviet Invasion to September 10, 2001* (New York: Penguin, 2005), 128–30.

100. Berkowitz and Goodman, "The logic of covert action." In fact, many covert actions were known. One study finds that the United States conducted sixty-four regime change covert operations during the Cold War, and in more than 70 percent of them, Washington was publicly accused of interfering in the domestic politics of the target state at the time. Lindsey A. O'Rourke, *Covert Regime Change* (Ithaca, N.Y.: Cornell University Press, 2018), 11. National Intelligence Council chairman Gregory Treverton wrote that by his estimate, at least half of the roughly forty covert actions underway in the mid-1980s had been the subject of a press account. Treverton, "Forward to the Past?" 7.

101. Robert M. Gates, *Duty: Memoirs of a Secretary at War* (New York: Knopf, 2014), 540–42.

102. Interview by author, July 28, 2020.

103. Matthew Aid with William Burr and Thomas Blanton, "Project Azorian: The CIA's Declassified History of the Glomar Explorer," National Security Archive, https://nsarchive2 .gwu.edu//nukevault/ebb305/index.htm; David H. Sharp, *The CIA's Greatest Covert Operation* (Lawrence, Kan.: University Press of Kansas, 2012).

104. Quoted in Theodore Sorensen, *Kennedy* (New York: Harper & Row, 1965), 309.

105. CIA Director William Casey had briefed the Senate Select Committee on Intelligence about the agency's Nicaraguan activities for more than two hours on March 8, 1984, but spent one sentence on the mining operation. According to historian Christopher Andrew, "the committee failed to realize that the CIA itself had mined the harbors until its involvement was revealed by the *Wall Street Journal*." See Andrew, *For the President's Eyes Only*, 478. In an angry letter to Director Casey, Intelligence Committee Chairman Barry Goldwater wrote that he was completely unaware of the mining operation. "Text of Goldwater's Letter to Head of C.I.A.," *New York Times*, April 11, 1984, https://www.nytimes.com/1984/04/11/world/text-of-goldwater-s-letter-to-the-head-of-cia .html. For "pissed off" expletive deleted by the *New York Times*, see Andrew, 478.

106. Malcolm Byrne, ed., "The Iran-Contra Affair 30 Years Later: A Milestone in Post-Truth Politics," National Security Archive, November 25, 2016, https://nsarchive.gwu.edu/briefing -book/iran/2016-11-25/iran-contra-affair-30-years-later-milestone-post-truth-politics.

107. Lydia Saad, "Gallup Vault: Reaction to Iran-Contra 30 Years Ago," Gallup, November 25, 2016, https://news.gallup.com/vault/198164/gallup-vault-reaction-iran-contra-years-ago.aspx (accessed December 16, 2020).

108. Quoted in Chris Whipple, *The Spymasters: How the CIA Directors Shape History and the Future* (New York: Scribner, 2020), 131.

109. Lawrence E. Walsh, "Summary of Prosecutions," Final Report of the Independent Counsel for Iran/Contra Matters, August 4, 1993, Washington, D.C., https://fas.org/irp/offdocs /walsh/summpros.htm.

110. The CIA has publicly confirmed its involvement in the coup. See National Security Archive Electronic Briefing Book No. 435, National Security Archive, August 19, 2013, https:// nsarchive2.gwu.edu/NSAEBB/NSAEBB435/ (accessed September 25, 2020).

111. Keating, "Don't try to convince yourself."

112. Participants included Sen. Daniel Patrick Moynihan (D-NY), former CIA Director William Colby, former Defense Department official Morton Halperin, former Under Secretary of State George Ball, *New York Times* national security correspondent Les Gelb, and several CIA operatives. See "Should the U.S. fight secret wars?" *Harper's*, September 1984.

113. George Kennan, "Morality and foreign policy," *Foreign Affairs* 64, no. 2 (Winter 1985): 214, https://www.law.upenn.edu/live/files/5139-kennanmoralityandforeignpolicyforeignaffairswinter.

114. Kennan, 214.

115. Halperin, in "Should the U.S. fight secret wars?" 37.

116. Gelb, in "Should the U.S. fight secret wars?" 38.

117. Ray Cline, in "Should the U.S. fight secret wars?" 44.

118. Elida Moreno, "Panama's Noriega: CIA Spy Turned Drug-Running Dictator," Reuters, May 30, 2017, https://www.reuters.com/article/us-panama-noriega-obituary/panamas-noriega -cia-spy-turned-drug-running-dictator-idUSKBN18Q0NW.

119. Ronald H. Cole, "OPERATION JUST CAUSE: The Planning and Execution of Joint Operations in Panama, February 1988–January 1990," Joint History Office, Office of the Chairman of the Joint Chiefs of Staff, November 1995, https://www.jcs.mil/Portals/36/Documents /History/Monographs/Just_Cause.pdf, 5–6.

120. Randal C. Archibold, "Manuel Noriega, Dictator Ousted by U.S. in Panama, Dies at 83," *New York Times*, May 30, 2017, https://www.nytimes.com/2017/05/30/world/americas/manuel -antonio-noriega-dead-panama.html; Moreno, "Panama's Noriega"; Colin Dwyer, "Former Panamanian Dictator Manuel Noriega Dies at 83," NPR, May 30, 2017, https://www.npr.org /sections/thetwo-way/2017/05/30/530666952/former-panamanian-dictator-manuel-noriega -dies-at-83.

121. Agence France-Presse, "Manuel Noriega Flown Home to Panama to Face Punishment," December 11, 2011, https://www.pri.org/stories/2011-12-11/manuel-noriega-flown-home -panama-face-punishment; Jon Lee Anderson, "Manuel Noriega, a thug of a different era," *New Yorker*, June 2, 2017, https://www.newyorker.com/news/daily-comment/manuel-noriega-a -thug-of-a-different-era.

122. Archibold, "Manuel Noriega, Dictator Ousted."

123. Snider, *Agency and the Hill*, 299–300.

124. Cole, "OPERATION JUST CAUSE," 27; Moreno, "Panama's Noriega."

125. Snider, *Agency and the Hill*, 299–300; Loch K. Johnson, "A conversation with former DCI William E. Colby: Spymaster during the 'Year of the Intelligence Wars,'" *Intelligence and National Security* 22, no. 2 (April 2007): 250–69, https://www.tandfonline.com/doi/full/10.1080 /02684520701303865?scroll=top&needAccess=true. For assassination bans in executive orders, see Elizabeth B. Bazan, "Assassination Ban and EO 12333: A Brief Summary," Congressional Research Service Report for Congress, RS21037, January 4, 2002.

126. Johnson, "A conversation with former DCI William E. Colby."

127. Panetta, *Worthy Fights*, 276.

128. Shannon Schwaller, "Operation Just Cause: The Invasion of Panama, December 1989," U.S. Army, November 17, 2008, https://www.army.mil/article/14302/operation_just_cause _the_invasion_of_panama_december_1989.

129. Andrew, *For the President's Eyes Only*, 515.

130. In 1992, Noriega was convicted and sentenced to forty years in prison. He was eventually extradited to France to serve time there, then sent to serve time in a Panamanian jail before he died in 2017. Archibold, "Manuel Noriega, Dictator Ousted."

131. Cole, "OPERATION JUST CAUSE," 65–66.

132. Johnson, "A conversation with former DCI William E. Colby."

133. Michael Hayden, *Playing to the Edge: American Intelligence in the Age of Terror* (New York: Penguin, 2016), 374.

134. The reference comes from a purported conversation on December 29, 1170, between King Henry II and Archbishop of Canterbury Thomas Becket in which the king exclaims, "Will no one rid me of this turbulent priest?" The next day, the archbishop was assassinated by four knights claiming to have a message from the king. The exact phrasing is disputed among historians, but the king did admit to saying something in anger that prompted his knights to go after Becket. Wilfred Lewis Warren, *Henry II* (Berkeley: University of California Press, 1973), 112.

135. The Church Committee investigation of 1975–1976 offers the most sweeping examination of covert action's early days; the complete collection of reports is available at https://www.intelligence.senate.gov/resources/intelligence-related-commissions. See also Zegart, *Flawed by Design*, 197; Jack Goldsmith, *Power and Constraint: The Accountable Presidency after 9/11* (New York: W. W. Norton, 2012), 84–86; Loch K. Johnson, *A Season of Inquiry Revisited: The Church Committee Confronts America's Spy Agencies* (Lawrence, Kan.: University Press of Kansas, 2015).

136. Church Committee, "Alleged Assassination Plots Involving Foreign Leaders," 109, 278–79.

137. Church Committee. See also Snider, *Agency and the Hill*, 255–311.

138. Church Committee, "Alleged Assassination Plots Involving Foreign Leaders," 10–12; Shimer, *Rigged*, 51.

139. For a more charitable view of early congressional oversight, see David Barrett, *The CIA and Congress: The Untold Story from Truman to Kennedy* (Lawrence, Kan.: University Press of Kansas, 2005).

140. Zegart, *Flawed by Design*, 193.

141. Quoted in Johnson, *Season of Inquiry Revisited*, 2.

142. Loch K. Johnson, ed., *Strategic Intelligence: Understanding the Hidden State of Government*, Vol. 3: Covert Action (Westport, Conn.: Praeger Publishers, 2007), xiii; Bazan, "Assassination Ban and E.O. 12333."

143. In August 2016, the Obama administration released an eighteen-page memo detailing the rules and procedures for targeting suspected terrorists for killing outside of war zones. See Charlie Savage, "U.S. Releases Rules for Airstrike Killing of Terror Suspects," *New York Times*, August 6, 2016. The document, known as the drone strike playbook, is *Procedures for Approving Direct Action against Terrorist Targets Located outside the United States and Areas of Active Hostilities*, May 22, 2013, declassified August 2016.

144. 50 U.S.C. section 3093a (2018).

145. Lowenthal, *Intelligence: From Secrets to Policy*, 253.

146. This is typically the "Gang of Eight": the chairs and vice chairs of the House and Senate Intelligence Committees as well as the majority and minority leaders of the House and Senate. When this occurs, the president must produce a written statement justifying more limited notification. 50 U.S.C. section 3093c (2018).

147. Sen. John D. Rockefeller, IV, Hearing about Congressional Oversight of Intelligence Activities, U.S. Senate Select Committee on Intelligence, 110th Cong., 1st sess., Nov. 13, 2007, 4.

148. National Commission on Terrorist Attacks Upon the United States, *The 9/11 Commission Report, Authorized Version* (New York: W. W. Norton, 2004), 133.

149. National Commission on Terrorist Attacks Upon the United States, "9/11 Commission Staff Statement Number Seven: Intelligence Policy," March 24, 2004, 8-9, https://govinfo.library.unt.edu/911/staff_statements/staff_statement_7.pdf; National Commission on Terrorist Attacks Upon the United States, *9/11 Commission Report*, 131–133.

150. 50 U.S.C. section 3093c (2018).

151. That said, Congress does not approve covert action funding before or at the time it is notified of a new or expanded program. Instead, the CIA can start spending immediately out of contingency or reprogrammed funds once a finding has been made and transmitted; Congress must wait until the next budget cycle to influence spending on that program. Perhaps the best-known

example of how Congress sought to use the power of the purse to end covert action were the Boland Amendments. Passed in the 1980s, the amendments cut off funding for CIA paramilitary operations and other support for the Nicaraguan Contras in their bid to overthrow the Sandinista regime. Members of the Reagan administration circumvented the law, funding the Contras out of arms sales to Iran in what became known as the Iran-Contra scandal.

152. Lowenthal, *Intelligence: From Secrets to Policy*, 254.

153. Douglas Jehl and David E. Sanger, "Plan Called for Covert Aid in Iraq Vote," *New York Times*, July 17, 2005, https://www.nytimes.com/2005/07/17/politics/plan-called-for-covert-aid-in-iraq-vote.html.

154. For details of how the authorization process worked in the Clinton and George W. Bush administrations, see Michael Morell with Bill Harlow, *The Great War of Our Time: The CIA's Fight against Terrorism—From al Qa'ida to ISIS* (New York: Twelve, 2015), 23–24.

155. Scott Shane and Sheryl Gay Stolberg, "A Brilliant Career with a Meteoric Rise and an Abrupt Fall," *New York Times*, November 10, 2012.

156. Schroen, *First In*.

157. George Tenet with Bill Harlow, *At the Center of the Storm: My Years at the CIA* (New York: HarperCollins, 2007), 187.

158. U.S. Senate Committee on Foreign Relations, "Tora Bora Revisited: How We Failed to Get Bin Laden and Why It Matters Today," 111th Cong., 1st sess., November 30, 2009, S. Prt. 111-35, https://www.govinfo.gov/content/pkg/CPRT-111SPRT53709/html/CPRT-111SPRT53709.htm; Tenet, *At the Center of the Storm*, 187, 225–26.

159. Robert Chesney, "A Revived CIA Drone Strike Program? Comments on the New Policy," Lawfare, March 14, 2017; Robert Chesney, "Shift to JSOC on Drone Strikes Does Not Mean the CIA Has Been Sidelined," Lawfare, June 16, 2016; Miller, "Why CIA Drone Strikes have Plummeted."

160. Jennifer Kibbe, "Covert Action and the Pentagon," in *Strategic Intelligence: Understanding the Hidden State of Government*, Vol. 3: Covert Action, edited by Loch K. Johnson (Westport, Conn.: Praeger Publishers, 2007), 131–35.

161. Technically, the CIA's targeted killing of Anwar al-Awlaki was a covert operation. Realistically, there wasn't much covert about it. Within hours, President Obama announced Awlaki's death without mentioning the CIA or drones. Office of the White House Press Secretary, "Remarks by the President at the 'Change of Office' Chairman of the Joint Chiefs of Staff Ceremony," September 30, 2011, https://obamawhitehouse.archives.gov/the-press-office/2011/09/30/remarks-president-change-office-chairman-joint-chiefs-staff-ceremony. But the *New York Times* did, revealing details about the operation the same day. Mazzetti, Schmitt, and Worth, "Two-Year Manhunt."

162. Samuel P. Huntington, *The Soldier and the State* (Cambridge, Mass.: Harvard University Press, 1957).

163. Interview by author, October 7, 2020.

Chapter 8: Congressional Oversight

Portions of this chapter were published as Amy B. Zegart, *Eyes on Spies: Congress and the United States Intelligence Community* (Stanford, Calif.: Hoover Institution Press, 2011).

1. Quoted in Loch K. Johnson, *A Season of Inquiry* (Lawrence, Kan.: University Press of Kansas, 1985), 263. Originally quoted in David M. Alpern, "America's secret warriors," *Newsweek*, October 10, 1983, 38.

2. U.S. Senate Select Committee on Intelligence hearing, November 13, 2007, 25.

3. John O. Brennan, *Undaunted: My Fight against America's Enemies, at Home and Abroad* (New York: Celadon Books, 2020), 318.

4. Dianne Feinstein, "Statement on the Intel Committee's CIA Detention, Interrogation Report," March 11, 2014, https://www.feinstein.senate.gov/public/index.cfm/2014/3/feinstein -statement-on-intelligence-committee-s-cia-detention-interrogation-report.

5. Feinstein.

6. Connie Bruck, "The inside war," *New Yorker*, June 22, 2015.

7. David B. Buckley, Office of Inspector General, Central Intelligence Agency, "Report of Investigation: Agency Access to the SSCI Shared Drive on RDINet," July 18, 2014, approved for release January 14, 2015, https://fas.org/irp/eprint/ig-access.pdf, i, iii, iv, 6. The CIA appointed a special accountability board, chaired by former Sen. Evan Bayh, which recommended against disciplining any CIA personnel. The board found all five CIA employees acted "reasonably under the complex and unprecedented circumstances involved in investigating a potential security breach in the highly classified shared computer network" between Congress and the CIA. The board also found the Senate Intelligence Committee and the Agency did not have a clear understanding of how such potential breaches would be handled. "Statement by Senator Evan Bayh Regarding the Findings of the Agency Accountability Board," Central Intelligence Agency, posted January 14, 2015, https://www.cia.gov/news-information/press-releases-statements/2015 -press-releases-statements/statements-on-agency-accountability-board-findings.html (accessed September 21, 2020).

8. Bruck, "Inside war."

9. Bruck.

10. Feinstein, "Statement."

11. Greg Miller, "CIA Director John Brennan Apologizes for Search of Senate Committee's Computers," *Washington Post*, July 31, 2014, https://www.washingtonpost.com/world/national -security/cia-director-john-brennan-apologizes-for-search-of-senate-computers/2014/07/31 /28004b18-18c6-11e4-9349-84d4a85be981_story.html.

12. "Report of the Senate Select Committee on Intelligence Committee Study of the Central Intelligence Agency's Detention and Interrogation Program" [hereafter "Senate Detention and Interrogation Program Report"], 113th Cong., 2nd sess., December 9, 2014, S. Report 113-288, https://www.intelligence.senate.gov/sites/default/files/publications/CRPT-113srpt288.pdf, xxi, xxv, 9–10. The declassified summary includes just five hundred pages; the full report remains classified.

13. These included cases of people who were swept up in the terrorist dragnet by mistake. "Senate Detention and Interrogation Program Report," 15–16.

14. Michael Hayden, *Playing to the Edge: American Intelligence in the Age of Terror* (New York: Penguin, 2016), 223. For descriptions of enhanced interrogation techniques, see Central Intelligence Agency Office of the Inspector General, "Special Review: Counterterrorism Detention and Interrogation Activities" (September 2001–October 2003), Report No. 2003-7123-IG,

May 7, 2004, redacted and declassified August 24, 2009, https://nsarchive2.gwu.edu/torture
_archive/comparison.htm, 15.

15. "Senate Detention and Interrogation Report," xii–xiii, xxv, 9-10, 40–46, 85–92, 115, 268,
412. Many considered these methods torture. See Leon Panetta with Jim Newton, *Worthy Fights:
A Memoir of Leadership in War and Peace* (New York: Penguin, 2014), 193; Sen. John McCain,
"SSCI Study of the CIA's R&I Program," remarks in the Senate, *Congressional Record*, daily edition, vol. 160, no. 149 (December 9, 2014), S6411; Barack Obama, "Press Conference by the
President," The White House, August 1, 2014, https://obamawhitehouse.archives.gov/the-press
-office/2014/08/01/press-conference-president (accessed September 16, 2020).

16. "Today's first session . . . had a profound effect on all staff members present," noted one
cable from a black site. "Senate Detention and Interrogation Report," 44.

17. "Senate Detention and Interrogation Report," iv. The full report ran 6,700 pages and included 35,000 footnotes, making it the longest and most heavily sourced report in committee
history. Feinstein, "Statement."

18. U.S. Senate Select Committee on Intelligence, "Committee Study of the CIA's Detention
and Interrogation Program: Minority Views of Vice Chairman Chambliss joined by Senators
Burr, Risch, Coats, Rubio, and Coburn," June 20, 2014, revised for redaction on December 5,
2014, https://fas.org/irp/congress/2014_rpt/ssci-rdi-min.pdf.

19. Comments on the Senate Select Committee on Intelligence's Study of the Central Intelligence Agency's Former Detention and Interrogation Program, approved for release December 8, 2014, Tab C, 2, https://fas.org/irp/congress/2014_rpt/cia-ssci.pdf. See also CIA, "Fact
Sheet Regarding the SSCI Study on the Former Detention and Interrogation Program," December 9, 2014.

20. See, for example, "Ex-CIA Directors: Interrogations Saved Lives," *Wall Street Journal*,
January 16, 2015, https://www.wsj.com/articles/ex-cia-directors-interrogations-saved-lives
-1421427169; Michael Morell with Bill Harlow, *The Great War of Our Time: The CIA's Fight against
Terrorism—From al Qa'ida to ISIS* (New York: Twelve, 2015), 277.

21. George Tenet, "Statement on the Release of the SSCI Report on CIA Rendition, Detention and Interrogation," December 9, 2014, https://www.ciasavedlives.com/statements.html.

22. The committee's investigation was originally approved by a vote of 14-1. The final report
was approved along partisan lines, 9-6, with all eight Democrats and a single committee Republican, Olympia Snowe, voting in favor. See Morell, *Great War of Our Time*, 262; Office of Senator
Susan Collins, "Sen. Collins' Views on Senate Intelligence Committee Report on CIA Interrogation Program," December 9, 2014, https://www.collins.senate.gov/newsroom/sen-collins-views
-senate-intelligence-committee-report-cia-interrogation-program.

23. Senate Select Committee on Intelligence, "Minority Views."

24. Central Intelligence Agency Office of the Inspector General, "Special Review," 16–22;
George W. Bush, *Decision Points* (New York: Crown, 2010), 168–71; George W. Tenet with Bill
Harlow, *At the Center of the Storm: My Years at the CIA* (New York: HarperCollins, 2007),
241–42; Morell, *Great War of Our Time*, 269–70. Several studies found, and the CIA agreed, that
the detention and interrogation program was poorly run in the beginning and that some personnel used methods that were not approved. These excesses led to the death of Gul Rahman in
November 2002. See Comments on the Senate Select Committee on Intelligence's Study, 3–7.

25. Bush, *Decision Points*, 168–71; Central Intelligence Agency Office of the Inspector General, "Special Review," 16–24; Comments on the Senate Select Committee on Intelligence's Study, 15–16; "Ex-CIA Directors: Interrogations Saved Lives." The CIA's independent inspector general issued a report in 2004 noting that "in the fall of 2002, the Agency briefed the leadership of the congressional Intelligence Oversight Committees" and that briefings continued. "Special Review," 23–24. In 2009, after House Speaker Nancy Pelosi claimed she had not been briefed about the use of waterboarding, CIA Director Leon Panetta released a memo listing thirty-three times that members of Congress had, in fact, been briefed on the detention and interrogation program, starting in 2002. For the controversy, see David Welna, "CIA: Pelosi Knew of Interrogation in '02," *All Things Considered*, NPR, May 8, 2009, https://www.npr.org/templates/story/story.php?storyId=103951579. For the CIA list of briefings, see https://fas.org/irp/congress/2009_cr/eit-briefings.pdf. For additional sources on the extent of congressional briefings, see "Ex-CIA Directors," 35–38.

26. Bush, *Decision Points*, 171; Morell, *Great War of Our Time*, 269; Central Intelligence Agency Office of the Inspector General, "Special Review," 23–24.

27. Jose A. Rodriguez Jr., "Today's CIA Critics Once Urged the Agency to Do Anything to Fight al-Qaeda," *Washington Post*, December 5, 2014, https://www.washingtonpost.com/opinions/todays-cia-critics-once-urged-the-agency-to-do-anything-to-fight-al-qaeda/2014/12/05/ac418da2-7bda-11e4-84d4-7c896b90abdc_story.html. For more on how congressional leaders went from advocating more aggressive CIA interrogations to criticizing them, see Bush, *Decision Points*, 171.

28. Comments on the Senate Select Committee on Intelligence's Study. See also CIA, "Fact Sheet Regarding the SSCI Study"; "Detainee Reporting Pivotal to the War Against Al-Qa'ida, June 3, 2005," approved for release October 28, 2014, https://www.ciasavedlives.com/effectiveness.html; Bush, *Decision Points*, 168–71.

29. The judicial and executive branches also engage in intelligence oversight through the courts, the Justice Department, and other positions such as agency lawyers and inspectors general.

30. James Madison, "Federalist 51: The Structure of the Government Must Furnish the Proper Checks and Balances between the Different Departments," February 8, 1788, https://avalon.law.yale.edu/18th_century/fed51.asp (accessed June 22, 2021).

31. Arthur M. Schlesinger Jr. and Roger Bruns, eds. *Congress Investigates: A Documented History, 1792–1794*, Vol. 1 (New York: Chelsea House, 1975), xix.

32. Jennifer Stisa Granick and Christopher Jon Sprigman, "The Criminal N.S.A.," *New York Times*, June 27, 2013, https://www.nytimes.com/2013/06/28/opinion/the-criminal-nsa.html.

33. Michael Morell, *Intelligence Matters*, Special Edition Episode on Congressional Oversight, with Sen. Saxby Chambliss, Sen. Bill Nelson, Rep. Jane Harman, and Rep. Mike Rogers, March 29, 2019.

34. To give some idea of the workload, in one twelve-month period, CIA officials answered 1,140 Questions for the Record, responded to 254 other congressional queries and letters, and wrote 29 congressionally mandated reports (Hayden, *Playing to the Edge*, 229). That's a lot of time spent writing products that likely went unread; we know that only a handful of Senators and Representatives bothered even to read the National Intelligence Estimate on Iraq before

voting to go to war. Dana Priest, "Congressional Oversight of Intelligence Criticized," *Washington Post*, April 27, 2004, https://www.washingtonpost.com/archive/politics/2004/04/27/congressional-oversight-of-intelligence-criticized/a306890e-4684-4ed4-99a0-c8ae7f47feb7/.

35. Zegart, *Eyes on Spies*, 31.

36. Christopher Andrew, *For the President's Eyes Only: Secret Intelligence and the American Presidency from Washington to Bush* (New York: Harper Perennial, 1996), 11; Edward F. Sayle, "The historical underpinnings of the U.S. Intelligence Community," *International Journal of Intelligence and CounterIntelligence* 1, no. 1 (1986): 9.

37. James S. Van Wagenen, "A review of congressional oversight," *Studies in Intelligence*, no. 1 (1997), https://apps.dtic.mil/sti/pdfs/ADA524502.pdf.

38. James D. Richardson, ed., *A Compilation of the Messages and Papers of the Presidents, 1789–1897*, 20 vols. (Washington, D.C.: GPO, 1897), 4:431–36.

39. Oversight was described by one observer as "benign neglect." Van Wagenen, "Review of congressional oversight," 98.

40. Frank J. Smist Jr., *Congress Oversees the United States Intelligence Community, 1947–1994*, 2nd ed. (Knoxville: University of Tennessee Press, 1994); CIA Draft Study, Vol. 1, 38, cited in L. Britt Snider, *The Agency and the Hill: The CIA's Relationship with Congress, 1946–2004* (Washington, D.C.: Center for the Study of Intelligence, 2008), 8.

41. Snider, 18. Sensitive matters were handled in one-on-one sessions between the CIA director and individual committee chairmen, but these, too, were infrequent and informal.

42. *Congressional Record*, daily edition, vol. 102, part 5 (April 9, 1956), 5924.

43. Quoted in Loch K. Johnson, *A Season of Inquiry Revisited: The Church Committee Confronts America's Spy Agencies* (Lawrence, Kan.: University Press of Kansas, 2015), 3.

44. Johnson, 3.

45. Snider interview of Pforzheimer, January 11, 1988, printed in *Agency and the Hill*, 9–10.

46. Quoted in Johnson, *Season of Inquiry Revisited*, 4.

47. We now know that the White House asked the CIA to interfere with the FBI's Watergate investigation but CIA Director Richard Helms refused. Snider, *Agency and the Hill*, 29.

48. Seymour M. Hersh, "C.I.A. Chief Tells House of $8-Million Campaign against Allende in 70–73," *New York Times*, September 8, 1974, https://www.nytimes.com/1974/09/08/archives/cia-chief-tells-house-of-8million-campaign-against-allende-in-7073.html.

49. Seymour M. Hersh, "Huge C.I.A. Operation Reported in U.S. against Antiwar Forces, Other Dissidents in Nixon Years," *New York Times*, December 22, 1974, https://www.nytimes.com/1974/12/22/archives/huge-cia-operation-reported-in-u-s-against-antiwar-forces-other.html.

50. For analysis of the documents, see Amy Zegart, *New York Times Room for Debate*, June 26, 2007, https://washington.blogs.nytimes.com/2007/06/26/hunt-requests-a-lockpicker/.

51. Mark Mazzetti and Tim Weiner, "Files on Illegal Spying Show C.I.A. Skeletons from Cold War," *New York Times*, June 27, 2007, https://www.nytimes.com/2007/06/27/washington/27cia.html?_r=1&adxnnl=1&oref=slogin&adxnnlx=1182972009-ar6ADyP9/dnr/FI%2B6HYzuA.

52. Zegart, *New York Times Room for Debate*. "The Family Jewels" can be found at https://www.cia.gov/readingroom/document/0001451843, 107.

53. U.S. Senate Select Committee to Study Governmental Operations with Respect to Intelligence Activities (Church Committee), "Intelligence Activities and the Rights of Americans, Book 2, Final Report," 94th Cong., 2nd sess., April 26, 1976, Report No. 94-755, 6. On legality issues, see 137–63.

54. U.S. Senate Select Committee to Study Governmental Operations with Respect to Intelligence Activities (Church Committee), "Intelligence Activities and the Rights of Americans, Book 2, Final Report," 94th Cong., 2nd sess., April 26, 1976, Report No. 94-755; Church Committee, "Intelligence Activities and the Rights of Americans" and "Supplementary Detailed Staff Reports on Intelligence Activities and the Rights of Americans, Book 3, Final Report," April 23, 1976. Congress found that the CIA had operated four mail opening programs that photographed more than 2.7 million letters and opened more than 200,000 of them. The FBI ran mail opening programs as well. "Supplementary Detailed Staff Reports," 565–71. Congress found the NSA's telegram interception program, code named SHAMROCK, was "probably the largest governmental interception program affecting Americans ever undertaken," running from 1945 to 1975 and involving an estimated 150,000 telegrams per month in its final two to three years. "Supplementary Detailed Staff Reports," 765.

55. Church Committee, "Supplementary Detailed Staff Reports," 3, 355–71; "Intelligence Activities and the Rights of Americans," 289.

56. National Security Act of 1947, sections 501-503, Public Law 235, July 26, 1947, https://www.dni.gov/index.php/ic-legal-reference-book/national-security-act-of-1947.

57. Interview by author, August 17, 2020.

58. Amy Zegart, Spying Blind: The CIA, the FBI, and the Origins of 9/11 (Princeton, N.J.: Princeton University Press, 2007); U.S. Senate Select Committee on Intelligence and House Permanent Select Committee on Intelligence, "Joint Inquiry into Intelligence Community Activities before and after the Terrorist Attacks of September 11, 2001," 107th Cong., 2nd sess., December 2002, S. Rept. No. 107-351 / H. Rept. No. 107-792; National Commission on Terrorist Attacks Upon the United States, The 9/11 Commission Report, Authorized Version (New York: W. W. Norton, 2004).

59. National Commission on Terrorist Attacks Upon the United States, 9/11 Commission Report, 420, 105.

60. Zegart, Spying Blind, 1–15, 61–100, 120–155.

61. Tenet memo quoted in Senate Select Committee on Intelligence and House Permanent Select Committee on Intelligence, "Joint Inquiry," 231; see Zegart, Spying Blind, 3–4, 80–88.

62. Zegart, 4, 83.

63. National Commission on Terrorist Attacks Upon the United States, 9/11 Commission Report, 106.

64. Joel Aberbach, Keeping a Watchful Eye: The Politics of Congressional Oversight (Washington, D.C.: Brookings Institute, 1990).

65. Mathew D. McCubbins and Thomas Schwartz, "Congressional oversight overlooked: Police patrol vs. Fire alarm," American Journal of Political Science 28 (February 1984): 165–79; Mathew D. McCubbins, Roger G. Noll, and Barry R. Weingast, "Administrative procedures as instruments of political control," Journal of Law, Economics, and Organization 3 (1987): 243–77. Others find a hybrid approach. See, for example, Mathew D. McCubbins, "The legislative design

of regulatory structure," *American Journal of Political Science* 29, no. 4 (1985): 721–48; Kathleen Bawn, "Political control versus Expertise: Congressional choices about administrative procedures," *American Political Science Review* 89, no. 1 (1994): 62–73.

66. Zegart, *Eyes on Spies*, 55–57. See also Aberbach, *Keeping a Watchful Eye*.

67. McCubbins, "Legislative design of regulatory structure," 728.

68. Terry M. Moe, "The Politics of Bureaucratic Structure," in *Can the Government Govern?* edited by J. E. Chubb and P. E. Peterson (Washington, D.C.: Brookings Institution Press, 1989).

69. Economists call these situations "principal–agent" problems. One party, the principal, delegates authority to an agent. Often, the interests of principals and agents diverge. Particularly in situations where the principal cannot observe the agent, shirking becomes likely.

70. Quoted in U.S. Senate Select Committee on Intelligence, Hearing on Congressional Oversight of Intelligence Activities (hereafter SSCI Hearing), 110th Cong., 1st sess., November 13, 2007.

71. Quoted in SSCI Hearing.

72. Zegart, *Eyes on Spies*, 75–76.

73. See Hon. Tim Roemer, testimony, SSCI Hearing.

74. SSCI Hearing.

75. Interview by author, August 12, 2020.

76. SSCI Hearing.

77. Morell, *Intelligence Matters*; Hayden, *Playing to the Edge*, 391.

78. Interview by author, August 19, 2009.

79. Jose A. Rodriguez Jr. with Bill Harlow, *Hard Measures: How Aggressive CIA Actions after 9/11 Saved American Lives* (New York: Threshold Editions, 2012), 193–94.

80. Morell, *Great War of Our Time*, 259.

81. Rodriguez, *Hard Measures*, 183–217; Morell, *Great War of Our Time*, 259; Hayden, *Playing to the Edge*, 240.

82. Rodriguez, *Hard Measures*, 193, 259–61. Rodriguez was concerned the tapes would reveal the identities of CIA officers, endangering their lives. Around Langley, Rodriguez was considered a hero. Hayden, *Playing to the Edge*, 240.

83. Hayden, 118.

84. James R. Clapper with Trey Brown, *Facts and Fears: Hard Truths from a Life in Intelligence* (New York: Penguin, 2018), 237.

85. Clapper, 207.

86. Stellarwind is named in Hayden, *Playing to the Edge*, 64.

87. Robert Chesney, "Telephone Metadata: Is the Contact-Chaining Program Unsalvageable?" Lawfare, March 6, 2019.

88. Hayden, *Playing to the Edge*, 64–91.

89. Bush, *Decision Points*, 162–64; Senate Select Committee on Intelligence and House Permanent Select Committee on Intelligence, "Joint Inquiry," 36.

90. Interview by author, August 26, 2020.

91. USA FREEDOM Act of 2015, https://www.congress.gov/bill/114th-congress/house-bill/2048.

92. U.S. Library of Congress Congressional Research Service, John W. Rollins and Edward C. Liu, "NSA Surveillance Leaks: Background and Issues for Congress," R43134, September 4, 2013, https://fas.org/sgp/crs/intel/R43134.pdf; Clapper, *Facts and Fears*, 198, 207–10, 251.

93. Loch K. Johnson, "A conversation with James R. Clapper, Jr., the Director of National Intelligence," *Intelligence and National Security* 30, no. 1 (2015): 15.

94. Office of Sen. Ron Wyden, "Wyden Statement on Director Clapper's Resignation," November 17, 2016, https://www.wyden.senate.gov/news/press-releases/-wyden-statement-on -director-clappers-resignation.

95. Clapper, *Facts and Fears*, 207–10, 251; Hayden, *Playing to the Edge*, 77.

96. Clapper, *Facts and Fears*, 243, 251.

97. Author's YouGov National Poll, October 5–7, 2013. See chapter 2 for further discussion.

98. Hayden, *Playing to the Edge*, 80.

99. Interview by author, August 17, 2020. Clapper later noted in an interview that had the IC been more transparent about the program, its needs, and its safeguards, "people would not have been any more disturbed . . . than they are about the fact that the FBI maintains fingerprint files on millions of U.S. persons." Loch K. Johnson, "Conversation with James R. Clapper, Jr.," 16.

100. David Mayhew, *Congress: The Electoral Connection* (New Haven, Conn.: Yale University Press, 1974), 16.

101. Polls show that voters care more about domestic issues than foreign policy. See Zegart, *Eyes on Spies*, 72–73; Halimah Abdullah and Joe Van Kanel, "Economy Tops Voter Concerns in Exit Polls, CNN, November 6, 2012, https://www.cnn.com/2012/11/06/politics/exit-polls /index.html; "Election 2016 Exit Polls," CNN, November 23, 2016, https://www.cnn.com /election/2016/results/exit-polls/national/house. The House Intelligence Committee concluded in a 1996 report, "Intelligence, unlike virtually all other functions of government, has no natural advocates in the public at large. Its direct effect on most citizens is largely unfelt or unseen; its industrial base is too rarified to build a large constituency in many areas." U.S. House Permanent Select Committee on Intelligence, *IC21: The Intelligence Community in the 21st Century* (Washington, D.C.: GPO, 1996), section 10.

102. Interview by author, August 20, 2009.

103. According to a 2017 U.S. Department of Agriculture report, a significant portion of farm aid goes to farmers with household incomes over $150,000. That's almost three times higher than the median U.S. household income. Tamar Haspel, "Why Do Taxpayers Subsidize Rich Farmers?" *Washington Post*, March 15, 2018, https://www.washingtonpost.com/lifestyle/food/why-do -taxpayers-subsidize-rich-farmers/2018/03/15/50e89906-27b6-11e8-b79d-f3d931db7f68_story.html. For more on the history of farm subsidies, see Congressional Budget Office, "Options to Reduce the Budgetary Costs of the Federal Crop Insurance Program," December 2017, https://www.cbo .gov/system/files/115th-congress-2017-2018/reports/53375-federalcropinsuranceprogram.pdf; Chris Edwards, "Reforming Federal Farm Policies," CATO Institute, April 12, 2018, https://www .cato.org/publications/tax-budget-bulletin/reforming-federal-farm-policies.

104. Interview by author, August 19, 2009.

105. For example, see Hayden, *Playing to the Edge*, 232–42.

106. Cofer Black, "Out of the shadows," *Men's Journal*, November 20, 2013, https://www .mensjournal.com/features/cofer-black-out-of-the-shadows-20131120/.

107. Interview by author, March 14, 2009.

108. Morell, *Intelligence Matters*.

109. Interview by author, August 20, 2019.

110. *Meet the Press*, NBC, February 12, 2006, http://www.nbcnews.com/id/11272634/ns/meet_the_press/t/transcript-february/#.X2JaPnZKhTZ.

111. Edward Wyatt, "Publisher Names 9/11 Charities," *New York Times*, July 21, 2005, https://www.nytimes.com/2005/07/21/books/publisher-names-911-charities.html.

112. Zegart, *Spying Blind*, 179.

113. SSCI Hearing, 25.

114. Chris Carney (D-PA) served as a Pentagon intelligence analyst and Mike Rogers (R-MI) worked as an FBI agent for six years. Zegart, *Eyes on Spies*, 88.

115. Congressman Peter Welch, "Welch Launches Congressional Dairy Farmers Caucus," press release, July 29, 2009, https://welch.house.gov/media-center/press-releases/welch-launches-congressional-dairy-farmers-caucus.

116. In 2004, the Senate passed Resolution 445 abolishing term limits: https://www.congress.gov/bill/108th-congress/senate-resolution/445#:~:text=S.-,Res.,108th%20Congress%20(2003%2D2004).

117. Michael E. DeVine, "Congressional Oversight of Intelligence: Background and Selected Options for Further Reform," Congressional Research Service, December 4, 2018, https://fas.org/sgp/crs/intel/R45421.pdf.

118. In the House, for example, only the Committee on the Budget and the Committee on Ethics have term limits, and these committees don't handle legislation.

119. Zegart, *Eyes on Spies*, 93–94. The committee is attractive to some. Legislators with presidential aspirations often like to join intelligence committees. For a few others, "it's just cool," as one staffer told me (interview by author, April 28, 2011).

120. Longtermers in the intelligence committees arise mostly from chairs and ranking members (who are allowed to serve longer) and legislators who accrue years of *discontinuous* service by rolling onto and off the committees. Karen L. Haas, Clerk of the House of Representatives, "Rules of the House of Representatives," 116th Cong., January 11, 2019, https://naturalresources.house.gov/imo/media/doc/116-House-Rules-Clerk.pdf (accessed September 21, 2020), 14.

121. Analysis by author.

122. Sharon Bradford Franklin, "Fulfilling the Promise of the USA Freedom Act: Time to Truly End Bulk Collection of Americans' Calling Records," Just Security, March 28, 2019, https://www.justsecurity.org/63399/fulfilling-the-promise-of-the-usa-freedom-act-time-to-truly-end-bulk-collection-of-americans-calling-records/.

123. Department of Homeland Security Press Office, "Joint Statement from the Department of Homeland Security and Office of the Director of National Intelligence on Election Security," October 7, 2016, https://www.dhs.gov/news/2016/10/07/joint-statement-department-homeland-security-and-office-director-national.

124. Interview by author, August 19, 2009.

125. SSCI Hearing.

126. Statement by Sen. Kit Bond, SSCI Hearing; Zegart, *Eyes on Spies*, 107–9.

127. Sen. John McCain, *Congressional Record*, October 7, 2004, S21334.

128. Interview by author, August 20, 2009.

129. An important exception was from 2011 to 2014, which was a period of unusual bipartisanship under HPSCI chairman Mike Rogers (R-MI) and ranking member Dutch Ruppersberger (D-CA). During that time, the committee passed five authorization bills, a landmark cybersecurity bill to increase information sharing between the government and tech companies, and a bipartisan bill to end the NSA's phone metadata program. See David Ignatius, "The House Intelligence Committee: A Rare Example of Bipartisanship," *Washington Post,* March 2, 2012, https://www.washingtonpost.com/opinions/the-house-intelligence-committee-a-rare-example -of-bipartisanship/2012/03/01/gIQAMfianR_story.html; John Fritze, "Ruppersberger Nearing End of 12-Year Run on House Intel Committee," *Baltimore Sun,* November 26, 2014, https://www .google.com/search?q=ruppersberger+rogers+bipartisan+best&sxsrf=ALeKk02awWc7vASdOu VbEEOxGqLztTLM6A:1600720489909&ei=aQ5pX_-IN4jz-gS665fYDw&start=0&sa=N&ved =2ahUKEwi_4b3BjPvrAhWIuZ4KHbr1Bfs4ChDyowN6BAgMEC0&biw=1397&bih=701.

130. Morell, *Intelligence Matters.*

131. Interview by author, August 12, 2020.

132. Saxby Chambliss, Lawfare podcast, March 23, 2019.

133. Gregory Krieg, "Bernie Sanders: GOP Senator James Inhofe Is a Friend," CNN, March 13, 2016, https://www.cnn.com/2016/03/13/politics/bernie-sanders-james-inhofe -friends/index.html.

134. See, for example, Chambliss, Lawfare podcast. Another key difference is the role of the vice chairman. In the House, the majority party always runs the show. If the chairman cannot run a hearing, the next most senior majority party committee member serves in her absence. But in the Senate Intelligence Committee, a vice chairman is chosen from the minority party and presides in the chairman's absence. Zegart, *Eyes on Spies,* 24.

135. Berkman Center for Internet & Society, Harvard University, "Don't Panic: Making Progress on the "Going Dark" Debate," February 1, 2016, https://cyber.harvard.edu/pubrelease /dont-panic/Dont_Panic_Making_Progress_on_Going_Dark_Debate.pdf.

136. This process is called the Vulnerabilities Equities Process. See White House, "Fact Sheet: Vulnerabilities Equities Process," November 2017, https://www.hsdl.org/?abstract&did =805727 (accessed April 25, 2021). For a history and discussion of key issues, see Ari Schwartz and Rob Knake, "Government's Role in Vulnerability Disclosure: Creating a Permanent and Accountable Vulnerability Equities Process," June 2016, https://www.belfercenter.org/sites/default /files/legacy/files/vulnerability-disclosure-web-final3.pdf; Sven Herpig and Ari Schwartz, "The Future of Vulnerabilities Equities Processes Around the World," Lawfare, January 4, 2019, https:// www.lawfareblog.com/future-vulnerabilities-equities-processes-around-world.

137. Nicole Perlroth, Jeff Larson, and Scott Shane, "N.S.A. Able to Foil Basic Safeguards of Privacy on Web," *New York Times,* September 5, 2013, https://www.nytimes.com/2013/09/06 /us/nsa-foils-much-internet-encryption.html.

138. Kevin Poulsen, "Apple's iPhone encryption is a godsend, even if cops hate it," *Wired,* October 8, 2014, https://www.wired.com/2014/10/golden-key/.

139. Berkman Center for Internet & Society, "Don't Panic."

140. Kim Zetter, "Apple's FBI battle is complicated. Here's what's really going on," *Wired,* February 18, 2016, https://www.wired.com/2016/02/apples-fbi-battle-is-complicated-heres -whats-really-going-on/.

141. Devlin Barrett, "FBI Paid More Than $1 Million to Hack San Bernardino iPhone," *Wall Street Journal*, April 21, 2016, https://www.wsj.com/articles/comey-fbi-paid-more-than-1-million -to-hack-san-bernardino-iphone-1461266641; "Source: Israeli Firm Helped FBI Hack San Bernardino Terrorist's iPhone," *NBC Nightly News*, March 29, 2016, https://www.nbcnews.com/video /source-israeli-firm-helped-fbi-hack-san-bernardino-terrorist-s-iphone-654582339974.

142. Roger Cheng, "Apple, FBI, Face Off before Congress over iPhone Encryption," CNET, March 1, 2016, https://www.cnet.com/news/apple-fbi-face-off-before-congress-over-iphone -encryption-san-bernardino-terrorist/; Lily Hay Newman, "The Apple-FBI fight is different from the last one," *Wired*, January 16, 2020, https://www.wired.com/story/apple-fbi-iphone -encryption-pensacola/.

143. Christopher Mims, "The Day When Computers Can Break All Encryption Is Coming," *Wall Street Journal*, June 4, 2019, https://www.wsj.com/articles/the-race-to-save-encryption -11559646737.

144. Amy Zegart and Kevin Childs, "The divide between Silicon Valley and Washington is a national-security threat," *Atlantic*, December 13, 2018, https://www.theatlantic.com/ideas /archive/2018/12/growing-gulf-between-silicon-valley-and-washington/577963/.

145. They are Martin Heinrich, David Perdue, and Steve Daines.

146. The hearing was held April 10, 2018. For a transcript, see https://www.washingtonpost .com/news/the-switch/wp/2018/04/10/transcript-of-mark-zuckerbergs-senate-hearing/.

147. Zegart and Childs, "Divide between Silicon Valley and Washington."

Chapter 9: Intelligence Isn't Just for Governments Anymore

The author gratefully acknowledges the support of the American Academy of Arts and Sciences for the project on which this chapter is based.

1. Interview by author, July 4, 2020.

2. Jon Gambrell, "Analysts: Fire at Iran Nuke Site Hit New Centrifuge Facility," ABC News, July 2, 2020, https://abcnews.go.com/International/wireStory/incident-damages-construction -iran-nuclear-site-71570921.

3. David Albright and Andrea Stricker, "Previously Identified: Iran's New Centrifuge Assembly Workshop," Institute for Science and International Security, June 6, 2018, https://isis -online.org/isis-reports/detail/previously-identified-irans-new-centrifuge-assembly-workshop/8; David Albright, Sarah Burkhard, and Frank Pabian, "Mysterious Fire and Explosion in the New Natanz Advanced Centrifuge Assembly Facility," Institute for Science and International Security, July 3, 2020.

4. Gambrell, "Analysts: Fire at Iran Nuke Site"; David E. Sanger, William J. Broad, Ronen Bergman, and Farnaz Fassihi, "Mysterious Explosion and Fire Damage Iranian Nuclear Enrichment Facility," *New York Times*, July 2, 2020, https://www.nytimes.com/2020/07/02/us/politics /iran-explosion-nuclear-centrifuges.html?action=click&module=Top%20Stories&pgtype =Homepage (accessed September 26, 2020). The shed's real purpose wasn't even much of a secret. In 2019, Iranian media carried a photograph showing the building's name: Iran Centrifuge Assembly Center. See Albright, Burkhard, and Pabian, "Mysterious Fire and Explosion."

5. Sanger et al., "Mysterious Explosion and Fire Damage." Whatever the cause, experts believe the blaze probably set back Iran's uranium enrichment significantly. Albright, Burkhard, and Pabian, "Mysterious Fire and Explosion."

6. Gambrell, "Analysts: Fire at Iran Nuke Site."

7. Michael Adler, "Iran and the IAEA," *The Iran Primer*, United States Institutes of Peace, October 11, 2010, https://iranprimer.usip.org/resource/iran-and-iaea (accessed September 26, 2020).

8. International Atomic Energy Agency, "IAEA and Iran: Chronology of Key Events," September 2020, https://www.iaea.org/newscenter/focus/iran/chronology-of-key-events (accessed September 26, 2020).

9. U.S. Department of State, "Joint Comprehensive Plan of Action," posted January 20, 2009, to January 20, 2017, https://2009-2017.state.gov/e/eb/tfs/spi/iran/jcpoa//index.htm; Arms Control Association, "The Joint Comprehensive Plan of Action (JCPOA) at a Glance," https://www.armscontrol.org/factsheets/JCPOA-at-a-glance (accessed September 26, 2020). In 2018, the Trump administration unilaterally withdrew from the nuclear deal.

10. Sanger et al., "Mysterious Explosion and Fire Damage"; Guilbert Gates, "How a Secret Cyberwar Program Worked," *New York Times*, June 1, 2012, https://archive.nytimes.com/www.nytimes.com/interactive/2012/06/01/world/middleeast/how-a-secret-cyberwar-program-worked.html?ref=middleeast; David E. Sanger, *The Perfect Weapon: War, Sabotage, and Fear in the Cyber Age* (New York: Crown, 2018), 9, 41.

11. For details, see Kim Zetter, *Countdown to Zero Day: Stuxnet and the Launch of the World's First Digital Weapon* (New York: Crown Publishers, 2014); Sanger, *Perfect Weapon*.

12. Sanger et al., "Mysterious Explosion and Fire Damage."

13. See July 2, 2020, Tweets by @fabhinz and @ThegoodISIS; Gambrell, "Analysts: Fire at Iran Nuke Site"; and Sanger et al., "Mysterious Explosion and Fire Damage."

14. Gambrell, "Analysts: Fire at Iran Nuke Site." The story first ran at 8:00 A.M. and was updated later in the day.

15. Sanger et al., "Mysterious Explosion and Fire Damage."

16. "Iran Warns Israel, U.S. after Fire at Nuclear Site, Amid Reports Bomb Caused Blaze," *Times of Israel*, July 2, 2020, https://www.timesofisrael.com/iran-issues-warning-to-israel-us-after-mystery-fire-at-nuclear-enrichment-site/ (accessed September 26, 2020).

17. R. Jeffrey Smith, "CIA Missed Signs of India's Tests, U.S. Officials Say," *Washington Post*, May 13, 1998, https://www.washingtonpost.com/archive/politics/1998/05/13/cia-missed-signs-of-indias-tests-us-officials-say/0967b27b-8f47-45ca-ae7a-f5d684e3d23f/ (accessed September 26, 2020).

18. Frank V. Pabian, "Commercial Satellite Imagery as an Evolving Open-Source Verification Technology," Joint Research Centre, European Commission, 2015, 34. See also Oleg A. Bukharin, "From the Russian perspective: The Cold War atomic intelligence game, 1945–1970," *Studies in Intelligence* 48, no. 2 (2004), https://www.cia.gov/static/826e930085a20f893b891b25417c0a1f/Cold-War-Atomic-Intel.pdf.

19. James H. Hansen, "Learning from the past: Soviet deception in the Cuban missile crisis," *Studies in Intelligence* 46, no. 1 (2002), https://www.cia.gov/resources/csi/studies-in-intelligence/volume-46-no-1/soviet-deception-in-the-cuban-missile-crisis/, 34–35.

20. George J. Tenet, "DCI Remarks on Iraq's WMD Programs," February 5, 2004, http://web
.archive.org/web/20201111195134/https://www.cia.gov/news-information/speeches-testimony
/2004/tenet_georgetownspeech_02052004.html (accessed April 25, 2021).

21. William Tobey, "Cooperation in the Libya WMD disarmament case," *Studies in Intelligence* 61, no. 4, December 2017, https://www.cia.gov/static/c134fac60c8d3634a28629e6082d19
eb/Cooperation-in-Libya-WMD.pdf.

22. Office of the Director of National Intelligence, "Iran: Nuclear Intentions and Capabilities," National Intelligence Estimate, November 2007, https://www.dni.gov/files/documents
/Newsroom/Reports%20and%20Pubs/20071203_release.pdf.

23. Gregory F. Treverton, "Support to Policymakers: The 2007 NIE on Iran's Nuclear Intentions and Capabilities," Center for the Study of Intelligence, Central Intelligence Agency,
May 2013, Appendix A, 19, https://psu.pb.unizin.org/app/uploads/sites/65/2018/01/support
-to-policymakers-2007-nie.pdf (accessed April 25, 2021).

24. Greg Simmons, "Bush Administration Credibility Suffers after Iran NIE Report," Fox
News, December 7, 2007.

25. George W. Bush, *Decision Points* (New York: Crown, 2010), 418.

26. Treverton, "Support to Policymakers," vi.

27. For an excellent discussion of limitations of academic studies of nuclear proliferation,
see Alexander H. Montgomery and Scott D. Sagan, "The perils of predicting proliferation,"
Journal of Conflict Resolution 53, no. 2 (April 2009): 302–28.

28. Eliot A. Cohen, "Why we should stop studying the Cuban missile crisis," *National Interest*
no. 2 (Winter 1985–1986): 3–13.

29. Alexander H. Montgomery and Adam Mount, "Misestimation: Explaining U.S. failures
to predict nuclear weapons programs," *Intelligence and National Security* 29, no. 3 (2014): Appendix 357–86, http://people.reed.edu/~ahm/Projects/ProlifIntel/ProlifIntelAppendix.pdf.

30. Montgomery and Mount.

31. Montgomery and Mount, 371.

32. Central Intelligence Agency, "The Chances of an Imminent Communist Chinese Nuclear
Explosion," Special National Intelligence Estimate (SNIE)13-4-64, August 26, 1964, https://fas
.org/irp/cia/product/frus_30_043.htm.

33. Cullen G. Nutt, "Proof of the bomb: The influence of previous failure on intelligence
judgments of nuclear programs," *Security Studies* 28, no. 2 (2019): 321–59.

34. Together these and other tools have been called "public technical means." Christopher
Stubbs and Sidney Drell, "Public domain treaty compliance verification in the digital age," *IEEE
Technology and Society Magazine*, Winter 2013.

35. Central Intelligence Agency, "CORONA: America's First Imaging Satellite Program,"
CIA Museum, November 21, 2012, https://www.cia.gov/legacy/museum/exhibit/corona
-americas-first-imaging-satellite-program/.

36. Quoted in Philip Taubman, *Secret Empire: Eisenhower, the CIA, and the Hidden Story of
America's Space Espionage* (New York: Simon & Schuster, 2003), 35.

37. Bukharin, "From the Russian perspective."

38. Peter A. Gorin, "ZENIT: Corona's Soviet Counterpart," in *CORONA between the Sun
and the Earth*, edited by Robert A. MacDonald (Bethesda, Md.: American Society for

Photogrammetry and Remote Sensing, 1997), excerpts republished by the Central Intelligence Agency, April 29, 2013, https://web.archive.org/web/20201017111249/https://www.cia.gov/library/publications/intelligence-history/corona-between-the-sun-and-the-earth/introduction.html (accessed April 25, 2021); Peter A. Gorin, "Zenit: The Soviet Response to CORONA," in *Eye in the Sky: The Story of the CORONA Spy Satellites*, edited by Dwayne A. Day, John M. Logsdon, and Brian Latell (Washington, D.C.: Smithsonian Institution Press, 1998), 157–72.

39. Allison Puccioni, "Commercial lift-off," *IHS Jane's Intelligence Review*, December 2015, 53.

40. China more recently has joined that elite group. See Amy Zegart and Michael Morell, "Spies, lies, and algorithms," *Foreign Affairs* 98, no. 3 (May/June 2019).

41. Pabian, "Commercial Satellite Imagery," 6, 10, 11. Satellite launch dates and resolution data from Satellite Imagine Corporation, https://www.satimagingcorp.com/satellite-sensors/. Philip Bump, "Here's Why the Resolution of Satellite Images Never Seems to Improve," *Washington Post*, April 21, 2017, https://www.washingtonpost.com/news/politics/wp/2017/04/21/heres-why-the-resolution-of-satellite-images-never-seems-to-improve/. Commercial satellite imagery resolution is both a matter of technology and law. Satellites operated by the United States Intelligence Community produce even sharper resolutions but the precise specifications are classified. Commercial satellite operators must be cleared to sell photographs at certain resolutions.

42. Pabian, "Commercial Satellite Imagery," 16; Allison Puccioni, "Penetrating vision," *IHS Jane's Intelligence Review*, May 2016; Wisconsin Project on Nuclear Arms Control, "More Eyes on More Data: Prospects for Restricting Iran's Missile Program Using Open Sources," February 13, 2019. Electro-optical imagery is inherently limited because 50 percent of the earth's surface is cloud-covered at any given time. Puccioni, "Penetrating vision," 54.

43. Puccioni, 57. Most non-governmental organizations rely on basic, inexpensive electro-optical imagery that can only capture imagery in clear weather. But some are starting to use SAR and other more advanced capabilities. U.S. Geospatial Intelligence Foundation, "2019 State and Future of GEOINT Report," https://trajectorymagazine.com/wp-content/uploads/2019/01/2019-SaFoG-Extended-Final.pdf, 8.

44. Daniel R. Coats, "Statement for the Record: Worldwide Threat Assessment of the U.S. Intelligence Community," Senate Select Committee on Intelligence, January 29, 2019, 17.

45. Maxime Puteaux and Alexandre Najar, "Are Smallsats Entering the Maturity Stage?" Space News, August 6, 2019, https://spacenews.com/analysis-are-smallsats-entering-the-maturity-stage/.

46. See Allison Puccioni and Neil Ashdown, "Raising standards," *IHS Jane's Intelligence Review*, December 2019, 8.

47. Pabian, "Commercial Satellite Imagery," 14.

48. See planet.com, a company that provides commercial satellite imagery: https://www.planet.com/products/monitoring/.

49. Caleb Henry, "BlackSky Launching Two Satellites on June Starlink Mission," Space News, June 5, 2020, https://spacenews.com/blacksky-launching-two-satellites-on-june-starlink-mission/. See also BlackSky's website, https://www.blacksky.com/.

50. Pabian, "Commercial Satellite Imagery."

51. Niall McCarthy, "Giant chart: Global Internet usage by the numbers," *Forbes*, August 27, 2014, https://www.forbes.com/sites/niallmccarthy/2014/08/27/giant-chart-global-internet -usage-by-the-numbers/#1cb1938a7f7b.

52. Zegart and Morell, "Spies, lies, and algorithms."

53. Wisconsin Project on Nuclear Arms Control, "More Eyes on More Data: Prospects for Restricting Iran's Missile Program Using Open Sources," February 13, 2019.

54. North Korea is 120,000 square kilometers. Fixed sites can be found by machines. Mobile launchers are harder and still require human skills. Sandra Erwin, "With Commercial Satellite Imagery, Computer Learns to Quickly Find Missile Sites in China," Space News, October 19, 2017.

55. Jeffrey Lewis, "Applying New Tools to Nonproliferation: A Nuclear Detective Story," Nuclear Threat Initiative, May 2, 2016, chap. 4.

56. "Exoplanet Explorers Discover Five-Planet System," Electronic Specifier, January 12, 2018, https://www.electronicspecifier.com/industries/aerospace-defence/exoplanet-explorers -discover-five-planet-system.

57. Philip J. Marshall et al., "SPACE WARPS—I. crowdsourcing the discovery of gravitational lenses," *Monthly Notices of the Royal Astronomical Society*, January 11, 2016, https://academic.oup .com/mnras/article/455/2/1171/1103277; Adam Hadhazy, "Crowdsourcing the Universe: How Citizen Scientists Are Driving Discovery (Kavli Roundtable)," January 15, 2016, https://www .space.com/31626-crowdsourced-astronomy-finding-faint-galaxies-in-deep-space.html.

58. Melissa Hanham, Jeffrey Lewis, Catherine Dill, Grace Liu, Joseph Rodgers, Octave Lepi-nard, Brendan Knapp, Olivia Hallam, and Ben McIntosh, "Geo4Nonpro 2.0," CNS Occasional Paper #38, October 2018, Middlebury Institute of International Studies at Monterey, 19–20.

59. Allison Puccioni and Melissa Hanham, "OSINT transparency raises ethical questions," *IHS Jane's Intelligence Review*, February 12, 2018, 5.

60. Allison Puccioni and Neil Ashdown, "Raising standards," *IHS Jane's Intelligence Review*, December 2019; Ben Loehrke, Laura Rockwood, Melissa Hanham, and Luisa Kenausis, "The Gray Spectrum: Ethical Decision Making with Geospatial and Open Source Analysis," work-shop sponsored by The Stanley Center for Peace and Security and the Open Nuclear Network, Readout & Recommendations, July 2019.

61. Interview by author, July 2, 2020.

62. Author interviews and emails with several open-source nuclear analysts, June–July 2020; Zegart and Morell, "Spies, lies, and algorithms," 91.

63. Puccioni and Ashdown, "Raising standards," 8; Allison Puccioni, "Steady gaze," *IHS Jane's Intelligence Review*, December 2017, 56–57. This capability gap is expected to narrow. See Zegart and Morell, "Spies, lies, and algorithms."

64. In 2019 U.S. intelligence agencies spent $300 million on commercial imagery, and experts expect spending to increase in the next several years. Sandra Erwin, "Analysts: NRO's Com-mercial Imagery Purchases Could Reach $400 Million by 2023," Space News, June 29, 2020, https://spacenews.com/analysts-nros-commercial-imagery-purchases-could-reach-400 -million-by-2023/; Sandra Erwin, "Satellite Imagery Startups to Challenge Maxar for Big

Government Contracts," Space News, June 6, 2019, https://spacenews.com/satellite-imagery
-startups-to-challenge-maxar-for-big-government-contracts/.

65. Puccioni and Ashdown, "Raising standards," 7.

66. Zachary Dorfman, "True detectives," *Middlebury Magazine*, May 3, 2018.

67. Pabian, "Commercial Satellite Imagery," 31–32; Lewis, "Applying New Tools to Nonproliferation," chap. 3.

68. Jeffrey Lewis, "That secret Iranian 'nuclear facility' you just found? Not so much," *Foreign
Policy*, March 3, 2015; Lewis, "Applying New Tools to Nonproliferation." Lewis's team has published several significant studies. One was instrumental in proving that North Korea's 2016
submarine-launched ballistic missile test had failed—and that Kim Jong-Un's claims of success
were based on a doctored video. James Pearson, "North Korea Faked Missile Test Footage: U.S.
Experts," January 11, 2016, https://www.reuters.com/article/us-northkorea-missile-analysis
-idUSKCN0UQ0CC20160112; Anna Fitfield, "With Technology, These Researchers Are Figuring Out North Korea's Nuclear Secrets," *Washington Post*, November 21, 2017. See also Ellen
Nakashima and Joby Warrick. "U.S. Spy Agencies: North Korea Is Working on New Missiles,"
Washington Post, July 30, 2018.

69. Pabian, "Commercial Satellite Imagery," 38.

70. Frank Pabian and Siegfried S. Hecker, "Contemplating a third nuclear test in North
Korea," *Bulletin of the Atomic Scientists*, August 6, 2012, https://thebulletin.org/2012/08
/contemplating-a-third-nuclear-test-in-north-korea/.

71. Frank Pabian, Joseph S. Bermudez Jr., and Jack Liu, "The Punggye-ri Nuclear Test Site
Destroyed: A Good Start but New Questions Raised about Irreversibility," 38 North, May 31,
2018, https://www.38north.org/2018/05/punggye053118/.

72. Niko Milonopoulos, Siegfried S. Hecker, and Robert Carlin, "North Korea from 30,000
Feet," *Bulletin of the Atomic Scientists*, January 6, 2012, https://thebulletin.org/2012/01/north
-korea-from-30000-feet/.

73. Geospatial Intelligence Foundation, "2019 State and Future of GEOINT," 9. Good unclassified technical intelligence also gives policymakers the ability to bring evidence to international
debates more quickly because they don't need to request declassification. Cortney Weinbaum,
John V. Parachini, Richard S. Girven, Michael H. Decker, and Richard C. Baffa, "Perspectives
and Opportunities in Intelligence for U.S. Leaders," RAND Corporation, 2018.

74. Center for Strategic & International Studies, "CSIS Korea Chair Announces Research
Partnership with National Geospatial-Intelligence Agency (NGA)," May 22, 2018, https://www
.csis.org/news/csis-korea-chair-announces-research-partnership-national-geospatial
-intelligence-agency-nga.

75. Pabian, "Commercial Satellite Imagery," 25, 27. What's more, different imagery technologies require different, specialized training and experience. Interpreting electro-optical imagery
is not the same as interpreting images taken by Synthetic Aperture Radar satellites. Puccioni,
"Penetrating vision," 56.

76. David Albright, Frank Pabian, and Andrea Stricker, "The Fordow Enrichment Plant, aka Al
Ghadir: Iran's Nuclear Archive Reveals Site Originally Purposed to Produce Weapon-Grade Uranium for 1-2 Nuclear Weapons per Year," Institute for Science and International Security, March 13,
2009, http://isis-online.org/isis-reports/detail/the-fordow-enrichment-plant-aka-al-ghadir/.

77. Pabian, "Commercial Satellite Imagery," 25.

78. David B. Sandalow, "Remote Sensing and Foreign Policy," paper delivered at Symposium on Viewing the Earth: The Role of Satellite Earth Observations and Global Monitoring in International Affairs, George Washington University, Washington, D.C., June 6, 2000. Quoted in Pabian, "Commercial Satellite Imagery," 29, and in Laurie J. Schmidt, "New Tools for Diplomacy," NASA, 2019, https://earthdata.nasa.gov/learn/sensing-our-planet/new-tools-for-diplomacy.

79. Jeffrey Lewis, "Collected Thoughts on Phil Karber," Arms Control Wonk, December 7, 2011, https://www.armscontrolwonk.com/archive/204799/collected-thoughts-on-phil-karber/.

80. William Wan, "Georgetown Students Shed Light on China's Tunnel System for Nuclear Weapons," Washington Post, November 29, 2011, https://www.washingtonpost.com/world/national-security/georgetown-students-shed-light-on-chinas-tunnel-system-for-nuclear-weapons/2011/11/16/gIQA6AmKAO_story.html.

81. Hui Zhang, "The Defensive Nature of China's Underground Great Wall," Bulletin of the Atomic Scientists, January 16, 2012, https://thebulletin.org/2012/01/the-defensive-nature-of-chinas-underground-great-wall/.

82. Lewis, "Collected Thoughts on Phil Karber."

83. Zhang, "Defensive Nature of China's Underground Great Wall."

84. Sandalow, "Remote Sensing and Foreign Policy."

85. Zegart and Morell, "Spies, lies, and algorithms."

86. Mike Isaac, "Facebook Finds New Disinformation Campaigns and Braces for 2020 Torrent," New York Times, October 21, 2019, https://www.nytimes.com/2019/10/21/technology/facebook-disinformation-russia-iran.html.

87. Jessica Brandt and Torrey Taussig, "The Kremlin's Disinformation Playbook Goes to Beijing," Brookings, https://www.brookings.edu/blog/order-from-chaos/2020/05/19/the-kremlins-disinformation-playbook-goes-to-beijing/ (accessed September 26, 2020); Mark Scott, Laura Kayali, and Laurens Cerulus, "Brussels Accuses China of Peddling Disinformation," Politico, June 10, 2020, https://www.politico.com/news/2020/06/10/brussels-accuses-china-of-peddling-disinformation-311303 (accessed September 26, 2020).

88. Gwynne Roberts, "Was This Saddam's Bomb?" Sunday Times, February 25, 2001.

89. For Iraq's failed nuclear program, see Målfrid Braut-Hegghammer, Unclear Physics: Why Iraq and Libya Failed to Build Nuclear Weapons (Ithaca, N.Y.: Cornell University Press, 2016); Charles Duelfer, "Comprehensive Report of the Special Advisor to the DCI on Iraq's WMD," September 30, 2004, https://www.govinfo.gov/app/details/GPO-DUELFERREPORT/context; Joseph Cirincione, Jessica T. Mathews, George Perkovich, with Alexis Orton, "WMD in Iraq: Evidence and Implications," Carnegie Endowment for International Peace, January 2004, https://carnegieendowment.org/files/Iraq3FullText.pdf.

90. Frank V. Pabian unclassified email to author, October 17, 2019; Frank V. Pabian, "Commercial Satellite Imagery: Another Tool in the Nonproliferation Verification and Monitoring Tool-Kit," in Nuclear Safeguards, Security, and Nonproliferation, edited by James Doyle (Burlington, Mass.: Elsevier, 2008), 247, http://www.elsevier.com/books/nuclear-safeguards-security-and-nonproliferation/doyle/978-0-7506-8673-0#description; Larry O'Hanlon, "Seismic sleuths," Nature 411 (June 14, 2001): 734–36, https://www.nature.com/articles/35081281.pdf.

91. Gwynne Roberts, "Saddam's Bomb," BBC News, March 2, 2001, http://news.bbc.co.uk /2/hi/programmes/correspondent/1191203.stm. For Iraq's failed nuclear program, see Braut-Hegghammer, *Unclear Physics*; Duelfer, "Comprehensive Report of the Special Advisor"; Cirincione et al., "WMD in Iraq."

92. It also made it harder for the Soviets to retaliate against Pakistan and Egypt for assisting the American covert effort.

93. Bruce D. Berkowitz and Allan E. Goodman, "The Logic of Covert Action," *National Interest*, March 1, 1998. See also Austin Carson, *Secret Wars: Covert Conflict in International Politics* (Princeton, N.J.: Princeton University Press, 2018); Lindsey A. O'Rourke, *Covert Regime Change* (Ithaca, N.Y.: Cornell University Press, 2018).

94. Wisconsin Project on Nuclear Arms Control, "More Eyes on More Data," 3.

95. Joseph Bermudez, Victor Cha, and Lisa Collins, "Undeclared North Korea: The Sino-ri Missile Operating Base and Strategic Force Facilities," CSIS, January 21, 2019, https:// beyondparallel.csis.org/undeclared-north-korea-the-sino-ri-missile-operating-base-and-strategic -force-facilities/.

96. Interview by author with two nonproliferation experts, October 2019.

97. Lena H. Sun, "Report Identifies Another Secret North Korea Missile Site, One of 20," *Washington Post*, January 21, 2019, https://www.washingtonpost.com/politics/report-identifies -another-secret-north-korea-missile-site-one-of-20/2019/01/21/4066aeec-1db0-11e9-9145 -3f74070bbdb9_story.html; David E. Sanger and William J. Broad, "In North Korea, Missile Bases Suggest a Great Deception," *New York Times*, November 12, 2018, https://www.nytimes .com/2018/11/12/us/politics/north-korea-missile-bases.html; Courtney Kube and Carol E. Lee, "Report Finds Another Undisclosed North Korea Missile Site, Says There Are 19 More," NBC News, January 21, 2019, https://www.nbcnews.com/news/north-korea/report-finds -another-undisclosed-north-korea-missile-site-says-there-n958801.

98. Interview by author, October 2019.

99. Pabian, "Commercial Satellite Imagery," 35.

100. Puccioni and Ashdown, "Raising standards," 9.

101. Anna Fifield, "With Technology, These Researchers Are Figuring Out North Korea's Nuclear Secrets," *Washington Post*, November 21, 2017.

102. For more on this point, see Wisconsin Project on Nuclear Arms Control, "More Eyes on More Data."

103. Puccioni and Ashdown, "Raising standards," 8.

104. Puccioni and Ashdown, "Raising standards"; Loehrke et al., "Gray Spectrum."

Chapter 10: Decoding Cyber Threats

1. Susan M. Gordon, keynote address, GEOINT 2018 Symposium, April 24, 2018, https:// trajectorymagazine.com/building-to-scale-and-creating-anew/ (accessed September 24, 2020).

2. Claire Allbright, "A Russian Facebook Page Organized a Protest in Texas. A Different Russian Page Launched the Counterprotest," *Texas Tribune*, November 1, 2017, https://www .texastribune.org/2017/11/01/russian-facebook-page-organized-protest-texas-different-russian -page-l/.

3. U.S. Senate Select Committee on Intelligence, Hearing on Social Media Influence in the 2016 United States Elections, 115th Cong., 1st sess., November 1, 2017; U.S. Senate Select Committee on Intelligence, "Russian Active Measures Campaigns and Interference in the 2016 Election," Vol. 2: Russia's Use of Social Media with Additional Views, 116th Cong., 1st sess., October 2019, https://www.intelligence.senate.gov/sites/default/files/documents/Report _Volume2.pdf, 47.

4. Senate Select Committee on Intelligence, Hearing on Social Media Influence.

5. Descriptions are based on pictures displayed at Senate Select Committee on Intelligence, Hearing on Social Media Influence, https://www.intelligence.senate.gov/sites/default/files /documents/Exhibits%20used%20by%20Chairman%20Burr%20during%20the%202017-11 -01%20hearing.pdf.

6. Allbright, "Russian Facebook Page Organized."

7. Senate Select Committee on Intelligence, "Russian Active Measures Campaigns," 46–47.

8. Senate Select Committee on Intelligence, Hearing on Social Media Influence; Senate Select Committee on Intelligence, "Russian Active Measures Campaigns"; Robert S. Mueller III, "Report on the Investigation into Russian Interference in the 2016 Presidential Election," Vol. 1, March 2019, https://www.justice.gov/storage/report.pdf.

9. Senate Select Committee on Intelligence, "Russian Active Measures Campaigns," 22–62; *United States v. Internet Research Agency et al.*, indictment, Case 1:18-cr-00032-DLF (D.D.C. Feb. 16, 2018); Adrian Chen, "The Agency," *New York Times*, June 2, 2015, https://www.nytimes .com/2015/06/07/magazine/the-agency.html. For around-the-clock and hundreds of trolls, see Neil MacFarquhar, "Inside the Russian Troll Factory: Zombies and a Breakneck Pace," *New York Times*, February 18, 2018, https://www.nytimes.com/2018/02/18/world/europe/russia-troll -factory.html.

10. Terms such as *influence operations, information warfare, active measures, disinformation,* and *deception* are often used interchangeably in both academic and popular discourse. The core idea is the intentional spread of false information to deceive. Senate Select Committee on Intelligence, "Russian Active Measures Campaigns," 11. Although this chapter focuses on deception across borders, it is worth noting that the use of half-truths and outright lies has a storied history in domestic American political campaigns and played a major role in the January 6, 2021, Capitol siege by pro-Trump rioters seeking to stop congressional certification of the 2020 presidential election. See Jill Lepore, *These Truths: A History of the United States* (New York: W. W. Norton, 2018).

11. Senate Select Committee on Intelligence, "Russian Active Measures Campaigns," 46.

12. Mueller, "Report on the Investigation into Russian Interference," 4; *United States v. Internet Research Agency*, indictment, 12–13; Senate Select Committee on Intelligence, "Russian Active Measures Campaigns," 5, 29–32.

13. Senate Select Committee on Intelligence, Hearing on Social Media Influence.

14. Senate Select Committee on Intelligence, Hearing on Social Media Influence.

15. Senate Select Committee on Intelligence, Hearing on Social Media Influence. See also Intelligence Community Assessment, "Assessing Russian Activities and Intentions in Recent US Elections," January 2017; Senate Select Committee on Intelligence, "Russian Active Measures Campaigns"; MacFarquhar, "Inside the Russian Troll Factory."

16. Senate Select Committee on Intelligence, "Russian Active Measures Campaigns," 45–48.

17. Colin Stretch, testimony before U.S. Senate Select Committee on Intelligence, Hearing on Social Media Influence, https://www.intelligence.senate.gov/sites/default/files/documents/os-cstretch-110117.pdf.

18. Intelligence Community Assessment, "Assessing Russian Activities and Intentions"; Senate Select Committee on Intelligence, "Russian Active Measures Campaigns and Interference in the 2016 Election," Vol. 4: Review of the Intelligence Community Assessment, 116th Cong., 1st sess., https://www.intelligence.senate.gov/sites/default/files/documents/Report_Volume4.pdf. Twitter found more than 3,800 accounts controlled by Russians and 50,000 suspected Russian bots, accounts that automatically generated 2.1 million election-related Tweets receiving 454.7 million impressions during the final ten weeks of the 2016 presidential election. "Update on Twitter's Review of the 2016 US Election," blog post, Twitter, January 19, 2018, https://blog.twitter.com/official/en_us/topics/company/2018/2016-election-update.html; Gerrit De Vynck and Selina Wang, "Russian bots retweeted Trump's Twitter 470,000 times," *Bloomberg*, January 26, 2018, https://www.bloomberg.com/news/articles/2018-01-26/twitter-says-russian-linked-bots-retweeted-trump-470-000-times.

19. Kent Walker, testimony before U.S. Senate Select Committee on Intelligence, Hearing on Social Media Influence, https://www.intelligence.senate.gov/sites/default/files/documents/os-kwalker-110117.pdf.

20. Google discovered that suspected Russian agents uploaded more than one thousand YouTube videos about divisive social issues. Martin Matishak, "What we know about Russia's election hacking," *Politico*, July 18, 2018, https://www.politico.com/story/2018/07/18/russia-election-hacking-trump-putin-698087.

21. Stretch testimony. See also Mueller, "Report on the Investigation into Russian Interference," 26.

22. Intelligence Community Assessment, "Assessing Russian Activities and Intentions"; U.S. Senate Select Committee on Intelligence, "Russian Active Measures Campaigns and Interference in the 2016 U.S. Election," Vol. 1: Russian Efforts against Election Infrastructure with Additional Views, 116th Cong., 1st sess., https://www.intelligence.senate.gov/sites/default/files/documents/Report_Volume1.pdf; Senate Select Committee on Intelligence, Hearing on Social Media Influence, vol. 2; Senate Select Committee on Intelligence, Hearing on Social Media Influence vol. 4: Review of the Intelligence Community Assessment.

23. Russia successfully penetrated voter registration databases in Arizona and Illinois and attempted to infiltrate election infrastructures in nearly a dozen other states. No evidence to date indicates that Russian activities changed any vote tallies in the election. U.S. Senate Select Committee on Intelligence, Hearing on Russian Interference in the 2016 U.S. Elections, 115th Cong., 1st sess., June 21, 2017 (see in particular statement by Sen. Mark Warner and testimony by Sam Liles, acting director, cyber division, Office of Intelligence and Analysis, Department of Homeland Security), https://www.intelligence.senate.gov/sites/default/files/hearings/Russian%20Interference%20in%20the%202016%20U.S.%20Elections%20S.%20Hrg.%20115-92.pdf); Intelligence Community Assessment, "Assessing Russian Activities and Intentions"; Nicole Perlroth, Michael Wines, and Matthew Rosenberg, "Russian Election Hacking Efforts,

Wider Than Previously Known, Draw Little Scrutiny, *New York Times*, September 1, 2017 https://www.nytimes.com/2017/09/01/us/politics/russia-election-hacking.html.

24. Intelligence Community Assessment, "Assessing Russian Activities and Intentions." See also Senate Select Committee on Intelligence, "Russian Active Measures Campaigns," Vols. 1–5; Senate Select Committee on Intelligence, Hearing on Social Media Influence; Mueller, "Report on the Investigation into Russian Interference."

25. Quoted in David Shimer, *Rigged: America, Russia and One Hundred Years of Covert Electoral Interference* (New York: Knopf, 2020), 162.

26. For the warning to Obama, see Amy Zegart and Michael Morell, "Spies, lies, and algorithms," *Foreign Affairs* (May/June 2019); James Clapper with Trey Brown, *Facts and Fears* (New York: Penguin, 2018), 349–50; Susan Rice, *Tough Love* (New York: Simon and Schuster, 2019), 441–42. A month before the election, Secretary of Homeland Security Jeh Johnson and DNI James Clapper issued a rare public statement, noting that the recent hacking and dumping of information stolen from the Democratic National Committee and the Clinton campaign were authorized by "Russia's senior-most officials" and "intended to interfere with the US election process." Joint Statement from the Department of Homeland Security and Office of the Director of National Intelligence on Election Security, October 7, 2016, https://www.dhs.gov/news/2016/10/07/joint-statement-department-homeland-security-and-office-director-national.

27. Zegart and Morell, "Spies, lies, and algorithms."

28. Joint Statement on Election Security.

29. Zegart and Morell, "Spies, lies, and algorithms," 86.

30. Clapper, *Facts and Fears*, 303; Zegart and Morell, "Spies, lies, and algorithms," 87.

31. In 2018, the Senate Intelligence Committee found that its own investigation "exposed a far more extensive effort to manipulate social media outlets to sow discord and to interfere in the 2016 election and American society" than the U.S. Intelligence Community had found as late as 2017. U.S. Senate Select Committee on Intelligence, "The Intelligence Community Assessment," July 3, 2018, https://www.justsecurity.org/wp-content/uploads/2018/07/SSCI-ICA-ASSESSMENT_FINALJULY3.pdf, 3–4; Zegart and Morell, "Spies, lies, and algorithms."

32. William A. Owens, Kenneth W. Dam, and Herbert S. Lin, eds., *Technology, Policy, Law, and Ethics Regarding U.S. Acquisition and Use of Cyberattack Capabilities* (Washington, D.C.: National Academies Press, 2009), 1.

33. "Services, value added (% of GDP)," The World Bank, https://data.worldbank.org/indicator/NV.SRV.TOTL.ZS.

34. Kai-Fu Lee, interview with Scott Pelley, *60 Minutes*, CBS, January 13, 2019, https://www.cbsnews.com/news/60-minutes-ai-facial-and-emotional-recognition-how-one-man-is-advancing-artificial-intelligence/.

35. Interview by author, August 26, 2020.

36. "The world's most valuable resource is no longer oil, but data," *Economist*, May 6, 2017, https://www.economist.com/leaders/2017/05/06/the-worlds-most-valuable-resource-is-no-longer-oil-but-data.

37. Mark Seal, "An exclusive look at Sony's hacking saga," *Vanity Fair*, February 4, 2015, https://www.vanityfair.com/hollywood/2015/02/sony-hacking-seth-rogen-evan-goldberg.

38. Seal; Richard Stengel, "The untold story of the Sony hack: How North Korea's battle with Seth Rogen and George Clooney foreshadowed Russian election meddling in 2016," *Vanity Fair*, October 6, 2019, https://www.vanityfair.com/news/2019/10/the-untold-story-of-the-sony-hack.

39. Cecilia King, Drew Harwell, and Brian Fung, "North Korean Web Goes Dark Days after Obama Pledges Response to Sony Hack," *Washington Post*, December 22, 2014, https://www.washingtonpost.com/business/economy/north-korean-web-goes-dark-days-after-obama-pledges-response-to-sony-hack/2014/12/22/b76fa0a0-8a1d-11e4-9e8d-0c687bc18da4_story.html.

40. Rebecca Hersher, "North Korea Accidentally Reveals It Only Has 28 Websites," NPR, September 21, 2016, https://www.npr.org/sections/thetwo-way/2016/09/21/494902997/north-korea-accidentally-reveals-it-only-has-28-websites.

41. Rick Newman, "Here's How Lousy Life Is in North Korea," *U.S. News*, April 12, 2013, http://www.usnews.com/news/blogs/rick-newman/2013/04/12/heres-how-lousy-life-is-in-north-korea; Anna Fifield, "North Korean Drought Is Hobbling the Power Supply, and the Economy with It," *Washington Post*, June 21, 2015, https://www.washingtonpost.com/world/asia_pacific/north-korean-drought-is-hobbling-the-power-supply-and-the-economy-with-it/2015/06/21/65e51c02-14ff-11e5-8457-4b431bf7ed4c_story.html; Kevin Stahler, "North Korea's Cell Phone Growth in Context," Peterson Institute for International Economics, September 30, 2014, https://www.piie.com/blogs/north-korea-witness-transformation/new-research-cell-phone-use-north-korea.

42. John D. Negroponte, testimony before U.S. House Permanent Select Committee on Intelligence, "Annual Threat Assessment of the Director of National Intelligence," 110th Cong., 1st sess., January 18, 2007, https://www.dni.gov/files/documents/Newsroom/Testimonies/20070118_testimony.pdf.

43. Dennis C. Blair, testimony before U.S. House Permanent Select Committee on Intelligence, Annual Threat Assessment Hearing, 111th Cong., 1st sess., February 25, 2009, https://fas.org/irp/congress/2009_hr/hpsci-threat.pdf.

44. James R. Clapper, testimony before U.S. House Permanent Select Committee on Intelligence, "Worldwide Threat Assessment," 112th Cong., 2nd sess., February 2, 2012, https://www.dni.gov/files/documents/Newsroom/Testimonies/20120202_HPSCI%20WWTA%20-%20Oral%20Remarks%20as%20delivered.pdf.

45. James R. Clapper, "Statement for the Record: Worldwide Threat Assessment of the US Intelligence Community," Senate Committee on Armed Services, 113th Cong., 1st sess., April 18, 2013, https://www.dni.gov/files/documents/Intelligence%20Reports/UNCLASS_2013%20ATA%20SFR%20FINAL%20for%20SASC%2018%20Apr%202013.pdf.

46. Leon Panetta, remarks to the Business Executives for National Security, New York City, October 11, 2012, https://www.hsdl.org/?view&did=724128 (accessed April 25, 2021).

47. Elisabeth Bumiller and Thom Shanker, "Panetta Warns of Dire Threat of Cyberattack on U.S.," *New York Times*, October 11, 2012, https://www.nytimes.com/2012/10/12/world/panetta-warns-of-dire-threat-of-cyberattack.html.

48. Importantly, Carter publicly revealed in that speech that Russia was behind a recent cyber intrusion of the Defense Department's unclassified networks. Defense Secretary Ashton Carter, "Remarks by Secretary Carter at the Drell Lecture Cemex Auditorium, Stanford

Graduate School of Business, Stanford California," April 23, 2015, https://www.defense.gov
/Newsroom/Transcripts/Transcript/Article/607043/remarks-by-secretary-carter-at-the-drell
-lecture-cemex-auditorium-stanford-grad/ (accessed January 12, 2021).

49. U.S. Department of Defense, *Cyber Strategy*, April 2015, 5.

50. According to April 2015 congressional testimony by Eric Rosenbach, principal cyber advisor to the secretary of defense, "significant cyber attacks" represented "the top 2 percent, the most serious" cyber attacks against the United States. U.S. Senate Committee on Armed Services, Subcommittee on Emerging Threats and Capabilities, Hearing on Military Cyber Program and Posture Review of the Defense Authorization Request for FY2016 and the Future Years Defense Program, 114th Cong., 1st sess., April 14, 2015.

51. Department of Defense, *Cyber Strategy*, 5.

52. For example, in one of the earliest known cyber operations, the 1999 Serbian bombing campaign, a Pentagon unit hacked into Serbia's air defense systems to make it appear U.S. planes were coming from a different direction than they really were. Michèle Flournoy and Michael Sulmeyer, "Battlefield Internet," *Foreign Affairs*, September/October 2018, https://www
.foreignaffairs.com/articles/world/2018-08-14/battlefield-internet.

53. U.S. Cyber Command, *Achieve and Maintain Cyberspace Superiority: Command Vision for US Cyber Command* (March 23, 2018), 3; Department of Defense, *Summary of the 2018 National Defense Strategy of the United States of America*, https://dod.defense.gov/Portals/1/Documents
/pubs/2018-National-Defense-Strategy-Summary.pdf.

54. Herbert Lin, "Thoughts on threat assessment in cyberspace," *I/S: A Journal of Law and Policy for the Information Society* 8, no. 2 (2012): 348–49.

55. For more on deterrence in the era of emerging technology, see Amy Zegart, "Cheap fights, credible threats," *Journal of Strategic Studies* 43, no. 1 (February 2018): 6–46.

56. Flournoy and Sulmeyer, "Battlefield Internet."

57. Paul M. Nakasone and Michael Sulmeyer, "How to compete in cyberspace," *Foreign Affairs*, August 25, 2020, https://www.foreignaffairs.com/articles/united-states/2020-08-25
/cybersecurity.

58. Cyber Command, *Achieve and Maintain Cyberspace*; Nakasone and Sulmeyer, "How to compete in cyberspace."

59. CSIS/McAfee, "Economic Impact of Cybercrime: No Slowing Down," February 2018, https://www.mcafee.com/enterprise/en-us/assets/reports/restricted/rp-economic-impact
-cybercrime.pdf.

60. Rebecca Hersher, "Meet Mafiaboy, the 'Bratty Kid' Who Took Down the Internet," NPR, February 7, 2015, http://www.npr.org/sections/alltechconsidered/2015/02/07/384567322
/meet-mafiaboy-the-bratty-kid-who-took-down-the-internet; Robert McMillan, "Mafiaboy grows up: A hacker seeks redemption," *Computer World*, October 13, 2008, http://www
.computerworld.com/article/2533517/mafiaboy-grows-up--a-hacker-seeks-redemption.html.

61. Kate Conger and Nathaniel Popper, "Florida Teenager Is Charged as 'Mastermind' of Twitter Hack," *New York Times*, July 31, 2020, https://www.nytimes.com/2020/07/31
/technology/twitter-hack-arrest.html.

62. Cyberspace Solarium Commission, "Final Report," March 2020, https://drive.google
.com/file/d/1ryMCIL_dZ30QyjFqFkkf10MxIXJGT4yv/view (accessed September 24, 2020).

63. Cyber Operations Tracker, database, Council on Foreign Relations, https://www.cfr.org/cyber-operations/.

64. Daniel R. Coats, "Statement for the Record: Worldwide Threat Assessment of the US Intelligence Community," Senate Select Committee on Intelligence, January 29, 2019.

65. CSIS/McAfee, "Economic Impact of Cybercrime."

66. Michelle Nichols, "North Korea Took $2 Billion in Cyberattacks to Fund Weapons Program: UN Report," Reuters, August 5, 2019, https://www.reuters.com/article/us-northkorea-cyber-un/north-korea-took-2-billion-in-cyberattacks-to-fund-weapons-program-u-n-report-idUSKCN1UV1ZX.

67. White House, "National Cyber Strategy of the United States of America," September 2018, https://trumpwhitehouse.archives.gov/wp-content/uploads/2018/09/National-Cyber-Strategy.pdf, 2.

68. *United States v. Su Bin*, plea agreement, No. SA CR 14-131 (C.D. Cal. Mar. 22, 2016), https://www.justice.gov/opa/file/834936/download.

69. Keith Alexander, testimony before U.S. Senate Armed Services Committee, "Future of Warfare," 114th Cong., 1st sess., November 3, 2015, https://www.armed-services.senate.gov/imo/media/doc/Alexander_11-03-15.pdf. FBI Director Christopher Wray issued a similar warning in 2020. Wray, remarks, "China's Attempt to Influence U.S. Elections," Hudson Institute, Washington, D.C., July 7, 2020, https://www.fbi.gov/news/speeches/the-threat-posed-by-the-chinese-government-and-the-chinese-communist-party-to-the-economic-and-national-security-of-the-united-states.

70. U.S. Department of Justice, press release, "U.S. Charges Five Chinese Military Hackers for Cyber Espionage Against U.S. Corporations and a Labor Organization for Commercial Advantage," May 19, 2014, https://www.justice.gov/opa/pr/us-charges-five-chinese-military-hackers-cyber-espionage-against-us-corporations-and-labor.

71. White House, Office of the Press Secretary, "Fact Sheet: President Xi Jinping's State Visit to the United States," September 25, 2015, https://obamawhitehouse.archives.gov/the-press-office/2015/09/25/fact-sheet-president-xi-jinpings-state-visit-united-states.

72. Ellen Nakashima, "Powerful NSA Hacking Tools Have Been Revealed Online," *Washington Post*, August 16, 2016, https://www.washingtonpost.com/world/national-security/powerful-nsa-hacking-tools-have-been-revealed-online/2016/08/16/bce4f974-63c7-11e6-96c0-37533479f3f5_story.html; Scott Shane, Matthew Rosenberg, and Andrew Lehren, "WikiLeaks Releases Trove of Alleged C.I.A. Hacking Documents," *New York Times*, March 7, 2017, https://www.nytimes.com/2017/03/07/world/europe/wikileaks-cia-hacking.html. A 2008 cyberattack compromised the Defense Department's classified and unclassified networks and gave rise to the creation of U.S. Cyber Command. Nakasone and Sulmeyer, "How to compete in cyberspace"; William J. Lynn III, "Defending a new domain: The Pentagon's cyberstrategy," *Foreign Affairs*, September/October 2010, https://www.foreignaffairs.com/articles/united-states/2010-09-01/defending-new-domain.

73. Chris Inglis, "Illuminating a New Domain," in *Bytes, Bombs and Spies*, edited by Herb Lin and Amy Zegart (Washington, D.C.: Brookings Institution Press, 2019).

74. Damian Paletta, "Former CIA Chief Says Government Data Breach Could Help China Recruit Spies," *Wall Street Journal*, June 15, 2015, https://www.wsj.com/articles/former-cia-chief-says-government-data-breach-could-help-china-recruit-spies-1434416996.

75. Nakasone and Sulmeyer, "How to compete in cyberspace."

76. Rosenbach testimony.

77. For attribution to Chinese government, see U.S. Department of Justice, "Attorney General William P. Barr Announces Indictment of Four Members of China's Military for Hacking into Equifax," February 10, 2020, https://www.justice.gov/opa/speech/attorney-general -william-p-barr-announces-indictment-four-members-china-s-military; Garrett M. Graff, "China's hacking spree will have a decades-long fallout," *Wired*, February 11, 2020, https://www .wired.com/story/china-equifax-anthem-marriott-opm-hacks-data/; Cyberspace Solarium Commission, "Final Report," 10.

78. Graff, "China's hacking spree."

79. Paletta, "Former CIA Chief."

80. Damian Paletta, "U.S. Intelligence Chief James Clapper Suggests China Behind OPM Breach," *Wall Street Journal*, June 25, 2015, https://www.wsj.com/articles/SB10007111583511843 69540458106986317089950 4.

81. David E. Sanger and Nicole Perlroth, "FireEye, a Top Cybersecurity Firm, Says It Was Hacked by a Nation-State," *New York Times*, December 8, 2020, https://www.nytimes.com/2020 /12/08/technology/fireeye-hacked-russians.html (accessed January 12, 2021); William Turton and Kartikay Mehrotra, "FireEye discovered SolarWinds breach while probing own hack," *Bloomberg*, December 14, 2020, https://www.bloomberg.com/news/articles/2020-12-15/fireeye -stumbled-across-solarwinds-breach-while-probing-own-hack (accessed January 12, 2021).

82. Dustin Volz and Robert McMillan, "SolarWinds Hack Breached Justice Department System," *Wall Street Journal*, January 6, 2021, https://www.wsj.com/articles/solarwinds-hack -breached-justice-department-systems-11609958761 (accessed January 12, 2021); Amy Zegart, "Everybody spies in cyberspace. The U.S. must plan accordingly," *Atlantic*, December 30, 2020, https://www.theatlantic.com/ideas/archive/2020/12/everybody-spies-cyberspace-us-must -plan-accordingly/617522/.

83. "Joint Statement by the Federal Bureau of Investigation (FBI), the Cybersecurity and Infrastructure Security Agency (CISA), the Office of the Director of National Intelligence (ODNI), and the National Security Agency (NSA)," January 5, 2021, https://www.cisa.gov /news/2021/01/05/joint-statement-federal-bureau-investigation-fbi-cybersecurity-and -infrastructure (accessed January 12, 2021).

84. Zegart, "Everybody spies in cyberspace."

85. Emily Tamkin, "10 years after the landmark attack on Estonia, is the world better prepared for cyber threats?" *Foreign Policy*, April 27, 2017, https://foreignpolicy.com/2017/04/27/10-years -after-the-landmark-attack-on-estonia-is-the-world-better-prepared-for-cyber-threats/.

86. Laurens Cerulus, "How Ukraine became a test bed for cyberweaponry," *Politico*, February 14, 2019, https://www.politico.eu/article/ukraine-cyber-war-frontline-russia-malware -attacks/.

87. Andy Greenberg, "New clues show how Russia's grid hackers aimed for physical destruc- tion," *Wired*, September 12, 2019, https://www.wired.com/story/russia-ukraine-cyberattack -power-grid-blackout-destruction/; Cyberspace Solarium Commission, "Final Report," 18.

88. Cerulus, "How Ukraine became a test bed for cyberweaponry;" Andy Greenberg, "The untold story of NotPetya, the most devastating cyberattack in history," Wired, August 22, 2018, https://www.wired.com/story/notpetya-cyberattack-ukraine-russia-code-crashed-the-world/.

89. For "into the wild," see David Sanger, *The Perfect Weapon: War, Sabotage, and Fear in the Cyber Age* (New York: Crown, 2018), 22. For "watershed," see Paul D. Shinkman, "Former CIA Director: Cyber Attack Game-Changers Comparable to Hiroshima," *U.S. News*, February 20, 2013, https://www.usnews.com/news/articles/2013/02/20/former-cia-director-cyber-attack-game-changers-comparable-to-hiroshima.

90. David Sanger, "Obama Order Sped Up Wave of Cyberattacks against Iran," *New York Times*, June 1, 2012, https://www.nytimes.com/2012/06/01/world/middleeast/obama-ordered-wave-of-cyberattacks-against-iran.html; Sanger, *Perfect Weapon*. Former CIA Director Michael Hayden acknowledges in his memoir only that "someone was destroying their centrifuges with a cyber weapon." Hayden, *Playing to the Edge: American Intelligence in the Age of Terror* (New York: Penguin, 2016), 307.

91. Panetta remarks.

92. Cyberspace Solarium Commission, "Final Report," 12.

93. Stengel, "Untold story of the Sony hack."

94. George W. Bush, *Decision Points* (New York: Broadway Books, 2010), 415–20; Hayden, *Playing to the Edge*, 290–309.

95. Sanger, "Obama Order Sped Up"; "Iran to Push for 50,000 Centrifuges," NTI, April 18, 2007, https://www.nti.org/gsn/article/iran-to-push-for-50000-centrifuges/.

96. Bush, *Decision Points*, 415–20; Robert Gates, *Duty: Memoirs of a Secretary at War* (New York: Crown, 2014), 189–92; Sanger, "Obama Order Sped Up."

97. Gates, *Duty*, 190–92. See also Sanger, "Obama Order Sped Up"; Sanger, *Perfect Weapon*, 21.

98. Sanger, "Obama Order Sped Up."

99. Carey Nachenberg, remarks, "A Forensic Discussion of Stuxnet," Center for International Security and Cooperation, Stanford University, April 23, 2012.

100. Sanger, "Obama Order Sped Up."

101. David Kushner, "The Real Story of Stuxnet," IEEE Spectrum, February 26, 2013, https://spectrum.ieee.org/telecom/security/the-real-story-of-stuxnet.

102. Sanger, *Perfect Weapon*, 21.

103. Nachenberg remarks; Ellen Nakashima and Joby Warrick, "Stuxnet Was Work of US and Israeli Experts, Officials Say," *Washington Post*, June 2, 2012, https://www.washingtonpost.com/world/national-security/stuxnet-was-work-of-us-and-israeli-experts-officials-say/2012/06/01/gJQAInEy6U_story.html.

104. Nakashima and Warrick; Sanger, "Obama Order Sped Up"; Hayden, *Playing to the Edge*, 151.

105. Shinkman, "Former CIA Director."

106. Amy Zegart, "The tools of espionage are going mainstream," *Atlantic*, November 27, 2017, https://www.theatlantic.com/international/archive/2017/11/deception-russia-election-meddling-technology-national-security/546644/.

107. Senate Select Committee on Intelligence, "Russian Active Measures Campaigns," Vol. 2, 12.

108. Christopher M. Andrew and Vasili Mitrokhin, *The Sword and the Shield: The Mitrokhin Archive & the Secret History of the KGB* (New York: Basic Books, 1985), 244–45.

109. Senate Select Committee on Intelligence, "Russian Active Measures Campaigns," Vol. 2, 15–20.

110. Senate Select Committee on Intelligence, "Russian Active Measures Campaign," Vol. 2.

111. RT is described in Intelligence Community Assessment, "Assessing Russian Activities and Intentions," as Russia's "principal international propaganda outlet" (13).

112. Christopher Paul and Miriam Matthews, "The Russian 'Firehose of Falsehood' Propaganda Model," RAND Perspective, 2016, https://www.rand.org/pubs/perspectives/PE198 .html, 2.

113. Analysis of YouTube news subscribers by author. As of February 18, 2019, RT had 3.3 million subscribers, while Fox News had 2.5 million, CBS News had 1.2 million, and NBC News had 1.1 million. CNN and ABC News surpassed RT, with 6 million and 5.3 million subscribers, respectively. As a RAND report noted, Russia has created a "disinformation chain" that reaches deep within targeted societies and consists of four key, often overlapping, links: (1) leadership from the Kremlin; (2) organs and proxies such as RT; (3) amplification channels such as social media platforms, fake and real accounts, bots, American news media, and unaffiliated websites that either intentionally or unintentionally amplify messages; and (4) consumers who spread the Russian narratives by retweeting, posting, or promoting content. Elizabeth Bodine-Baron, Todd C. Helmus, Andrew Radin, and Elina Treyger, "Countering Russian Social Media Influence," RAND, 2018, https://www.rand.org/pubs/research_reports/RR2740.html.

114. Paul and Matthews, "Russian 'Firehose of Falsehood.'"

115. Stephanie Bodoni, "China, Russia are spreading virus misinformation, EU says," *Bloomberg,* June 10, 2020, https://www.bloomberg.com/news/articles/2020-06-10/eu-points-finger -at-china-russia-for-covid-19-disinformation. See also "EEAS Special Report Update: Short Assessment of Narratives and Disinformation Around the COVID-19 Pandemic," EUvsDiS-iNFO, May 20, 2020, https://euvsdisinfo.eu/eeas-special-report-update-short-assessment-of -narratives-and-disinformation-around-the-covid19-pandemic-updated-23-april-18-may/; Kathy Gilsinian, "How China is planning to win back the world," *Atlantic,* May 28, 2020, https:// www.theatlantic.com/politics/archive/2020/05/china-disinformation-propaganda-united -states-xi-jinping/612085/.

116. "Statement by NCSC Director William Evanina: 100 Days Until Election 2020," press release, Office of the Director of National Intelligence, July 24, 2020, https://www.dni.gov/index .php/newsroom/press-releases/item/2135-statement-by-ncsc-director-william-evanina-100 -days-until-election-2020; "Statement by NCSC Director William Evanina: Election Threat Update for the American Public," press release, Office of the Director of National Intelligence, August 7, 2020, https://www.dni.gov/index.php/newsroom/press-releases/item/2139 -statement-by-ncsc-director-william-evanina-election-threat-update-for-the-american-public; Robert Draper, "Unwanted Truths: Inside Trump's Battles with U.S. Intelligence Agencies," *New York Times,* August 8, 2020, https://www.nytimes.com/2020/08/08/magazine/us-russia -intelligence.html?.

117. Adam Entous and Ronan Farrow, "Private Mossad for hire," *New Yorker,* February 11, 2019, https://www.newyorker.com/magazine/2019/02/18/private-mossad-for-hire.

118. Mark Mazzetti, Ronen Bergman, David D. Kirkpatrick, and Maggie Haberman, "Rick Gates Sought Online Manipulation Plans from Israeli Intelligence Firm for Trump Campaign," *New York Times,* October 8, 2018, https://www.nytimes.com/2018/10/08/us/politics/rick-gates -psy-group-trump.html.

119. Quoted in Entous and Farrow, "Private Mossad for hire."

120. David Bauder and Calvin Woodward, "Expert: Acosta Video Distributed by White House Was Doctored," Associated Press, November 8, 2018, https://apnews.com/c575bd1cc3b 1456cb3057ef670c7fe2a; Drew Harwell, "White House Shares Doctored Video to Support Punishment of Journalist Jim Acosta," *Washington Post*, November 8, 2018, https://www .washingtonpost.com/technology/2018/11/08/white-house-shares-doctored-video-support -punishment-journalist-jim-acosta/.

121. Drew Harwell, "Fake Pelosi Videos, Slowed to Make Her Appear Drunk, Spread across Social Media," *Washington Post*, May 24, 2019, https://www.washingtonpost.com/technology /2019/05/23/faked-pelosi-videos-slowed-make-her-appear-drunk-spread-across-social-media/.

122. Cade Metz, "A Fake Zuckerberg Video Challenges Facebook's Rules," *New York Times*, June 11, 2019, https://www.nytimes.com/2019/06/11/technology/fake-zuckerberg-video -facebook.html.

123. Tero Karras, Timo Aila, Samuli Laine, and Jaako Lehtinen, "Progressive Growing of GANS for Improved Quality, Stability, and Variation," conference paper at ICLR 2018, https:// research.nvidia.com/sites/default/files/pubs/2017-10_Progressive-Growing-of/karras2018iclr -paper.pdf.

124. Catherine Stupp, "Fraudsters Used AI to Mimic CEO's Voice in Unusual Cybercrime Case," *Wall Street Journal*, August 30, 2019, https://www.wsj.com/articles/fraudsters-use-ai-to -mimic-ceos-voice-in-unusual-cybercrime-case-11567157402.

125. Kaylee Fagan, "A Viral Video That Appeared to Show Obama Calling Trump a 'Dips—' Shows a Disturbing New Trend Called 'Deepfakes,'" *Business Insider*, April 17, 2018, https://www .businessinsider.com/obama-deepfake-video-insulting-trump-2018-4; Supasorn Suwajanakorn, Steven M. Seitz, and Ira Kemelmacher-Shlizerman, "Synthesizing Obama: Learning Lip Sync from Audio," *ACM Transactions on Graphics* 36, no. 4 (July 2017), http://grail.cs.washington.edu /projects/AudioToObama/siggraph17_obama.pdf; Drew Harwell, "Top AI Researchers Race to Detect 'Deepfake' Videos: 'We Are Outgunned,'" *Washington Post*, June 12, 2019, https://www .washingtonpost.com/technology/2019/06/12/top-ai-researchers-race-detect-deepfake-videos -we-are-outgunned/.

126. Martin Giles, "The GANfather: The man who's given machines the gift of imagination," *MIT Technology Review*, February 21, 2018, https://www.technologyreview.com/s/610253/the -ganfather-the-man-whos-given-machines-the-gift-of-imagination/.

127. Harwell, "Top AI Researchers Race."

128. "FaceIt," Github, March 6, 2018, https://github.com/goberoi/faceit; Zegart and Morell, "Spies, lies, and algorithms."

129. U.S. Senate Select Committee on Intelligence, Hearing to Consider Worldwide Threats, 116th Cong., 1st sess., January 29, 2019, https://www.intelligence.senate.gov/hearings/open -hearing-worldwide-threats; U.S. House Permanent Select Committee on Intelligence, Hearing: National Security Challenges of Artificial Intelligence, Manipulated Media and Deepfakes, 116th Cong., 1st sess., June 13, 2019.

130. Adam Schiff, remarks, House Permanent Select Committee on Intelligence, Hearing: National Security Challenges of Artificial Intelligence, Manipulated Media and Deepfakes, 116th Cong., 1st sess., June 13, 2019.

131. Sanger, *Perfect Weapon*; Kim Zetter, *Countdown to Zero Day: Stuxnet and the Launch of the World's First Digital Weapon* (New York: Crown, 2015). Cybersecurity experts at Symantec believe a version of the Stuxnet virus was deployed as early as 2005 but the virus was not publicly discovered until 2010. Jim Finkle, "Researchers Say Stuxnet Was Deployed against Iran in 2007," Reuters, February 26, 2013, https://www.reuters.com/article/us-cyberwar-stuxnet/researchers-say-stuxnet -was-deployed-against-iran-in-2007-idUSBRE91P0PP20130226.

132. Sanger, *Perfect Weapon*, 268–85.

133. David Sanger and William Broad, "Trump Inherits a Secret Cyberwar against North Korean Missiles," *New York Times*, March 4, 2017, https://www.nytimes.com/2017/03/04 /world/asia/north-korea-missile-program-sabotage.html.

134. Robert McMillan, "Hackers Lurked in SolarWinds Email System for at Least 9 Months, CEO Says," *Wall Street Journal*, February 2, 2021.

135. Herbert Lin, "The existential threat from cyber-enabled info warfare," *Bulletin of Atomic Scientists* 74, no. 4 (July 2019).

136. John Markoff, "Chip Error Continuing to Dog Officials at Intel," *New York Times*, December 6, 1994, https://www.nytimes.com/1994/12/06/business/chip-error-continuing-to -dog-officials-at-intel.html.

137. David Manners, "How much will the flaws cost Intel," *Electronics Weekly*, January 8, 2018, https://www.electronicsweekly.com/blogs/mannerisms/shenanigans/much-will-flaws-cost -intel-2018-01/; Desire Athow, "Pentium, FDIV: The Processor Bug that Shook the World," TechRadar, October 30, 2014, https://www.techradar.com/news/computing-components /processors/pentium-fdiv-the-processor-bug-that-shook-the-world-1270773.

138. Interview by author, September 13, 2020.

139. Inglis, "Illuminating a New Domain," 25.

140. Inglis.

141. "The IoT Rundown for 2020: Stats, Risks, and Solutions," Security Today, January 13, 2020, https://securitytoday.com/Articles/2020/01/13/The-IoT-Rundown-for-2020.aspx?Page=2.

142. Hackers broke into more than 100,000 consumer gadgets, such as home-networking routers, televisions, and at least one refrigerator, sending more than 750,000 malicious emails worldwide. See "Your Fridge Is Full of SPAM: Proof of an IoT-Driven Attack," blog post, Proof-Point, January 16, 2014, https://www.proofpoint.com/us/threat-insight/post/Your-Fridge-is -Full-of-SPAM.

143. Andy Greenberg, "Hackers remotely kill a Jeep on the highway—with me in it," *Wired*, July 21, 2015, http://www.wired.com/2015/07/hackers-remotely-kill-jeep-highway/.

144. Called MIRAI botnet, the October 2016 attack was the first IoT-based massive cyberattack.

145. Saleh Solton, Prateek Mittal, and H. Vincent Poor, "BlackIoT: IoT Botnet of High Wattage Devices Can Disrupt the Power Grid," presented at USINEX Security Symposium, August 2018, https://www.princeton.edu/~pmittal/publications/blackiot-usenix18.pdf.

146. These software weaknesses are known as *zero day* vulnerabilities because they were originally unknown to the vendor.

147. U.S. Cyber Command, *Achieve and Maintain Cyberspace*, 4.

148. Inglis, "Illuminating a New Domain," 24.

149. Robert M. Gates, remarks, United States Military Academy, West Point, New York, February 25, 2011. For other military leaders issuing similar remarks, see Micha Zenko, "100% right 0% of the time," *Foreign Policy*, October 16, 2012, https://foreignpolicy.com/2012/10/16/100-right-0-of-the-time/.

150. Amy Zegart, *Spying Blind: The CIA, the FBI, and the Origins of 9/11* (Princeton, N.J.: Princeton University Press, 2007), 97.

151. Inglis, "Illuminating a New Domain," 24.

152. Lin, "Thoughts on threat assessment in cyberspace," 344.

153. Ellen Nakashima, "Dismantling of Saudi-CIA Web site illustrates need for clearer cyberwar policies," *Washington Post*, March 19, 2010, https://www.washingtonpost.com/wp-dyn/content/article/2010/03/18/AR2010031805464_pf.html.

154. Rajesh De, remarks at Georgetown University Law School, February 27, 2013, https://www.nsa.gov/news-features/speeches-testimonies/Article/1620139/remarks-of-rajesh-de-general-counsel-national-security-agency-georgetown-law-sc/.

155. Hayden, *Playing to the Edge*, 147.

156. Flournoy and Sulmeyer, "Battlefield Internet."

157. Hayden, *Playing to the Edge*, 147.

158. Senate Select Committee on Intelligence, "Russian Active Measures Campaigns," Vol. 2, 73, 78.

159. "Former Top DNI Official Sue Gordon Discusses Circumstances of Her Departure from ODNI—Transcript," interview by Michael Morell, *Intelligence Matters*, CBS, February 14, 2020, https://www.cbsnews.com/news/former-top-dni-official-sue-gordon-discusses-circumstances-of-her-departure-from-odni-transcript/.

160. Gordon interview by Morell.

161. U.S. Senate Committees on the Judiciary and Commerce, Science, and Transportation, "Facebook, Social Media Privacy, and the Use and Abuse of Data," 115th Cong., 2nd sess., April 10, 2018, https://www.washingtonpost.com/news/the-switch/wp/2018/04/10/transcript-of-mark-zuckerbergs-senate-hearing/.

162. Amy Zegart and Kevin Childs, "The divide between Silicon Valley and Washington is a national-security threat," *Atlantic*, December 13, 2018; Sheera Frenkel et al., "Delay, Deny and Deflect: How Facebook's Leaders Fought through Crisis," *New York Times*, November 14, 2018, https://www.nytimes.com/2018/11/14/technology/facebook-data-russia-election-racism.html.

163. Liam Tung, "Google: Here's Why We're Pulling Out of Pentagon's $10bn JEDI Cloud Race," ZDNet, October 9, 2018, https://www.zdnet.com/article/google-heres-why-were-pulling-out-of-pentagons-10bn-jedi-cloud-race/; Kate Conger, David E. Sanger, and Scott Shane, "Microsoft Wins Pentagon's $10 Billion JEDI Contract, Thwarting Amazon," *New York Times*, October 25, 2019, https://www.nytimes.com/2019/10/25/technology/dod-jedi-contract.html.

164. Google Employees Against Dragonfly, "We Are Google Employees. Google Must Drop Dragonfly," Medium, November 27, 2018, https://medium.com/@googlersagainstdragonfly/we-are-google-employees-google-must-drop-dragonfly-4c8a30c5e5eb; Letter from Marco Rubio et al. to Google CEO Sundar Pichai, August 3, 2018, https://www.rubio.senate.gov/public/_cache/files/9b139bf6-d0c1-4969-aaf2-4a4aede8ed35/397FE4632728A13B6EEABDB5956550

AC.8-3-18-letter-to-mr.-pichai-re-censorship-in-china.pdf; Olivia Solon, "Google's 'Project Dragonfly' Censored Search Engine Triggers Protests," NBC News, January 18, 2019, https:// www.nbcnews.com/tech/tech-news/google-s-project-dragonfly-censored-search-engine -triggers-protests-n960121; Jeb Su, "Confirmed: Google terminated Project Dragonfly, its censored Chinese search engine," *Forbes*, July 19, 2019, https://www.forbes.com/sites/jeanbaptiste /2019/07/19/confirmed-google-terminated-project-dragonfly-its-censored-chinese-search -engine/#6454c4567e84.

165. U.S. Senate Committee on the Judiciary, Subcommittee on the Constitution, Hearing on Google and Censorship, 116th Cong., 1st sess., July 16, 2019.

166. Zegart and Childs, "Divide between Silicon Valley and Washington."

167. Zegart and Childs.

SELECTED READING

Aberbach, Joel. 1990. *Keeping a Watchful Eye: The Politics of Congressional Oversight*. Washington, D.C.: Brookings Institution Press.

Alexander, Keith. 2015. Testimony before the Senate Armed Services Committee, "Future of Warfare." 114th Cong., 1st sess., November 3.

Allen, Michael. 2013. *Blinking Red: Crisis and Compromise in American Intelligence after 9/11*. Dulles, Va.: Potomac Books.

Allison, Graham and Philip Zelikow. 1999. *Essence of Decision: Explaining the Cuban Missile Crisis*, 2nd edition. New York: Longman Press.

Andrew, Christopher. 1996. *For the President's Eyes Only: Secret Intelligence and the American Presidency from Washington to Bush*. New York: Harper Perennial.

Andrew, Christopher. 2018. *The Secret World: A History of Intelligence*. New Haven, Conn.: Yale University Press.

Andrew, Christopher M. and Vasili Mitrokhin. 1985. *The Sword and the Shield: The Mitrokhin Archive & the Secret History of the KGB*. New York: Basic Books.

Baer, Robert. 2002. *See No Evil: The True Story of a Ground Soldier in the CIA's War on Terrorism*. New York: Crown.

Bakos, Nada. 2019. *The Targeter*. New York: Little, Brown.

Bamford, James. 1982. *The Puzzle Palace*. New York: Penguin.

Bamford, James. 2001. *Body of Secrets: Anatomy of the Ultra-Secret National Security Agency*. New York: Doubleday.

Bamford, James. 2008. *The Shadow Factory: The Ultra-Secret NSA from 9/11 to the Eavesdropping on America*. New York: Anchor Books.

Barrett, David M. 2005. *The CIA and Congress: The Untold Story from Truman to Kennedy*. Lawrence, Kan.: University Press of Kansas.

Bennett, Gina. 2008. *National Security Mom*. Deadwood, Ore.: Wyatt-MacKenzie.

Bergen, Peter. 2011. *The Longest War: The Enduring Conflict between America and Al Qaeda*. New York: Free Press.

Bergen, Peter. 2013. *Manhunt: The Ten-Year Search for Bin Laden from 9/11 to Abbottabad*. New York: Broadway Books.

Berkowitz, Bruce D. and Allan E. Goodman. 2000. *Best Truth: Intelligence in the Information Age*. New Haven, Conn.: Yale University Press.

Bernsten, Gary and Ralph Pezzullo. 2005. *Jawbreaker*. New York: Crown Publishers.

Blair, Dennis C. 2009. Testimony before the House Permanent Select Committee on Intelligence, "Annual Threat Assessment," 111th Cong., 1st sess., February 25.

Blair, Dennis C. 2010. Testimony before the Senate Select Committee on Intelligence, "Annual Threat Assessment of the US Intelligence Community," 111th Cong., 2nd sess., February 2.

Blight, James G. and David A. Welch, eds. 1999. *Intelligence and the Cuban Missile Crisis*. London: Frank Cass.

Blum, Howard. 2014. *Dark Invasion: 1915: Germany's Secret War and the Hunt for the First Terrorist Cell in America*. New York: Harper.

Braut-Hegghammer, Målfrid. 2016. *Unclear Physics: Why Iraq and Libya Failed to Build Nuclear Weapons*. Ithaca, N.Y.: Cornell University Press.

Brennan, John O. 2020. *Undaunted: My Fight against America's Enemies, at Home and Abroad*. New York: Celadon Books.

Brown, Anthony Cave. 1994. *Treason in the Blood: H. St. John Philby, Kim Philby, and the Spy Case of the Century*. Boston: Houghton Mifflin.

Bush, George W. 2010. *Decision Points*. New York: Crown.

Carson, Austin. 2018. *Secret Wars: Covert Conflict in International Politics*. Princeton, N.J.: Princeton University Press.

Center for Strategic and International Studies (CSIS). 2021. "Maintaining the Intelligence Edge: Reimagining and Reinventing Intelligence through Innovation." January 17.

Central Intelligence Agency. 2004. "Comprehensive Report of the Special Advisor to the DCI on Iraq's WMD" (also known as the "Duelfer Report," and the "Iraq Survey Group Nuclear Report"), September 30.

Central Intelligence Agency, Office of the Inspector General. 2004. "Special Review: Counterterrorism Detention and Interrogation Activities (September 2001–October 2003)." May 7.

Central Intelligence Agency, Office of the Inspector General. 2013. "Report of Investigation: Potential Ethics Violations Involving Film Producers." September 16.

Chauhan, Sharad. 2004. *Inside CIA: Lessons in Intelligence*. New Delhi: APH Publishing.

Chesney, Robert. 2010. "Who May Be Killed? Anwar Al-Awlaki as a Case Study in the International Legal Regulation of Lethal Force." *Yearbook of International Humanitarian Law* 13 (August 15).

Clapper, James. 2010. "Declaration in Support of Formal Claim of State Secrets Privilege." In United States District Court for the District of Columbia, *Nasser al-Aulaqi v. Barack Obama, Robert Gates, and Leon Panetta*. Civ. A. No. 10-cv-1469. September 24.

Clapper, James R. 2011. Testimony before the Senate Committee on Armed Services, "Worldwide Threat Assessment of the US Intelligence Community," 112th Cong., 1st sess., March 10.

Clapper, James R. 2012. Testimony before the House Permanent Select Committee on Intelligence, "Worldwide Threat Assessment," 112th Cong., 2nd sess., February 2.

Clapper, James R. 2013. Testimony before the Senate Committee on Armed Services, "Worldwide Threat Assessment of the US Intelligence Community," 113th Cong., 1st sess., April 18.

Clapper, James R. 2014. Testimony before Senate Armed Services Committee, "Current and Future World Threats to the National Security of the United States," 113th Cong., 2nd sess., February 11.

Clapper, James R. 2015. Testimony before Senate Armed Services Committee, "Worldwide Threat Assessment of the US Intelligence Community," 114th Cong., 1st sess., February 26.

Clapper, James R. 2016. Testimony before Senate Select Committee on Intelligence, "Worldwide Threat Assessment of the US Intelligence Community," 114th Cong., 2nd sess., February 9.

Clapper, James R. with Trey Brown. 2018. *Facts and Fears: Hard Truths from a Life in Intelligence*. New York: Penguin.

Coats, Daniel R. 2017. Testimony before Senate Select Committee on Intelligence, "Worldwide Threat Assessment of the US Intelligence Community," 115th Cong., 1st sess., May 11.

Coats, Daniel R. 2018. Testimony before Senate Select Committee on Intelligence, "Worldwide Threat Assessment of the US Intelligence Community," 115th Cong., 2nd sess., February 13.

Coats, Daniel R. 2019. Testimony before Senate Select Committee on Intelligence, "Worldwide Threat Assessment of the US Intelligence Community," 116th Cong., 1st sess., January 29.

Cohen, Eliot A. 1988. "The Chinese intervention in Korea, 1950." *Studies in Intelligence* 32, no. 3.

Colby, William. 1984. "Should the U.S. fight secret wars?" *Harper's Magazine*. September.

Cole, Ronald H. "OPERATION JUST CAUSE: The Planning and Execution of Joint Operations in Panama, February 1988–January 1990," Joint History Office, Office of the Chairman of the Joint Chiefs of Staff, November 1995.

Commission on Protecting and Reducing Government Secrecy (Moynihan Commission). 1997. "Report of the Commission on Protecting and Reducing Government Secrecy," 103rd Cong. March 3. Washington, D.C.: GPO.

Commission on the Intelligence Capabilities of the United States Regarding Weapons of Mass Destruction (Silberman-Robb Commission). 2005. "Report to the President of the United States." Washington, D.C.: GPO.

Commission to Review the Department of Defense Security Policy and Practices. 1985. "Keeping the Nation's Secrets: A Report to the Secretary of Defense." November 19.

Crumpton, Henry. 2012. *The Art of Intelligence: Lessons from a Life in the CIA's Clandestine Service*. New York: Penguin.

Cyberspace Solarium Commission. 2020. "Cyberspace Solarium Commission Report."

Daigler, Kenneth A. 2014. *Spies, Patriots, and Traitors: American Intelligence in the Revolutionary War*. Washington, D.C.: Georgetown University Press.

Department of Justice, Office of the Inspector General. 2002. "A Review of the Federal Bureau of Investigation's Counterterrorism Program: Threat Assessment, Strategic Planning, and Resource Management." Audit Report 02-38. Executive summary declassified and redacted September.

Department of Justice, Office of the Inspector General. 2003. "A Review of the FBI's Performance in Deterring, Detecting, and Investigating the Espionage Activities of Robert Philip Hanssen." August 14.

Devine, Jack. 2021. *Spymaster's Prism: The Fight against Russian Aggression*. Dulles, Va.: Potomac Books.

Duelfer, Charles and Central Intelligence Agency. 2004. "Comprehensive Report of the Special Advisor to the DCI on Iraq's WMD." September 30.

Earley, Pete. 1997. *Confessions of a Spy: The Real Story of Aldrich Ames.* New York: Berkley Books.

Executive Order 11905. 1976. February 18.

Executive Order 13526. 2009. 75 Fed. Reg. 705. December 29.

Federal Bureau of Investigation. 1998. "Keeping Tomorrow Safe: Draft FBI Strategic Plan, 1998–2003," unclassified version. May 8.

Fischhoff, Baruch and Cherie Chauvin, eds., National Research Council of the National Academies. 2011. *Intelligence Analysis: Behavioral and Social Scientific Foundations.* Washington, D.C.: National Academies Press.

Fishel, Edwin C. 1996. *The Secret War for the Union: The Untold Story of Military Intelligence in the Civil War.* New York: Houghton Mifflin Harcourt.

Flournoy, Michèle and Michael Sulmeyer. 2018. "Battlefield Internet." *Foreign Affairs.* September/October.

Garthoff, Raymond L. 1998. "U.S. Intelligence in the Cuban missile crisis." *Intelligence and National Security* 13, no. 3.

Gates, Robert M. 1996. *From the Shadows: The Ultimate Insider's Story of Five Presidents and How They Won the Cold War.* New York: Simon & Schuster.

Gates, Robert M. 2014. *Duty: Memoirs of a Secretary at War.* New York: Knopf.

Gofman, Michael and Zhao Jin. 2020. "Artificial Intelligence, Human Capital, and Innovation." University of Rochester.

Goldsmith, Jack. 2012. *Power and Constraint: The Accountable Presidency after 9/11.* New York: W. W. Norton.

Gorin, Peter A. 1998. "Zenit: The Soviet Response to CORONA." In *Eye in the Sky: The Story of the CORONA Spy Satellites,* edited by Dwayne A. Day, John M. Logsdon, and Brian Latell. Washington, D.C.: Smithsonian Institution Press.

Halberstam, David. 2008. *The Coldest Winter: America and the Korean War.* Great Britain: Macmillan.

Hamrick, S. J. 2004. *Deceiving the Deceivers: Kim Philby, Donald Maclean, and Guy Burgess.* New Haven, Conn.: Yale University Press.

Hayden, Michael V. 2016. *Playing to the Edge: American Intelligence in the Age of Terror.* New York: Penguin.

Heuer, Richards J. and Randolph H. Pherson. 2010. *Structured Analytic Techniques for Intelligence Analysis.* Washington, D.C.: CQ Press.

Hoffman, David E. 2016. *The Billion Dollar Spy: A True Story of Cold War Espionage and Betrayal.* New York: Anchor Books.

Huntington, Samuel P. 1957. *The Soldier and the State.* Cambridge, Mass.: Harvard University Press.

Inglis, Chris. 2019. "Illuminating a New Domain." In *Bytes, Bombs, and Spies,* edited by Herbert Lin and Amy Zegart. Washington, D.C.: Brookings Institution Press.

Intelligence Authorization Act of 1991. Public Law 102-88. 102nd Cong., August 14.

Intelligence Community Assessment. 2017. "Assessing Russian Activities and Intentions in Recent US Elections." January.

Intelligence Science Board. 2006. "Educing Information: Interrogation: Science and Art Foundations for the Future, Phase I Report." Washington, D.C.: National Defense Intelligence College.

Isaacson, Walter. 2008. *Benjamin Franklin: An American Life*. Simon & Schuster.

Janis, Irving. 1982. *Groupthink: Psychological Studies of Policy Decisions and Fiascoes*. Boston: Houghton Mifflin.

Jervis, Robert. 1976. *Perception and Misperception in International Politics*. Princeton, N.J.: Princeton University Press.

Johnson, Loch K. 1989. *America's Secret Power: The CIA in a Democratic Society*. New York: Oxford University Press.

Johnson, Loch K. 2015. *A Season of Inquiry Revisited: The Church Committee Confronts America's Spy Agencies*. Lawrence, Kan.: University Press of Kansas.

Joint Security Commission. 1994. "Redefining Security: A Report to the Secretary of Defense and the Director of Central Intelligence." February 28.

Kahn, David. 1996. *The Codebreakers: The Comprehensive History of Secret Communication from Ancient Times to the Internet*. New York: Scribner.

Kahneman, Daniel. 2011. *Thinking, Fast and Slow*. New York: Farrar, Straus and Giroux.

Kennedy, David M. 2014. "Thinking Historically about Grand Strategy." In *Grand Strategy: Ideas and Challenges in a Complex World*. Stanford, Calif.: Hoover Institution.

Kent, Sherman. 1964. "A crucial estimate relived." Declassified and Approved for Release July 10, 2013.

Kessler, Ronald. 2003. *The Bureau: The Secret History of the FBI*. New York: St. Martin's.

Ketchum, Richard M. 2004. *Victory at Yorktown: The Campaign that Won the Revolution*. New York: Henry Holt and Company.

Knott, Stephen F. 1996. *Secret and Sanctioned: Covert Operations and the American Presidency*. Oxford, U.K.: Oxford University Press.

Kreps, Sarah E. 2016. *Drones: What Everyone Needs to Know*. New York: Oxford University Press.

Kuhns, Woodrow J. 1997. *Assessing the Soviet Threat: The Early Cold War Years*. Washington, D.C.: Center for the Study of Intelligence.

Leary, William M., ed. 1984. *The Central Intelligence Agency: History and Documents*. Tuscaloosa: University of Alabama Press.

Lepore, Jill. 2018. *These Truths: A History of the United States*. New York: W. W. Norton.

Lin, Herbert and Amy Zegart, eds. 2019. *Bytes, Bombs, and Spies*. Washington, D.C.: Brookings Institution Press.

Lord, Charles G., Lee Ross and Mark R. Lepper. 1979. "Biased assimilation and attitude polarization: The effects of prior theories on subsequently considered evidence." *Journal of Personality and Social Psychology* 37, no. 11.

Lowenthal, Mark M. 2017. *Intelligence: From Secrets to Policy*. 7th edition. Thousand Oaks, Calif.: CQ Press.

Lynn, William J. III. 2010. "Defending a new domain: The Pentagon's cyberstrategy." *Foreign Affairs*. September/October.

Mattis, Jim and Kori N. Schake, eds. 2016. *Warriors & Citizens: American Views of Our Military*. Stanford, Calif.: Hoover Institution Press.

Mayhew, David. 1974. *Congress: The Electoral Connection*. 2nd edition. New Haven, Conn.: Yale University Press.

Mazzetti, Mark. 2013. *The Way of the Knife: The CIA, a Secret Army, and a War at the Ends of the Earth*. New York: Penguin.

McConnell, Michael. 2008. Testimony before the Senate Select Committee on Intelligence, "Worldwide Threat Assessment," 110th Cong., 2nd sess., February 5.

McDermott, Rose and Uri Bar-Joseph. 2017. *Intelligence Success and Failure: The Human Factor.* New York: Oxford University Press.

McKinsey Global Institute. 2020. "The Bio Revolution."

Millman, Chad. 2006. *The Detonators: The Secret Plot to Destroy America and an Epic Hunt for Justice.* New York: Little, Brown.

Morell, Michael with Bill Harlow. 2015. *The Great War of Our Time: The CIA's Fight against Terrorism—From al Qa'ida to ISIS.* New York: Twelve.

Mueller, Robert S. 2019. "Report on the Investigation Into Russian Interference in the 2016 Presidential Election." Vol. 1. March.

Muskie, Edmund S., John Tower and Brent Scowcroft. 1997. "Report of the President's Special Review Board."

Nagy, John A. 2013. *Dr. Benjamin Church, Spy: A Case of Espionage on the Eve of the American Revolution.* Yardley, Pa.: Westholme Publishing.

Nagy, John A. 2016. *George Washington's Secret Spy War: The Making of America's First Spymaster.* New York: St. Martin's Press.

Nakasone, Paul M. and Michael Sulmeyer. 2020. "How to compete in cyberspace." *Foreign Affairs*, August 25.

Nasser al-Aulaqi v. Barack Obama, Robert Gates, and Leon Panetta. 2010. Civ. A. No. 10-cv-1469. District Court for the District of Columbia. September 24.

National Academies of Sciences, Engineering, and Medicine. 2018. *Biodefense in the Age of Synthetic Biology.* Washington D.C.: National Academies Press.

National Commission on Terrorist Attacks Upon the United States. 2004. "9/11 Commission Staff Statement Number Seven: Intelligence Policy." March 24.

National Commission on Terrorist Attacks Upon the United States. 2004. *The 9/11 Commission Report, Authorized Version.* New York: W. W. Norton.

National Counterintelligence and Security Center, Office of the Director of National Intelligence. 2017. "Fiscal Year 2017 Annual Report on Security Clearance Determinations."

National Intelligence Estimate 2002-16HC. 2002. "Iraq's Continuing Programs for Weapons of Mass Destruction." Washington, D.C.: National Intelligence Council. Redacted and declassified April 2004.

National Research Council. 2011. *Intelligence Analysis for Tomorrow: Advances from the Behavioral and Social Sciences.* Washington, D.C.: National Academies Press.

National Research Council Committee to Review the Scientific Evidence on the Polygraph, Division of Behavioral and Social Sciences and Education. 2003. *The Polygraph and Lie Detection.* Washington, D.C.: National Academies Press.

National Security Commission on Artificial Intelligence. 2019. "Interim Report." July.

National Security Commission on Artificial Intelligence. 2019. "Interim Report." November.

National Security Commission on Artificial Intelligence. 2020. "First Quarter Recommendations." March.

National Security Commission on Artificial Intelligence. 2020. "Interim Report and Third Quarter Recommendations." October.

Negroponte, John D. 2007. Testimony before the House Permanent Select Committee on Intelligence, "Annual Threat Assessment of the Director of the National Intelligence," 110th Cong., 1st sess., January 18.

Office of the Director of National Intelligence. 2010. "Implementation Plan of Executive Order 13526." Washington, D.C.: ODNI. December 31.

Office of the Director of National Intelligence. 2015. "Intelligence Community Policy Guidance 704.6: Conduct of Polygraph Examinations for Personnel Security Vetting," February 4.

Office of the Director of National Intelligence. 2015. *Principles of Transparency for the Intelligence Community.*

Office of the Director of National Intelligence. 2020. *ODNI FOIA Handbook.* Washington, D.C.: ODNI.

Office of the Director of National Intelligence, National Counterintelligence and Security Center. 2016. "National Counterintelligence Strategy of the United States of America." Washington, D.C.

Olson, James M. 2006. *Fair Play: The Moral Dilemmas of Spying.* Dulles, Va.: Potomac Books.

Olson, James. 2019. *To Catch a Spy: The Art of Counterintelligence.* Washington, D.C.: Georgetown University Press.

O'Rourke, Lindsey A. 2018. *Covert Regime Change.* Ithaca, N.Y.: Cornell University Press.

Owens, William A., Kenneth W. Dam and Herbert S. Lin., eds. 2009. *Technology, Policy, Law, and Ethics Regarding U.S. Acquisition and Use of Cyberattack Capabilities.* Washington, D.C.: National Academies Press.

Pabian, Frank. 2015. "Commercial Satellite Imagery as an Evolving Open-Source Verification Technology," Joint Research Centre, European Commission.

Panetta, Leon E. and Jeremy Bash. 2016. "The former head of the CIA on managing the hunt for Bin Laden." *Harvard Business Review.* May 2.

Panetta, Leon with Jim Newton. 2014. *Worthy Fights: A Memoir of Leadership in War and Peace.* New York: Penguin.

Pappas, Aris. 2004. "Ryszard Kuklinski: A Case Officer's View." Seminar on Intelligence, Command, and Control. Incidental Paper. Center for Information Policy Research, Harvard University. April 29.

Paul, Christopher and Miriam Matthews. 2016. "The Russian 'Firehose of Falsehood' Propaganda Model." RAND Perspective.

People's Republic of China. 2017. State Council Notice, "A Next Generation Artificial Intelligence Plan." Translated by Graham Webster, Rogier Creemers, Paul Triolo, and Elsa Kania. August 1.

Philbrick, Nathaniel. 2018. *In the Hurricane's Eye: The Genius of George Washington and the Victory at Yorktown.* New York: Penguin.

Phillippi v. CIA. 1976. 546 F.2d 1009, 1013 (D.C. Cir.).

Poznansky, Michael. 2020. *In the Shadow of International Law.* New York: Oxford University Press.

President's Review Group on Intelligence and Communications Technologies. 2013. "Liberty and Security in a Changing World: Report and Recommendations of the President's Review Group on Intelligence and Communications Technologies." December 12.

Priest, Dana and William M. Arkin. 2011. *Top Secret America: The Rise of the New American Security State*. New York: Little, Brown.

Puccioni, Allison. 2015. "Commercial lift-off." *IHS Jane's Intelligence Review*.

Puccioni, Allison. 2016. "Penetrating vision." *IHS Jane's Intelligence Review*.

Puccioni, Allison. 2017. "Steady gaze." *IHS Jane's Intelligence Review*.

Puccioni, Allison and Neil Ashdown. 2019. "Raising standards." *IHS Jane's Intelligence Review*.

Raines, Rebecca Robbins. 2011. *Getting the Message Through: A Branch History of the U.S. Army Signal Corp. Army Historical Series*. Washington, D.C.: Center of Military History, United States Army.

Ranelagh, John. 1986. *The Agency: The Rise and Decline of the CIA*. New York: Simon & Schuster.

Rice, Condoleezza and Amy B. Zegart. 2018. *Political Risk*. New York: Twelve.

Richelson, Jeffrey T. 1995. *A Century of Spies: Intelligence in the Twentieth Century*. New York: Oxford University Press.

Rogers, Michael. 2015. Testimony before the Senate Select Committee on Intelligence, "National Security Agency Activities and its Ability to Meet its Diverse Mission Requirements," 114th Cong., 1st sess., September 24.

Rohde, David. 2020. *In Deep: The FBI, the CIA, and the Truth about America's "Deep State."* New York: W. W. Norton.

Rosenbach, Eric. 2015. Testimony before Senate Committee on Armed Services, Hearing on Military Cyber Program and Posture Review of the Defense Authorization Request for FY2016 and the Future Years Defense Programs, 114th Cong., 1st sess., April 14.

Sanger, David. 2018. *The Perfect Weapon: War, Sabotage, and Fear in the Cyber Age*. New York: Crown.

Sayle, Edward F. 1986. "The historical underpinnings of the US Intelligence Community." *International Journal of Intelligence and Counter Intelligence* 1, no. 1: 1–27.

Schaeper, Thomas J. 2011. *Edward Bancroft: Scientist, Author, Spy*. New Haven, Conn.: Yale University Press.

Schiff, Adam. 2019. Remarks, House Permanent Select Committee on Intelligence. Hearing on National Security Challenges of Artificial Intelligence, Manipulated Media, and Deepfakes. 116th Cong., 1st sess., June 13.

Schlesinger, Arthur M. Jr. and Roger Bruns. 1975. *Congress Investigates: A Documented History, 1792–1794*. Vol. 1. New York: Chelsea House.

Schmitt, Eric and Thom Shanker. 2011. *Counterstrike: The Untold Story of America's Secret Campaign against Al Qaeda*. New York: Times Books.

Schroen, Gary C. 2005. *First In: An Insider's Account of How the CIA Spearheaded the War on Terror in Afghanistan*. New York: Random House.

Schwartz, Peter. 1991. *The Art of the Long View*. New York: Doubleday.

Schwartz, Peter. 2011. *Learnings from the Long View*. San Francisco: Global Business Network.

Scowcroft, Brent. 2002. Testimony, Joint Inquiry of the House Permanent Select Committee on Intelligence and Senate Select Committee on Intelligence, 107th Cong., 2nd sess., September 19.

Shane, Scott. 2015. *Objective Troy: A Terrorist, a President, and the Rise of the Drone*. New York: Tim Duggan Books.

Sharot, Tali. 2012. *Optimism Bias*. New York: Vintage Books.

Sharp, David H. 2012. *The CIA's Greatest Covert Operation*. Lawrence, Kan.: University Press of Kansas.

Shimer, David. 2020. *Rigged: America, Russia, and One Hundred Years of Covert Electoral Interference*. New York: Knopf.

Silber, Mitchell D. and Arvin Bhatt. 2007. *Radicalization in the West: The Homegrown Threat*. New York Police Department.

Smist, Frank J. Jr. 1994. *Congress Oversees the United States Intelligence Community, 1947–1994*. 2nd edition. Knoxville: University of Tennessee Press.

Snider, L. Britt. 2008. *The Agency and the Hill: The CIA's Relationship with Congress, 1946–2004*. Washington, D.C.: Center for the Study of Intelligence.

Sorensen, Theodore. 1965. *Kennedy*. New York: Harper & Row.

Spanier, John W. 1965. *The Truman-MacArthur Controversy*. New York: W. W. Norton.

Stimson, Henry L. and McGeorge Bundy. 1947. *On Active Service in Peace and War*. New York: Harper & Brothers.

Stretch, Colin. 2017. Testimony before U.S. Senate Select Committee on Intelligence, Hearing on Social Media Influence, 115th Cong., 1st sess., November 1.

Stueck, William. 2002. *Rethinking the Korean War: A New Diplomatic and Strategic History*. Princeton, N.J.: Princeton University Press.

Sulick, Michael. 2012. *Spying in America: Espionage from the Revolutionary War to the Dawn of the Cold War*. Washington, D.C.: Georgetown University Press.

Taubman, Philip. 2003. *Secret Empire: Eisenhower, the CIA, and the Hidden Story of America's Space Espionage*. New York: Simon & Schuster.

Taylor, Philip M. 2003. *Munitions of the Mind: A History of Propaganda from the Ancient World to the Present Day*. 3rd edition. Manchester, U.K.: Manchester University Press.

Tenet, George with Bill Harlow. 2007. *At the Center of the Storm: My Years at the CIA*. New York: HarperCollins.

Tetlock, Philip E. and Dan Gardner. 2015. *Superforecasting: The Art and Science of Prediction*. New York: Crown Publishing Group.

Thompson, E. R. 1991. *Secret New England: Spies of the American Revolution*. New England Chapter, Association of Former Intelligence Officers.

Treverton, Greg. 1987. *Covert Action: The Limits of Intervention in the Postwar World*. New York: Basic Books.

Troy, Thomas F. 1981. *Donovan and the CIA: A History of the Establishment of the Central Intelligence Agency*. Frederick, Md.: University Publications of America.

Turner, Stansfield. 1985. *Secrecy and Democracy: The CIA in Transition*. Boston: Houghton Mifflin.

Tversky, Amos and Daniel Kahneman. 1983. "Extensional versus Intuitive reasoning: The conjunction fallacy in probability judgement." *Psychological Review* 90, no. 4 (October).

Tzu, Sun. 2003. *The Art of War*. Translated by Lionel Giles. New York: Barnes & Noble.

United States v. Internet Research Agency et al. 2018. Case 1:18-cr-00032-DLF (D.D.C. Feb. 16, 2018).

United States v. Jerry Chun Shing Lee. 2018. Criminal No. 1:15-cr-89-TSE. U.S. District Court for the Eastern District of Virginia. May 8.

United States v. Kevin Patrick Mallory. 2017. Affidavit. Case 1:17-cr-00154-TSE. U.S. District Court for the Eastern District of Virginia. June 21.

United States v. Su Bin. 2016. Plea agreement. No. SA CR 14-131 (C.D. Cal. Mar. 22, 2016).

USA Freedom Act. 2014. H.R.3361. 113th Cong., 2nd sess.

USA Freedom Act. 2015. Public Law 114-23. June 2.

U.S. Cyber Command. 2018. *Achieve and Maintain Cyberspace Superiority: Command Vision for US Cyber Command*. March 23.

U.S. Department of Defense. 2015. *Cyber Strategy*. April.

U.S. Department of Defense. 2018. *Summary of the 2018 National Defense Strategy of the United States of America*.

U.S. Department of Defense, Katherine L. Herbig. 2017. "The Expanding Spectrum of Espionage by Americans, 1947–2015." Defense Personnel and Security Research Center (PERSEREC), Office of People Analytics.

U.S. Department of Homeland Security and Office of the Director of National Intelligence. 2016. Joint Statement on Election Security. October 7.

U.S. Department of State. 2009–2017. "Joint Comprehensive Plan of Action."

U.S. Geospatial Intelligence Foundation. "2019 State and Future of GEOINT Report."

U.S. Government Accountability Office. 2019. "Intelligence Community: Actions Needed to Improve Planning and Oversight of the Centers for Academic Excellence Program" (GAO-19-529).

U.S. House of Representatives Committee on Government Reform. 2004. Hearing before the Subcommittee on National Security, Emerging Threats, and International Relations. 108th Cong., 2nd sess., August 24. Serial No. 108-263.

U.S. House of Representatives Committee on the Judiciary. 2007. "Torture and the Cruel, Inhuman and Degrading Treatment of Detainees: The Effectiveness and Consequences of 'Enhanced' Interrogation." Hearing before the Subcommittee on the Constitution, Civil Rights, and Civil Liberties. 110th Cong., 1st sess., November 8. Serial No. 110-94.

U.S. House of Representatives Committee on the Judiciary. 2008. "Department of Justice to Guantanamo Bay: Administration Lawyers and Administration Interrogation Rules (Part I)." Hearing before the Subcommittee on the Constitution, Civil Rights, and Civil Liberties of the House Judiciary Committee. 110th Cong., 2nd sess., May 6. Serial No. 110-97.

U.S. House of Representatives Permanent Select Committee on Intelligence. 2016. "Review of the Unauthorized Disclosures of Former National Security Agency Contractor Edward Snowden." 114th Cong., 2nd sess., December 23. H. Rpt. 114-891.

U.S. House of Representatives Permanent Select Committee on Intelligence. 2019. Hearing on National Security Challenges of Artificial Intelligence, Manipulated Media and Deepfakes. 116th Cong., 1st sess., June 13.

U.S. Library of Congress Congressional Research Service, Michael R. DeVine. 2019. "Covert Action and Clandestine Activities of the Intelligence Community: Selected Definitions in Brief." RL45175.

U.S. Library of Congress Congressional Research Service, John W. Rollins and Edward C. Liu. 2013. "NSA Surveillance Leaks: Background and Issues for Congress." R43134.

U.S. Senate. 1946. "Report of the Joint Committee on the Investigation of the Pearl Harbor Attack." 79th Cong., 2nd sess., July 20. Document 244. Washington, D.C.: GPO.

U.S. Senate. 2004. "A resolution to eliminate certain restrictions on service of a Senator on the Senate Select Committee on Intelligence." 108th Cong., 2nd sess., October 1. S. Res. 445.

U.S. Senate. 2012. Letter from Senators Dianne Feinstein, Carl Levin, and John McCain to Acting CIA Director Michael Morell. December 19.

U.S. Senate Committee on Armed Services. 2008. "Inquiry into the Treatment of Detainees in U.S. Custody: Report." 110th Cong., 2nd sess., November 20.

U.S. Senate Committee on Foreign Relations. 2007. Extraordinary Rendition, Extraterritorial Detention and Treatment of Detainees Hearing. 110th Cong., 1st sess., July 26.

U.S. Senate Committee on Foreign Relations. 2009. "Tora Bora Revisited: How We Failed to Get Bin Laden and Why It Matters Today." 111th Cong., 1st sess., November 30. S. Prt. 111-35.

U.S. Senate Committee on Homeland Security and Governmental Affairs. 2009. *The Fort Hood Attack: A Preliminary Assessment.* 111th Cong., 1st sess., November 19.

U.S. Senate Committee on Homeland Security and Governmental Affairs. 2011. "A Ticking Time Bomb: Counterterrorism Lessons from the U.S. Government's Failure to Prevent the Fort Hood Attack, A Special Report by Joseph I. Lieberman, Chairman and Susan M. Collins, Ranking Member." 112th Cong., 1st sess., February 3.

U.S. Senate Committee on the Judiciary. 2005. Confirmation Hearing on the Nomination of Alberto R. Gonzales to be Attorney General of the United States. 109th Cong., 1st sess., January 6. Serial No. J-109.

U.S. Senate Committee on the Judiciary, Subcommittee on the Constitution. 2019. Hearing on Google and Censorship. 116th Cong., 1st sess., July 16.

U.S. Senate Committees on the Judiciary and Commerce, Science, and Transportation. 2018. "Facebook, Social Media Privacy, and the Use and Abuse of Data." 115th Cong., 2nd sess., April 10.

U.S. Senate Select Committee on Intelligence. 1994. "An Assessment of the Aldrich H. Ames Espionage Case and Its Implications for U.S. Intelligence: Report." 103rd Cong., 2nd sess. S. Rep. 84-046.

U.S. Senate Select Committee on Intelligence. 2006. "Postwar Findings about Iraq's WMD Programs and Links to Terrorism and How They Compare with Prewar Assessments, together with Additional and Minority Views." 109th Cong., 2nd sess.

U.S. Senate Select Committee on Intelligence. 2007. Hearing on the Congressional Oversight of Intelligence Activities. 110th Cong., 1st sess., November 13. S. Hrg. 110-794.

U.S. Senate Select Committee on Intelligence. 2009. Hearing on the Nomination of Leon Panetta to be Director of Central Intelligence Agency. 111th Cong., 1st sess., February 5.

U.S. Senate Select Committee on Intelligence. 2014. "Committee Study of the Central Intelligence Agency's Detention and Interrogation Program." 113th Cong., 2nd sess., December 9.

U.S. Senate Select Committee on Intelligence. 2014. "Committee Study of the Central Intelligence Agency's Detention and Interrogation Program: Minority Views of Vice Chairman

Chambliss joined by Senators Burr, Risch, Coats, Rubio, and Coburn." 113th Cong., 2nd sess., December 5.

U.S. Senate Select Committee on Intelligence. 2014. Hearing on National Security Threats. 113th Cong., 1st sess., January 29.

U.S. Senate Select Committee on Intelligence. 2017. Hearing on Social Media Influence in the 2016 United States Elections. 115th. Cong., 1st sess., November 1.

U.S. Senate Select Committee on Intelligence. 2018. "The Intelligence Community Assessment: Assessing Russian Activities and Intentions in Recent U.S. Elections, Summary of Initial Findings." July 3.

U.S. Senate Select Committee on Intelligence. 2019. Hearing on Global Threats and National Security. 116th Cong., 1st sess., January 29.

U.S. Senate Select Committee on Intelligence. 2019. "Report on the Investigation into Russian Interference in the 2016 Presidential Election," Vol. 2. March.

U.S. Senate Select Committee on Intelligence. 2019. "Russian Active Measures Campaigns and Interference in the 2016 Election," Vol. 2: Russia's Use of Social Media with Additional Views. 116th Cong., 1st sess., October.

U.S. Senate Select Committee on Intelligence. 2021. Hearing on Worldwide Threats, 117th Cong., 1st sess., April 24.

U.S. Senate Select Committee on Intelligence and House Permanent Select Committee on Intelligence. 2002. "Joint Inquiry into Intelligence Community Activities before and after the Terrorist Attacks of September 11, 2001." 107th Cong., 2nd sess. S. Rep. 107-351 / H. Rep. 107-792.

U.S. Senate Select Committee to Study Governmental Operations with Respect to Intelligence Activities. 1975. "Alleged Assassination Plots Involving Foreign Leaders." 94th Cong., 1st sess., November 20. Rep. 94-465.

U.S. Senate Select Committee to Study Government Operations with Respect to Intelligence Activities. 1975. "Covert Action in Chile 1963–1965." 94th Cong., 1st sess.

U.S. Senate Select Committee to Study Governmental Operations with Respect to Intelligence Activities, 1975–1976. 1976. "Final Report." 94th Cong., 2nd sess., April 26. S. Rept. 940-775, Serial 13133–3–3.

U.S. Senate Select Committee to Study Government Operations with Respect to Intelligence Activities. 1976. "Supplementary Detailed Staff Reports on Foreign and Military Intelligence." 94th Cong., 2nd sess., April 23.

Walker, Kent. 2017. Testimony before Senate Select Committee on Intelligence. Hearing on Social Media Influence. 115th Cong., 1st sess., November 1.

Walsh, Lawrence E. and Federation of American Scientists. 1993. "Summary of Prosecutions, Final Report of the Independent Counsel for Iran/Contra Matters." August 4.

Webster (William H.) Commission. 2012. "The Federal Bureau of Investigation, Counterterrorism Intelligence, and the Events at Fort Hood, Texas, on November 5, 2009, Final Report," redacted version released July 19, 2012.

Weiner, Tim. 2008. *Legacy of Ashes: The History of the CIA*. New York: Anchor Books.

Weiner, Tim. 2012. *Enemies: A History of the FBI*. New York: Random House.

Weiner, Tim, David Johnston and Neil A. Lewis. 1995. *Betrayal: The Story of Aldrich Ames, an American Spy*. New York: Random House.

Weintraub, Stanley. 2000. *MacArthur's War: Korea and the Undoing of an American Hero.* New York: Free Press.

Whipple, Chris. 2020. *The Spymasters: How the CIA Directors Shape History and the Future.* New York: Scribner.

White House. 2018. "National Cyber Strategy of the United States of America." September.

Whiting, Allen and Harvey de Weerd. 1960. *China Crosses the Yalu: The Decision to Enter the Korean War.* Palo Alto, Calif.: Stanford University Press.

Wise, David. 2002. *Spy: The Inside Story of How the FBI's Robert Hanssen Betrayed America.* New York: Random House.

Wohlstetter, Roberta. 1962. *Pearl Harbor: Warning and Decision.* Palo Alto, Calif.: Stanford University Press.

Woods, David L. 1965. *A History of Tactical Communication Techniques.* Orlando, Fla.: Martin-Marietta Corp.

Woodward, Bob. 2002. *Bush at War.* New York: Simon & Schuster.

Wright, Lawrence. 2016. *The Terror Years: From Al-Qaeda to the Islamic State.* New York: Penguin.

Zegart, Amy B. 1999. *Flawed by Design: The Evolution of the CIA, JCS, and NSC.* Palo Alto, Calif.: Stanford University Press.

Zegart, Amy B. 2007. *Spying Blind: The CIA, the FBI, and the Origins of 9/11.* Princeton, N.J.: Princeton University Press.

Zegart, Amy B. 2011. *Eyes on Spies: Congress and the United States Intelligence Community.* Stanford, Calif.: Hoover Institution Press.

Zegart, Amy B. 2018. "Cheap fights, credible threats." *Journal of Strategic Studies* 43, no. 1 (February): 6–46.

Zegart, Amy B. 2020. "Intelligence isn't just for government anymore." *Foreign Affairs,* November 2.

Zegart, Amy B. and Kevin Childs. 2018. "The divide between Silicon Valley and Washington is a national-security threat." *Atlantic,* December 13.

Zegart, Amy B. and Michael Morell. 2019. "Spies, lies, and algorithms." *Foreign Affairs* 98, no. 3 (May/June).

Zelizer, Julian E. 2010. *Arsenal of Democracy.* New York: Basic Books.

Zenko, Micah. 2015. *Red Team: How to Succeed by Thinking Like the Enemy.* New York: Basic Books.

Zetter, Kim. 2014. *Countdown to Zero Day: Stuxnet and the Launch of the World's First Digital Weapon.* New York: Crown Publishers.

INDEX

Note: page numbers followed by *f* and *t* refer to figures and tables respectively. Those followed by n refer to notes, with note number.

academic study of IC, 35–36, 299–300n125, 299n121

Afghanistan: bin Laden escape to, after 9/11, 99; Clinton administration policy on, 272; covert action in, 63, 100, 104, 174, 184; drone strikes in, 175; intelligence gathering in, after 9/11, 100; search for al Qaeda in, 100; Soviet occupation of, 178, 181, 183–84; as terrorism stronghold, 183

Afghanistan War: CIA and, 192–93, 246; and counterinsurgency doctrine, 192; and Manning documents, 31; Obama and, 179; and operation to kill bin Laden, 181; and regime change, 176

AI. *See* artificial intelligence

Alexander, Keith, 262

Alphabet. *See* Google

al Qaeda: interrogation of leaders of, 100–101; origins of, 183; and planning of 9/11, 37, 69; post-911 campaign against, 99–101, 170, 186; search for, in Afghanistan, 100; in Yemen, 170. *See also* bin Laden, Osama

"alternative competing hypotheses" process, 133

Amazon: and big data, 8; Prime, spytainment on, 25; refusal to cooperate with government, 276

American Protective League, 59

Ames, Aldrich, 150, 154, 155, 157–60

analysis of intelligence data: asymmetric information and, 113–15; coloring of, by personal experience, 105, 122–23; data shortages and, 111–13; deception and, 104, 116–17; failure of, in Korean War, 109–10; and general difficulty of predicting future, 111; and mental shortcut errors, 117–18; in search for bin Laden, 103–5; and success or failure, lack of feedback on, 115–16; superforecasting analysis techniques, 137–39

analysis, improvement of, 131–39; artificial intelligence and, 139–41, 235–36; format of information and, 134–36, 135*f*; identifying bias, ineffectiveness of, 131; Structured Analytic Techniques to force re-perception, 131–34; superforecasting techniques and, 137–39; testing of methods for effectiveness, 136–38. *See also* biases, and data analysis

Angleton, James Jesus, 160–64

Apple: and big data, 8; and encryption of data, 222–23; founding of, 121; influence on U.S. policy, 75; refusal to cooperate with government, 222–23

Arnold, Benedict, 44, 52, 54, 155

artificial intelligence (AI): challenges created by, 2; and competition for advantage, 141; and deepfake audio and video, 223, 243–46, 268; and improved data analysis, 139–41, 235–36; limitations of, 140; obstacles to

congressional oversight of IC (*continued*)
190–92, 346–47n151, 346n146; creation of
dedicated committees for, 204; era of
routinization (1970s–1990s), 202; era of
strategic weakness (1990s–now), 205–6;
era of undersight (1770s–1970s), 201–2;
failures of, post-9/11, 206; fire alarm type
of, 207; good, characteristics of, 199–200;
information asymmetry and, 207–12;
as inherently difficult, 198; investigation
of harsh interrogations, 195–98, 348n7,
349n22, 350n25; lack of expertise and,
216–18; lack of reelection benefits for
oversight committee members, 212–15;
as not mentioned in Constitution, 199;
partisanship and, 220–21, 356n129; police
patrol type of, 207; poor, characteristics
of, 200; secrecy as barrier to, 207–12; and
September 11th terrorist attacks, 205–6;
technological advances and, 221–24;
term limits on oversight committee
positions and, 216–18, 217f, 218f; three
eras of, 200–206; underlying factors
affecting, 198

conspiracy theories, 300n130; Internet and,
37–38; public's belief of, 37, 38–39;
spytainment and, 36–40

Coolidge Committee, 29

coordination of U.S. intelligence: asymmetric
information and, 114–15; Director of
National Intelligence and, 70–73; failures
of, before 9/11 attacks, 69, 205; ongoing
problems with, 73–74; push for, 61, 63, 65,
70; reports recommending (1991–2001),
67–69, 68t; resistance to, 67, 71

CORONA satellite program, 232–33

Cotton, Tom, 43

counterintelligence: Chinese destruction
of U.S. spy network, 166–68; defensive,
148–51; definition of, 145; and excessive
mistrust, 160–64; and excessive trust,
156–60, 164; increased difficulty in digital
age, 164–66, 167–68; methods used in,

145; offensive, 151–53; screening of
employees as, 149–51; spies, capture of,
143–44

counterterrorism interrogation methods:
congressional investigation of, 195–98,
348n7, 349n24, 350n25; defenders, arguments of, 197; destruction of videotapes
of, 210; public's lack of interest in, 21; in
search for bin Laden, 100; spytainment's
influence on support for, 19, 22–24,
40–43; and *Zero Dark Thirty* film, 27–28

covert action by CIA: in Afghanistan, 63,
100, 104, 174, 184; assassination as, 22, 64,
76, 171, 174–75, 189; bin Laden killing as,
105–6; in Brazil, 64; in Chile, 174, 202; in
Cold War, 174, 176, 180, 186; in Congo, 64,
175; congressional oversight of, 190–92,
346–47n151, 346n146; in Cuba, 63, 64,
174; defining characteristics of, 172–73;
and democratic accountability, 185; as
distraction from other CIA functions,
193–94; in early years, 63–64; efficacy of,
182–84; fig leaf and, 181; in Guatemala, 63,
174; in Iran, 63, 174, 176, 183, 184; in Iraq,
174, 175, 176, 192; in Italy, 64, 174, 180; and
military action, blurring of line between,
192–94; moral issues in, 97, 184–89; and
"neither confirm nor deny" response, 7,
284n39; in Nicaragua, 63, 174, 182–83;
non-covert versions of, 175–77; number
conducted, 64; as outside original CIA
mandate, 63–64. 65; in Pakistan, 175,
176–77, 179; in Panama, 188–89; and
plausible deniability, 172–73, 180–81, 190,
343n100; presidential support for, 172,
177–81; procedures for authorizing,
190–92; *vs.* secret action, 339–40n35;
in Serbia, 174, 369n52; in Somalia, 175,
176–77; and targeted killing, rules for, 191,
346n143; types of, 171–72, 173–75; and
unintended consequences, 183–84; as
unique in U.S. government, 74; within
U.S., as illegal, 173; against U.S. anti-war